The Princeton Review®

TOEFL iBT®

PREP

2022 Edition

The Staff of The Princeton Review

PrincetonReview.com

Penguin Random House

The Princeton Review, Inc.
110 East 42nd Street, 7th Floor
New York, NY 10017
E-mail: editorialsupport@review.com

ISBN: 978-0-525-57210-7
ISSN: 2687-8925

Editor: Selena Coppock
Production Editors: Kathy Carter, Emma Parker
Production Artist: Jason Ullmeyer
Content Contributors: Chad Chasteen, Clarissa Constantine, and Sarah Kass

Printed in the United States of America.

10 9 8 7 6 5 4 3 2 1

2022 Edition

Editorial

Rob Franek, Editor-in-Chief
David Soto, Director of Content Development
Stephen Koch, Student Survey Manager
Deborah Weber, Director of Production
Jason Ullmeyer, Production Design Manager
Selena Coppock, Director of Editorial
Aaron Riccio, Senior Editor
Meave Shelton, Senior Editor
Chris Chimera, Editor
Orion McBean, Editor
Patricia Murphy, Editor
Alexa Schmitt Bugler, Editorial Assistant

Penguin Random House Publishing Team

Tom Russell, VP, Publisher
Alison Stoltzfus, Senior Director, Publishing
Brett Wright, Senior Editor
Emily Hoffman, Assistant Managing Editor
Ellen Reed, Production Manager
Suzanne Lee, Designer
Eugenia Lo, Publishing Assistant

For customer service, please contact **editorialsupport@review.com**, and be sure to include:

- full title of the book
- ISBN
- page number

Acknowledgments

The Princeton Review would also like to thank Clarissa Constantine, Chad Chasteen, and Sarah Kass for their contributions to this book.

Special thanks to Adam Robinson, who conceived of and perfected the Joe Bloggs approach to standardized tests and many of the other successful techniques used by The Princeton Review.

Our gratitude also goes out to Jason Ullmeyer, Emma Parker, and Kathy G. Carter for their careful attention to every page.

Contents

Get More (Free) Content
at **PrincetonReview.com/prep**

As easy as **1·2·3**

1 Go to PrincetonReview.com/prep or scan the **QR code** and enter the following ISBN for your book:
9780525572107

2 Answer a few simple questions to set up an exclusive Princeton Review account. *(If you already have one, you can just log in.)*

3 Enjoy access to your **FREE** content!

Once you've registered, you can...

- Access 29 audio tracks for important practice for the Listening, Speaking, and Writing Sections

- Access a Reading Practice Drill with complete Answer Explanations

- Download a Study Guide to help you maximize your TOEFL prep and manage your calendar

- Access useful strategy and learning documents

- Check for any updates to the TOEFL or this book

Need to report a potential **content** issue?

Contact **EditorialSupport@review.com** and include:

- full title of the book
- ISBN
- page number

Need to report a **technical** issue?

Contact **TPRStudentTech@review.com** and provide:

- your full name
- email address used to register the book
- full book title and ISBN
- Operating system (Mac/PC) and browser (Firefox, Safari, etc.)

Look For These Icons Throughout The Book

 MORE GREAT BOOKS

 HEADPHONES ON!

 PROVEN TECHNIQUES

 APPLIED STRATEGIES

 STUDY BREAK

Part I: Orientation

Chapter 1
Introduction

WELCOME!

Welcome to The Princeton Review's thorough test preparation guide for the Test of English as a Foreign Language (TOEFL). In this book, you will find everything you need to prepare for the TOEFL—information on the test format, test-taking strategies, practice drills, and, of course, a full-length practice exam.

Part I of this book gives a brief outline of how the test is organized. Part II helps you familiarize yourself with the basic concepts tested on the TOEFL. Part III presents you with strategies and tips for the questions and tasks on the test. Part IV provides you with a full-length practice exam with corresponding answers and explanations.

WHAT IS THE TOEFL?

The TOEFL is a test that assesses your proficiency in the type of English used in an academic environment. The test is administered on the Internet, which we'll explain in more detail on page 5.

The exam takes about three hours to complete and integrates four essential skills: reading, listening, speaking, and writing. This means that any given question or task may require you to use one or more of these skills. For example, before attempting a writing task on the TOEFL, you may have to first read a passage and listen to a lecture on the topic.

Fortunately, the TOEFL is not as daunting as it may seem because it tests each of the four skills in a fairly specific way. By working through this book in its entirety, you'll become comfortable with the type of reading, listening, speaking, and writing skills that are required to achieve a good score on the exam.

Stop!

If it is difficult for you to understand the material on this page, it's best that you continue your study of basic English before taking the TOEFL. This book is intended to prepare students who already have knowledge of basic English, and our recommendation is that you should feel very comfortable with the language before you attempt to take the TOEFL.

The Structure of the Test

The TOEFL is broken down into four distinct sections, one for each of the skills listed. However, each section may require you to use more than one of the above four skills.

The structure of the test is as follows:

- One **Reading** section, consisting of three to four passages that are roughly 700 words each. Each passage will be followed by 10 multiple-choice questions about the content of the passage. Most of these questions will be worth one point each, though a few toward the end of the section may be worth more. You will have 54–72 minutes to complete the entire section.

- One **Listening** section, consisting of five to seven audio selections, each of which is three to five minutes long. Each selection will be either an academic lecture or a casual conversation. After each academic lecture selection, there will be six multiple-choice questions about the content of the lecture. After each conversation selection, there will be five questions about the content of the discussion. You will have 41–57 minutes to complete the entire section.

- One **Speaking** section, consisting of four speaking tasks. Most speaking tasks will also require some listening and some reading. Each task will ask you to speak for 45 or 60 seconds, depending on the task, and you will have 17 minutes to complete the entire section.

- One **Writing** section, consisting of two writing assignments. The Writing section, like the Speaking section, also requires listening and reading. You will have 50 minutes to complete the entire section.

Which Test Should You Take?

As you may know, there are two versions of the TOEFL: The TOEFL iBT (Internet-based test) and the TOEFL Essentials. Most students will take the iBT, which is offered more than 60 times a year at centers around the world and several days a week using the Home Edition. Because the iBT assesses all four areas of communication and focuses on on academic English, it is the preferred test at many universities. Therefore, we strongly recommend that you take the TOEFL iBT. If you are interested in finding out more about the TOEFL Essentials test, visit the ETS website at www.ets.org/toefl. If you do not have Internet access, you can call ETS at 1-877-863-3546 or 1-609-771-7100. It is important to remember that this book is designed to help you study for the TOEFL iBT. While some of the strategies and English vocabulary taught in this book will help with other versions of the TOEFL, all information on format and scoring applies to the iBT.

The TOEFL® Essentials test measures four skills using the some different types of questions from the TOEFL iBT test: Reading, Listening, Speaking, and Writing. More information and testing updates related to Covid-19 can be found at: https://www.ets.org/toefl/test-takers/

How Is the Test Scored?

After finishing the TOEFL iBT, you will receive a score from 0 to 30 for each of the four sections and a total score on a 0 to 120 scale calculated by adding the four section scores. Each score corresponds to a percentile ranking. This number shows how your score compares with the scores of other test takers. For example, a total score of 100 would put you in the 89th percentile, meaning that you scored higher than 89 out of 100 test takers, whereas a score of 50 would put you in the 26th percentile. The average TOEFL score is around 81.

Notice that the 0 to 30 scores are *scaled* scores, meaning that the 0 to 30 number doesn't represent the number of questions you answered correctly or the number of points your essay was awarded. For example, the Reading and Listening sections contain roughly 30–40 questions each. You will get one point for each correct answer (some Reading section questions will be worth two points), but there is no penalty for incorrect answers. At the end of the section, your *raw* score, which represents the number of points you've earned, is tallied and converted to a number on the 0 to 30 scale.

For help finding the right college for you, go online to PrincetonReview.com!

The Writing and Speaking sections are scored somewhat differently. Each Writing sample receives a score between 0 and 5. These raw scores are then converted to the 0 to 30 scale. Similarly, each Speaking task receives a score from 0 to 4. The scores from all six Speaking tasks are averaged and converted to the 0–30 scale.

Understanding Your Scores

In order to maximize your performance, it's important to understand what your scores mean to schools. ETS breaks down your scores so that schools can, at least theoretically, get a better grasp of how well you really know English.

In Reading, the 0–30 scale is subdivided into four sections:

- Advanced (24–30)
- High-Intermediate (18–23)
- Low-Intermediate (4–17)
- Below Low-Intermediate (0–3)

In Listening, the 0–30 scale is subdivided into four sections:

- Advanced (22–30)
- High-Intermediate (17–21)
- Low-Intermediate (9–16)
- Below Low-Intermediate (0–8)

In Speaking, the 0–30 scale is broken down into five sections:

- Advanced (25–30)
- High-Intermediate (20–24)
- Low-Intermediate (16–19)
- Basic (10–15)
- Below Basic (0–9)

In Writing, the 0–30 scale is broken down into five sections:

- Advanced (24–30)
- High-Intermediate (17–23)
- Low-Intermediate (13–16)
- Basic (7–12)
- Below Basic (0–6)

Why is it important to understand these breakdowns? Well, if you're right on the border of "High-Intermediate" and "Advanced," for example, you're going to really want to make sure that you focus on developing skills that will push your score above the dividing line.

For more information on these subdivisions, please refer to the appropriate Cracking chapter in Part III: Cracking Each Section of the TOEFL.

Do You Need Rock Star Status?

Well, it would be awesome if you could be a rock star in every section of the test. Most students, though, find that one section is significantly easier than the others or that one is noticeably harder. The good news is that since most schools want a COMBINED score, you just need to get to that total any way you can. So, let's say that you're starting out with scores in this range:

- Reading: 23
- Listening: 24

- Speaking: 18
- Writing: 17

And let's say the school you're applying to wants to see a combined score of 90 points. Well, you have 82 right now. You could absolutely spend time and energy working to bring up the Speaking and Writing, since those are your lowest scores. But, since you likely feel that the Reading and Listening are easier, you might find that it's easier to earn another 6 points between those two sections (maybe 3 in each), and then bring the Speaking and Writing up by 1 point each—that would give you 90 points.

Now, we're certainly NOT saying to just brush off the areas that you find challenging! But, we ARE saying that you shouldn't ignore the areas in which you're already doing well. A point is a point, no matter its source, so make sure to focus just as much on the areas you're doing well on as you do on the areas you find difficult.

How Are the Scores Used?

Colleges and universities will look at your TOEFL score when considering your application. Of course, your TOEFL score is not the only factor that affects your chance of admission. Colleges and universities also look at your academic performance, letters of recommendation, application essays, and scores on other standardized tests. Although a high TOEFL score will not guarantee admission to a particular program, a low test score could jeopardize your chances.

Some schools and programs may require students with TOEFL scores below a certain cutoff score to take supplemental English classes. Others may accept only applicants who score better than a particular cutoff score. Make sure you check with the programs to which you are applying for specific information.

The Computer-Based Format Used for Internet-Based Testing (iBT)

The TOEFL iBT is a computer-based test that is delivered to testing centers via the Internet. Therefore, the TOEFL can be offered at locations throughout the world. The test is administered by Educational Testing Service (ETS), the same testing organization that administers the GRE, SAT, and other standardized tests. According to ETS, Internet-based testing (iBT) is an easier and fairer way to capture speech and score responses. It also makes it possible for them to greatly expand access to test centers.

The iBT format will be new to the untrained eye and may seem intimidating, especially if you have never taken a test on a computer. A brief tutorial is offered at the beginning of the TOEFL to allow you time to familiarize yourself with the format. Still, the iBT presents some challenges. For example, when working on a reading passage, you will see something like the following.

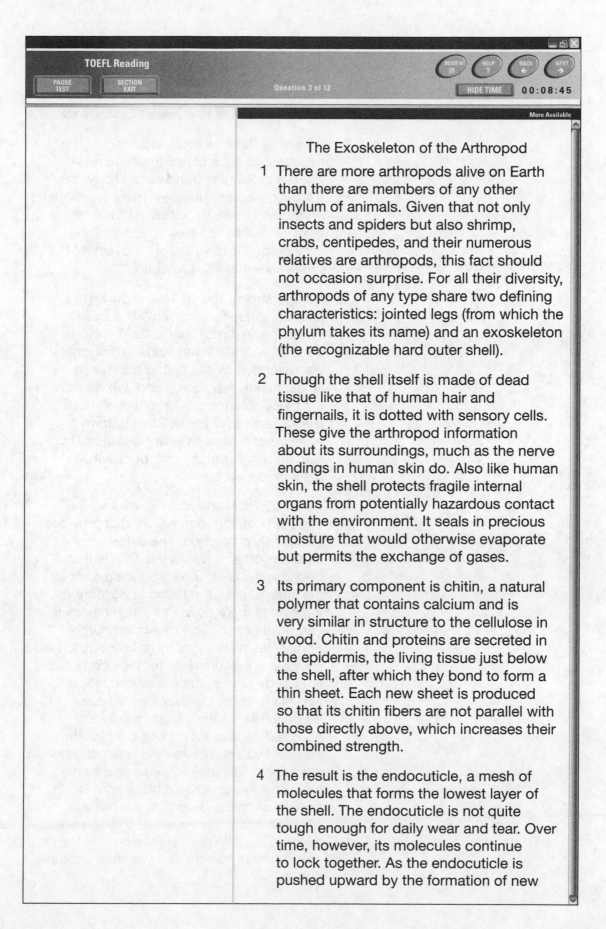

More Available

The Exoskeleton of the Arthropod

1   There are more arthropods alive on Earth than there are members of any other phylum of animals. Given that not only insects and spiders but also shrimp, crabs, centipedes, and their numerous relatives are arthropods, this fact should not occasion surprise. For all their diversity, arthropods of any type share two defining characteristics: jointed legs (from which the phylum takes its name) and an exoskeleton (the recognizable hard outer shell).

2   Though the shell itself is made of dead tissue like that of human hair and fingernails, it is dotted with sensory cells. These give the arthropod information about its surroundings, much as the nerve endings in human skin do. Also like human skin, the shell protects fragile internal organs from potentially hazardous contact with the environment. It seals in precious moisture that would otherwise evaporate but permits the exchange of gases.

3   Its primary component is chitin, a natural polymer that contains calcium and is very similar in structure to the cellulose in wood. Chitin and proteins are secreted in the epidermis, the living tissue just below the shell, after which they bond to form a thin sheet. Each new sheet is produced so that its chitin fibers are not parallel with those directly above, which increases their combined strength.

4   The result is the endocuticle, a mesh of molecules that forms the lowest layer of the shell. The endocuticle is not quite tough enough for daily wear and tear. Over time, however, its molecules continue to lock together. As the endocuticle is pushed upward by the formation of new

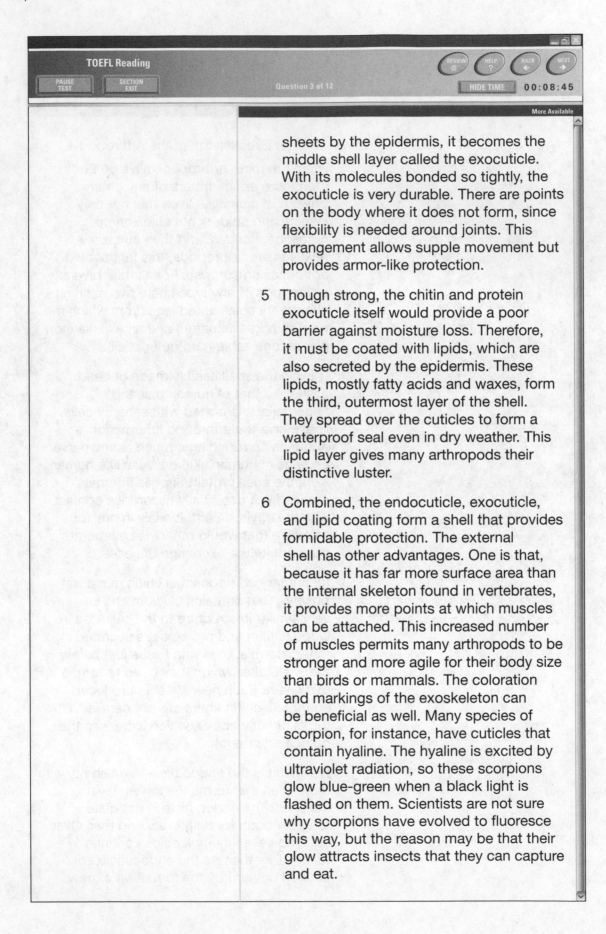

sheets by the epidermis, it becomes the middle shell layer called the exocuticle. With its molecules bonded so tightly, the exocuticle is very durable. There are points on the body where it does not form, since flexibility is needed around joints. This arrangement allows supple movement but provides armor-like protection.

5 Though strong, the chitin and protein exocuticle itself would provide a poor barrier against moisture loss. Therefore, it must be coated with lipids, which are also secreted by the epidermis. These lipids, mostly fatty acids and waxes, form the third, outermost layer of the shell. They spread over the cuticles to form a waterproof seal even in dry weather. This lipid layer gives many arthropods their distinctive luster.

6 Combined, the endocuticle, exocuticle, and lipid coating form a shell that provides formidable protection. The external shell has other advantages. One is that, because it has far more surface area than the internal skeleton found in vertebrates, it provides more points at which muscles can be attached. This increased number of muscles permits many arthropods to be stronger and more agile for their body size than birds or mammals. The coloration and markings of the exoskeleton can be beneficial as well. Many species of scorpion, for instance, have cuticles that contain hyaline. The hyaline is excited by ultraviolet radiation, so these scorpions glow blue-green when a black light is flashed on them. Scientists are not sure why scorpions have evolved to fluoresce this way, but the reason may be that their glow attracts insects that they can capture and eat.

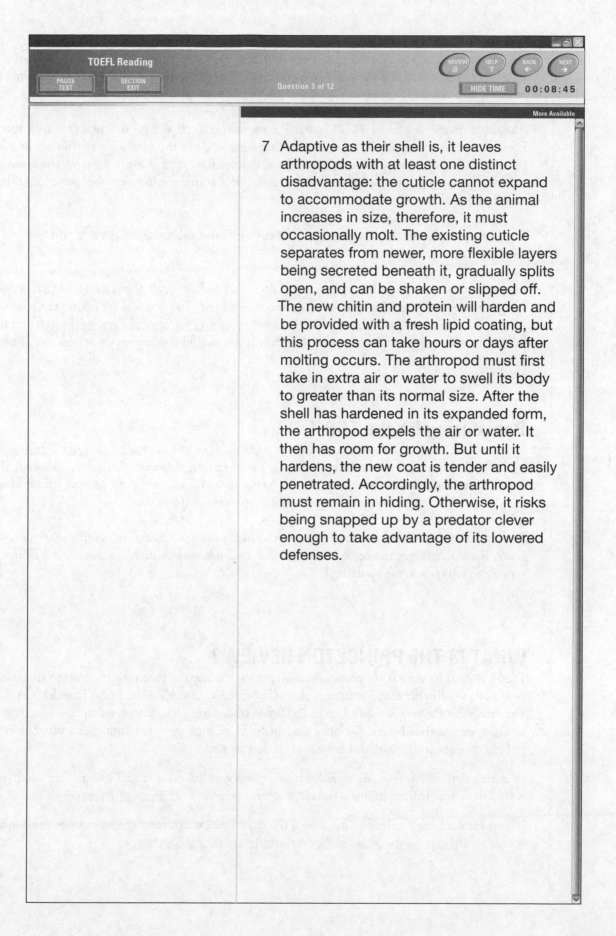

PAUSE TEST   SECTION EXIT

Question 3 of 12

HIDE TIME   00:08:45

More Available

7   Adaptive as their shell is, it leaves arthropods with at least one distinct disadvantage: the cuticle cannot expand to accommodate growth. As the animal increases in size, therefore, it must occasionally molt. The existing cuticle separates from newer, more flexible layers being secreted beneath it, gradually splits open, and can be shaken or slipped off. The new chitin and protein will harden and be provided with a fresh lipid coating, but this process can take hours or days after molting occurs. The arthropod must first take in extra air or water to swell its body to greater than its normal size. After the shell has hardened in its expanded form, the arthropod expels the air or water. It then has room for growth. But until it hardens, the new coat is tender and easily penetrated. Accordingly, the arthropod must remain in hiding. Otherwise, it risks being snapped up by a predator clever enough to take advantage of its lowered defenses.

Clearly, you cannot approach an Internet-based TOEFL reading passage the same way you would approach a paper-based test. For one thing, you won't be able to underline, circle, or otherwise make marks on the text (well, you could, but the testing center probably wouldn't be happy if you ruined its computer screens!).

Also, on the Internet-based TOEFL, you'll have to take each section of the test in its entirety. Therefore, you cannot skip part of the Reading section, go to the Listening section, and return to the Reading section. However, you can skip questions *within* some parts of the Reading section. You may want to skip questions that you do not understand in order spend more time on other questions.

The audio portions of the test are also Internet-based, and the speaking portion will ask you to speak into a recording device.

Even though this book contains paper-based drills and questions, all of the strategies in this book are geared toward preparing you for an Internet-based test. To get a feel for taking the test on a computer, you should practice at the TOEFL website: http://toeflpractice.ets.org. Even if you live in an area where accessing the Internet is difficult, you should try to practice at least once online before your testing day.

Registering for the TOEFL

Make sure to register early!

The easiest way to register for the TOEFL is online at www.ets.org/toefl/ibt/register. Because the test is Internet-based, many testing times are available, although this isn't necessarily true everywhere. Make sure you register early so that you receive a testing time and location with which you are comfortable.

You may take the TOEFL as many times as you like. Many programs will simply take your best score, but don't forget to check for specific information with admissions counselors from the schools to which you are applying.

WHAT IS THE PRINCETON REVIEW?

The Princeton Review is *the* premier test-preparation company that prepares tens of thousands of students each year for tests such as the TOEFL, SAT, GMAT, GRE, LSAT, and MCAT. At The Princeton Review, we spend countless hours researching tests and determining exactly how to crack standardized tests. We offer students proven, high-powered strategies and techniques to help them beat the tests and achieve their best scores.

In addition to our books, we offer both live classroom instruction and online courses. If you would like more information about our programs, visit us at PrincetonReview.com.

If you are looking for information on Princeton Review courses offered outside the United States, go to http://www.princetonreview.com/international/locations.

WHAT'S IN THIS BOOK

TOEFL iBT Prep contains four parts.

- **Orientation:** What you're reading now.

- **Core Concepts:** The basic skills necessary to successfully complete the exam. By working through the exercises in this section, you will have a greater understanding of how the integrated tasks on the TOEFL fit together.

- **Cracking:** The appropriate strategies to crack each question type on the TOEFL. Questions in the Listening, Speaking, and Writing sections are accompanied by audio tracks that you can listen to online (in your Student Tools).

- **Full-Length Practice Test:** After you've worked through all the exercises and drills in the previous two sections, you'll have a chance to practice under real testing conditions. After the practice exam, we provide detailed explanations for every question, as well as sample speaking and writing responses. In addition, the online audio files include samples of the types of conversations and lectures that you will hear on the test to give you a good idea of what to expect and help you develop your listening skills.

  Note: Please refer to the two-page spread (titled Get More (Free) Content) at the beginning of this book for step-by-step directions on how to register your book and access these online audio files.

For even more vocabulary practice, check out our *Essential TOEFL Vocabulary* flashcards!

WHAT'S NOT IN THIS BOOK

This book is primarily designed to aid you in preparing to take the TOEFL. By working through the book, you'll be able to pick up new vocabulary and some grammar rules, but if you need more help with the basics, there are a number of other resources available.

- The Princeton Review's *Grammar Smart*, *More Word Smart*, and *TOEFL Power Vocab* books provide extensive help with grammar and vocabulary. These books are available wherever you purchased this book, including at online retailers.
- Television, radio, film, and podcasts are enjoyable ways to learn the language. Almost any show or program will be helpful. Remember, the TOEFL asks you to listen to casual conversations, so be sure to look up words and phrases you don't understand.
- Even if you live in a non-English-speaking country, your city may have an English-language newspaper. Try reading that instead of your native-language paper.
- Reading magazines such as *Time*, *Vogue*, *Entertainment Weekly*, and *Sports Illustrated*, and newspapers such as *USA Today*, *The New York Times*, and *The Wall Street Journal* will help your comprehension and vocabulary.
- Similarly, read about current events and news online through trusted news sources. If you have a smart phone, you may wish to set news alerts so that stories of interest will be sent directly to your phone and you can read them in any spare time you may have, whether you are on the bus or waiting in line or killing time before an appointment or class.
- A quick search on the Internet will turn up a number of helpful websites devoted to helping people learn English.

This book is more useful if you are comfortable with the English language. If you are still having trouble with English, build up your confidence with the language first, and then work through this book.

HOW TO USE THIS BOOK

The material in *TOEFL iBT Prep* is provided to help students of all levels achieve higher scores on the test. Ideally, all students should work through the sections of the book in the order in which they are presented. Even students who are fairly comfortable speaking, reading, and writing in English will benefit from the information in the Core Concepts section (Part II).

Of course, if you feel that you have a strong grasp of the material, you are free to skip ahead to the Cracking section (Part III) to start working on TOEFL questions. If you find you are not progressing as you'd hoped, return to Part II and work through it first.

The best way to prepare for the TOEFL is to practice as much as possible, and this book gives you the chance to work through more than 200 sample questions. However, to get maximum value from this book, you must use the strategies and techniques we present. Many of these strategies will feel awkward or inefficient at first, but trust us: they *do* work.

CAN I REALLY IMPROVE MY SCORE?

Yes! Doing well on the TOEFL is a skill, and as with any skill, it can be learned. This book provides the tools necessary to do better on the TOEFL, but it is up to you to apply them. Work through the book at a comfortable pace. Take time to understand the strategies and techniques and *use* them. Look back at the questions you've answered: both the ones you answered correctly and the ones you answered incorrectly. Figure out what your strengths and weaknesses are on the test. Many test takers find that if they fail to use the strategies we offer, their scores don't change. However, test takers who *do* master our techniques and strategies will improve their scores.

Stages of Learning a New Language

While you have progressed through at least some of these stages already, it's important to recognize where you are in the process of learning a new language in order to maximize your preparation for the TOEFL. We map out these stages (named Stages 1 through 5) below. If at all possible, you should not attempt to take the TOEFL until you are at least comfortably into Stage 3, and preferably into Stage 4. Certainly, the more comfortable you are speaking, writing, and thinking in English, the more you can expect to gain from the time you spend preparing for the TOEFL, and therefore the higher score you can expect to earn.

1. Silent/Receptive/Pre-Production
    * You are not necessarily *silent*, but you definitely do more listening and absorbing than speaking.
    * You have a minimal comprehension in a second language.
2. Early Production
    * You begin to develop a vocabulary of about 1,000 words.
    * You start speaking in short phrases of one or two words, although not necessarily grammatically accurate.
    * You develop a limited comprehension but may use familiar phrases comfortably.
3. Speech Emergence
    * Your vocabulary grows to about 3,000 words (or more!).
    * Your comprehension improves significantly.
    * You begin to develop phrases, sentences, and questions, although they still may not necessarily be grammatically correct.
    * You might continue to make grammar and pronunciation errors (and that's okay!).
    * You should begin reading and writing in your second language.
4. Intermediate Fluency
    * Your vocabulary is as large as 6,000 words.
    * You have developed excellent comprehension and make few grammatical errors.
    * You begin writing in more complex sentences.
    * You begin thinking in the second language, which impacts proficiency significantly.
5. Continued Language Development/Advanced Fluency
    * Your comprehension and communication are nearly the same as those of a native speaker of the language.
    * It may take some time when learning a new language to get to this stage, depending on how intensively you have been studying and how frequently you have been communicating and reading in your second language.

Before We Begin

Before we discuss the TOEFL, there are a few basic principles to keep in mind for any standardized, multiple-choice test.

Wrong Answers

One of the advantages of a multiple-choice test is that the answer to every question is right there on the screen! To minimize this advantage, test writers have to make the wrong answers *seem* correct; often, the wrong answers are particularly appealing, and test takers fall into the trap of picking answers that seem too good to be true.

Learning to recognize and avoid these trap answers is one of the keys to your success on the TOEFL. For each question in this book, be sure to review both the right and wrong answers so you have an idea of what both good and bad answers look like. Also, pay close attention to our discussion of common trap answers in the Reading and Listening sections.

Increase Your Odds

Identifying wrong answers greatly improves your chances of getting a question correct. On the TOEFL, each multiple-choice question has four answer choices, which means you have a 25 percent (1 in 4) chance of guessing correctly. However, by using Process of Elimination (POE) to cross off wrong answers, you greatly increase your odds. (We discuss POE thoroughly in the "Cracking the Reading Section" chapter later in this book.) Finding and eliminating just *one* wrong answer means you have a 33 percent (1 in 3) chance of guessing correctly, and eliminating *two* answers raises your odds of guessing correctly to 50 percent (1 in 2)! This is an important fact to remember. Although you may not be able to answer every question on the TOEFL correctly, you can increase your score simply by increasing your odds when guessing.

Answer of the Day

Speaking of guessing, let me introduce another Princeton Review strategy, Answer of the Day. You will undoubtedly encounter multiple-choice questions for which you have NO idea what the right answer might be. You may be at the end of the test period and you are scrambling to fill in answers. When this happens, choose any answer (first, second, third, or fourth) and fill it in for all of your blank questions. Because there is no penalty for incorrect answers, be sure to answer every question, no matter what! When you're scrambling and wrapping up, use Answer of the Day for every question that you have not yet answered.

POOD—PERSONAL ORDER OF DIFFICULTY

POOD Across the Test

We've already talked about not needing Rock Star Status on every section, and now that we're discussing Personal Order of Difficulty, it's worth mentioning again. Remember that many schools indicate a combined score they'd like to see, and typically don't break that total down among the four sections. So, that means that you do NOT have to get the highest score possible on EVERY section in order get the score you need.

Proven Techniques
Check out these signature Princeton Review techniques to help you maximize points on the TOEFL.

Personal Order of Difficulty Within Each Section

In Reading and Listening, the passages and lectures/conversations are not presented in any particular order of difficulty. That means YOU have to decide—BEFORE TEST DAY!—which types of questions are easiest for YOU, and which ones are tougher. So it's important to remember that you need to walk in with a plan, knowing what types of Reading questions, for example, are easier for YOU, and which ones aren't worth your time.

Check out Part III: Cracking Each Section of the TOEFL to map out your test day strategy.

GENERAL STRATEGIES TO IMPROVE YOUR ENGLISH AND PREPARE FOR THE TOEFL

There are many strategies you can employ that will not only help you prepare for the TOEFL, but also help you improve your fundamental English skills. Many of these approaches can also impact several sections of the TOEFL, all at once. Here are a few suggestions. Read on for advice on how to space these out, depending upon how much time you have until your test date.

Read Articles Online or in Magazines

Go online and read—read anything! But don't just READ. As you read, ask yourself the following questions:

- When you see a pronoun, ask yourself to whom or what is the pronoun referring? What noun is it replacing?
  - This is an important skill to develop for everyday conversation, but questions that ask what noun a pronoun replaces are very common on the TOEFL!
- Summarize every paragraph—put it into your own words, and then WRITE it down! This will give you practice putting ideas into your own words, and it will also give you practice writing in English too.

- Summarize the entire article—what's the main point? Why do you think the author wrote the article? What is the author's opinion?
- Ask a friend who speaks English to read the same articles and then have a conversation about them—in English, of course! Summarize the articles, ask each other's opinion, think about what the people involved in the situation might think.

Watch TV or Listen to the Radio (or a Podcast!)

Watch one episode of a TV show or listen to a radio show or podcast in English. During and after the show, complete the following activities:

- Every time there is a scene change, pause the show and summarize what just happened.
  - What did the characters talk about?
  - Is one of them having a problem? If so, what is it?
  - Did one of them offer a solution? If so, what was the solution?
  - Are the characters happy? Sad? Angry? Why?
    - Discuss the TV/radio show/podcast with a friend, just like you did with the articles mentioned above.
    - As you watch/listen, make notes of what the characters are saying, just like you'll have to do on the TOEFL. Then write a 3–4 paragraph summary of the show to practice your writing skills.

Headphones On!

Build Your Vocabulary

- Look up words you don't know when you come across them in your reading.
- Study Greek and Latin root words—they form the basis for a large number of words in the English language! If you're not familiar with them, get your hands on a copy of *TOEFL Power Vocab*, published by The Princeton Review.

Practice Brainstorming for the Speaking Section

Using the following prompts, brainstorm your responses for the independent speaking tasks.

Personal Preference

1. What is your favorite book/movie? Describe it and explain why it is your favorite.
2. Who is your least favorite actor/musician? Describe this person and explain why she/he is your least favorite.
3. What do you like to do in your free time? Describe this activity and explain why you like to do it.
4. Where do you like to go on vacation? Describe this place and explain why you like to go there.
5. What is your favorite academic subject? Describe the subject and explain why you like to study it.

6. Who is an influential person from your country? Describe this person and explain why she/he is influential.

7. Talk about a person in your life who has been inspirational to you. Describe this person and explain how she/he has inspired you.

8. What is your favorite memory from your youth? Describe the memory and explain why it stands out to you.

9. What is the most important holiday in your country? Describe the holiday and explain why it is important.

10. Talk about a situation in which you felt uncomfortable. Describe the situation and explain why you were uncomfortable.

11. What do you like to do to relax? Describe this activity and explain how it helps you relax.

12. What do you find difficult to study? Describe this subject and explain why you struggle with it.

13. Talk about your favorite type of food. Describe this food and explain why it is your favorite.

14. What is the best advice you have ever received? Describe the advice and explain why it meant so much to you.

15. What is a popular tourist attraction in your country? Describe this attraction and explain why it is popular.

16. What do you enjoy doing with your family? Describe this activity and explain why your family enjoys doing it.

17. Where would you like to travel in the future? Describe this place and explain why you would like to go there.

18. What is your favorite athletic activity? Describe this activity and explain why it's your favorite.

19. What is your favorite mode of transportation around your hometown? Describe this mode and explain why it's your favorite.

20. What is your favorite type of animal? Describe this animal and explain why you like it.

Choose an Option

1. Some people prefer to attend a university that has fairly small class sizes, while others prefer to attend large institutions that have more lecture-style classes with hundreds of students. Which do you prefer, and why? Support your answer with specific reasons or examples.

2. Some high schools require students to wear uniforms, while others allow students to choose their own attire. Which do you prefer, and why? Use specific examples to support your opinion.

3. In some cities, public transportation is a reliable way to get around. Do you prefer to use public transit or your own vehicle? Use specific reasons and examples to support your opinion.

4. Some educators believe that students should participate in physical exercise every single day, while others feel that students should focus all of their attention on academics. Which do you feel is more helpful for students? Use specific examples to support your opinion.

5. Some people like to go out with large groups of friends to have fun. Others prefer to spend time with just a few friends and have a quiet dinner. Which do you prefer, and why? Use specific reasons to explain your preference.

6. People work in different ways: some prefer to go to a job where they sit at a desk for most of the work day, while others prefer to spend time traveling from job site to job site. Which do you prefer? Use specific reasons and examples to explain your answer.

7. Some people believe that a student must go to college in order to be successful in life. Others feel that going to a vocational school to learn a trade is a better option. Which do you feel is the better option? Use specific reasons to explain your opinion.

8. Some people prefer to listen to music while exercising, while others prefer to listen to the sounds around them. Which do you prefer to do? Use specific examples and reasons to explain your preference.

9. Some people like to stay up late at night and then sleep late in the mornings. Others prefer to go to bed earlier and get up earlier the next day. Which do you prefer? Use specific examples and reasons to explain your preference.

10. Some parents are very involved in their children's academic lives, helping with homework, talking with teachers, and volunteering at school. Other parents choose to take a lesser role in their children's academic programs. Do you prefer your parents to be more involved in your schooling or less? Use specific reasons and examples to support your opinion.

11. Some people prefer to talk on the phone, but others prefer to text. Which manner of communication do you prefer? Use specific reasons and examples to explain your opinion.

12. Some people prefer to be surrounded by large groups of friends and family for special events, like weddings or graduations. Others prefer to have smaller gatherings, perhaps without any friends or family at all. Which do you prefer? Use specific examples and reasons to explain your opinion.

13. Some people really like living in a big city. Others prefer living in a small town. Which do you like better? Use specific reasons to support your opinion.

14. Is it more valuable to be able to work with others or to be able to set your own goals and deadlines as you work independently? Why? Use specific reasons and examples to support your opinion.

15. Do you prefer to spend money as soon as you earn it, or would you rather save it to buy something at a later time? Why? Use specific reasons and examples to support your opinion.

16. Traveling the world can be very insightful and educational. Do you prefer to travel by yourself or with other companions? Why? Use specific examples to support your opinion.

17. Moving from place to place can be stressful, but can also bring new opportunities. Do you prefer to live in one place for a long time or to move someplace new every few years? Use specific examples and reasons to explain your opinion.

18. Which would you prefer: a job that pays a lot of money but that you don't really enjoy, or a job that you really love that doesn't pay as well? Use specific examples and reasons to explain your opinion.

19. Many colleges give students the flexibility to choose to live in dorms on campus or in apartments in nearby communities. Would you prefer to live on campus or off campus, and why? Use specific reasons and examples to support your opinion.

20. As we progress into the 21st century, educational opportunities are expanding. Some students have found great success in studying online at their own pace. Other students prefer a more traditional education in a typical school building. Which manner of studying do you think is better? Use specific examples and reasons to support your opinion.

Practice Brainstorming for the Writing

Use any of the "choice" prompts, reprinted below: write a brief outline of your response and then, if you are feeling ambitious and have the time, write a full essay. You can do it!

Choose an Option

1. Some people prefer to attend a university that has fairly small class sizes, while others prefer to attend large institutions that have more lecture-style classes with hundreds of students. Which do you prefer, and why? Support your answer with specific reasons or examples.

2. Some high schools require students to wear uniforms, while others allow students to choose their own attire. Which do you prefer, and why? Use specific examples to support your opinion.

3. In some cities, public transportation is a reliable way to get around. Do you prefer to use public transit or your own vehicle? Use specific reasons and examples to support your opinion.

4. Some educators believe that students should participate in physical exercise every single day, while others feel that students should focus all of their attention on academics. Which do you feel is more helpful for students? Use specific examples to support your opinion.

5. Some people like to go out with large groups of friends to have fun. Others prefer to spend time with just a few friends and have a quiet dinner. Which do you prefer, and why? Use specific reasons to explain your preference.

6. People work in different ways: some prefer to go to a job where they sit at a desk for most of the work day, while others prefer to spend time traveling from job site to job site. Which do you prefer? Use specific reasons and examples to explain your answer.

7. Some people believe that a student must go to college in order to be successful in life. Others feel that going to a vocational school to learn a trade is a better option. Which do you feel is the better option? Use specific reasons to explain your opinion.

8. Some people prefer to listen to music while exercising, while others prefer to listen to the sounds around them. Which do you prefer to do? Use specific examples and reasons to explain your preference.

9. Some people like to stay up late at night and then sleep late in the mornings. Others prefer to go to bed earlier and get up earlier the next day. Which do you prefer? Use specific examples and reasons to explain your preference.

10. Some parents are very involved in their children's academic lives, helping with homework, talking with teachers, and volunteering at school. Other parents choose to take a lesser role in their children's academic programs. Do you prefer your parents to be more involved in your schooling or less? Use specific reasons and examples to support your opinion.

Applied Strategies
What is the best way to prepare for the Writing section of the TOEFL? Practice, practice, practice and by that we mean write, write, write!

11. Some people prefer to talk on the phone, but others prefer to text. Which manner of communication do you prefer? Use specific reasons and examples to explain your opinion.

12. Some people prefer to be surrounded by large groups of friends and family for special events, like weddings or graduations. Others prefer to have smaller gatherings, perhaps without any friends or family at all. Which do you prefer? Use specific examples and reasons to explain your opinion.

13. Some people really like living in a big city. Others prefer living in a small town. Which do you like better? Use specific reasons to support your opinion.

14. Is it more valuable to be able to work with others or to be able to set your own goals and deadlines as you work independently? Why? Use specific reasons and examples to support your opinion.

15. Do you prefer to spend money as soon as you earn it, or would you rather save it to buy something at a later time? Why? Use specific reasons and examples to support your opinion.

16. Traveling the world can be very insightful and educational. Do you prefer to travel by yourself or with other companions? Why? Use specific examples to support your opinion.

17. Moving from place to place can be stressful, but can also bring new opportunities. Do you prefer to live in one place for a long time or to move someplace new every few years? Use specific examples and reasons to explain your opinion.

18. Which would you prefer: a job that pays a lot of money but that you don't really enjoy, or a job that you really love that doesn't pay as well? Use specific examples and reasons to explain your opinion.

19. Many colleges give students the flexibility to choose to live in dorms on campus or in apartments in nearby communities. Would you prefer to live on campus or off campus, and why? Use specific reasons and examples to support your opinion.

20. As we progress into the 21st century, educational opportunities are expanding. Some students have found great success in studying online at their own pace. Other students prefer a more traditional education in a typical school building. Which manner of studying do you think is better? Use specific examples and reasons to support your opinion.

Computer Practice

The TOEFL iBT is offered only online, so make sure you're comfortable with basic computer functions. No specialized knowledge is required, but you should know how to use a keyboard and mouse. Some basic typing skills will also be helpful on the Writing section.

STUDY PLANS

Regardless of how much time you have until you take the TOEFL, you should start by taking a practice test to identify your current score level.

Then, you need to find out what scores are required at the schools where you plan to apply. Be sure to identify whether there is a *minimum* score requirement, or whether they are looking for an *average* score. This is important to determine which areas you should focus on between now and the test. Also find out whether the school pays more attention to one sub-score over the others. Most schools simply want to see a combined score (all 4 sections added together).

Here are our suggestions about how to structure your time based on the length of time between now and your test date. Once you've determined which structure works best for you, be sure to set a day-by-day plan, even if you're spending only a half hour per day. Put appointments in your calendar, just as you would put a work meeting in. You may also want to consider finding a study partner (even if they aren't preparing for the TOEFL!) or an accountability partner. It's easier to stick to a plan when you have someone to help you stay focused.

8 Weeks Out

With a solid 8 weeks to get ready, you can likely see improvement in all four areas of the test. You should dedicate one hour a day and choose one day of the week on which to invest two hours. This will allow you to invest 2 hours per subject, per week.

During the first week, start with the practice test in this book to identify your stronger and weaker subject areas. Then, invest equal amounts of time in each section so you're working to improve all of them. Feel free to start with the section that you feel least comfortable with, but don't abandon your areas of strength—they all count toward your total score!

During the second and third weeks, continue to practice all four subject areas.

Proven Techniques
Plan your studying—it's the best way to stay organized and meet your goals.

In the fourth week, take your second practice test. ETS offers one free online practice test. *The Official Guide to the TOEFL® Test* has four additional practice tests or you can purchase additional practice exams through ETS online. Continue to study all four areas, but feel free to start spending more time on the areas you feel less comfortable with and lessen the amount of time you spend on your stronger areas.

During the fifth and sixth weeks, continue studying all four areas, with more time dedicated to the areas that you find more difficult.

At the beginning of the seventh week, take your third practice test. At this point, focus mostly on any area you still find challenging, as this will be the last week you can spend a lot of time on it.

At the beginning of the eighth week, take your final practice test. At this point, go back to focusing on all four content areas, with a primary focus on the areas you feel strongest in. Going into the official exam, you want to ensure that you have your stronger areas as sharp as can be so you can get the most points possible out of them!

4 Weeks Out

With four weeks to prepare for the TOEFL, you'll need to prioritize your studying a bit.

During the first week, take the first practice test. Then dedicate 6 hours this week to the two areas that you feel least comfortable with. Spend 1 or 2 hours doing a bit of practice on your two stronger areas.

At the beginning of the second week, take the second practice test. Then invest 6 hours this week on the two subjects that are lowest on this test. Spend another 2 hours reviewing the areas that you feel better about.

At the beginning of the third week, take the third practice test. This week, though, you're going to shift gears and focus on the areas that are the strongest so you can get as many points out of them as possible.

> ETS's free official practice test is available at https://www.ets.org/toefl/ibt/prepare/free_practice_test

At the beginning of the fourth week, take the last practice test. This week, you won't focus on any particular area. Instead, you'll spend 15 to 20 minutes each day on every subject area. This way, you'll end up spending between an hour and an hour and a half, total, each day.

2 Weeks Out

If your test is two weeks away, your best bet is to focus on the areas you're strongest in—it doesn't matter where the points come from, and you're more likely to see significant improvement over a short time frame in the areas you feel most confident about already.

At the beginning of the first week, take the first practice test. Once you identify the two areas with the highest scores, invest an hour each day in each subject. That means you'll be studying at least 2 hours each day. If you have the time, also spend some time on the areas you feel less comfortable with.

At the beginning of the second week, take the second practice test. This week you're going to continue focusing on your stronger areas. Spend at least 2 hours each, divided into 1 hour per subject. Also do everything you can to spend at least 15–30 minutes on the areas you feel less comfortable with.

The Week Before the Test

You should allow yourself about four to six weeks of preparation before you take the TOEFL. You cannot cram for the TOEFL, but there are some things you can do in the final week before the test.

1. **Review strategies:** Look back over the strategies in this book. Make sure you are comfortable with them.
2. **Review tasks:** Before the test, review the four different tasks on the TOEFL (Reading, Listening, Speaking, and Writing). Familiarize yourself with the format and the question types you'll see on test day.
3. **Know the directions:** Don't waste time on test day reading the directions for each task. Learn the directions ahead of time. They won't change.
4. **Warm-up questions:** Look back at the questions you've completed. Review how you approached each one. Note any trap answers and question types that were particularly difficult for you.
5. **Have a plan:** Make sure you know the format for your speaking and writing tasks. Review the structure of your responses. Also make sure you've reviewed your Personal Order of Difficulty for Reading and Listening so you have a plan for which questions to tackle and which ones will get Answer of the Day.

Beyond the Test

Many students focus so much on the academic prep for their upcoming tests that they totally forget other areas that are just as important.

- **Sleep!** Your brain won't function very well if you're not well rested. Make sure you get a good night's sleep every night for at least 3–4 nights before the test. The more the better!

- **Exercise!** Especially if you think you may be nervous going into the test, make sure to stick to a healthy exercise schedule. Exercise is a fantastic stress reliever! It's also a great way to get focused before a study session. Even 10 minutes of brisk walking can help you learn more effectively and remember more. Of course, make sure you ask your doctor for insight before you begin any exercise program.

- **Eat!** Just as your brain won't work very well without sleep, it certainly won't function without nourishment. Make sure to eat a healthy breakfast before you start the test.

- **Prepare Mentally!** Many of the world's most successful athletes spend time visualizing themselves executing their sport perfectly. You can do the same thing! Picture yourself sitting at the desk, reading a passage comfortably and using Process of Elimination easily on the answers. Envision yourself listening comfortably to the recordings and making brief notes about the important parts of the lectures and conversations. Imagine yourself speaking calmly and smoothly during the Speaking section. See yourself using your templates (more on that later) in the Writing section.

Study Break
In the midst of your hours and hours of studying, be sure to give yourself a break—a study break—and take a walk, listen to a song you love, eat a snack. Giving yourself some time to chill and disengage is an important part of studying and preparing for the test.

Test Day

On the night before the test, put your practice materials aside and give yourself a break. Make sure you know where your test center is, and plan to arrive at least 30 minutes before your scheduled test time. Be sure to dress comfortably and take a valid photo ID (such as a passport) to the test center. You should also take two pencils to take notes, although many centers will provide pencils. You may not take anything else into the testing center, so do not take food, backpacks, suitcases, cell phones, or laptops. You should also plan time to take a walk or do some kind of exercise to get your blood flowing, and definitely do a bit of a mental warm-up. You could do a puzzle, read a chapter of a book, or review notes about things you want to remember for the test.

Option to Cancel Your Scores

When you've completed the TOEFL iBT, you will have the option to cancel your scores. There are a few really important points to consider before deciding to cancel:

- You will NOT get your money back.
- Your scores will NOT be reported to schools.
- You can't pick and choose parts of the test to cancel—either you keep the whole thing or you cancel the whole thing.
- Your test CAN be reinstated within 60 days for a US$20 fee (please check http://www.ets.org/toefl/ibt/about/fees/ for current fees).

You should also conduct your research in advance to inquire about how schools view multiple tests.

Part II:
Core Concepts

Chapter 2
Core Concept: Reading

The TOEFL is an integrated exam, which means that each task may measure more than one skill. But the TOEFL is also a standardized test, which means that it consists of definite patterns. Your goal when taking the TOEFL is to make sure your responses conform to the patterns present on the test. The reading selections in this chapter will form the foundation for your listening and writing goals. Likewise, the skills needed to perform well in listening, speaking, and writing are closely intertwined. You'll find that mastering the core concepts of one section will also help you on other sections of the test.

READING ON THE TOEFL

The TOEFL has three to four reading passages, each around 700 words. Each passage will is followed by 10 questions. Although the TOEFL writers attempt to simulate the type of reading you will do in a university or graduate school program, the reading skills required on the test are very different from the skills used in an academic environment. Let's take a look at a passage.

1 Scientists at Michigan State University are asking a most challenging question. Can a computer program be considered alive? The members of the Digital Evolution Laboratory say yes. Computer scientists at the laboratory have created a program called Avida that has intrigued not only scientists and engineers but biologists and philosophers as well.

2 The Avida project began in the late 1990s, when Chris Adami, a physicist, sought to create computer programs that could evolve to do simple addition problems and reproduce inside a digital environment. Adami called these programs "digital organisms." Whenever a digital organism replicates, it has a chance to alter the program of the newly created offspring. In this way, the programs mutate and evolve. The goal of the Avida program is to create a model that could simulate the evolutionary process.

3 Initially, the digital creations were unable to process numbers in any way. But Adami designed Avida to reward digital organisms that were able to work with the numbers in some way. The digital organisms that could process numbers were allowed to reproduce in higher numbers. In only six short months, the primitive program had evolved a number of mechanisms to perform addition. And, most surprisingly, not all of the digital creatures performed addition in the same way.

4 The Avida program now resides at Michigan State University, where it has been growing and changing for years. The digital creatures number in the billions and have colonized more than two hundred computers. The organisms compete with one another for resources, and the most successful ones are able to make more copies of themselves. Just like living creatures, the digital entities also undergo mutations. Mutations that are beneficial ensure greater reproduction; harmful mutations have the opposite effect.

5 As a model for studying evolution, the Avida project has been a great success. Adami's digital organisms have suggested solutions to some of evolution's biggest mysteries. For example, Avida has helped disprove the theory of "irreducible complexity." Opponents of evolutionary theory have suggested that some structures, such as the eye, are too complex to have been created in piecemeal stages. The evolution of Avida's digital organisms proves that even extremely complex structures can be developed in stages over time.

6 The Avida program's success has also raised some unintentional philosophical dilemmas. Does Avida just simulate evolution, or are digital organisms a new form of life? According to the director of the Avida project, the processes undergone by the digital creatures are the same as those experienced by biological organisms. The only difference is that biological entities are based on strings of DNA, whereas the digital creations from

Avida are based on strings of ones and zeros. In a living creature, different sequences of DNA instruct cells to create certain proteins. In one of the Avida creations, different sequences of computer code instruct the program to perform certain functions. In both cases, the reproduction of the organisms is subject to forces such as competition and mutation.

7　Now, some biologists are maintaining that the programs in the Avida project are alive. The programs live, die, reproduce, compete, cooperate, and evolve—activities that many biologists consider the hallmarks of life. One prominent biologist says, "They don't have a metabolism—at least not yet. But otherwise, they're alive."

8　Of course, not everyone agrees that the program's creations are alive. One difficulty is that biologists do not even agree on the definition of life. The diversity of life on Earth constantly surprises scientists, and there are simply too many characteristics and qualities to provide one simple definition of life.

9　Despite these misgivings, the directors of the Avida program remain optimistic that their program, even if not considered alive, is leading to a greater understanding of life in all its forms. It may even facilitate future searches for life on other planets. According to one member of the Avida team, "The problem that we have now is that we are focused on looking for DNA-based life. But there may be other kinds of life out there that we have never dreamed of." The Avida program may provide biologists with another avenue to explore.

This passage is typical of the passages on the TOEFL. It's about 700 words long, and it discusses an academic topic. It contains some challenging vocabulary words and requires you to read about a topic in which you may have no interest or knowledge. Although you may end up reading passages such as this at a university or graduate program, your approach for the TOEFL should be very different. For example, in a college course, you would need to read this passage very carefully, paying close attention to the details and facts presented in it. That type of close reading, however, is neither possible nor necessary on the TOEFL. You should employ a tactic called "active reading" rather than close reading.

Working on Active Reading

In this chapter, we focus a lot on active reading. You might ask yourself how active reading differs from the way you ordinarily read. Active reading requires you to read with purpose; analyzing the material and looking for specific things within that material is something you will be asked to do on this section of the TOEFL. We want to make sure you get into the habit now so on test day you'll be prepared. The reading skills necessary for the TOEFL really are different from the skills you need for other types of reading that you do. Therefore, to do well on the TOEFL, you have to work on active reading. You will have to face many challenges in the Reading section. You've already seen an example of the level of content and vocabulary you may encounter. Perhaps the greatest challenge, however, is to attempt to both read the passages and answer the questions in the limited time provided. If you tackle every question, you have only about a minute and a half per question, and that's without allowing any time for actually reading the passage!

Therefore, instead of attempting to retain all of the information in the passage, you should focus on the big picture. Active reading involves completing three major steps.

1. **State the main idea:** Figure out what the passage is about.
2. **Understand the structure:** Figure out key information by mapping the passage.
3. **Find the purpose:** Figure out why the author wrote the piece.

By mastering the skill of active reading, you'll be able to not only find the most important information in a passage but also effectively and accurately answer the questions that follow the passage. After all, you gain no points on the TOEFL for simply reading the passages; you get points only for answering the questions correctly.

STEPS TO MASTERING ACTIVE READING

Step 1: State the Main Idea

All passages on the TOEFL have a main idea. The main idea is the central message or point of the passage. Finding the main idea answers this question: what is the author writing about?

Let's take a look at a passage and work on learning how to find the main idea.

To find the main idea, read the first sentence or two of the introduction, the first sentence of each body paragraph, and then the first and last sentence of the conclusion. After reading each sentence again ask yourself, "What is the author writing about?"

1 Sometimes it appears that the human mark on this planet is indelible. In only a blink of geological time, 200 years or so, human construction and expansion has resulted in the destruction of more than one-fifth of the world's forests, the recession of the polar icecaps, and the creation of a huge hole in the ozone layer. Additionally, industrial activity has damaged rivers and oceans, as well as groundwater supplies. Environmental scientists and activists warn that if Earth's future is not taken into account, humankind could very well destroy the planet.

What is the author writing about? _____

_____

2 However, Earth is an amazingly resilient place. In its 4.5-billion-year lifespan, Earth has endured bombardment by cosmic rays and meteors, violent earthquakes, volcanism, and frigid ice ages. In light of all these catastrophic events, many geologists and ecologists say that Earth could recover from any damage caused by human actions.

What is the author writing about? _____

_____

3 The author Alan Weisman has gone so far as to predict exactly what would happen on Earth if all humans were to disappear. Without upkeep, the concrete jungles of the world's largest cities would be slowly reclaimed by the wilderness around them. Harsh temperatures would cause pavement to crack. Plants would return to areas covered by streets and sidewalks.

What is the author writing about?

_____

_____

4 Different fates would await humankind's other creations. Litter and leaf matter would accumulate, and it would take only one chance lightning strike to start a raging fire. Many structures would burn to the ground. The steel foundations supporting larger buildings and bridges would corrode and buckle, especially with the rise in groundwater that would accompany the clogging of sewer systems.

What is the author writing about?

_____

_____

5 Without human interference, many of the threatened or endangered fauna would reclaim their ecological niches. Unfortunately, household pets would suffer. In addition, the rat, one of the greatest pests in large cities, would not have the waste of humankind to feed on and would be hunted mercilessly by growing populations of hawks and falcons. And the cockroach, which to many a city dweller seems to symbolize invincibility, would disappear from all but the warmest climes without artificial heat to sustain it.

What is the author writing about?

_____

_____

6 Within 500 years, again barely a heartbeat in geological time, most of humankind's monuments would be gone, covered over by plants and trees. It's happened before; the Mayan civilization in Northern Guatemala survived for 2,000 years but was swallowed up by the jungle at its end. And after a few thousand years, if earthquakes and volcanic eruptions have not obliterated everything made by humans, the glaciers would come, sweeping down from the mountains, slowly and inexorably destroying everything in their path. Several times in its history, Earth has been swept clean by these giant sheets of ice. The legacy of humankind would be wiped from Earth.

What is the author writing about?

_____

_____

7 Of course, not every man-made artifact would be reclaimed by nature. Plastic is a synthetic material that does not occur in nature. The strong bonds that hold plastic together are virtually impervious to natural erosion. Long after concrete and glass have turned back into sand and all processed metals have rusted away, plastics will still be cycling through the Earth's ecosystem, resilient to even the most destructive of natural forces. Some scientists believe that plastic molecules may eventually break down entirely, but there is no reliable data on just how long complete re-assimilation into the environment might take. Furthermore, it is impossible to predict just what sort of resources Mother Nature might develop in the distant future. There is always the possibility that, given enough time, some microbe or bacteria may evolve the capability to digest plastic. If nature somehow evolved a way to process plastics, then even humanity's most enduring artifacts might vanish in the space of a few hundred years.

What is the author writing about? _____

_____

8 The question of plastics aside, there is some evidence that Weisman's view may be true. Since 1953, a 150-mile-long tract of land separating North and South Korea has been declared a no-man's-land. After only a little more than 50 years, there is almost no trace of the rice paddies that farmers had created and used for almost 5,000 years. Even more spectacular are the flocks of red-crowned cranes that now inhabit the zone. These birds are the second rarest of all birds, but they have flourished in this area, free from human interference of all kinds.

What is the author writing about? _____

_____

Let's gather up the first sentences of each paragraph and the last sentence of the conclusion to see what we have. Your notes should be similar to the following.

Paragraph 1   Sometimes it appears that the human mark on this planet is indelible.
Paragraph 2   However, Earth is an amazingly resilient place.
Paragraph 3   The author Alan Weisman has gone so far as to predict exactly what would happen on Earth if all humans were to disappear.
Paragraph 4   Different fates would await humankind's other creations.
Paragraph 5   Without human interference, many of the threatened or endangered fauna would reclaim their ecological niches.
Paragraph 6   Within 500 years, again barely a heartbeat in geological time, most of humankind's monuments would be gone, covered over by plants and trees.
Paragraph 7   Of course, not every man-made artifact would be reclaimed by nature.
Paragraph 8   The question of plastics aside, there is some evidence that Weisman's view may be true.
Last sentence These birds are the second rarest of all birds, but they have flourished in this area, free from human interference of all kinds.

When stating the main idea, we must try to tie together all of these topics. Take a look at the sentences above and write down what you think the main idea is.

_____

_____

_____

A good answer to this question might be as follows:

If humans were to disappear, plants and animals would soon take over Earth again.

Notice how this sentence brings together all of the elements. The sentence from paragraph 4 mentions people; the sentences from paragraph 2 mentions Earth; and the sentences from paragraphs 1, 3, 5, 6, 7, and 8 mention both.

Let's try it one more time. Try to find the main idea of the following passage, which we saw at the beginning of this chapter. Write your notes about each paragraph in the space provided and note your thoughts on the main idea after the passage.

1 Scientists at Michigan State University are asking a most challenging question. Can a computer program be considered alive? The members of the Digital Evolution Laboratory say yes. Computer scientists at the laboratory have created a program called Avida that has intrigued not only scientists and engineers but biologists and philosophers as well.

What is the author writing about? _____

_____

2 The Avida project began in the late 1990s, when Chris Adami, a physicist, sought to create computer programs that could evolve to do simple addition problems and reproduce inside a digital environment. Adami called these programs "digital organisms." Whenever a digital organism replicates, it has a chance to alter the program of the newly created offspring. In this way, the programs mutate and evolve. The goal of the Avida program is to create a model that could simulate the evolutionary process.

What is the author writing about? _____

_____

3 Initially, the digital creations were unable to process numbers in any way. But Adami designed Avida to reward digital organisms that were able to work with the numbers in some way. The digital organisms that could process numbers were allowed to reproduce in higher numbers. In only six short months, the primitive program had evolved a number of mechanisms to perform addition. And, most surprisingly, not all of the digital creatures performed addition in the same way.

What is the author writing about? _____

_____

4 The Avida program now resides at Michigan State University, where it has been growing and changing for years. The digital creatures number in the billions and have colonized more than two hundred computers. The organisms compete with one another for resources, and the most successful ones are able to make more copies of themselves. Just like living creatures, the digital entities also undergo mutations. Mutations that are beneficial ensure greater reproduction; harmful mutations have the opposite effect.

What is the author writing about? _____

_____

5 As a model for studying evolution, the Avida project has been a great success. Adami's digital organisms have suggested solutions to some of evolution's biggest mysteries. For example, Avida has helped disprove the theory of "irreducible complexity." Opponents of evolutionary theory have suggested that some structures, such as the eye, are too complex to have been created in piecemeal stages. The evolution of Avida's digital organisms proves that even extremely complex structures can be developed in stages over time.

What is the author writing about? _____

_____

6 The Avida program's success has also raised some unintentional philosophical dilemmas. Does Avida just simulate evolution, or are digital organisms a new form of life? According to the director of the Avida project, the processes undergone by the digital creatures are the same as those experienced by biological organisms. The only difference is that biological entities are based on strings of DNA, whereas the digital creations from Avida are based on strings of ones and zeros. In a living creature, different sequences of DNA instruct cells to create certain proteins. In one of the Avida creations, different sequences of computer code instruct the program to perform certain functions. In both cases, the reproduction of the organisms is subject to forces such as competition and mutation.

What is the author writing about? _____

_____

7 Now, some biologists are maintaining that the programs in the Avida project are alive. The programs live, die, reproduce, compete, cooperate, and evolve—activities that many biologists consider the hallmarks of life. One prominent biologist says, "They don't have a metabolism—at least not yet. But otherwise, they're alive."

What is the author writing about? _____

_____

8 Of course, not everyone agrees that the program's creations are alive. One difficulty is that biologists do not even agree on the definition of life. The diversity of life on Earth constantly surprises scientists, and there are simply too many characteristics and qualities to provide one simple definition of life.

What is the author writing about? _____

_____

9 Despite these misgivings, the directors of the Avida program remain optimistic that their program, even if not considered alive, is leading to a greater understanding of life in all its forms. It may even facilitate future searches for life on other planets. According to one member of the Avida team, "The problem that we have now is that we are focused on looking for DNA-based life. But there may be other kinds of life out there that we have never dreamed of." The Avida program may provide biologists with another avenue to explore.

What is the author writing about? _____

_____

Write down what you think the main idea is:

_____

_____

_____

Here are the first sentences of each paragraph and the last sentence of the conclusion.

Paragraph 1   Scientists at Michigan State University are asking a most challenging question.
Paragraph 2   The Avida project began in the late 1990s, when Chris Adami, a physicist, sought to create a computer program that could evolve to do simple addition problems and reproduce inside a digital environment.
Paragraph 3   Initially, the digital creations were unable to process numbers in any way.
Paragraph 4   The Avida program now resides at Michigan State University, where it has been growing and changing for years.
Paragraph 5   As a model for studying evolution, the Avida project has been a great success.
Paragraph 6   The Avida program's success has raised some unintentional philosophical dilemmas.
Paragraph 7   Now, some biologists are maintaining that the programs in the Avida project are alive.
Paragraph 8   Of course, not everyone agrees that the program's creations are alive.
Paragraph 9   Despite these misgivings, the directors of the Avida program remain optimistic that their program, even if not considered alive, is leading to a greater understanding of life in all its forms.
Last sentence   The Avida program may provide biologists with another avenue to explore.

We could state our main idea as follows:

> The features of the Avida computer program have led some biologists to consider the program alive.

Because the Avida program is mentioned in sentences from paragraphs 2, 4, 5, 6, 7, 8, and 9, we definitely need it in our main idea. The sentences from paragraphs 2 and 4 talk about the program "evolving," "changing," and "growing." Later, the program is described as "alive" and likened to a "biological organism." So we also need to put this concept into our main idea.

Main Idea: Paying Attention to Direction Markers

When finding the main idea, pay close attention to direction markers.

Look for the following common direction words:

Same Direction	
And	For example
Because	One reason
Even	Due to
Therefore	Also
Another	

Opposite Direction	
Although	In contrast to
However	On the other hand
Yet	Rather
Despite	Even though
But	

Here's an example. Circle any direction markers you can find. Also note the main idea of each paragraph, as you did in the last exercise.

1 Art has always occupied a special place in society. Many people consider artists to be the ultimate authorities on aesthetics, the nature and expression of beauty. For much of history, the practice of art was inscrutable, and artists were viewed as being somewhat strange and often mad. Even the word most commonly associated with artists—inspiration—has its own magical overtones. Literally, "inspiration" is the breathing in of a spirit. Artists were thought of as people who were divinely inspired to create.

What is the author writing about? _____

_____

Did you find any direction markers? If so, list them here. _____

_____

2 Of course, artists contributed to this mythology. Many artists ascribed their talents to the presence of some supernatural agent or "muse." Whole movements of art have centered on the supposedly otherworldly nature of art. For example, the Romantic poets believed that art was the search for the sublime, a term for them that meant an ultimate expression of beauty and truth. The search for this ideal led them to explore both natural and supernatural themes in their works.

What is the author writing about? _____

_____

Did you find any direction markers? If so, list them here. _____

_____

3 Another persistent view of art regarded its divorce from rationality. Reason and logic were the province of scientists and philosophers, whereas creativity and intuition were the domain of the artists. The two separate spheres of the mind were supposed to remain distinct.

What is the author writing about? _____

_____

Did you find any direction markers? If so, list them here. _____

_____

4 But in 1704, a major transgression occurred. Sir Isaac Newton, mathematician and physicist extraordinaire, published his study of light, *Opticks*. One of Newton's major discoveries was on the nature of color. Using a prism, Newton found that white light is actually composed of all the colors of the rainbow. He even provided a scientific explanation for the presence of rainbows. The artistic community was shocked. A scientist had taken a beautiful and magical experience and reduced it to the simple refraction of beams of light through the prism of a raindrop. A scientist had intruded into their sacred territory.

What is the author writing about? _____

_____

Did you find any direction markers? If so, list them here. _____

_____

5 More than a hundred years later, John Keats, one of the most famous Romantic poets, accused Newton of diminishing beauty by "unweaving the rainbow." His colleague, Samuel Taylor Coleridge, famously remarked that the souls of five hundred Newtons would be needed to make one Shakespeare. And yet, from another perspective, Newton did not diminish the beauty of the rainbow; he enhanced it. In his quest to uncover the secrets of the rainbow, Newton demonstrated the wonder, creativity, and inspiration of an artist. He also gave the world another opportunity to experience the sublime. Newton's discovery paved the way for the development of the science of spectroscopy, a way of analyzing the chemical makeup of light. Now scientists can look at the stars and discern their composition. The sense of wonder this ability creates is not much different from the wonder the poet or artist feels when gazing at those same stars.

What is the author writing about? _____

_____

Did you find any direction markers? If so, list them here. _____

_____

Take a look at the topic sentences from the first three paragraphs. (Note: The first sentence of a paragraph is often known as the topic sentence.)

Paragraph 1   Art has always occupied a special place in society. (No direction markers.)
Paragraph 2   Of course, artists contributed to this mythology. (No direction markers.)
Paragraph 3   Another persistent view of art regarded its divorce from rationality. ("Another" is a direction marker that tells us the author is going in the same direction.)

At this point, you may predict that the main idea of the passage will be about views of art and artists. But look at the remaining topic sentences.

Paragraph 4   But in 1704, a major transgression occurred. ("But" is a direction marker that tells you the author is about to change the direction of the passage.)
Paragraph 5   More than a hundred years later, John Keats, one of the most famous Romantic poets, accused Newton of diminishing beauty by "unweaving the rainbow." (No direction markers.)
Last sentence   The sense of wonder this ability creates is not much different from the wonder the poet or artist feels when gazing at those same stars. (No direction markers.)

The sentence from paragraph 4 is an important one because it contains the direction marker "but." The author is introducing an important new idea contrary to the prior topics. We should figure out this new idea. In paragraph 4, the author discusses science's relationship to art. We need to make sure this idea is part of our main idea. Look through the passage again. Do you see any other direction markers that may clue us in to the main idea?

You may have noticed the following sentence in the last paragraph:

> And yet, from another perspective, Newton did not diminish the beauty of the rainbow; he enhanced it.

See if you can come up with a main idea that incorporates these elements. Write down what you think the main idea is.

_____

_____

_____

Your answer should look something like the following:

> Science does not diminish art but instead provides another source of wonder. Thus, it is important to incorporate all parts of the passage. The first part of this passage establishes the view of art, whereas the second discusses the intersection of art and science.

Drill #1: State the Main Idea

For each of the following passages, try to find the main idea. Read the topic sentences of each paragraph and paraphrase them. Then, try to state the main idea. Be on the lookout for direction markers! Check your answers with those at the end of this drill.

Passage A

1 Plants reproduce by seeding. The seed of the plant contains all the necessary genetic information to create a new plant, and more important, it is designed to start growing only when the surrounding conditions are perfect. For example, the seed of a plant growing in a temperate area will "wait" until the cold winter passes before growing. When spring arrives, the seed responds to environmental triggers such as water intake, rising air temperature, humidity levels, and amount of sunlight. Some seeds are programmed in such a way that they will not grow until they've passed through a period of cold weather.

2 A germinating seed will first display tiny leaves, called cotyledons. Plants are either monocotyledons, producing just a single leaf, or dicotyledons, producing two leaves. These tiny leaves quickly grow into a mature leaf system, which then begins gathering energy for the young plant. Plants gather the light of the Sun and transform it into energy in a process called photosynthesis. This process allows the plant to produce glucose, which the plant then uses to both further its growth and to produce cellulose and starch, two compounds essential to a plant. Cellulose is a strong, fibrous material that gives shape and structure to the cell walls. Starch is stored in the cells and used for energy.

3 Beneath the surface, the plant's root system grows and provides not only an anchor for the plant but a constant supply of food as well. Some plants possess what is called a taproot system, in which there is one main root. Others have a more dispersed root system, which lacks a main root. In either case, the roots of the plant are covered with microscopic hairs, which spread into the surrounding soil. These hairs greatly increase the surface area of the root system and allow the plant to absorb water and essential nutrients from the soil.

4 Water drawn in through the roots undergoes a process called transpiration. During this process, minerals are carried up to the leaves of the plant, while oxygen and water vapor escape through tiny pores, called stomata, on the surface of the leaves. Interestingly, the movement of water through the plant is also responsible for keeping the plant upright; a plant that lacks water will wilt and may die. Too much water may also harm the plant by saturating the soil and preventing the roots from absorbing oxygen.

5 Once a plant reaches full maturity, its energy is devoted to reproduction. The plant forms flowers and fruits, the structures essential to reproduction. The flowers of a plant are typically hermaphrodites, meaning that they contain both male and female reproductive organs. Thus, many plants are able to fertilize themselves. The flowers of some plants are unisexual, being all male or all female. These plants require another plant for fertilization. Some plants are polygamous, meaning they have both hermaphrodite and unisexual flowers. Fruits are created from the ovaries of flowering plants. The main purpose of the fruit is to protect the seed, but many fruits aid in the seed's dispersal as well. For example, a soft, fleshy fruit attracts animals, which eat the fruit and thus spread the seeds. Or a pod or capsule will split open and scatter its seeds. Some of the seeds distributed in this manner will take hold in favorable soil, and the entire process begins anew.

Paragraph 1: _____

Paragraph 2: _____

Paragraph 3: _____

Paragraph 4: _____

Paragraph 5: _____

Last sentence: _____

Did you find any direction markers? List them: _____

_____

_____

Main idea: _____

_____

_____

Passage B

1 The business practices of the Intel Corporation, a technology company best known for the production of microprocessors for computers, illustrate the importance of brand marketing. Intel was able to achieve a more than 1,500 percent increase in sales, moving from $1.2 billion in sales to more than $33 billion, in a little more than 10 years. Although the explosion of the home-computer market certainly accounted for some of this dramatic increase, the brilliance of its branding strategy also played a significant role.

2 Intel became a major producer of microprocessor chips in 1978, when its 8086 chip was selected by IBM for use in its line of home computers. The 8086 chip and its successors soon became the industry standard, even as Intel's competitors sought to break into this potentially lucrative market. Intel's main problem in facing its competitors was its lack of trademark protection for its series of microchips. Competitors were able to exploit this lack by introducing clone products with similar sounding names, severely inhibiting Intel's ability to create a brand identity.

3 In an effort to save its market share, Intel embarked on an ambitious branding program in 1991. The corporation's decision to invest more than $100 million in this program was greeted with skepticism and controversy. Many within the company argued that the money could be better spent researching and developing new products, while others argued that a company that operated within such a narrow consumer niche had little need for such an aggressive branding campaign. Despite these misgivings, Intel went ahead with its strategy, which in a short time became a resounding success.

4 One of the keys to the success of Intel's new branding initiative was its close partnership with computer manufacturers. Intel involved the manufacturers in its plan by first offering them a rebate on the purchase of an Intel microprocessor. The money saved on the purchase of microprocessors was redirected into advertising, with Intel offering to pay fully half of manufacturers' advertising costs, provided their computers prominently featured the Intel brand logo. In an even more effective

strategy, Intel also required computer manufacturers to produce products using competitors' chips. These products noticeably lacked the prominent Intel logo, which had a negative effect on consumers, who had come to expect to see Intel's brand on the computer.

5   Intel's successful branding campaign led to two important developments. The first was Intel's positioning of itself as the leader in microprocessors, recognized for creating products that were both reliable and ubiquitous, appearing in many different computer brands. This occurred despite the public's general lack of understanding of exactly what a microprocessor was or how Intel's processor was better than its competitors' chips. Second, Intel's campaign led to a boom in computer advertising. Prior to Intel's branding initiative, many advertisers avoided the computer industry, which generally spent far more of its money on research and development. But the success of Intel's branding program led to a new and eminently profitable relationship between computer manufacturers and advertisers.

6   Ironically, the success of Intel's branding strategy led to a marketing dilemma for the company. In 1992, Intel was prepared to unveil its new line of microprocessors. However, the company faced a difficult decision: release the new product under the current brand logo and risk consumer apathy or give the product a new name and brand and risk undoing all the work put into the branding strategy. In the end, Intel decided to move forward with a new brand identity. It was a testament to the strength of Intel's earlier branding efforts that the new product line was seamlessly integrated into the public consciousness.

Paragraph 1: _____

Paragraph 2: _____

Paragraph 3: _____

Paragraph 4: _____

Paragraph 5: _____

Paragraph 6: _____

Last sentence: _____

Did you find any direction markers? List them: _____

_____

_____

Main idea: _____

_____

_____

Passage C

1 On December 18, 1912, an amateur geologist named Charles Dawson and paleontologist Arthur Smith Woodward presented a stunning finding to the Geological Society of London. One year earlier, Dawson had found a piece of a human cranium in a gravel pit near Piltdown Common, Sussex. Further searching by Dawson uncovered remnants of what appeared to be flint tools and the remains of prehistoric animals. Excited by his discovery, Dawson took the fossils to Woodward at the British Museum, and the two men returned to the gravel pit for a systematic excavation.

2 In the summer of 1912, Dawson and Woodward made the discoveries that would later shock the assembled scientists at the Geological Society. Among the animal bones and primitive tools, the two men found another skull and an almost entirely intact jawbone. The geologic and biologic evidence dated the site to the Pleistocene era, and the bones were clearly of a creature that resembled no other known at that time. Although the skull resembled those of other finds, including the famous ape-men of Java, the jaw appeared to come from some type of heretofore unknown species of ape. Startlingly, however, the teeth were worn down in a human fashion.

3 Dawson and Woodward's announcement of the so-called Missing Link between man and apes, which they called Piltdown Man, set off an immediate firestorm. Across the Atlantic, *The New York Times* reported the story with the dramatic headline "Paleolithic Skull Is a Missing Link." The ensuing controversy over human origins eventually led the *Times* to publish an editorial that cautioned readers from seeing Piltdown Man as the missing link; instead, the editors advised readers to see Piltdown Man as a link to man's prehistoric past, but not necessarily proof of evolution.

4 Similar editorials sprang up across the United States, and the American public was divided over the issue of human origins. Although no fossil could conclusively prove evolution, scientists had amassed a huge collection of fossils in the early twentieth century. These fossils seemed to indicate a pattern of evolution and demanded attention. In the United States during the 1920s, a movement sprang up to counter the theory of evolution. This movement culminated in one of the most famous trials in history, the Scopes "Monkey" Trial.

5 John T. Scopes was a biology teacher in a Tennessee school. The textbook he used in his class contained a chapter on evolution and natural selection, a violation of Tennessee law. Scopes was brought to trial for the offense, and the ensuing confrontation riveted the American public. Scopes was defended by Clarence Darrow, a noted lawyer, and William Jennings Bryan, a former secretary of state, worked for the prosecution. After a confrontational trial, which even included Darrow calling Bryan as a witness, Scopes was ultimately found guilty.

6 Although Scopes's conviction was later overturned, the precedent set by the case endured. It wasn't until 1967 that Tennessee repealed its law forbidding the teaching of evolution. And even today, the reverberations of the trial are still visible. One school district in Georgia recently began placing stickers on its biology textbooks disavowing the validity of evolution. The Supreme Court eventually decided that the stickers were unconstitutional, but a cultural battle over the validity of evolution still rages in the United States.

Paragraph 1: _____

Paragraph 2: _____

Paragraph 3: _____

Paragraph 4: _____

Paragraph 5: _____

Paragraph 6: _____

Last sentence: _____

Did you find any direction markers? List them: _____

_____

_____

Main idea: _____

_____

_____

_____

Passage D

1 One of the most commonplace instructional strategies in elementary and middle schools is that of oral reading. Virtually all teachers, at some point in the school day, engage in this activity, whether by reading aloud to the class or by having the students read to one another. Although some recent educational theorists have challenged the efficacy of oral reading, its popularity in schools and classrooms is unchallenged.

2 The history of oral reading in the classroom is inextricably linked with the history of the culture that engendered it. Prior to the development of computers, television, and radio, reading was the predominant form of family entertainment. However, printed books were often scarce, and literacy rates were often low. Thus, families would gather around and listen to a book being read to them. Early classrooms were modeled after this phenomenon, and oral reading was such a part of academic life that schools were sometimes called blab schools. In these schools, students often read their lessons aloud simultaneously, even when the students had different lessons. At other times, all students read the same text aloud.

3 With the increasing availability of books, schools began using textbooks to teach reading in the classroom. By the nineteenth century, the focus had moved to teaching students "eloquent reading." Students were expected to recite stories, poems, and prayers for the class, and the teacher graded them on their articulation and pronunciation, as well as their abilities to recall what they had just read. This method persisted into the twentieth century and became known as the story method of instruction. Oral reading was such a focal point of instruction that philosopher William James stated "…the teacher's success or failure in teaching reading is based…upon the oral reading method."

4 However, as the twentieth century progressed, the effectiveness of oral reading was called into question. Educational scholars in both Europe and the United States wondered exactly what oral reading was teaching students. With oral reading focusing excessively on pronunciation and dynamics, educators doubted that students were even able to comprehend what they were saying. One scholar quoted a study that claimed that eleven-twelfths of students did not understand what

they were reciting when they read orally. Friedrich Froebel, a German education specialist, argued that oral reading inappropriately placed emphasis on expression, when the emphasis should be placed on process.

5 Also at this time, science was gaining increasing prominence, and across all fields researchers were placing a premium on empirical studies. Many long-standing beliefs and views were challenged, and educational theories were no exception. Behavioral scientists studied reading practices and determined that oral reading was no longer in fashion. In fact, they concluded that the only time students read orally was in school. Most individuals read silently, and this finding led many schools to change their methods to reflect this change.

6 The new preponderance of written texts also played a role in the history of oral reading. With the amount of printed material rapidly expanding, silent reading, which was more efficient, became the reading model of choice. For a number of years, oral reading was absent from many a classroom. But in time, new research and studies brought oral reading back to the forefront of education. Pressley's and Afflerbach's influential book *Verbal Protocols of Reading* emphasizes the importance of oral reading, tracing its history back to the methods of Aristotle and Plato. In many ways, however, the new research reiterates what most teachers already know. For them, the necessity and effectiveness of oral reading was never in doubt.

Paragraph 1: _____

Paragraph 2: _____

Paragraph 3: _____

Paragraph 4: _____

Paragraph 5: _____

Paragraph 6: _____

Last sentence: _____

Did you find any direction markers? List them: _____

_____

_____

Main idea: _____

_____

_____

ANSWERS TO DRILL #1

Passage A

Paraphrased Topic Sentences

Paragraph 1: "Plants reproduce by seeding." For short sentences like this one, don't worry about paraphrasing. Keep things simple.

Paragraph 2: "Seed first has tiny leaves." When finding the main idea, don't worry about strange or difficult vocabulary words (cotyledons). They are not important to the main idea.

Paragraph 3: "Plants have a root system that helps growth." When paraphrasing, you don't necessarily have to note the exact functions of the root system. Details are not important. All we need to know is that the root system is helpful to the plant.

Paragraph 4: "Water comes through the roots." Again, ignore the fancy term *transpiration*.

Paragraph 5: "After maturity, plants focus on reproduction."

Last sentence: "Process starts all over again."

Pay attention to the last sentence. Look for the author's final word. Is there a definite conclusion? The author wraps up things nicely, but some passages may end with a question or a call for more information or research on the topic.

Direction Markers

(We use boldface for same-direction markers and underline opposite-direction markers.)

> **For example**, the seed of a plant growing in a temperate area will "wait" until the cold winter passes before growing.

> During this process, minerals are carried up to the leaves of the plant, <u>while</u> oxygen and water vapor escape through tiny pores, called stomata, on the surface of the leaves.

> The main purpose of the fruit is to protect the seed, <u>but</u> many fruits aid in the seed's dispersal as well.

> **Thus**, many plants are able to fertilize themselves.

> **For example**, a soft, fleshy fruit attracts animals, which eat the fruit and thus spread the seeds.

Main Idea

"A plant reproduces with a seed, which grows from a tiny leaf into a mature plant capable of making its own seeds."

Each of our topic sentences discusses reproduction and the steps. Notice we did not mention the root system. That's because the root system is mentioned as a part of the growth process. We don't need to explicitly discuss each detail when stating the main idea, especially if the author is not introducing any contrasting ideas.

Passage B

Paraphrased Topic Sentences

Paragraph 1: "Intel is an example of good brand marketing." By reading the first sentence, we may be able to predict what's coming in the passage. It looks as if we're going to read a description of this company's business practices.

Paragraph 2: "Intel became a major producer in 1978." In addition to direction markers, time markers are also helpful. We know that we're going to read some of the background story.

Paragraph 3: "To save its market share, Intel started a new program." This sentence supports paragraph 1.

Paragraph 4: "One key to Intel's success." When the author presents an example, don't worry too much about what the example is. You don't need to know exactly what the details are for the main idea; it's enough to know that this paragraph will describe it.

Paragraph 5: "Two important developments from the program." Again, don't worry too much about what the developments are. The important thing is that the author is giving the results of the program.

Paragraph 6: "Success led to a problem." The author introduces a problem, but the problem is in the last paragraph. Therefore, you can correctly assume that the problem isn't a main focus of the passage.

Last sentence: "New product introduced with no problems." This last sentence indicates that everything ended well. The earlier problem was mentioned only to show how good the company's strategy was. Even the problem fits into the overall direction of the passage.

Direction Markers

(Again, we use **boldface** for same-direction markers and <u>underline</u> opposite-direction markers.)

> <u>Although</u> the explosion of the home-computer market certainly accounted for some of this dramatic increase, the brilliance of its branding strategy also played a significant role.

> <u>Despite</u> these misgivings, Intel went ahead with its strategy, which in a short time became a resounding success.

In an even more effective strategy, Intel **also** required computer manufacturers to produce products using competitors' chips.

<u>But</u> the success of Intel's branding program led to a new and eminently profitable relationship between computer manufacturers and advertisers. <u>However</u>, the company faced a difficult decision: release the new product under the current brand logo and risk consumer apathy or give the product a new name and brand and risk undoing all the work put into the branding strategy.

This passage contains quite a few opposite-direction markers. Notice how each one serves to indicate how successful Intel's branding campaign was.

Main Idea

"Intel's branding strategy was important to its success and also led to some important developments in the market."

As we predicted from the first sentence, we were going to read about a successful business strategy. We also brought in the developments mentioned later in the passage. The problem mentioned in the final paragraph doesn't need special mention because it again illustrates how successful Intel's campaign was.

Passage C

Paraphrased Topic Sentences

Paragraph 1: "Two scientists made a stunning finding." This is a good "teaser" introduction: the author doesn't tell us right away what the topic is. In this case, you may want to read another sentence or two to figure out what the finding is.

Paragraph 2: "The discoveries were made in 1912." This is another reference to the shocking discovery.

Paragraph 3: "The announcement set off controversy." If you are not sure what the word *firestorm* means, keep reading! You'll find hints in the next two sentences.

Paragraph 4: "The public was divided over human origins." Now the author is adding another dimension to the discussion. Often, a passage will introduce a controversy or problem, as is the case here.

Paragraph 5: "Scopes was a teacher." This sentence appears to be off the topic. We should read another sentence to discover why the author brings up Scopes. Scopes was using a textbook that violated Tennessee's law regarding evolution and natural selection.

Paragraph 6: "Lasting effects from the case." Don't be thrown off by the vocabulary! If you are not sure of some of the words in the sentence, read another line or two. The passage makes it clear that the situation lasted for many years.

Last sentence: "A battle still rages over the subject." The passage ends without a nice resolution; the author indicates that the situation is ongoing.

Direction Markers

(Again, we use **boldface** for same-direction markers and <u>underline</u> opposite-direction markers.)

> <u>Although</u> the skull resembled those of other finds, including the famous ape-men of Java, the jaw appeared to come from some type of heretofore unknown species of ape.

> The ensuing controversy over human origins eventually led the *Times* to publish an editorial that cautioned readers from seeing Piltdown Man as the missing link; <u>instead</u>, the editors advised readers to see Piltdown Man as a link to man's prehistoric past, <u>but</u> not necessarily proof of evolution.

> <u>Although</u> no fossil could conclusively prove evolution, scientists had amassed a huge collection of fossils in the early twentieth century.

> **And** even today, the reverberations of the trial are still visible.

This passage presents a rather controversial topic. There are two sides to the discussion, and the author indicates them by using the direction markers highlighted above.

Main Idea

"The discovery of fossils that supported evolution led to a battle over the theory of evolution, which continues to this day."

This passage is neatly divided into three large areas. The first two paragraphs talk about the discovery, the next two talk about the controversy, and the final two talk about the court case and its effects. Our main idea should touch on each of these topics.

Passage D

Paraphrased Topic Sentences

Paragraph 1: "Oral reading is used a lot in schools." This sentence prepares us to read about an educational topic. We'll learn shortly to think about the author's purpose—why the author is writing. The author may want to support oral reading, attack it, or just give a history of it. Did you spot any clues that indicate what this passage will do?

Paragraph 2: "The history of oral reading is linked to culture." This paragraph discusses the history of oral reading.

Paragraph 3: "Schools started to use textbooks to teach reading." This continues the history and indicates a change in the way reading was taught.

Paragraph 4: "The usefulness of oral reading is questioned." The author introduces a problem.

Paragraph 5: "Changes in research and science." If you're not sure how this sentence fits into the rest of the passage, read another sentence or two. It appears that new research was against oral reading.

Paragraph 6: "Written books played a role in oral reading." Check the following sentence to see how this fits into the discussion. The author states that silent reading was taking over.

Last sentence: "Good things about oral reading were never in doubt." This final sentence seems to go against what we've been reading. The last three paragraphs all discussed negative aspects of oral reading. But the author ends on a positive note. To understand this ending, let's check our direction markers.

Direction Markers

(Again, we use **boldface** for same-direction markers and <u>underline</u> opposite-direction markers.)

<u>Although</u> some recent educational theorists have challenged the efficacy of oral reading, its popularity in schools and classrooms is unchallenged.

<u>However</u>, printed books were often scarce, and literacy rates were often low. **Thus**, families would gather around and listen to a book being read to them.

In fact, they concluded that the only time students read orally was in school.

For a number of years, oral reading was absent from many a classroom. <u>But in time</u>, new research and studies brought oral reading back to the forefront of education.

By looking at these direction markers, you can see that the main idea (and the author's purpose) becomes much clearer. The author wishes to show how oral reading has persisted despite challenges. This explains why three paragraphs discuss negative aspects, but the final sentence is positive.

Main Idea

"Despite challenges to its usefulness, oral reading remains an important educational technique."

If your main idea isn't similar to the one above, you may have missed some of the direction markers. This passage isn't presenting oral reading in a negative manner, but rather supporting it. The last sentence of the first paragraph is a very important one.

Summary: State the Main Idea

1. Read the first sentence of each paragraph. State what topic the author is writing about.
2. Skim the rest of the paragraph for direction markers. Pay particular attention to opposite-direction markers.
3. Remember to read both the first sentence of each paragraph in the passage and the last sentence of the conclusion. The last sentence will contain the author's final point.
4. The main idea should connect all the ideas found in the first sentences of the paragraphs and the last sentence of the conclusion. (If you're having trouble connecting all of the topics, ask yourself what the purpose of the passage is to help you put all the pieces together.)

Step 2: Understand the Structure

Once you've found the purpose as discussed in Step 1, you'll have a better idea of the structure of the passage. The structure refers to the organization or layout of the passage. On the TOEFL, different types of questions will address different parts of the passage. If you are familiar with the types of structures on the TOEFL, you'll know where to look to find the information you need.

What Is the Structure of a TOEFL Passage?

On the TOEFL, all passages will follow a very similar structure, which will look like the following:

1. An introduction paragraph that contains the basic topic of the passage
2. Four or five body paragraphs that provide more information about the topic
3. A conclusion that brings the passage to a close with a final statement

Let's look at the structure of each of these paragraphs in detail.

What Is the Structure of the Introduction?

Here's the introduction of a passage you've already read.

(1) Sometimes it appears that the human mark on this planet is indelible. (2) In only a blink of geological time, 200 years or so, human construction and expansion has resulted in the destruction of more than one-fifth of the world's forests, the recession of the polar icecaps, and the creation of a huge hole in the ozone layer. (3) Additionally, industrial activity has damaged rivers and oceans, as well as groundwater supplies. (4) Environmental scientists and activists warn that if Earth's future is not taken into account, humankind could very well destroy the planet.

Now let's look at this very same paragraph in terms of its structure, or what each sentence contributes to the passage.

(1) This sentence introduces the topic the author is addressing.
(2) This sentence provides information to support the first sentence.
(3) This sentence also provides information to support the first sentence.
(4) This sentence uses the information in sentences 1, 2, and 3 to make a point.

As you can see, stripping down the paragraph in terms of its structure makes it easier to comprehend. Many of the passages on the TOEFL will conform to this basic structure. That means for your purposes, when reading the introduction, you should proceed as follows:

1. Read the first sentence—and the last sentence— of the introduction very carefully. They will most likely contain key information about the passage.
2. Skim through the sentences in the middle. They typically contain background information that merely supports the author's first or last sentence.

Reading the introduction is helpful for answering questions about the main idea or the primary purpose of the passage. The introduction may also contain background information about the topic, ask a question, or answer a question posed by important details in the body paragraphs.

Drill #2: Analyze the Structure

For each of the following introduction paragraphs, write down what role each sentence plays in the paragraph. Check your answers at the end.

Introduction A

(1) Scientists at Michigan State University are asking a most challenging question. (2) Can a computer program be considered alive? (3) The members of the Digital Evolution Laboratory say yes. (4) Computer scientists at the laboratory have created a program called Avida that has intrigued not only scientists and engineers but biologists and philosophers as well.

(1) _____

(2) _____

(3) _____

(4) _____

Introduction B

(1) After a seven-year journey, the *Cassini* spacecraft approached the planet Saturn in June 2004. (2) The spacecraft's successful entry into orbit around the world represented the culmination of a vision that took more than 20 years to realize. (3) Launched amid controversy in October 1997, the *Cassini* spacecraft traveled more than one billion miles in its journey. (4) Despite all the public and technological challenges, the *Cassini* mission has been more successful than even its planners imagined.

(1) _____

(2) _____

(3) _____

(4) _____

Introduction C

(1) What causes hallucinations, vivid perceptions of sights or sounds that appear quite real to the person experiencing them? (2) These mystical experiences have long fascinated psychologists, neuroscientists, and anthropologists alike. (3) In many cultures, shamans, prophets, and seers are marked by their susceptibility to hallucinations. (4) Are hallucinations caused by ghosts or spirits? (5) Are they messages from another world? (6) Although researchers don't have all the answers, there is some intriguing information on the topic.

(1) _____

(2) _____

(3) _____

(4) _____

(5) _____

(6) _____

Introduction D

(1) In the Arctic tundra, temperatures are below freezing for nine months out of the year.
(2) Soil in the Arctic, called permafrost, remains permanently frozen, making agriculture
impossible. (3) Travel over the land, whether covered in snow and ice in the winter or in
boggy marshes during the summer, is extremely difficult. (4) And perhaps most distressing
of all, the Sun shines for only six months out of the year. (5) Yet this foreboding landscape
has been inhabited for more than 12,000 years, longer than any other part of North America.

(1) _____

(2) _____

(3) _____

(4) _____

(5) _____

Introduction E

(1) Alexis de Tocqueville's *Democracy in America* studies the interplay between political
power and society. (2) The treatise was the first of its kind and was revolutionary for its use
of empirical methods, which were more common in the "hard" sciences—chemistry, biology,
and physics—than in the social sciences. (3) Tocqueville distinguished himself from his
colleagues by viewing democracy not as a system based on freedom but as one based on
power. (4) In fact, Tocqueville argues that democracy is a form of government with more
power than any other governmental system.

(1) _____

(2) _____

(3) _____

(4) _____

Answers to Drill #2

As is always the case with our sample written answers, your answers do not have to look exactly like ours. Just be sure the main ideas are similar.

Introduction A
(1) This sentence introduces the main question of the passage.
(2) This sentence states what the question is.
(3) This sentence gives an answer to the question.
(4) This sentence makes a more specific statement about the topic.

Introduction B
(1) This sentence introduces the topic of the passage.
(2) This sentence provides background about the topic.
(3) This sentence provides more background about the topic.
(4) This sentence makes a statement about the topic.

Introduction C
(1) This sentence asks a question about the topic.
(2) This sentence states who is interested in the topic.
(3) This sentence provides more information about the topic.
(4) This sentence asks another question about the topic.
(5) This sentence asks another question about the topic.
(6) This sentence states that some answers will be provided about the topic.

Introduction D
(1) This sentence introduces the topic.
(2) This sentence gives more support for sentence 1.
(3) This sentence gives more support for sentence 1.
(4) This sentence gives more support for sentence 1.
(5) This sentence indicates a contrast to the previous sentences.

Introduction E
(1) This sentence introduces the topic.
(2) This sentence explains why the topic is important.
(3) This sentence indicates why the topic is different.
(4) This sentence states a viewpoint.

You should notice that all of these paragraphs have similar structures. The important stuff is at the beginning and the end, which is typical: the TOEFL is a standardized test and therefore uses the same types of passages and questions repeatedly. So, you should expect to see a similar structure on your test.

What Is the Structure of a Body Paragraph?

Body paragraphs, just like introduction paragraphs, also share a similar structure. Here's an example of a typical body paragraph.

(1) The harsh terrain demanded much of its inhabitants. (2) Many residents of the tundra were nomadic, moving about in small bands, following the migrations of caribou, seals, and whales. (3) Cooperation among groups was essential for survival in this land, and the cultures developed elaborate rituals of reciprocity. (4) Groups of hunters often waited patiently at the various breathing holes used by seals. (5) If one hunter caught a seal, all would eat of it. (6) Bravery was also rewarded, as evidenced by the Inupiaq people, who risked death by wandering far across sea ice to hunt seals.

Now we'll look at this paragraph in terms of its structure.

(1)   This sentence states the specific topic discussed (that much is demanded of people).
(2)   This sentence gives an example of something demanded.
(3)   This sentence gives an example of how the people adapted.
(4)   This sentence provides a detail related to sentence 3.
(5)   This sentence provides an additional detail related to sentence 3.
(6)   This sentence gives an example of something else demanded.

Looking at the paragraph this way, you can clearly see that these body paragraphs are all about details. Of course, these details are all closely related to the topic sentence. This means that when dealing with body paragraphs on the TOEFL, you should proceed as follows:

1.   Read the topic sentence carefully.
2.   Sort through the specific details until you find what you need. It is easy to get distracted by all the information in a body paragraph. Stay focused on the information you need. Reading the body paragraphs will help you answer lead word and inference questions.

When answering main idea or primary purpose questions, do not read more than the first sentence of the body paragraphs. The information found in the body paragraphs is too narrow. We'll cover these question types more thoroughly in Chapter 7.

Types of Body Paragraphs

The body paragraph we just read supports the author's views. Most body paragraphs on the TOEFL will be of this type. However, some passages have body paragraphs that present an opposing point of view. Usually, these show up in passages that try to resolve a dilemma or convince the reader of something. By stating contradictory opinions, an author provides a more complete understanding of a topic and makes the main point stronger.

You can usually tell when you are reading a body paragraph that contradicts the author by reading the first sentence. The first sentence may have a transition word that indicates the author is now discussing an opposing point of view. Here's an example of such a paragraph.

> (1) Of course, not everyone agrees that the program's creations are alive.
> (2) One difficulty is that biologists do not even agree on the definition of life.
> (3) The diversity of life on Earth constantly surprises scientists, and there are simply too many characteristics and qualities to provide one simple definition of life.

Again, here's the structure of the paragraph.

(1)   This sentence presents an opposite point of view.
(2)   This sentence explains why some biologists disagree with the author's position.
(3)   This sentence supports sentence 2.

The first sentence states, "Of course, not everyone agrees...." This sentence indicates that this paragraph will contradict the author. It is important to recognize these types of paragraphs, especially when answering main idea or primary purpose questions on the TOEFL.

Drill #3: Analyzing Body Paragraphs

State the role of each sentence in the following paragraphs. Also note whether the paragraph appears to support or contradict the passage. Check your answers with those at the end of the drill.

Body Paragraph A

(1) The harsh terrain demanded much of its inhabitants. (2) Many residents of the tundra were nomadic, moving about in small bands, following the migrations of caribou, seals, and whales. (3) Cooperation among groups was essential for survival in this land, and the cultures developed elaborate rituals of reciprocity. (4) Groups of hunters often waited patiently at the various breathing holes used by seals. (5) If one hunter caught a seal, all would eat of it. (6) Bravery was also rewarded, as evidenced by the Inupiaq people, who risked death by wandering far across sea ice to hunt seals.

(1) _____

(2) _____

(3) _____

(4) _____

(5) _____

(6) _____

Supports or contradicts?

_____

Body Paragraph B

(1) Without human interference, many of the threatened or endangered fauna would reclaim their ecological niches. (2) Unfortunately, household pets would suffer. (3) In addition, the rat, one of the greatest pests in large cities, would not have the waste of humankind to feed on and would be hunted mercilessly by growing populations of hawks and falcons. (4) And the cockroach, which to many a city dweller seems to symbolize invincibility, would disappear from all but the warmest climes without artificial heat to sustain it.

(1) _____

(2) _____

(3) _____

(4) _____

Supports or contradicts?

_____

Body Paragraph C

(1) According to surveys, anywhere from 10 to 25 percent of the population has experienced at least one hallucination. (2) Most often, the hallucination comes in the form of some visual experience, but some people report hearing a sound or even voices. (3) Even rarer, but not unheard of, is a hallucination of a particular smell or aroma. (4) It is not known exactly what causes hallucinations, although one commonly accepted theory is that hallucinations occur when the external stimulus received by the senses no longer matches the level of activity occurring in the brain. (5) Sensory deprivation is one of the surest ways to elicit hallucinations.

(1) _____

(2) _____

(3) _____

(4) _____

(5) _____

Supports or contradicts?

_____

Body Paragraph D

(1) Another connection between the lower classes and the centralization of power is literacy, or more accurately, illiteracy. (2) In aristocratic societies, widespread illiteracy did not result in the consolidation of power because the social structure was so segmented. (3) But in an egalitarian society, the intermediate agencies vanish. (4) Without these agencies acting on behalf of the less-informed citizenry, the responsibility falls to the government. (5) Centralization is therefore necessary to aid and provide for citizens who may otherwise have nowhere else to turn to for assistance.

(1) _____

(2) _____

(3) _____

(4) _____

(5) _____

Supports or contradicts?

_____

Answers to Drill #3

Body Paragraph A

 (1) This sentence states that much is demanded of people.
 (2) This sentence gives an example of something demanded.
 (3) This sentence gives an example of how the people adapted.
 (4) This sentence provides a detail related to sentence 3.
 (5) This sentence provides an additional detail related to sentence 3.
 (6) This sentence gives an example of something else demanded.

This paragraph supports the passage.

Body Paragraph B

 (1) This sentence gives a consequence of a situation.
 (2) This sentence gives a contrast to sentence 1.
 (3) This sentence gives another contrast to sentence 1.
 (4) This sentence gives another contrast to sentence 1.

This paragraph contradicts the passage.

Body Paragraph C

 (1) This sentence gives a fact about the topic.
 (2) This sentence provides more information related to sentence 1.
 (3) This sentence provides more information related to sentence 1.
 (4) This sentence provides another fact about the topic.
 (5) This sentence provides more information related to sentence 4.

This paragraph supports the passage.

Body Paragraph D

 (1) This sentence introduces another connection.
 (2) This sentence provides a detail related to sentence 1.
 (3) This sentence explains sentences 1 and 2 more fully.
 (4) This sentence also explains sentences 1 and 2 more fully.
 (5) This sentence summarizes the other sentences.

This paragraph supports the passage.

As you can see, body paragraphs start with a narrow topic followed by details that are closely related to that narrow topic. Sometimes, as in paragraph C, there are two topics (the percentage of the population experiencing hallucinations; potential causes of hallucinations), but most body paragraphs deal with only one topic. Most times, the body paragraphs support the author, but occasionally they are used to present contradictory information.

What Is the Structure of a Conclusion Paragraph?

Many of the passages on the TOEFL are edited versions of longer passages. Thus, the last paragraph will usually provide some additional details and a final wrap-up of the topic. Let's revisit a conclusion paragraph.

(1) Of course, other factors increase the centralization of a democracy.
(2) Tocqueville points out that war is an important agent of centralization.
(3) To succeed in war, contends Tocqueville, a nation must be able to focus its resources around a single point. (4) Countries with a centralization of power are far more able to accomplish this task than are countries with fragmented power structures. (5) But it is interesting how Tocqueville sees democracy as a vehicle not for freedom but for power, driven by the very people the democracy is designed to empower.

Again, here's the structure of the conclusion.

(1)   This sentence provides a detail that contrasts with the main point of the passage.
(2)   This sentence provides more information on sentence 1.
(3)   This sentence provides a detail related to sentence 1.
(4)   This sentence provides a detail related to sentence 1.
(5)   This sentence states the author's final point.

As you can see, the conclusion paragraph offers some specific details similar to a body paragraph. However, it also contains an important final statement that should apply to the passage as a whole. Therefore, when reading a conclusion paragraph, you should proceed as follows:

1.   Read the first sentence. If the topic sentence introduces more details, skim through them.
2.   Read the very last sentence. Try to figure out what the author's final message or point is.

Conclusion paragraphs can be very useful for primary purpose questions. In addition to containing extra details, conclusions can also provide contradictory points and ask final questions about the topic.

Drill #4: Analyzing Conclusions

For each of the following conclusion paragraphs, specify the role each sentence plays. Also, write down the author's final point or message. Check your answers with those at the end of the drill.

Conclusion Paragraph A

(1) Despite these misgivings, the directors of the Avida program remain optimistic that their program, even if not considered alive, is leading to a greater understanding of life in all its forms. (2) It may even facilitate future searches for life on other planets. (3) According to one member of the Avida team, "The problem that we have now is that we are focused on looking for DNA-based life. (4) But there may be other kinds of life out there that we have never dreamed of." (5) The Avida program may provide biologists with another avenue to explore.

(1) _____

(2) _____

(3) _____

(4) _____

Final point: _____

Conclusion Paragraph B

(1) Newcomers to the Arctic region required the use of advanced technology to make a living in the region. (2) But the native inhabitants of the tundra existed there for generations without the need for guns, steel knives, vehicles, or modern clothing. (3) Rather than struggling against the harsh environment around them, the original inhabitants found ways to live in harmony with it. (4) The Arctic offers an abundance of riches, and these people, through their resourcefulness, were able to harvest them.

(1) _____

(2) _____

(3) _____

Final point: _____

Conclusion Paragraph C

(1) The question of plastics aside, there is some evidence that Weisman's view may be true. (2) Since 1953, a 150-mile-long tract of land separating North and South Korea has been declared a no-man's-land. (3) After only a little more than 50 years, there is almost no trace of the rice paddies that farmers had created and used for almost 5,000 years. (4) Even more spectacular are the flocks of red-crowned cranes that now inhabit the zone. (5) These birds are the second rarest of all birds, but they have flourished in this area, free from human interference of all kinds.

(1) _____

(2) _____

(3) _____

(4) _____

Final point: _____

Conclusion Paragraph D

(1) Regardless of the causes of hallucinations, the effects they have on their subjects are very real. (2) Hallucinations can cause the aforementioned change in heart rate and body temperature, and they can also lead a person to act on the hallucination. (3) Psychologists have found that the memories created by a hallucination are processed by the same part of the brain that handles normal memories. (4) Thus, for the subject of a hallucination, the experience is as real as any other.

(1) _____

(2) _____

(3) _____

Final point: _____

Answers to Drill #4

Conclusion Paragraph A

(1)   This sentence provides information on the future of the topic.
(2)   This sentence provides more information related to sentence 1.
(3)   This sentence presents a quote to support sentence 2.
(4)   This sentence supports sentence 2.

Final point: The Avida program is providing biologists with new things to explore.

Conclusion Paragraph B

(1)   This sentence introduces new information about the topic.
(2)   This sentence contrasts the two subjects.
(3)   This sentence contrasts the two subjects.

Final point: The inhabitants of the Arctic are able to use its many resources.

Conclusion Paragraph C

(1)   This sentence introduces evidence to support a view.
(2)   This sentence provides details about the evidence.
(3)   This sentence provides more details about the evidence.
(4)   This sentence presents a new piece of evidence.

Final point: Without human interference, the land and animals can flourish.

Conclusion Paragraph D

(1)   This sentence introduces another point about the main topic.
(2)   This sentence provides a detail related to sentence 1.
(3)   This sentence provides a detail related to sentence 1.

Final point: Hallucinations are experienced as real.

Following the Direction of the Passage

We've been practicing all these steps to mastering active reading. Based on our analysis of passages so far, you should begin to see that each passage on the TOEFL is broken down into pieces, each with a main topic and supporting details. The key to active reading is to focus only on the larger topics and not be distracted by details that you can come back for if a question requires more detail.

Now let's do some more practice on paying attention to the direction of the passage. We've already seen paragraphs that either support or contradict an author's position. We say a passage is going in the same direction if the information or paragraph supports the author. If a paragraph contradicts the author, we say that it is going in the opposite direction. Read the passage below, and circle the changes in direction.

1 Art has always occupied a special place in society. Many people consider artists to be the ultimate authorities on aesthetics, the nature and expression of beauty. For much of history, the practice of art was inscrutable, and artists were viewed as being somewhat strange and often mad. Even the word most commonly associated with artists—inspiration—has its own magical overtones. Literally, "inspiration" is the breathing in of a spirit. Artists were thought of as people who were divinely inspired to create.

2 Of course, artists contributed to this mythology. Many artists ascribed their talents to the presence of some supernatural agent or "muse." Whole movements of art have centered on the supposedly otherworldly nature of art. For example, the Romantic poets believed that art was the search for the sublime, a term for them that meant an ultimate expression of beauty and truth. The search for this ideal led them to explore both natural and supernatural themes in their works.

3 Another persistent view of art regarded its divorce from rationality. Reason and logic were the province of scientists and philosophers, whereas creativity and intuition were the domain of the artists. The two separate spheres of the mind were supposed to remain distinct.

4 But in 1704, a major transgression occurred. Sir Isaac Newton, mathematician and physicist extraordinaire, published his study of light, *Opticks*. One of Newton's major discoveries was on the nature of color. Using a prism, Newton found that white light is actually composed of all the colors of the rainbow. He even provided a scientific explanation for the presence of rainbows. The artistic community was shocked. A scientist had taken a beautiful and magical experience and reduced it to the simple refraction of beams of light through the prism of a raindrop. A scientist had intruded into their sacred territory.

5 More than a hundred years later, John Keats, one of the most famous Romantic poets, accused Newton of diminishing beauty by "unweaving the rainbow." His colleague, Samuel Taylor Coleridge, famously remarked that the souls of five hundred Newtons would be needed to make one Shakespeare. And yet, from another perspective, Newton did not diminish the beauty of the rainbow; he enhanced it. In his quest to uncover the secrets of

the rainbow, Newton demonstrated the wonder, creativity, and inspiration of an artist. He also gave the world another opportunity to experience the sublime. Newton's discovery paved the way for the development of the science of spectroscopy, a way of analyzing the chemical makeup of light. Now scientists can look at the stars and discern their composition. The sense of wonder this ability creates is not much different from the wonder the poet or artist feels when gazing at those same stars.

Here's the passage again, with the direction changes indicated. To make it easier to tell them apart, in this passage the same-direction words are **bolded**, whereas the opposite-direction words are underlined.

Applied Strategies

1 Art has always occupied a special place in society. Many people consider artists to be the ultimate authorities on aesthetics, the nature and expression of beauty. For much of history, the practice of art was inscrutable, and artists were viewed as being somewhat strange and often mad. **Even** the word most commonly associated with artists—inspiration—has its own magical overtones. Literally, "inspiration" is the breathing in of a spirit. Artists were thought of as people who were divinely inspired to create.

2 **Of course**, artists contributed to this mythology. Many artists ascribed their talents to the presence of some supernatural agent or "muse." Whole movements of art have centered on the supposedly otherworldly nature of art. **For example**, the Romantic poets believed that art was the search for the sublime, a term for them that meant an ultimate expression of beauty and truth. The search for this ideal led them to explore both natural and supernatural themes in their works.

3 **Another** persistent view of art regarded its divorce from rationality. Reason and logic were the province of scientists and philosophers, whereas creativity and intuition were the domain of the artists. The two separate spheres of the mind were supposed to remain distinct.

4 But in 1704, a major transgression occurred. Sir Isaac Newton, mathematician and physicist extraordinaire, published his study of light, *Opticks*. One of Newton's major discoveries was on the nature of color. Using a prism, Newton found that white light is actually composed of all the colors of the rainbow. He **even** provided a scientific explanation for the presence of rainbows. The artistic community was shocked. A scientist had taken a beautiful and magical experience and reduced it to the simple refraction of beams of light through the prism of a raindrop. A scientist had intruded into their sacred territory.

5 More than a hundred years later, John Keats, one of the most famous Romantic poets, accused Newton of diminishing beauty by "unweaving the rainbow." His colleague, Samuel Taylor Coleridge, famously remarked that the souls of five hundred Newtons would be needed to make one Shakespeare. **And** yet, from another perspective, Newton did not diminish the beauty of the rainbow; he enhanced it. In his quest to uncover the secrets of the rainbow, Newton demonstrated the wonder, creativity, and inspiration of an artist. He

also gave the world another opportunity to experience the sublime. Newton's discovery paved the way for the development of the science of spectroscopy, a way of analyzing the chemical makeup of light. Now scientists can look at the stars and discern their composition. The sense of wonder this ability creates is not much different from the wonder the poet or artist feels when gazing at those same stars.

When reading actively, use direction words to help you understand the organization of the information in the passage. Same-direction markers mean that the information you are about to read supports the topic. Once you notice this, you can often skim through this information. However, pay particular attention to changes of direction in a passage. These indicate an important shift.

Here again are the common direction words we presented earlier. Look for them as you read the passages.

Same Direction		Opposite Direction	
And	For example	Although	In contrast to
Because	One reason	However	On the other hand
Even	Due to	Yet	Rather
Therefore	Also	Despite	Even though
Another		But	

Drill #5: Finding Directions

Read each paragraph, circle the direction markers, and identify whether they are same-direction or opposite-direction words. Check your answers with those at the end of the drill.

Direction Paragraph A

Hallucinations can also be elicited in a number of other ways. Some of the most common experiences of hallucinations happen when a person is in the throes of an epileptic fit or suffering from a high fever. Other methods of bringing about a hallucination include fasting or sleeplessness. Admiral Richard Byrd reported having hallucinations after spending several months alone in the Antarctic. Hallucinations can be so powerful that members of many cultures seek them out, undertaking "vision quests" in the hopes of having a hallucinatory experience. Usually, the participants who go on these quests journey out into the elements without food or shelter.

Direction Paragraph B

Another connection between the lower classes and the centralization of power is literacy, or more accurately, illiteracy. In aristocratic societies, widespread illiteracy did not result in the consolidation of power because the social structure was so segmented. But in an egalitarian society, the intermediate agencies vanish. Without these agencies acting on behalf of the less-informed citizenry, the responsibility falls to the government. Centralization is therefore necessary to aid and provide for citizens who may otherwise have nowhere else to turn to for assistance.

Direction Paragraph C

It is also suspected that the brain has its own chemicals designed to produce hallucinations. For example, some patients suffer from delirium tremens, a violent period of hallucinations accompanied by sweating, an increase in heart rate, and a rise in body temperature. Through experience treating episodes such as this, it is also known that certain chemicals can stop hallucinations. The drug Thorazine is often used to treat patients suffering from psychotic disorders that involve hallucinations.

Direction Paragraph D

The career of Phillip Johnson, one of America's foremost architects, was a study in contrasts. Initially, Johnson was a staunch proponent of the Modernist school of architecture, and he achieved his early fame by working in this style. After a time, however, Johnson apparently became bored with Modernism, even though he claimed that he loved the experience of the new above all things. Johnson decided to move from Modernism to Classicism, a style that he explored thoroughly. He soon tired of the Classical school as well and moved back toward Modernism, although his later works still incorporate Classical elements.

Answers to Drill #5

Direction Paragraph A

Hallucinations can (also) (same direction) be elicited in a number of other ways. Some of the most common experiences of hallucinations happen when a person is in the throes of an epileptic fit or suffering from a high fever. (Other) (same direction) methods of bringing about a hallucination include fasting or sleeplessness. Admiral Richard Byrd reported having hallucinations after spending several months alone in the Antarctic. Hallucinations can be so powerful that members of many cultures seek them out, undertaking "vision quests" in the hopes of having a hallucinatory experience. Usually, the participants who go on these quests journey out into the elements without food or shelter.

Direction Paragraph B

(Another) (same direction) connection between the lower classes and the centralization of power is literacy, or more accurately, illiteracy. In aristocratic societies, widespread illiteracy did not result in the consolidation of power (because) (same direction) the social structure was so segmented. (But) (opposite direction) in an egalitarian society, the intermediate agencies vanish. Without these agencies acting on behalf of the less-informed citizenry, the responsibility falls to the government. Centralization is (therefore) (same direction) necessary to aid and provide for citizens who may otherwise have nowhere else to turn to for assistance.

Direction Paragraph C

It is (also) (same direction) suspected that the brain has its own chemicals designed to produce hallucinations. (For example) (same direction), some patients suffer from delirium tremens, a violent period of hallucinations accompanied by sweating, an increase in heart rate, and a rise in body temperature. Through experience treating episodes such as this, it is (also) (same direction) known that certain chemicals can stop hallucinations. The drug Thorazine is often used to treat patients suffering from psychotic disorders that involve hallucinations.

Direction Paragraph D

The career of Phillip Johnson, one of America's foremost architects, was a study in contrasts. (Initially) (same direction), Johnson was a staunch proponent of the Modernist school of architecture, and he achieved his early fame by working in this style. After a time, (however) (opposite direction), Johnson apparently became bored with Modernism, (even though) (opposite direction) he claimed that he loved the experience of the new above all things. Johnson decided to move from Modernism to Classicism, a style that he explored thoroughly. He soon tired of the Classical school as well and moved back toward Modernism, (although) (opposite direction) his later works still incorporate Classical elements.

Summary: Understanding Structure

1. Identify the structure of the passage because this knowledge will help you to find information quickly.
2. Remember, TOEFL passages are made up of the following paragraph types: introduction, body, and conclusion. Know what type of information is usually found in each type of paragraph.
3. Use the first sentence of the paragraph as a guide to the information contained in the rest of the paragraph.
4. Keep in mind that the remaining sentences provide details about the topic.
5. Pay attention to direction markers. Same-direction markers indicate the author is continuing the discussion. Opposite-direction markers highlight contrasting ideas.

Step 3: Find the Purpose

People write for many reasons. Some write to entertain, whereas others write to inform. If you know the purpose of a passage, then you know what the writer is trying to accomplish, and you can determine what is important and unimportant about the piece.

The majority of passages on the TOEFL will do one of the following:

- **Explain:** The purpose of these passages is to present you with information on specific topics, and they contain mostly facts.
- **Resolve:** The purpose of these passages is to find solutions for some sort of dilemma. There is usually a debate or question that needs an answer.
- **Convince:** The purpose of these passages is to try to argue the validity of a certain viewpoint or idea. They give opinions and support these opinions with evidence.

As you've just learned, a written passage can be broken down into three basic parts: the introduction, the body, and the conclusion. The introduction seeks to give the reader background about the topic. The body of a passage provides details and explanations of what is covered in the introduction. The conclusion summarizes everything in the passage and usually leaves the reader with a few new thoughts on the topic. In the next section, we will practice active reading by looking at each part of a passage. To find the purpose of the passage, we'll start with the introduction (the first paragraph).

The Introduction Paragraph

Let's return to the sample passage at the beginning of this chapter. Here's the first paragraph again.

> 1 Scientists at Michigan State University are asking a most challenging question. Can a computer program be considered alive? The members of the Digital Evolution Laboratory say yes. Computer scientists at the laboratory have created a program called Avida that has intrigued not only scientists and engineers but biologists and philosophers as well.

The introduction paragraph is one of the most important paragraphs in the passage—it should give you a pretty good idea of what the author wants to accomplish. Look at it sentence by sentence and identify clues that will help you find the purpose.

First, examine the opening sentence.

> Scientists at Michigan State University are asking a most challenging question.

Now, focus on the important stuff. You do this by asking yourself what and why. The first question to ask yourself is this: what are you reading about? This is the subject of the sentence. Write down the subject.

_____

Now ask yourself this question: why is the author writing about this? Write down what you think the author wants you to know. _____

_____

So far, you are reading about the scientists. And why are you reading about them? Because they are asking a question. If you are still unsure about this information after reading the first sentence, then continue to the second sentence.

> Can a computer program be considered alive?

This clarifies the first sentence. Now you know that the passage is about scientists and a computer program that may be considered alive. Do you think the author wrote this passage to inform, to resolve, or to argue? Write it down.

_____

Now move on to the body paragraphs.

The Body Paragraphs

When looking for the purpose, don't get bogged down in the details. For most passages, you can get everything you need by reading just the first sentence or two of each paragraph. Try that on the passage below. Here are the first four body paragraphs.

2 The Avida project began in the late 1990s, when Chris Adami, a physicist, sought to create computer programs that could evolve to do simple addition problems and reproduce inside a digital environment. Adami called these programs "digital organisms." Whenever a digital organism replicates, it has a chance to alter the program of the newly created offspring. In this way, the programs mutate and evolve. The goal of the Avida program is to create a model that could simulate the evolutionary process.

3 Initially, the digital creations were unable to process numbers in any way. But Adami designed Avida to reward digital organisms that were able to work with the numbers in some way. The digital organisms that could process numbers were allowed to reproduce in higher numbers. In only six short months, the primitive program had evolved a number of mechanisms to perform addition. And, most surprisingly, not all of the digital creatures performed addition in the same way.

4 The Avida program now resides at Michigan State University, where it has been growing and changing for years. The digital creatures number in the billions and have colonized more than two hundred computers. The organisms compete with one another for resources, and the most successful ones are able to make more copies of themselves. Just like living creatures, the digital entities also undergo mutations. Mutations that are beneficial ensure greater reproduction; harmful mutations have the opposite effect.

5 As a model for studying evolution, the Avida project has been a great success. Adami's digital organisms have suggested solutions to some of evolution's biggest mysteries. For example, Avida has helped disprove the theory of "irreducible complexity." Opponents of evolutionary theory have suggested that some structures, such as the eye, are too complex to have been created in piecemeal stages. The evolution of Avida's digital organisms proves that even extremely complex structures can be developed in stages over time.

For paragraph 2, write down what the author's subject is and what you think the author is telling you about it.

What? _____

What about it? _____

Do the same for the other three paragraphs.

What? _____

What about it? _____

What? _____

What about it? _____

What? _____

What about it? _____

Please note that your answers may be worded differently from ours and still be correct. Just check to be sure they share the same general idea. Your answers should look something like this.

What? Avida project
What about it? To tell us how it began

What? Digital creatures
What about it? They are able to work with numbers.

What? Avida program
What about it? It's been changing.

What? Studying evolution
What about it? Digital creatures can help scientists learn more about evolution.

Check back on the prediction you made earlier. Does this new information change it? Let's look at the remaining body paragraphs.

6 The Avida program's success has also raised some unintentional philosophical dilemmas. Does Avida just simulate evolution, or are digital organisms a new form of life? According to the director of the Avida project, the processes undergone by the digital creatures are the same as those experienced by biological organisms. The only difference is that biological entities are based on strings of DNA, whereas the digital creations from Avida are based on strings of ones and zeros. In a living creature, different sequences of DNA instruct cells to create certain proteins. In one of the Avida creations, different sequences of computer code instruct the program to perform certain functions. In both cases, the reproduction of the organisms is subject to forces such as competition and mutation.

7 Now, some biologists are maintaining that the programs in the Avida project are alive. The programs live, die, reproduce, compete, cooperate, and evolve—activities that many biologists consider the hallmarks of life. One prominent biologist says, "They don't have a metabolism—at least not yet. But otherwise, they're alive."

8 Of course, not everyone agrees that the program's creations are alive. One difficulty is that biologists do not even agree on the definition of life. The diversity of life on Earth constantly surprises scientists, and there are simply too many characteristics and qualities to provide one simple definition of life.

Again, read only the first sentence or two of each paragraph and answer the questions.

What? _____

What about it? _____

What? _____

What about it? _____

What? _____

What about it? _____

Take a look at your responses. Do they match the following?

What? Are digital organisms a form of life?
What about it? The digital creatures meet many of the criteria for life.

What? Biologists
What about it? They think the program is alive.

What? Other people
What about it? They don't agree with the biologists.

By now, you should have a pretty good idea of why the author has written this passage.

Write down your reason here. _____

_____

You'll check your final prediction in a moment, but before you do so, you have one more paragraph to review.

The Conclusion

Here's the final paragraph, but for this paragraph, read both the first and the last sentence.

9 Despite these misgivings, the directors of the Avida program remain optimistic that their program, even if not considered alive, is leading to a greater understanding of life in all its forms. It may even facilitate future searches for life on other planets. According to one member of the Avida team, "The problem that we have now is that we are focused on looking for DNA-based life. But there may be other kinds of life out there that we have never dreamed of." The Avida program may provide biologists with another avenue to explore.

Now answer the questions regarding the first and last sentences in this conclusion.

What? _____

What about it? _____

What? _____

What about it? _____

Here are our answers.

What? Directors of the program
What about it? The program is helping people understand life.

What? The Avida program
What about it? The program gives biologists something to explore.

Putting It All Together

Look back at what you've written. Based on only the six or seven sentences you've read, does it seem as if the author is trying to argue a point, resolve a dilemma, or simply provide you with information? The purpose of this passage is to provide us with information—to explain something. It introduces the scientists and their Avida program. Next, it describes the beginning of the project and the current state of the Avida program. After that, the author talks about how the director of the project and other people view the project. Finally, the author indicates that scientists hope Avida will lead to new avenues of exploration. Thus, we could write down the following for the purpose:

Purpose: To present a brief overview of the Avida computer program and its implications

Remember, you won't have time to read and comprehend every single word and sentence on the TOEFL. Therefore, with active reading, you'll read fewer sentences, but your comprehension will increase because you'll read only the important parts.

Drill #6: Find the Purpose

In the following passages, read the first sentence or two of each paragraph and the first and last sentence of the conclusion. Then, fill in the information required for each paragraph. Use this information to develop the overall purpose of each passage. Check your answers at the end of the drill.

Passage A

1 Alexis de Tocqueville's *Democracy in America* studies the interplay between political power and society. The treatise was the first of its kind and was revolutionary for its use of empirical methods, which were more common in the "hard" sciences—chemistry, biology, and physics—than in the social sciences. Tocqueville distinguished himself from his colleagues by viewing democracy not as a system based on freedom but as one based on power. In fact, Tocqueville argues that democracy is a form of government with more power than any other governmental system.

2 Born in France in 1805, Tocqueville had a conflicted relationship with his reformist ideals. His grandfather, a liberal aristocrat, lawyer, and politician, was a powerful force for social reforms prior to and during the French Revolution. Despite this, he was condemned as a counterrevolutionary and executed along with several members of his family. Tocqueville adopted his grandfather's liberal ideals, but never lost a profound distrust for the potentially violent extremes to which the drive for democracy can push a nation. Tocqueville's famous study of the United States was the product of a nine-month trip to the young republic, beginning in 1831. Tocqueville had traveled to the United States to produce a study of America's prisons. That initial study was published in 1833, a year after he returned to France. He then labored another nine years over *Democracy in America*. The book itself was written in two distinct volumes. The first volume focused specifically on Tocqueville's observations of American culture. He stressed the growth of social equality promoted by a stable social order, an issue that was close to his heart given France's repeated violent efforts to establish a lasting democracy. The second volume, written four years after the first had been completed, was more abstract. Tocqueville turned his attention to the conflict of individuality and centrality in democratic cultures.

3 Tocqueville ascribes the power of a democracy to its tendency to centralize power. In a democracy, there are no guilds, estates, or sharply defined social classes. These institutions, in earlier times, represented a check on the powers of kings and tyrants. But in their absence, the government holds the ultimate authority. According to Tocqueville, it is the lower classes that primarily drive the centralization of power in a democracy.

4 One reason the lower classes prefer a centralization of power relates to the historical role of the aristocratic class. In many class-based societies, the lower classes were subject to the rule of classes above them. Local affairs were overseen by aristocrats, who often acted like petty tyrants. Only by surrendering authority to a central government could the lower classes achieve equality.

5 Another connection between the lower classes and the centralization of power is literacy, or more accurately, illiteracy. In aristocratic societies, widespread illiteracy did not result in the consolidation of power because the social structure was so segmented. But in an egalitarian society, the intermediate agencies vanish. Without these agencies acting on behalf of the

less-informed citizenry, the responsibility falls to the government. Centralization is therefore necessary to aid and provide for citizens who may otherwise have nowhere else to turn to for assistance.

6 But perhaps the most profound effect the lower classes can have on the centralization of power in a democracy concerns the nature of the democratic leader. In an aristocracy or a monarchy, the ruler was always viewed as a person apart from the lower classes, a person whose birth made him (or her) superior to his subjects. In a democracy, the lower classes can identify more closely with a leader whom they can view as one of them and thus are willing to rally around him (or her) more readily.

7 Of course, other factors increase the centralization of a democracy. Tocqueville points out that war is an important agent of centralization. To succeed in war, contends Tocqueville, a nation must be able to focus its resources around a single point. Countries with a centralization of power are far more able to accomplish this task than are countries with fragmented power structures. But it is interesting how Tocqueville sees democracy as a vehicle not for freedom but for power, driven by the very people the democracy is designed to empower.

Paragraph 1

What? _____

What about it? _____

Paragraph 2

What? _____

What about it? _____

Paragraph 3

What? _____

What about it? _____

Paragraph 4

What? _____

What about it? _____

Paragraph 5

What? _____

What about it? _____

Paragraph 6

What? _____

What about it? _____

Paragraph 7

What? _____

What about it? _____

Overall Purpose? _____

Passage B

1 Sometimes it appears that the human mark on this planet is indelible. In only a blink of geological time, 200 years or so, human construction and expansion has resulted in the destruction of more than one-fifth of the world's forests, the recession of the polar icecaps, and the creation of a huge hole in the ozone layer. Additionally, industrial activity has damaged rivers and oceans, as well as groundwater supplies. Environmental scientists and activists warn that if Earth's future is not taken into account, humankind could very well destroy the planet.

2 However, Earth is an amazingly resilient place. In its 4.5-billion-year lifespan, Earth has endured bombardment by cosmic rays and meteors, violent earthquakes, volcanism, and frigid ice ages. In light of all these catastrophic events, many geologists and ecologists say that Earth could recover from any damage caused by human actions.

3 The author Alan Weisman has gone so far as to predict exactly what would happen on Earth if all humans were to disappear. Without upkeep, the concrete jungles of the world's greatest cities would be slowly reclaimed by the wilderness around them. Harsh temperatures would cause pavement to crack. Plants would return to areas covered by streets and sidewalks.

4 Different fates would await humankind's other creations. Litter and leaf matter would accumulate, and it would take only one chance lightning strike to start a raging fire. Many structures would burn to the ground. The steel foundations supporting larger buildings and bridges would corrode and buckle, especially with the rise in groundwater that would accompany the clogging of sewer systems.

5 Without human interference, many of the threatened or endangered fauna would reclaim their ecological niches. Unfortunately, household pets would suffer. In addition, the rat, one of the greatest pests in large cities, would not have the waste of humankind to feed on and would be hunted mercilessly by growing populations of hawks and falcons. And the cockroach, which to many a city dweller seems to symbolize invincibility, would disappear from all but the warmest climes without artificial heat to sustain it.

6 Within 500 years, again barely a heartbeat in geological time, most of humankind's monuments would be gone, covered over by plants and trees. It's happened before; the Mayan civilization in Northern Guatemala survived for 2,000 years but was swallowed up by the jungle at its end. And after a few thousand years, if earthquakes and volcanic eruptions have not obliterated everything made by humans, the glaciers would come, sweeping down from the mountains, slowly and inexorably destroying everything in their path. Several times in its history, Earth has been swept clean by these giant sheets of ice. The legacy of humankind would be wiped from Earth.

7 Of course, not every man-made artifact would be reclaimed by nature. Plastic is a synthetic material that does not occur in nature. The strong bonds that hold plastic together are virtually impervious to natural erosion. Long after concrete and glass have turned back into sand and all processed metals have rusted away, plastics will still be cycling through the Earth's ecosystem, resilient to even the most destructive of natural forces. Some scientists believe that plastic molecules may eventually break down entirely, but there is no reliable data on just how long complete re-assimilation into the environment might take. Furthermore, it is impossible to predict just what sort of resources Mother Nature might develop in the distant future. There is always the possibility that, given enough time, some microbe or bacteria may evolve the capability to digest plastic. If nature somehow evolved a way to process plastics, then even humanity's most enduring artifacts might vanish in the space of a few hundred years.

8 The question of plastics aside, there is some evidence that Weisman's view may be true. Since 1953, a 150-mile-long tract of land separating North and South Korea has been declared a no-man's-land. After only a little more than 50 years, there is almost no trace of the rice paddies that farmers had created and used for almost 5,000 years. Even more spectacular are the flocks of red-crowned cranes that now inhabit the zone. These birds are the second rarest of all birds, but they have flourished in this area, free from human interference of all kinds.

Paragraph 1

What? _____

What about it? _____

Paragraph 2

What? _____

What about it? _____

Paragraph 3

What? _____

What about it? _____

Paragraph 4

What? _____

What about it? _____

Paragraph 5

What? _____

What about it? _____

Paragraph 6

What? _____

What about it? _____

Paragraph 7

What? _____

What about it? _____

Paragraph 8

What? _____

What about it? _____

Overall Purpose? _____

Passage C

1 What causes hallucinations, vivid perceptions of unreal sights or sounds that appear quite real to the person experiencing them? These mystical experiences have long fascinated psychologists, neuroscientists, and anthropologists alike. In many cultures, shamans, prophets, and seers are marked by their susceptibility to hallucinations. Are hallucinations caused by ghosts or spirits? Are they messages from another world? Although researchers don't have all the answers, there is some intriguing information on the topic.

2 According to surveys, anywhere from 10 to 25 percent of the population has experienced at least one hallucination. Most often, the hallucination comes in the form of some visual experience, but some people report hearing a sound or even voices. Even rarer, but not unheard of, is a hallucination of a particular smell or aroma. It is not known exactly what

causes hallucinations, although one commonly accepted theory is that hallucinations occur when the external stimulus received by the senses no longer matches the level of activity occurring in the brain. Sensory deprivation is one of the surest ways to elicit hallucinations.

3   Hallucinations can also be elicited in a number of other ways. Some of the most common experiences of hallucinations happen when a person is in the throes of an epileptic fit or suffering from a high fever.

4   Other methods of bringing about a hallucination include fasting or sleeplessness. Admiral Richard Byrd reported having hallucinations after spending several months alone in the Antarctic. Hallucinations can be so powerful that members of many cultures seek them out, undertaking "vision quests" in the hopes of having a hallucinatory experience. Usually the participants who go on these quests journey out into the elements without food or shelter.

5   Not all hallucinations are the product of extreme physical conditions. Some very complex hallucinations can be triggered by nothing more unusual than everyday memories. People who have lost limbs often report that they continue to feel physical sensations as if the limb were still there. These "phantom limbs" are most likely the result of the brain interpreting signals it receives from severed nerve endings in the context of its memories of the missing limb. An even stranger phenomenon involves hallucinations produced by the memories of recently departed loved ones. Called grief hallucinations, these vivid visions can be simple visual hallucinations or more complex fantasy interactions. In one reported case, a woman reported receiving multiple visits from her departed children. The woman claimed that she and her "ghosts" regularly held long and involved conversations. Neuroscientists theorize that grief hallucinations may be the product of vivid memories that last in the mind long after a loved one has passed away. As bizarre as grief hallucinations may sound, the experience is quite common. Some researchers estimate that up to 80 percent of people will experience some form of grief hallucination in their lifetime.

6   Although neuroscientists may not be sure of the exact mechanism in the brain that causes hallucinations, they have isolated activity in the left temporal lobe of the brain that appears to play a part in the phenomenon. Certain drugs that affect this region of the brain are known for their ability to cause hallucinations. Drugs such as LSD, psilocybin, and mescaline gained popularity with the 1960s Western youth culture for their ability to provide vivid hallucinatory experiences.

7   It is also suspected that the brain has its own chemicals designed to produce hallucinations. For example, some patients suffer from delirium tremens, a violent period of hallucinations accompanied by sweating, an increase in heart rate, and a rise in body temperature. Through experience treating episodes such as this, it is also known that certain chemicals can stop hallucinations. The drug Thorazine is often used to treat patients suffering from psychotic disorders that involve hallucinations.

8   Regardless of the causes of hallucinations, the effects they have on their subjects are very real. Hallucinations can cause the aforementioned change in heart rate and body temperature, and they can also lead a person to act on the hallucination. Psychologists have found that the memories created by a hallucination are processed by the same part of the brain that handles normal memories. Thus, for the subject of a hallucination, the experience is as real as any other.

Paragraph 1

What? _____

What about it? _____

Paragraph 2

What? _____

What about it? _____

Paragraph 3

What? _____

What about it? _____

Paragraph 4

What? _____

What about it? _____

Paragraph 5

What? _____

What about it? _____

Paragraph 6

What? _____

What about it? _____

Paragraph 7

What? _____

What about it? _____

Paragraph 8

What? _____

What about it? _____

Overall Purpose? _____

Passage D

1 In the Arctic tundra, temperatures are below freezing for nine months out of the year. Soil in the Arctic, called permafrost, remains permanently frozen, making agriculture impossible. Travel over the land, whether covered in snow and ice in the winter or in boggy marshes during the summer, is extremely difficult. And perhaps most distressing of all, the Sun shines for only six months out of the year. Yet this foreboding landscape has been inhabited for more than 12,000 years, longer than any other part of North America.

2 Natives of this frozen land benefited from the ample food provided by the marine animals of the region. Indeed, one reason people settled in the Arctic was the almost continuous availability of seals. And although the Arctic is above the tree line, meaning that no trees can grow there, the summer months brought a rich growth of lichen (a form of plant composed of fungi and algae) and other plants. Herds of caribou would migrate north to feed on these plants, providing more food to the Arctic peoples.

3 Inhabitants of the Arctic and sub-Arctic regions cleverly used the environment to their advantage. The constant wind drove the snow into compact masses that in some ways resembled stone. Since they had no wood or rock from which to build structures, inhabitants built their homes from the snow itself. Using knives and tools made from the antlers of caribou, a native of the Arctic could build a home that was both elegant and warm.

4 The harsh terrain demanded much of its inhabitants. Many residents of the tundra were nomadic, moving about in small bands, following the migrations of caribou, seals, and whales. Cooperation among groups was essential for survival in this land, and the cultures developed elaborate rituals of reciprocity. Groups of hunters often waited patiently at the various breathing holes used by seals. If one hunter caught a seal, all would eat of it. Bravery was also rewarded, as evidenced by the Inupiaq people, who risked death by wandering far across sea ice to hunt seals.

5 To survive the brutal cold, Arctic dwellers devised special clothing. Most people wore parkas made of double layers of caribou hide, with boots and pants also made of the same material. The natives fashioned the coats so that caribou hair on the inner layer faced outward, while that on the outer layer faced inward. This provided a high degree of insulation and allowed a hunter to remain outside all day.

6 Among the many other innovations of the people living in the Arctic were the seal-oil lamps, to compensate for the lack of natural sunlight, and snow goggles, to prevent snow blindness. These remarkable people also developed snowshoes, kayaks, and harpoons with detachable heads. Such resourcefulness was necessary to thrive in the unforgiving conditions of the tundra.

7 The Arctic inhabitants also developed a body of knowledge adapted to their unique living conditions. When American and European explorers first began long-term expeditions in the Arctic, they ignored the knowledge and survival skills of the Arctic's native inhabitants at their own peril. For example, some animals suited to frozen climates process nutrients from their food differently than animals in more hospitable environments. One of the notable differences is the concentration of vitamin A in the livers of Arctic mammals. In small doses, vitamin A is an essential nutrient. In large doses, it can be toxic. Vitamin A poisoning causes hair loss, brittle bones, skin lesions, nausea, and the build-up of potentially fatal pressure on the brain. Arctic hunters had long ago learned to avoid eating the liver of certain animals.

The newly arrived explorers rarely trusted native folklore and did not benefit from their wisdom. Famed explorers Douglas Mawson and Xavier Mertz both suffered from vitamin A poisoning. Only Mawson survived the experience.

8 Later arrivals to the Arctic region required the use of advanced technology to make a living in the region. But the native inhabitants of the tundra existed there for generations without the need for guns, steel knives, vehicles, or modern clothing. Rather than struggling against the harsh environment around them, the original inhabitants found ways to live in harmony with it. The Arctic offers an abundance of riches, and these people, through their resourcefulness, were able to harvest them.

Paragraph 1

What? _____

What about it? _____

Paragraph 2

What? _____

What about it? _____

Paragraph 3

What? _____

What about it? _____

Paragraph 4

What? _____

What about it? _____

Paragraph 5

What? _____

What about it? _____

Paragraph 6

What? _____

What about it? _____

Paragraph 7

What? _____

What about it? _____

Paragraph 8

What? _____

What about it? _____

Overall Purpose? _____

Answers to Drill #6

Passage A

The purpose of this passage is to describe one person's view of a government system. Right away, we know we are reading about someone's book. That's the "what." The "why" requires a little more reading, but once again, the body paragraphs help us figure out why the author wrote the passage. Each one mentions something about the centralization of power in a democracy. The passage ends by again mentioning centralization of power and that Tocqueville's view of democracy is "interesting."

Notice how we were able to take a 700-word passage and condense it into a brief description. The key point is to ignore the details! All we need to worry about is the big picture.

Passage B

The purpose of passage B is to convince the reader of the outcome of a situation. The first paragraph states that humans have made a mark on the planet. But notice how the second paragraph starts.

> However, Earth is an amazingly resilient place.

The use of the word *however* indicates that the author is now going to discuss the opposite of the idea that humans have left their mark on the planet. Each of the next paragraphs then mentions what the theorist thinks will happen if people were to disappear. The final paragraph states there may be evidence for the view, and it ends by repeating the idea of a world free from human interference.

Passage C

The purpose of this passage is to answer questions about the nature of hallucinations. The introduction begins with a brief description of hallucinations. We also learn that hallucinations are related to supernatural experiences. The topic sentences of the next two body paragraphs tell us that many people experience hallucinations and mention how they are caused. Next, the passage mentions the causes of hallucinations and the area of the brain where hallucinations occur. The passage ends by stating that the subjects of hallucinations perceive them as real.

Passage D

The purpose of this passage is to explain how people survived in the Arctic. The introduction provides information only on the Arctic. So if you weren't sure exactly why the author is writing about this topic, that's okay. Once you get to the next paragraph, you have a clearer idea of the author's direction. The first body paragraph talks about the available food, and the next one mentions clever use of the environment. After that, there is another mention of the harsh terrain and a paragraph about the clothes that natives wore. The final body paragraph talks of the people's other inventions, and the conclusion contrasts the resourcefulness of the native inhabitants of the land with modern inhabitants.

Summary: How to Find the Purpose

1. Read the first two sentences of the first paragraph. Note what the topic is and what the author is writing about it.
2. Read the first sentence of each body paragraph. Again, note what the topic is and why the author introduces it.
3. Read the first and last sentence of the final paragraph. Pay particular attention to how the author ends the passage.
4. Look back at your notes. What's the common idea? Is the author presenting facts? Examining different views? Answering questions?

DEALING WITH DIFFICULT PASSAGES

One of the greatest challenges of the TOEFL is dealing with passages that are written for native speakers. Because the TOEFL is designed to measure your ability to perform at an academic institution, you can expect to see passages that contain some difficult vocabulary and complicated structures. Don't be intimidated by them! Keep in mind that even native English speakers often have difficulties with the types of passages found on standardized tests such as the TOEFL. If you find yourself struggling with a passage on the TOEFL, use the following helpful strategies.

Tip #1: Skim, Don't Read!

Now that you've practiced finding the main idea and purpose of a passage, you have seen how little of the passage you actually have to read to understand what an author is writing about. If you find yourself getting lost as you are reading, move on to another part of the passage. Often, you can still figure out the main idea even if you're not sure what one or two paragraphs are about. Focus on the big picture!

Tip #2: Trim the Fat!

"Trim the fat" is an English idiom meaning "to get rid of extra parts you don't want." Think about a piece of meat you're preparing to eat. You have to cut off most of the fat before you can get to the delicious part, right? It's the same with understanding a sentence. A sentence is a simple thing. All it requires is a subject, usually a noun (for example, a person, place, or thing) and a verb (an action). Writers like to make sentences more complicated by adding all sorts of words to this basic formula. Though it does make sentences more beautiful, it may also make them much more difficult to understand. By cutting out all the extra parts—"trimming the fat"—you will be left with the "meat" of a sentence, making it much easier to understand.

Let's look at two sample sentences.

Joe ran.

Joe, a competitive runner for nearly 20 years, ran perhaps the best race of his entire life last week when he narrowly defeated his arch rival in a stunning showdown.

These two sentences have the same subject (Joe) and the same verb (ran). The second sentence has a lot more information in it, but they are basically telling us the same thing. One way to increase your comprehension is to ignore all the extra words in a sentence—trim the fat. When faced with a difficult sentence, look for the following three basic parts:

- **Subject.** This is who or what is performing the action.
- **Verb.** This is the action being performed.
- **Object.** This receives the action of the verb.

Here's another example.

Scientists using NASA's Spitzer Space Telescope have found a new class of stellar object, miniature stars too small to initiate fusion but large enough to have their own planets orbiting them.

That's quite a mouthful, but if we trim the fat, the sentence basically says:

Scientists…have found…a new object.

That's it! All of the other words provide some useful details, but the most important ones are the subject, verb, and object. Let's try this a few more times.

Drill #7: Trim the Fat

For each of the following sentences, find the subject, verb, and object. Write down a simpler version of each sentence. Check your answers at the end of the drill.

1. Wild horses, which once roamed freely over the grasslands of Europe, Asia, and Africa, are found only in isolated patches of Southeastern Africa and Eastern Asia now.

   Simple version: _____

2. In a digital camera, light entering the camera is focused on a charged coupled device, or CCD, which converts light energy into a charged electron.

   Simple version: _____

3. A major stumbling block in the development of a viable hydrogen-fueled car is the expectation of many drivers that the vehicle will travel at least 300 miles before needing to refuel.

   Simple version: _____

4. Prior to the development of germ theory, John Snow, a London physician, was able to halt an outbreak of cholera by restricting access to a water pump that he suspected was contributing to the spread of the disease.

   Simple version: _____

5. Cores of ice, drilled from glaciers in Greenland and the Antarctic, provide climatologists with valuable data on Earth's prehistoric climate, including changes in the concentration of greenhouse gases in the atmosphere.

   Simple version: _____

6. In 1899, Nikola Tesla, famed inventor of the alternating current electrical system, shocked an assembled audience at a conference by operating a six-foot radio-controlled electric boat.

   Simple version: _____

7. Fainting, which can be a sign of a serious ailment such as heart failure or a result of something as harmless as standing up too quickly, results from an insufficient supply of oxygen to the brain.

   Simple version: _____

8. One of the main provisions of the Taft-Hartley Labor Act was the government's ability to prevent a strike by any workers it considered essential to the nation's health or safety.

   Simple version: _____

9. After spending nearly 26 years in jail, South African statesman Nelson Mandela was elected president of South Africa in that country's first multiracial election in 1994.

    Simple version: _____

10. On Shrove Tuesday in 217 B.C.E., soldiers in Derby, England celebrated a victory over Roman soldiers by playing the first recorded soccer match, starting an annual event that lasted for almost 1,000 years.

    Simple version: _____

Answers to Drill #7

If your answers include a bit more information, that's fine. The important thing with trimming the fat is to cut out as much as you can while still keeping the parts that are important to the meaning of the sentence. If you're not sure if a phrase is important, leave it.

1. Wild horses, which once roamed freely over the grasslands of Europe, Asia, and Africa, are found only in isolated patches of Southeastern Africa and Eastern Asia now.

   Simple version: Wild horses are found in patches of Africa and Asia.

   Watch out for phrases that begin with the word *which*. These phrases are not essential to the sentence and can be ignored.

2. In a digital camera, light entering the camera is focused on a charged coupled device, or CCD, which converts light energy into a charged electron.

   Simple version: Light is focused onto a device.

   Fancy technical terms are always good candidates for trimming. Ignore them whenever possible.

3. A major stumbling block in the development of a viable hydrogen-fueled car is the expectation of many drivers that the vehicle will travel at least 300 miles before needing to refuel.

   Simple version: A block is the expectation that the vehicle will travel 300 miles.

   This sentence contains numerous prepositional phrases. These are phrases that start with words like *in, of,* and *at*. When you see short phrases that start with these words, you can usually cut their phrases out of the sentence.

4. Prior to the development of germ theory, John Snow, a London physician, was able to halt an outbreak of cholera by restricting access to a water pump that he suspected was contributing to the spread of the disease.

   Simple version: John Snow was able to halt an outbreak.

   Often, a phrase in the beginning of a sentence that is set off with a comma ("Prior to the development of germ theory,") can be trimmed away.

5. Cores of ice, drilled from glaciers in Greenland and the Antarctic, provide climatologists with valuable data on Earth's prehistoric climate, including changes in the concentration of greenhouse gases in the atmosphere.

   Simple version: Cores of ice provide valuable data.

   Similarly, phrases at the end of a sentence that are set off with a comma ("including changes in…atmosphere") can be removed as well.

6. In 1899, Nikola Tesla, famed inventor of the alternating current electrical system, shocked an assembled audience at a conference by operating a six-foot radio-controlled electric boat.

    Simple version: Nikola Tesla shocked an audience by operating a boat.

    When trimming the fat, locate the subject first. Then find the verb. Once you do that, you can almost always cut out everything in between them.

7. Fainting, which can be a sign of a serious ailment such as heart failure or a result of something as harmless as standing up too quickly, results from an insufficient supply of oxygen to the brain.

    Simple version: Fainting results from an insufficient supply of oxygen.

    Once again, we have another phrase using the word *which*. Get rid of it!

8. One of the main provisions of the Taft-Hartley Labor Act was the government's ability to prevent a strike by any workers it considered essential to the nation's health or safety.

    Simple version: One provision was the government's ability to prevent a strike.

    This sentence has a bunch of prepositional phrases: "of the main...," "of the Taft-Hartley Labor Act...," "by any workers...," and "to the nation's health or safety." These can all be trimmed away.

9. After spending nearly 26 years in jail, South African statesman Nelson Mandela was elected president of South Africa in that country's first multiracial election in 1994.

    Simple version: Nelson Mandela was elected president.

    You can also eliminate any words that provide descriptions, such as "South African statesman" and "first multiracial." Although these words provide more details, they are not essential to the sentence.

10. On Shrove Tuesday in 217 B.C.E., soldiers in Derby, England celebrated a victory over Roman soldiers by playing the first recorded soccer match, starting an annual event that lasted for almost 1,000 years.

    Simple version: Soldiers celebrated by playing soccer.

    There are many phrases that can be trimmed here. As you can see, most of the words in this sentence only provide more details. Ignore them and focus on the important stuff.

Tip #3: Dealing with Difficult Vocabulary

Passages on the TOEFL may contain a number of difficult or unfamiliar words. It's easy to become frustrated with these words and lose track of what you've read. Fortunately, you often do not need to understand these words to determine the passage's main idea. As we just saw, trimming the fat eliminates many of the words in a sentence because they are not crucial to understanding it. Let's look at some examples of sentences with difficult vocabulary words.

> Despite the preponderance of evidence debunking this outdated notion, many people continue to vigorously defend it.

First, let's trim the fat. Remember, we said that phrases at the beginning of a sentence that are set off with commas can be cut. That eliminates two of the difficult words, leaving us with the following sentence:

> Many people continue to vigorously defend it.

Now the sentence isn't so complicated. Let's just focus on the subject, verb, and object. Our sentence now reads as follows:

> People continue to defend it.

The other words are just adjectives—modifiers. They add detail, but they're not essential to understanding the basic idea. In some cases, the difficult vocabulary word is the subject or the verb. In these cases, trimming the fat won't be too helpful. Here's an example.

> The gentry of Victorian England viewed work as the domain of men and often limited women's access to various jobs and professions.

Let's trim away some of the unnecessary phrases. Start by eliminating some of the prepositional phrases (those phrases beginning with words such as *on, of, in,* and so forth) and modifiers. That leaves us with the following sentence:

> The gentry viewed work as the domain of men and often limited women's access to jobs and professions.

Our first verb is "viewed," and our subject is "gentry," a difficult vocabulary word. However, to understand this sentence, we don't need to know exactly what "gentry" means. You can tell by the meaning of the word "view"—to see or to look at—that "gentry" probably means some kind of people. So, let's just replace "gentry" as shown below:

> Some people viewed work as the domain of men.

This is good enough for understanding the author's general idea. This even works when the difficult vocabulary takes the form of a verb. Here's an example.

> In time, the Scythians were able to subjugate the Slavs, a people who throughout their history suffered under the dominion of many foreign rulers.

Using the same "trimming" process, we can reduce this sentence to the following:

> The Scythians were able to subjugate the Slavs.

Then we can replace our difficult word with a simple phrase.

> The Scythians were able to do something to the Slavs.

Most likely, you'll find some information in another part of the passage that will help you figure out what the difficult word means. But when you are looking for the main idea or purpose, don't focus on what you don't know—work with what you do know.

Drill #8: Difficult Vocabulary

The following sentences contain one or more difficult vocabulary words. Paraphrase each sentence, cutting out extra phrases. Then simplify the sentence, taking difficult words and replacing them with more familiar ones whenever possible. Check your answers with those at the end of the drill.

1. The authorship of *The Art of War*, an influential treatise on war, tactics, and espionage, is often attributed to Sun Tzu, but the tome was more likely penned by a number of writers.

   Simplify: _____

2. One of the more controversial incidents of government intervention into the private sector occurred when, during the early 1970s, the government imposed a cap on wages to combat inflation.

   Simplify: _____

3. Saccharin, a white crystalline compound that tastes more than 100 times sweeter than sugar, was discovered by accident in 1879.

   Simplify: _____

4. The writ of habeas corpus functions not to ascertain a detainee's guilt or innocence, but to determine if the prisoner has been accorded due process.

   Simplify: _____

5. Theodor Adorno, Walter Benjamin, and Herbert Marcuse, distinguished philosophers of the Frankfurt School, were instrumental in formulating seminal critical theories on capitalism.

   Simplify: _____

6. Based on his observations of the Andromeda galaxy and others like it, Walter Baade inferred the existence of ancient stars in the Milky Way that were formed from primordial hydrogen and helium.

   Simplify: _____

7. Most critics consider *Dracula* the archetypal horror novel, the one from which all other macabre stories originate.

   Simplify: _____

8. Archaeologists usually employ two types of dating methods: one that attempts to determine the temporal order of a sequence of events and one that strives to date an object or event in terms of absolute calendar years.

   Simplify: _____

9. A modem operates by converting discrete digital data into an analog signal that varies continuously in reference to a standard reference point.

    Simplify: _____

10. Abstract expressionism emerged from the turbulent 1940s New York City art scene and quickly captivated critics with its stylistic diversity and nonrepresentational framework.

    Simplify: _____

Answers to Drill #8

Many of these examples are similar to the exercises in Drill #7.

1. The authorship of *The Art of War*, an influential treatise on war, tactics, and espionage, is often attributed to Sun Tzu, but the tome was more likely penned by a number of writers.

    Words such as "treatise," "espionage," and "tome" are not important to the general idea of this sentence.

    Simplify: The writing is often said to be that of Sun Tzu, but many writers probably wrote it.

2. One of the more controversial incidents of government intervention into the private sector occurred when, during the early 1970s, the government imposed a cap on wages to combat inflation.

    In this sentence, it is necessary to realize that a controversial incident occurred. Thus, it is not important what words such as "intervention" and "sector" mean. If you are unsure of what "imposed" means, you can still get the basic idea. You can make this sentence very simple, which may help you to understand the overall meaning of its passage on the test.

    Simplify: Something happened when the government did something.

3. Saccharin, a white crystalline compound that tastes more than 100 times sweeter than sugar, was discovered by accident in 1879.

    In this example, one of our difficult words—"saccharin"—is the subject. But don't dwell on it. The sentence's message is that it was discovered by accident. Even if you have no idea what saccharin is, you can get the meaning of the whole sentence by substituting the word "something" for "saccharin" and then following the clues in the phrase—that it's something like sugar.

    Simplify: Something like sugar was discovered by accident.

4. The writ of habeas corpus functions not to ascertain a detainee's guilt or innocence, but to determine if the prisoner has been accorded due process.

    Some passages may contain jargon, specialized terminology relating to a particular field of study. Ignore it. In this sentence, we can cut out "writ of habeas corpus" and "due process" and read the sentence as follows:

    Simplify: This thing functions to determine one thing.

5. Theodor Adorno, Walter Benjamin, and Herbert Marcuse, distinguished philosophers of the Frankfurt School, were instrumental in formulating seminal critical theories on capitalism.

   This sentence has a lot of information packed into it: the names of three men, who they were (philosophers), and what they did. To avoid a lot of trouble and to help you find the main idea, simply paraphrase the sentence.

   Simplify: Some guys were doing something with theories.

6. Based on his observations of the Andromeda galaxy and others like it, Walter Baade inferred the existence of ancient stars in the Milky Way that were formed from primordial hydrogen and helium.

   "Inferred" and "primordial" do not affect the meaning of this sentence in a major way.

   Simplify: Walter Baade did something with the existence of stars.

7. Most critics consider *Dracula* the archetypal horror novel, the one from which all other macabre stories originate.

   Many times, an author will provide clues as to the meaning of a word in the rest of the sentence. In this case, "archetypal" is defined as something from which other things originate. Even so, the meaning of the word is not important to the sentence. "Macabre" is also not necessary.

   Simplify: Critics consider *Dracula* the horror story from which all others originate.

8. Archaeologists usually employ two types of dating methods: one that attempts to determine the temporal order of a sequence of events and one that strives to date an object or event in terms of absolute calendar years.

   Once again, the important stuff is surrounded by lots of extra information. Don't worry about words such as "temporal" or "strive."

   Simplify: Archaeologists use two types of methods.

9. A modem operates by converting discrete digital data into an analog signal that varies continuously in reference to a standard reference point.

   There are a few parts of this sentence that may be difficult to understand. Let's simplify it.

   Simplify: A thing operates by changing one type of thing into another.

10. Abstract expressionism emerged from the turbulent 1940s New York City art scene and quickly captivated critics with its stylistic diversity and nonrepresentational framework.

    Sometimes the entire sentence is filled with difficult vocabulary or jargon. If you encounter this type of sentence on the test, move on. No single sentence will be absolutely essential to understanding an author's main idea, so look for your information elsewhere. For this sentence, you need to know the following:

    Simplify: Something came from art and did something to critics.

Final Exam

Now it's time to try out all the strategies you've learned. For the following passage, identify the main idea, structure, and author's primary purpose in writing it. Briefly paraphrase each paragraph after you read it. Check your answers at the end of the exercise.

1 Since 1979, there has been a consensus that a doubling of carbon dioxide would raise global temperatures 1.5 to 4.5 degrees Celsius. Emissions of methane, nitrous gases, and other gases that absorb infrared radiation could speed this process further. Although attention has been given to strategies intended to limit global warming, most climatologists feel an average temperature increase of one to two degrees Celsius is inevitable.

2 A potentially hazardous consequence of even a slight increase in worldwide temperature was identified in the early 1970s. Scientists predicted a nearly 20-foot rise in global sea levels as a result of the Antarctic ice sheet melting. Although this prediction has since been discredited by new research that shows such an occurrence would take place over a span of roughly 500 years, more recent studies have identified several sites, including smaller glaciers and large parts of the ice sheet in Greenland, that are more susceptible to rapid thawing. Based on data compiled from researchers, a seven-foot rise in sea level is possible by the year 2100.

3 Even a small rise in sea level, an average of two feet worldwide, would result in inundation, erosion, flooding, and saltwater intrusion. Coastal areas of the United States would lose a significant amount of land: Scientists predict a 50- to 100-foot loss in New Jersey, and up to 1,000 feet of shore areas flooded in Florida. According to some studies, the rise in water levels could contribute to a loss of 50 to 90 percent of U.S. Wetlands.

4 Currently, two major policy approaches are being considered by coastal communities. The first, known as the no-protection approach, is based on a philosophy of nonintervention. Communities in coastal regions simply zone areas they anticipate losing land to erosion within the next 30 to 60 years. No new buildings are permitted to be built in zones likely to be lost to flooding or erosion, and the current structures are left to their fates. Communities that take a no-protection approach acknowledge the coming danger, but they are often unwilling or unable to incur the financial losses associated with condemning and removing beachfront property. However, it should be noted that communities that elect a no-protection approach place the financial burden on the federal government, which compensates homeowners for homes lost to floods or storms.

5 The second option, and certainly the more appealing one, involves raising the land level along the shore. This approach, although a far costlier one, offers several advantages. First, it does not require the removal or demolition of buildings. Instead, the entire land mass is raised to protect it from the ocean. Second, the federal government does not have to intervene in the form of land buys or flood insurance. Despite these benefits, many communities choose not to raise the land because of the great cost and large amount of labor involved. To raise the land, sand must be pumped onto the beach (including the underwater part of the beach) until the land level gradually rises. In addition, roads, houses, and other structures must be gradually raised again. The size of this undertaking prevents many communities from considering it.

6 One of the major hurdles facing policy makers is the lack of urgency surrounding the onset of global warming and rising sea levels. Many communities do not see the need to take action in response to effects that will not materialize for 100 years. However, considering the possible consequences of inaction, community leaders would be wise to begin serious discussions about their preferred strategy.

Paragraph 1: _____

_____

Paragraph 2: _____

_____

Paragraph 3: _____

_____

Paragraph 4: _____

_____

Paragraph 5: _____

_____

Paragraph 6: _____

_____

Main idea: _____

_____

Purpose: _____

_____

Answers to Final Exam

Paragraph 1: This paragraph indicates that a doubling of carbon dioxide leads to an increase in temperature. The "although" near the end of the passage should be noted. The sentence states that the warming seems inevitable.

More Great Books
If you need more reading and writing drills and practice, check out another Princeton Review page-turner, *TOEFL Reading & Writing Workout.*

Paragraph 2: The author gives information on the consequence: a rise in sea levels. Remember, you don't need to pay too much attention to the details.

Paragraph 3: This paragraph continues the discussion of results of the rise in sea level. Note the word "even." This is a direction word.

Paragraph 4: Now the author introduces two major approaches to solving the problem. The first possible solution is the no-protection approach. Did you find the direction word ("however") at the end of the paragraph? Note that this approach places a financial burden on the government.

Paragraph 5: This is the second option, and it is important to note that the author favors it ("more appealing"). The second option involves raising the land level. There are quite a few direction markers in this paragraph.

Paragraph 6: The author ends with a "hurdle," or obstacle, to solving the problem. The author thinks people should decide on the best solution soon and act on it.

Main idea: There are two main approaches to dealing with rising sea levels caused by global warming, and communities should give thought to which strategy they will use.

Purpose: The purpose of this passage is to provide a possible solution to a problem. The first paragraph introduces a situation that would cause Earth's temperature to rise. The next two paragraphs reveal consequences of the warming. After that, the author discusses two possible solutions. Finally, the author states that leaders need to act soon.

The Last Word on Reading

We've spent a lot of time working with passages, but the time has been well spent. The elements of reading we've reviewed in this chapter form the core of the skills required to do well on the TOEFL. Reading skills will also prove invaluable on two other sections of the TOEFL— Speaking and Writing. But first, let's look at the core concepts you'll need to master the next section—Listening.

Chapter 3
Core Concept: Listening

The TOEFL is an integrated exam, which means that each task may measure more than one skill. Now that you've learned about the reading section of the exam, continue mastering the core concepts of the TOEFL in this Listening chapter. Pay attention to how some of the strategies you learned for Reading can be applied to Listening questions as well.

The Listening section will have 3–4 lectures with 6 questions each and 2–3 casual conversations with 5 questions each. The entire Listening section will last 41–57 minutes.

The Listening section can seem like one of the most intimidating sections on the TOEFL. The tasks in the Listening section require you to sort through lectures and conversations that are filled with distracting pauses and brief digressions—a very frustrating experience, but a very realistic scenario. Don't be discouraged! The Listening section does follow some common patterns. The key to getting a good score is to find these patterns; this chapter is going to teach you how to do exactly that.

LISTENING ON THE TOEFL

In this section, you'll be asked to listen to *lectures* and *conversations*. These listening tasks will have a definite structure, which is similar to the reading passages you just studied. There will be an introduction, supporting details or examples, and a conclusion.

Let's take a closer look at the structure of these lectures and conversations.

In a *lecture,* you can expect to hear the following:

1. **Opening:** The teacher or professor will greet the class and announce the topic of the lecture.
2. **Purpose of the lecture:** After stating the topic, the speaker will usually mention the focus of this particular lecture.
3. **Details and/or examples:** The lecture will usually include several supporting details and/or examples.
4. **Conclusion:** Conclusions in the lectures will not always be obvious. Some lectures or talks will end rather abruptly.

An academic lecture or talk on the TOEFL is also likely to contain the following additional element:

5. **Questions and/or comments:** During the lecture, a student will often ask a question or make a comment. The answers to these questions typically reinforce the speaker's purpose.

In a *conversation,* you can expect to hear the following:

1. **Greeting:** The two people talking will first exchange greetings.
2. **Statement of problem/issue:** Conversations on the TOEFL typically revolve around a problem or an issue faced by one of the speakers.
3. **Response:** After the problem or issue is raised, one of the speakers will respond, usually by making a suggestion to the other.
4. **Resolution:** The conversation will end with some sort of closing or resolution to the problem.

Your challenge in the Listening section is similar to your challenge in the Reading section of the TOEFL. When listening to a conversation or lecture, you need to do the following:

1. Identify *what* the topic is.
2. Figure out *why* the topic is being addressed.
3. Note the supporting *examples*.

You've practiced identifying these parts in the previous chapter. Now the challenge is to apply what you've learned to the Listening section. There are some things, however, that make the listening tasks especially difficult.

CHALLENGES IN THE LISTENING SECTION

In the Speaking and Writing sections (which you'll learn about in the other Core Concepts chapters in this book), you will be required to listen to lectures and respond, just as you will in the Listening section. However, there is a difference between the tasks in other sections and those in the Listening section.

The difference is that the tasks in the Listening section have intentional distractions. These distractions are pauses, interruptions, and interjections that disrupt the flow of the speaker's talk. Interestingly, if you were to respond on the Speaking section in the same way the speakers talk on the Listening section, you would receive a fairly low score.

For example, you may hear something like the three brief statements that follow, which include common distractions (try reading them aloud, or ask a friend to read them to you).

> "Okay, so, uh…today we're going to discuss the hunting practices of the umm…Trobriand Islanders. As you remember, we uh…last week, last week we talked about their social structure, now we're moving into their day-to-day activities."

> "So let's take our example of…what did we say? Right, our example is the proposed flat tax rate. Now this example isn't a perfect one because, well… it's only a hypothetical example, but it'll do for this discussion."

> "Therefore—and this is an important point—the New Historicism Movement— didn't um, didn't come out of nowhere. It was a product of its time. Okay?"

Another characteristic that makes the Listening section different from the others is that you will have to follow conversations between multiple speakers. It can be difficult to identify the purpose or the supporting details of a conversation when the speaker changes.

TAKING NOTES

You are allowed to take notes on the TOEFL. Of course, you must balance your note taking with your ability to comprehend the speech or lecture. A common mistake is to try to write too much; this often causes you to miss hearing some important information. Therefore, keep your note taking to a minimum and focus only on major points.

Here's a suggestion on how to organize your notes.

I.   What? _____

II. Why? _____

III. Reasons/examples _____

1. _____

2. _____

3. _____

IV. Conclusion _____

Whether or not you take notes, you will need to listen actively to do well on this part of the TOEFL.

ACTIVE LISTENING

Active listening strategies are similar to the *active reading* strategies that you learned in Chapter 2. Of course, active listening is more difficult than active reading. However, by familiarizing yourself with the overall structure of the lectures and conversations, you'll have an easier time understanding the main points.

When listening actively, pay attention to the following:

1. **Purpose:** The speaker will usually state the purpose of the lecture or conversation within the first few lines of the talk.

2. **Reasons/examples:** The rest of the conversation or lecture will contain reasons or examples related to the purpose.

The next sections provide you with some practice in listening actively to lectures and conversations. Let's start with lectures.

Listening to Lectures

Track 1 available in your Student Tools online is a lecture in a sociology class. As you listen to the lecture, try to identify the purpose and the reasons or examples. How is this lecture similar to the reading passages you've looked at? How is it different?

Play Track 1. A transcript of the lecture can be found on page 114.

Purpose: _____

Examples: _____

_____

_____

Headphones On!

Lecture Analysis

Lectures typically follow the format of reading passages. The speaker will provide an introduction, supporting reasons and examples, and some sort of conclusion. Of course, as you're listening to the lecture, you won't be aware of when a paragraph ends, but you should still know what to expect based on the part of the lecture to which you're listening.

Here's the introduction of the lecture, broken down piece by piece.

> (1) Okay, class, let's get started. (2) Today, um, today we're going to talk about the ah...structural functionalist theory in sociology. (3) You guys remember last week we discussed the interactionist perspective, right? (4) Now that theory, the interactionist theory, focused on how people get along with one another and, uh, the way that interactions um...create behaviors.

Now, let's analyze what's going on in this first part of the introduction.

(1) **Introduction.** On the TOEFL, the lectures and conversations usually start with a greeting of some sort. This greeting is not important to the lecture.
(2) **Topic.** At some point early in the lecture, the professor will probably state what the class is going to talk about "today" or "in this class." This is very important. Note the topic on your scrap paper.
(3) **Background.** Usually, the professor will refer to a prior lecture or topic. The professor will state that the class talked about this topic "last time," "last class," or something along those lines. This information may be important to the lecture or it may be a distraction; it depends on what the purpose of the lecture is.
(4) **More background.** This sentence provides more background information.

Here's the second part of the introduction.

> (1) This theory...the structural functionalist theory...I'm just going to call it the functionalist theory...is very different. (2) Now, we'll talk about the historical context of this theory a little bit later, (3) but first I would like to just...um, go over the main tenets of the theory.

Let's analyze what's going on in this second part of the introduction.

(1) **Transition:** Speeches and lectures tend to have transitions. These transitions don't add any new information.
(2) **Digression:** You will also notice a digression (an off-topic comment) or two during the lectures. Usually, the professor will refer to something that will be "discussed later" or "at another time." Sometimes the professor will say, "I'm not going to get into this now." This information is unimportant.
(3) **Purpose:** Listen for the statement of purpose early in the lecture. If you figure out the purpose, write it down on your scrap paper.

This is the next part of the lecture.

> (1) The basic view of functionalism is that our behaviors and actions can be best explained with...explained by the role...or function, if you will...that they

perform for the society as a whole. (2) Now, I know that may be a little vague. (3) What do I mean by that? (4) Well, let's look at some different behaviors and, uh, see how a functionalist would explain them.

Let's analyze what's happening in this part of the lecture.

(1) **Definition/explanation:** The purpose of many of the lectures is to define or explain a term.

(2, 3) **Digression:** Neither sentence 2 nor sentence 3 adds anything to the lecture. As you're listening, try to focus on the topic and the examples given to support/explain it.

(4) **Transition:** Here's another transition. Note how the speaker is about to discuss examples. Typically, the lecturer will say something such as, "Now, let's look at…" or "Now, I want to talk about…." These words let you know that examples are coming.

Here's the next section.

(1) A good example would be the, uh, drug use. (2) A functionalist wouldn't really um…judge a drug user as a deviant, a bad person. Instead, the functionalist would try to ah…figure out what role the drug user, the person, fills in society. (3) This seems a little strange at first, I know, but bear with me. (4) Think about what role a drug user fills in society. (5) You may automatically think that the role, um, the role is always negative—crime, the cost of treatment, maybe more jails—but the functionalist tries to see the positives as well.

And here's the analysis of this section.

(1) **Example:** Once the lecturer begins discussing examples, the structure is very similar to a reading passage. There will be an example followed by specific details.

(2) **Detail:** Many of the questions will ask about details, so try to note some of them.

(3, 4) **Digression:** These two sentences address the class. They emphasize the lecturer's example, but they are relatively unimportant.

(5) **Detail:** This is similar to sentence 2. Don't try to write down or memorize everything the lecturer says. You won't have time.

Here is the next part of the lecture.

(1) I bet you're thinking that drug use doesn't have too many positives, right? (2) Well, here's what a functionalist would say. (3) While a drug user may be harming himself or herself, to be fair, he is also benefiting society. Having drug users means we need to have more police, which means obviously, more jobs.

(4) And also…if you think about it…more doctors, nurses, and social workers. (5) Even drug counselors. (6) All these people would be out of work, probably, if we didn't have a drug problem. (7) Let's keep going…without drug users, we wouldn't need the entire Drug Enforcement Agency, that bureau employs thousands of people, you know, and there's also the border patrol, customs agents, and so on, and so on.

And here's what's happening in this section.

(1, 2)　**Transition:** This sentence acts as a bridge from one paragraph (which describes negative factors) to the next sentences (which describe positive factors).

(3)　**Detail:** This sentence brings the discussion back to the topic.

(4–7)　**Detail:** The rest of the sentences give details about the topic. Again, you can't possibly note every single part, so just try to note down one or two important points.

Finally, here is the last part of the lecture.

(1) So I think our example has given you a pretty good idea of how a functionalist views behaviors. (2) Again, the important thing is that they don't really judge behaviors as good or bad...they only view them based on their role or function in society.

(3) And I think we can probably guess then, that to a functionalist, all behaviors...no matter how good or bad you may think they are...are necessary to society. (4) It's really a, uh, pretty interesting viewpoint, if you think about it.

Here's what's going on in this last part.

(1)　**Conclusion:** Listen for the conclusion of the lecture. The speaker may say something such as, "So..." or "Thus..." or "And so...."

(2, 3)　**Summary:** Some lectures will end with a brief summary of the important points.

(4)　**Digression:** This sentence contains no new or important information.

As this exercise shows, many of the parts of the lecture are similar to the reading passages. While you listen to the sample lectures, think about their purpose and structure, just as you would with a reading passage.

Summary: Lectures

Try to identify the main parts of the lecture. Listen for the following:

1.　**What?** This should appear early in the lecture, after the greeting.
2.　**Why?** Shortly after the topic is introduced, the purpose of the lecture will be stated.
3.　**Reasons/Examples:** The majority of the lecture will be examples and details. Don't try to write down or memorize every single one.
4.　**Conclusion:** Note any final points or summaries.

Listening to Conversations

Now let's listen to a conversation similar to what you'll hear on the TOEFL and see how this form works.

Play Track 2 in your Student Tools online. A transcript can be found on page 115.

Conversation Analysis

Headphones On!

Conversations have the basic elements of reading passages. There should be some basic purpose to the conversation and reasons or examples related to that purpose. Here is a breakdown of the conversation you just heard.

Computer Lab Monitor:	Hi. Do you need help with something?
Student:	Yes. I'm supposed to use this program for my statistics class, but I'm not sure how.

Conversations also start with a greeting. Usually, the purpose will appear right at the beginning. Note this purpose on your scrap paper. Let's see what's next.

CLM:	Okay. Do you have the program with you?
S:	Sure, here it is.
CLM:	Okay, let's bring this over to a computer and see how it works.
S:	I think there's something wrong with the program. When I tried to run it on my computer, nothing happened.

These lines provide a detail about the problem the student is having. The questions will often ask about this type of detail, so be sure to note it.

CLM:	Hmm. That's interesting. Well, let's see what happens here. It looks like it's running fine on this computer.
S:	Weird. My computer freezes every time I try to open the program.
CLM:	You mean the entire computer locks up? Have you had this type of problem before?
S:	Yeah, I guess. Sometimes when I try to use certain programs, they just don't seem to work correctly. I don't know why though.

More specific details are provided about the problem. Note that in a conversation, you'll have to pay attention to the roles of the speakers. In this case, one speaker is describing a problem, and the other is trying to help find a solution.

CLM:	You can always use the computers here in the lab, you know. That way you won't have to worry about it.
S:	I know. But I'd rather figure out what the problem is with my computer. The computer lab can be busy, and I need to work on this project often. It's going to be one-third of our grade.
CLM:	What class is this for?
S:	It's for Statistics 101, with Professor Lee.

> *CLM:* And this program is required for the course?
>
> *S:* Yep. Professor Lee even got the campus bookstore to stock a bunch of copies. That's where I bought it.
>
> *CLM:* Do you use your computer for a lot of things? Maybe you should clear up some memory before you run the program.
>
> *S:* Yeah, I've tried that actually. I do have a lot of programs on my computer, but I should have enough memory to run this program.

Here, the lab monitor proposes a solution. This is an important part of the conversation, so make sure to note it. Also note the student's response to the solution. Many of the other details, such as the course or the professor's name, are not important. Focus only on details that relate back to the purpose. Let's see how the conversation wraps up.

> *CLM:* Well, I'm not quite sure what the problem could be. But you're welcome to use the program here.
>
> *S:* Okay.
>
> *CLM:* And you should definitely come back later and talk to my supervisor. She's a computer whiz. I bet she can solve your problem.

Conversations should have a fairly definite conclusion. You should pay attention to how the conversation ends. Has the purpose been achieved? Note this on your scrap paper.

Summary: Conversations

Conversations have a definite structure. When listening to a conversation, pay attention to the following:

1. **Purpose:** What do the people in the conversation hope to achieve? Why are these people having this conversation?
2. **Details:** What specific details or examples are offered? How do these examples relate back to the purpose?
3. **Conclusion:** Is there any resolution? Do the people achieve their purpose?

TRANSCRIPTS

Track 1

Professor: Okay, class, let's get started. Today, um, today we're going to talk about the ah... structural functionalist theory in sociology. You guys remember last week we discussed the interactionist perspective, right? Now that theory, the interactionist theory, focused on how people get along with one another and, uh, the way that interactions um...create behaviors.

This theory...the structural functionalist theory...I'm just going to call it the functionalist theory...is very different. Now, we'll talk about the historical context of this theory a little bit later, but first I would like to just...um, go over the main tenets of the theory.

The basic view of functionalism is that our behaviors and actions can be best explained with...explained by the role...or function, if you will...that they perform for the society as a whole. Now, that may be a little vague. What do I mean by that? Well, let's look at some different behaviors and uh, see how a functionalist would explain them.

A good example would be the, uh, drug use. A functionalist wouldn't really um... judge a drug user as a deviant, a bad person. Instead, the functionalist would try to uh...figure out what role the drug user, the person, fills in society. This seems a little strange at first but bear with me. Think about what role a drug user fills in society. You may automatically think that the role, um the role is always negative— crime, the cost of treatment, maybe more jails—but the functionalist tries to see the positives as well.

I bet you're thinking that drug use doesn't have too many positives, right? Well, here's what a functionalist would say. While a drug user may be harming himself... or herself, to be fair...he is also benefiting society. Having drug users means we need to have more police, which means obviously, more jobs.

And also...if you think about it...more doctors, nurses, and social workers. Even drug counselors. All these people would be out of work, probably, if we didn't have a drug problem. Let's keep going...without drug users, we wouldn't need the entire Drug Enforcement Agency...that bureau employs thousands of people, you know...and there's also the border patrol, customs agents, and so on, and so on.

So I think our example has given you a pretty good idea of how a functionalist views behaviors. Again, the important thing is that they don't really judge behaviors as good or bad...they only view them based on their role or function in society.

And I think we can probably guess then, that to a functionalist, all behaviors...no matter how good or bad you may think they are...are necessary to society. It's really a, uh, pretty interesting viewpoint, if you think about it.

Track 2

Computer Lab Monitor:	Hi. Do you need help with something?
Student:	Yes. I'm supposed to use this program for my statistics class, but I'm not sure how.
CLM:	Okay. Do you have the program with you?
S:	Sure, here it is.
CLM:	Okay, let's bring this over to a computer and see how it works.
S:	I think there's something wrong with the program. When I tried to run it on my computer, nothing happened.
CLM:	Hmm. That's interesting. Well, let's see what happens here. It looks like it's running fine on this computer.
S:	Weird. My computer freezes every time I try to open the program.
CLM:	You mean the entire computer locks up? Have you had this type of problem before?
S:	Yeah, I guess. Sometimes when I try to use certain programs, they just don't seem to work correctly. I don't know why though.
CLM:	You can always use the computers here in the lab, you know. That way you won't have to worry about it.
S:	I know. But I'd rather figure out what the problem is with my computer. The computer lab can be busy, and I need to work on this project often. It's going to be one-third of our grade.
CLM:	What class is this for?
S:	It's for Statistics 101, with Professor Lee.
CLM:	And this program is required for the course?
S:	Yep. Professor Lee even got the campus bookstore to stock a bunch of copies. That's where I bought it.
CLM:	Do you use your computer for a lot of things? Maybe you should clear up some memory before you run the program.
S:	Yeah, I've tried that actually. I do have a lot of programs on my computer, but I should have enough memory to run this program.
CLM:	Well, I'm not quite sure what the problem could be, but you're welcome to use the program here.
S:	Okay.
CLM:	And you should definitely come back later and talk to my supervisor. She's a computer whiz. I bet she can solve your problem.

Chapter 4
Core Concept: Speaking

Continue mastering the core concepts of the TOEFL in this Speaking section. In the previous chapter, you learned how to interpret the communication of others. Here you'll learn how to prepare your own thoughts to communicate them to the world.

As mentioned earlier, the TOEFL is an integrated exam, which means that each individual section will measure several abilities. You'll be learning Speaking skills that you will use in concert with the Reading, Listening, and Writing skills.

SCORING FOR THE SPEAKING SECTION

Although the Speaking section is different from the Writing section in some ways, many of the guidelines for scoring it are similar. The Speaking section is graded on a scale of 0 to 4, while the scale for the Writing section is 0 to 5. In both Speaking and Writing, a score of 0 is reserved for a response that simply repeats the prompt, is in a foreign language, or is left blank, whereas a score of 4 on the Speaking section is judged to have accomplished the following:

- The response fulfills the demands of the task.
- The response presents a clear progression of ideas.
- The response includes appropriate details.

These standards conform to our three basic Core Concept Reading skills: *purpose, main idea,* and *structure.*

The main difference on the Speaking section is that the graders will also consider the quality of your speech. While they don't expect perfect English, they expect a top response to:

- use speech that is clear, fluid, and sustained, although it may contain minor lapses in pronunciation or intonation. Pace may vary at times, but overall intelligibility remains high.
- demonstrate good control of basic and complex grammatical structures and contain generally effective word choice. Minor errors or imprecise use may be noticeable, but they neither require listener effort nor do they obscure meaning.

The best way to make sure you meet these guidelines is to *practice.* We'll give you suggestions and tips on how to achieve these goals, but there's no substitute for continued repetition.

PART 1: STATING YOUR PURPOSE

You remember that you needed to find a purpose in Reading passages and listen for a purpose in lectures on the Listening section. Well, the best way to succeed on the Speaking section of the TOEFL is to use those skills you've learned in the reading and listening exercises.

Purpose and the Speaking Section

The speaking tasks on the TOEFL usually require you to do one of the following:

- Present your opinion on an issue.
- Explain facts presented in a lecture or reading.
- Summarize someone else's position.
- Describe something of importance to you.

Your speech on the TOEFL will need an introduction, just as you've observed in reading passages. Let's look at some ways to come up with an effective introduction.

Clearly Expressing Purpose on the Speaking Section

Let's look at a sample speaking task.

> Describe a job that you've held, and explain why it was important.

Now, here are the steps to follow.

Step 1: Decide What Your Purpose Is

Make sure you take a moment to decide what your purpose is; otherwise, you will not be able to communicate it effectively. As you have seen in the previous bullet points, there are four different types of tasks that you may encounter on the Speaking section of the TOEFL.

Step 2: State the Topic

For speaking tasks that ask you to present your opinion or to describe something personal to you, use the following introductory phrases:

I believe	*I think*	*I feel*
My view is	*My opinion is*	*My preference is*

After each of these statements, mention the topic and whatever example you're going to use. For the sample task about a job you've held, your first sentence could be as follows:

> I think that the most important job I've had was working at a library.
> *(introductory statement)*   *(topic)*   *(specific example)*

State your topic in a clear, direct way. Also, note that on opinion questions, there is no right or wrong answer. Your purpose is to convince the listener that your position is correct, whatever your position may be.

For speaking tasks that require you to summarize someone else's opinion or to explain facts, the following introductions are appropriate:

This person believes that	*This person holds that*	*This person argues that*
This person's view is that	*This person's point is that*	*The lecture stated*
The reading stated	*The reading presented*	*The lecture offered*

After each statement, fill in what the topic or position is. For example, a TOEFL task may ask you to summarize facts from a reading. Your introduction may sound like the example below.

> The reading presented facts on…(topic)

Step 3: State *What* or *Why*

For speaking tasks that ask your opinion, you will have to state *why* you believe something. For speaking tasks that require you to summarize facts or someone else's position, you'll have to say *what* his or her reasons are. Use the following words to indicate *what* and *why*:

Because	*The reason*	*Due to*	*For*

Once you put it all together, the introduction to your speech may look like the following:

> I think that the most important job I've had was working at a library. I believe this because I met many interesting people at this job.

Spoken responses on the TOEFL are only 45 or 60 seconds, so most of your time will be used presenting details or examples. Therefore, your introduction should be brief and to the point.

Drill #1: Practice Speaking an Introduction to a Speech

Practice speaking introductions for each of the following tasks. If possible, record yourself so that you can review and evaluate your responses later. Compare your responses to those at the end of the drill.

1. If you could have any job in the world, which job would you choose?

2. Describe a person you admire, and explain why you admire him or her.

3. A university has recently received a large sum of money. The university desperately needs to improve housing on campus, but students have also complained that the library needs to be fixed. Do you think that the money should be spent on housing or the library? Provide examples and reasons for your choice.

4. Read the following short passage:

    The cane toad, a poisonous species of toad, is causing problems in Australia. The cane toad was brought to Australia in 1935 to help control the population of greyback beetles. Unfortunately, the toads did nothing to reduce the beetle population. Now, however, cane toads number in the millions and are threatening native animal populations.

    The cane toad has two poisonous sacs located near its head and is so toxic that dingoes, snakes, and even crocodiles die within fifteen minutes of eating a cane toad. Now, conservationists are forced to transport some endangered species of animals to islands free from cane toads so that the endangered species can breed in safety.

    The passage above describes a problem. Explain what the problem is and what steps are being taken to fix it.

5. Read the following conversation between two coworkers:

    Employee A: I'm really swamped at work. I don't know if I'm going to be able to finish all of my projects by the deadline.

    Employee B: I know. We really need to hire some more people around here. What are you going to do?

    Employee A: I don't know. My boss said I have to finish the budget analysis by Friday, but he just gave me a new project that he needs completed right away.

    Employee B: Well, if I were you, I'd tell your boss that there's no way you can finish both in time. I'd ask for more time.

    Employee A: Yeah, I guess I could do that.

    Employee B: Or maybe you can ask your boss to assign the project to someone else. That way you can focus on the budget analysis.

    Employee B offers two possible solutions to Employee A's problems. Describe the problem, and state which of the two solutions you prefer. Explain why.

Sample Responses to Drill #1

Read the following responses and practice speaking them aloud:

1. If I could have any job, I think that I would like to be an ambassador. I think this because I enjoy visiting other countries and meeting and interacting with other people.

2. One person whom I admire very much is Mohandas Gandhi. I admire him for many reasons, especially his strong sense of justice and rightness.

3. In my opinion, the university should spend its money on the library. I think this because a university should be an institution of learning and a good library is essential to that.

4. The passage states that the problem is the poisonous cane toad. The toad is threatening many of the species in Australia.

5. The problem the employee has is that he or she cannot finish his or her work on time. In my opinion, the better solution is to ask the boss to assign the project to someone else. I think this because it is better to get the work done on time than to extend the deadline.

Summary: Stating Your Purpose

Your introduction is the first chance you have to make a good impression on your listener—so make it solid. Since you won't have much time to give your spoken response, make your introduction quick and concise.

The three points you need to convey in your introduction are as follows:

1. **Purpose**: Your task.
2. **Thesis**: Your topic. The thesis is basically a statement of your position or belief on a topic or your main idea. It will be slightly different based on what you are trying to accomplish in your spoken response.
3. **Why**: After introducing the topic, state why you are discussing it. The answer to this *why* question should relate back to the purpose.

In your introduction, don't go into specific details about your examples. You'll get to those later in the body of your speech. Also, avoid repeating the prompt word for word.

PART 2: ORGANIZING YOUR IDEAS

Before you begin speaking, take a few seconds to think about how you will organize your response. Make sure to follow the same guidelines that you saw in the Reading passages. You should include the following in every spoken response:

> - **Introduction**: State your purpose, which is what we practiced earlier.
> - **Body**: Take the majority of your time to give examples and details that refer back to your purpose. (We will focus next on the body of your response.)
> - **Conclusion**: Finally, summarize your thoughts. We will take a look at conclusions toward the end of this chapter.

Developing Body Paragraphs When Speaking

Everything you learned about body paragraphs in the Reading section applies to speaking. Body paragraphs are the place where the author, or speaker, develops his or her ideas. While the introduction states the purpose, the body paragraphs provide specific details to support that purpose.

Note that your responses on the Speaking section will be only 45 or 60 seconds, which means you will have a limited amount of time to develop your body paragraphs.

Articulating Your Body Paragraphs

As we've seen from the reading exercises, the body paragraphs are where an author attempts to accomplish his or her purpose by presenting facts, arguments, and evidence.

A good body paragraph contains the following elements:

1. A **topic sentence** that introduces the main point of the paragraph
2. **Examples, facts, and evidence** that help the author achieve his or her purpose

Step 1: Provide a Topic Sentence

A good topic sentence does two things: it provides a transition between ideas and clearly states the main idea of the paragraph.

Let's look back at the introduction we established before.

> "I think the most important job I've had was working at a library. I believe this because I met many interesting people at this job."

Now, each spoken body paragraph should begin with a topic sentence that supports your introduction.

Therefore, a good topic sentence for the first body paragraph might be this one:

"Working at the library was my most important job because I met Professor Martin, who has become my advisor this semester."

The topic sentence is introducing your idea (the job was important because you met Professor Martin), and then the rest of your body paragraph will give details that support your example. Perhaps Professor Martin convinced you to change your major, suggested you submit an article to the school's literary magazine, or hinted at a promotion on the library staff. These are all details that support your topic sentence.

Another good topic sentence is one that indicates a progression of ideas by using the phrase "One reason…"

In this instance, a good topic sentence might be as follows:

"One reason that my job at the library was important is that I met Professor Martin, who has become my advisor this semester."

Other phrases that accomplish this progression are as follows:

Another reason	*Additionally*	*First*	*Moreover*
Second	*Third*	*Furthermore*	

These are transition statements that help you move from one idea to the next. Each succeeding topic sentence should have a transition statement that connects back to the thesis.

The topic sentence for your next body paragraph might use the following transition:

"Another reason that my job at the library was important is that I met Dr. Lucas, who asked me to edit the book he was writing."

And then the rest of your body paragraph will provide details that support this example.

By writing topic sentences that connect ideas in this way, your response will sound well structured and will be easy to follow.

Step 2: Make Your Case with Examples

《STEP 2

To support your thesis statement, you should provide details or information, usually in the form of facts or reasons.

Your examples should be:

- **Specific:** Don't use examples that are vague or too general.
- **Explained:** Make sure you give details to support your examples.

Use the following template to articulate your examples:

Statement 1: State your example and tie it back to your thesis.
Statement 2: Give one reason why your example is relevant to your thesis.
Statement 3: Add detail to reason #1.
Statement 4: Give another reason why your example is relevant to your thesis.
Statement 5: Add detail to reason #2.
Statement 6 (optional): Provide a summary of your reasons and relate them
to your thesis.

Drill #2: Practice Speaking with Examples

For each task, speak aloud using two examples to support your point. Use the template above as a guide while you articulate your thoughts. Compare your responses with those at the end of the drill.

Record your answers so you can review and evaluate your responses based on our sample answers.

1.   Do you agree or disagree with the following statement?

      It is better for students to gain real-world experience than to spend their time in a classroom.

2.   Describe an influential person, and explain why you feel this person is a positive role model.

3.   Some schools require first-year students to take the same courses, whereas other schools allow students to select the classes they want. Which policy do you think is better for first-year students and why?

4.   Do you agree or disagree with the following statement?

      The most important education occurs not during adulthood but during childhood.

5.   Read the following passage about insect behavior:

> Many insects are social creatures, living in large groups containing literally millions of individuals. Social insects, which include ants, termites, bees, and wasps, are the prime example of unselfish behavior in animals.
>
> In any insect social system, each insect performs a specialized duty that is necessary for the survival of the hive as a whole. For example, among ants, there are certain types of ants that are soldiers—large, fearsome creatures with terrible jaws. Other ants, called drones, do not reproduce, instead devoting their time to taking care of the hive and the young of the queen. Each ant selflessly performs its role, not for its own benefit, but for the benefit of all the other ants.
>
> Now entomologists have found an interesting case of this sort of cooperation in a nonsocial insect, the cricket. Crickets are a prime example of a "selfish" insect, leading a very isolated existence. They typically interact with other crickets only when mating or fighting over territory. But scientists have observed a species of cricket that undergoes periodic mass migrations. Every so often, the crickets set off to find more favorable living areas. When these migrations occur, the crickets band together into a huge caravan. Surely at a time like this, the crickets realize there is safety in numbers and put aside their selfish instinct for the good of all members.

Now read the following lecture on the same subject:

Professor: One of the biggest misconceptions in biology is the belief that organisms act out of concern for the "greater good" of the species. It is somewhat amazing how people assume that an ant or a mouse has enough sense to figure out how its actions impact all the members of its species!

Still, it is understandable why many people might believe this erroneous view. Many actions can be misinterpreted as being for the "good of the species." A classic example found in many early biology textbooks discussed the behavior of the stag. During mating season, a stag typically battles with other males, and the winner of these contests gains access to the females, while the loser walks away. Some people believed that the loser realizes that his offspring will be weaker, so the defeated stag "allows" the winner to mate to ensure the survival of the stag species.

This couldn't be further from the truth. The defeated stag wants to mate just as much as the winner does; the only problem is that he doesn't want to risk his life for the chance to mate. The stag is better off looking for other females to mate with. Thus, both stags—the winner and the loser—are acting not for the good of the species, but for their own selfish reasons.

Another good example of this is a recent study on the behavior of crickets. Scientists noted that crickets occasionally band together, traveling in huge swarms from location to location. The easy assumption was that the crickets believed in strength in numbers. But a researcher showed this is not the case. He attached tags to a sampling of crickets. Some of the tagged crickets were allowed to travel with the group. But some of them were separated from the rest. All the crickets that were separated were eaten by birds or rodents, whereas the tagged crickets in the group survived.

Apparently, there is safety in numbers, but the crickets aren't looking to help their fellow travelers. They want to avoid being eaten, and what better way is there than to disappear into a group of thousands of other tasty morsels?

Summarize the points in the professor's lecture, and explain how the points cast doubt on the reading.

_____

_____

_____

_____

_____

_____

_____

_____

_____

_____

_____

_____

_____

_____

Sample Responses to Drill #2

See how your responses compare to the suggested answers below. When you review the answers, read them aloud for more practice speaking.

1. Real-world experience is usually better than time spent in a classroom. I believe this because experience is the best teacher.

   One example of a way in which real-world experience is valuable is that students studying auto mechanics cannot just read about an engine. Instead, they have to practice taking that engine apart piece by piece and then put it back together. Only then will students understand the concept.

   A second example of a way in which real-world experience is valuable can be applied to learning a foreign language. If students in a classroom never have a chance to practice the language, they may forget the skills they were taught. In this instance, it would also be helpful to practice their skills in a real-world environment.

2. I believe that Mikhail Gorbachev is both an influential person and a positive role model.

   One reason Mikhail Gorbachev is a role model is because he is willing to work for change. Many people are content to have things stay the same, but he worked hard to change the Communist system. Even though his reforms were not as helpful as he would have liked, his willingness for change makes him a good role model.

   Another reason that Mikhail Gorbachev is a positive role model is because of his devotion to ideals that are larger than himself. For instance, he reached out to Ronald Reagan when he wanted to end the Cold War, instead of just following in the footsteps of Soviet leaders who came before him. Ensuring the future success of the Soviet Union was more important than simply concentrating on his personal power.

3. I would support mandatory classes for freshman instead of allowing the students to pick whatever classes they want.

   First, this will ensure a certain quality of education. With standardized classes, universities can make sure that all of their students are familiar with important intellectual works. That way, all students will have a basic educational level.

   Moreover, required classes will serve to increase the camaraderie of students. Universities are good places for students to meet each other and make connections that will help them later in life. Freshmen can sometimes have difficulty fitting in, so required classes will help them make friends.

4. I agree that the most important education happens when one is a child.

   One reason why I agree with this statement is that younger children are very open to ideas and perceptions. A young child is very impressionable, so the lessons learned at this age can have a great impact.

   Furthermore, childhood is a time when education focuses on the essentials of our society. Although children may not be learning advanced skills, they are learning basic life lessons. At this age, children learn important lessons, such as the difference between right and wrong and how to treat other people.

5. The points made in the professor's lecture cast doubt on the reading.

The first point the professor makes that casts doubt on the reading is his point about the behavior of stags. For example, some people interpret the stag's action as being for the "good of the species," but the professor shows that the stag is actually acting in self-interest. Likewise, the professor talks about how crickets act only in self-interest, which does not support the example in the reading.

The second point the professor makes that casts doubt on the reading is his point about the intelligence of animals and insects. He states that it would require a lot of intelligence for an animal or insect to evaluate how its behavior will affect an entire species. Therefore, his argument is that the cricket is acting only out of self-preservation, which again casts doubt on the reading.

Summary: Choosing Examples and Developing Body Paragraphs When Speaking

Good examples are important for your responses. Make sure your examples and your structure are organized.

Remember to do the following:

- **State** the example.
- **Explain** how the example supports your position.
- **Transitions:** Provide a topic sentence or transition statement to move from one example to the next.
- **Details:** Support each example with details.

Focus on stating just a few examples and explaining their significance. Always provide specific details for each example, and articulate the ways in which your examples relate to your purpose.

PUTTING IT ALL TOGETHER

Now take what you learned about organizing your ideas, stating your purpose, providing topic sentences, and making your case with examples to articulate both an introduction and a full body paragraph for each of the following tasks.

Drill #3: Practice Speaking an Introduction and Body Paragraph

Speak a body paragraph for each of the following tasks. It may help to repeat your introduction statement first. If possible, record your responses and evaluate them when you are finished. Then practice speaking by reading the sample responses that follow this drill.

1. If you could have any job in the world, which job would you choose?
2. Describe a person you admire, and explain why you admire him or her.
3. A university has recently received a large sum of money. The university desperately needs to improve housing on campus, but students have complained that the library needs to be fixed. Do you think that the money should be spent on housing or the library? Provide reasons and examples for your choice.
4. Read the following short passage:

The cane toad, a poisonous species of toad, is causing problems in Australia. The cane toad was brought to Australia in 1935 to help control the population of greyback beetles. Unfortunately, the toads did nothing to reduce the beetle population. Now, however, cane toads number in the millions and are threatening native animal populations.

The cane toad has two poisonous sacs located near its head and is so toxic that dingoes, snakes, and even crocodiles die within fifteen minutes of eating a cane toad. Now, conservationists are forced to transport some endangered species of animals to islands free from cane toads so that the endangered species can breed in safety.

The passage above describes a problem. Explain what the problem is and what steps are being taken to fix it.

5. Read the following conversation between two coworkers:

Employee A: I'm really swamped at work. I don't know if I'm going to be able to finish all of my projects by the deadline.

Employee B: I know. We really need to hire some more people around here. What are you going to do?

Employee A: I don't know. My boss said I have to finish the budget analysis by Friday, but he just gave me a new project that he needs completed right away.

Employee B: Well, if I were you, I'd tell your boss that there's no way you can finish both in time. I'd ask for more time.

Employee A: Yeah, I guess I could do that.

Employee B: Or maybe you can ask your boss to assign the project to someone else. That way you can focus on the budget analysis.

Employee B offers two possible solutions to Employee A's problems. Describe the problem, and state which of the two solutions you prefer. Explain why.

Sample Responses to Drill #3

Read the following responses aloud, and practice speaking them until you're comfortable. Pay attention to the use of transitions and direction markers.

1. (Introduction) If I could have any job, I think that I would like to be an ambassador. I think this because I enjoy visiting other countries and meeting and interacting with other people.

   (Body) The primary role of an ambassador is to represent your nation's country in one other country. I would enjoy doing this very much because I love learning about new cultures. I have traveled to many countries already, and I would like the opportunity to visit more.

   (Body) Another reason that I would like to be an ambassador is to have the opportunity to meet and interact with new people. An ambassador's job is to represent his or her country to other people, and I think this would be an exciting role.

2. (Introduction) One person whom I admire very much is Mohandas Gandhi. I admire him for many reasons, especially his strong sense of justice and rightness.

   (Body) The main reason I admire Gandhi is his commitment to his ideas. Gandhi was convinced that his country should be free and devoted his life to that goal. He went on a hunger strike and led many protests.

   (Body) A second reason I admire Gandhi is for his use of nonviolent protest. Even though Gandhi was devoted to his ideas, he realized that there was a right way of achieving them. He rejected violence as a method, and I admire this very much.

3. (Introduction) In my opinion, the university should spend its money on the library. I think this because a university should be an institution of learning, and a good library is important for that.

   (Body) The first reason I would spend money on the library is to benefit the students. It would be a disservice to students if they couldn't perform the type of research required for their classes. To do well in school, students need a good library.

   (Body) Furthermore, I think it is a good idea to spend money on a library to help the reputation of the school. If a university has a top library, it can attract more students. This will bring more money to the university.

4. (Introduction) The passage states that the problem is the poisonous cane toad. The toad is threatening many of the species in Australia.

   (Body) According to the passage, the problem is that the cane toad is very poisonous. The cane toad can kill animals that eat it. This is making it very dangerous for many species in Australia.

   (Body) To fix the problem, conservationists have decided to move some animals to other islands. They think this will allow the animals to breed in safety.

5. (Introduction) The problem the employee has is that he or she cannot finish his or her work on time. In my opinion, the better solution is to ask the boss to assign the project to someone else. I think this because it is better to get the work done on time than to extend the deadline.

(Body) I believe the employee should ask the boss to assign the project to someone else for two reasons. First, it is more important that the job get done on time and correctly. If the employee doesn't have enough time, the job may be finished late or the work may not be of good quality.

(Body) Second, I believe that an employee who can admit when he or she has too much work to do is a very responsible employee. It is better to be honest with your boss about what you can do instead of making him or her think you can do everything.

WRAPPING THINGS UP: THE CONCLUSION

The conclusion is essential to a well-organized speech or essay. Without a conclusion, it will seem to end abruptly, or worse yet, trail off and your score will be lower. Fortunately, the conclusion is probably the easiest part to create. A conclusion has to do one thing and one thing only.

- **Restate** your thesis.

The conclusion is your last chance to make your point to the reader. You want to remind the reader that you accomplished your purpose. As with body paragraphs, conclusions still need to have good transitions. Here are some good words and phrases to use for your final paragraph.

And so	*In conclusion*	*Finally*	*Thus*
Ultimately	*As I've stated*	*Clearly*	*To sum up*
	As this essay has demonstrated		

Here's a sample conclusion from our practice prompt.

In conclusion, if I could have any job, I would choose to be an ambassador. As I mentioned before, I feel this would be a perfect fit for my skill set because I love traveling to other countries and meeting new people.

Drill #4: Develop Conclusions for Speaking

Practice conclusions for your speeches, on the same topics we've practiced before. Compare your conclusions with those at the end of the drill.

1. If you could have any job in the world, which job would you choose?
2. Describe a person you admire, and explain why you admire him or her.
3. A university has recently received a large sum of money. The university desperately needs to improve housing on campus, but students have complained that the library needs to be fixed as well. Do you think that the money should be spent on housing or the library? Provide reasons and examples for your choice.
4. Read the following short passage:

> The cane toad, a poisonous species of toad, is causing problems in Australia. The cane toad was brought to Australia in 1935 to help control the population of greyback beetles. Unfortunately, the toads did nothing to reduce the beetle population. Now, however, cane toads number in the millions and are threatening native animal populations.
>
> The cane toad has two poisonous sacs located near its head and is so toxic that dingoes, snakes, and even crocodiles die within fifteen minutes of eating a cane toad. Now, conservationists are forced to transport some endangered species of animals to islands free from cane toads so that the endangered species can breed in safety.

The passage above describes a problem. Explain what the problem is and what steps are being taken to fix it.

5. Read the following conversation between two coworkers:

> *Employee A:* I'm really swamped at work. I don't know if I'm going to be able to finish all of my projects by the deadline.
>
> *Employee B:* I know. We really need to hire some more people around here. What are you going to do?
>
> *Employee A:* I don't know. My boss said I have to finish the budget analysis by Friday, but he just gave me a new project that he needs completed right away.
>
> *Employee B:* Well, if I were you, I'd tell your boss that there's no way you can finish both in time. I'd ask for more time.
>
> *Employee A:* Yeah, I guess I could do that.
>
> *Employee B:* Or maybe you can ask your boss to assign the project to someone else. That way you can focus on the budget analysis.

Employee B offers two possible solutions to Employee A's problems. Describe the problem, and state which of the two solutions you prefer. Explain why.

Sample Responses to Drill #4

Read the following responses aloud, and practice speaking them until you're comfortable.

1. For all the reasons I have stated, I feel that being an ambassador would be my dream job. I think that it is the perfect match for my interests and skills.

2. As I have stated, there are many reasons that I admire Gandhi. His values and ideas are things that I find very important in a person.

3. So, to conclude, it is my opinion that the money would be best spent on a library. Spending money on a library is the right thing to do for an academic institution.

4. In conclusion, the conservationists think the best solution to the problem of the cane toad is to move the animals to a different place.

5. Ultimately, I believe the best solution is to ask the boss to reassign the project. This is best for the company and is what a responsible employee would do.

Summary: Concluding Your Response

Because you have only 45 or 60 seconds for a spoken response, you won't have a lot of time to wrap up your thoughts. But you always need a concluding sentence, so make it short and simply restate your thesis.

One important point to remember is this: don't introduce any new ideas or examples in the conclusion. It will leave your listener or reader feeling as though you should have explained those new examples in more detail.

Now you have all the tools you need to give great spoken responses on the TOEFL!

Chapter 5
Core Concept:
Writing

In the real world, speaking and writing are two very different skills. But on the TOEFL, these basic skills are graded on very similar rubrics. Many of the constructions that you used in your speaking can easily be transferred to your writing. Similarly, many of the forms you use when writing can also be used when speaking.

SCORING FOR THE WRITING SECTION

By examining the scoring guidelines for the Writing section, we can gain a better understanding of what our goals should be for this section.

The writing responses will be graded on a scale of 0 to 5. On the TOEFL, according to ETS, an essay receiving a score of 5 has the following characteristics:

- It effectively addresses the topic and the task.
- It is well organized and well developed, with clearly appropriate explanations, exemplifications, and/or details.
- It displays unity, progression, and coherence.
- It displays consistent facility in the use of language, demonstrating syntactic variety, appropriate word choice, and idiomaticity, although it may have minor lexical or grammatical errors. (In essence, it shows that you understand how to use the language, how to use a variety of sentence structures, how to use idioms or common phrases within the language, but it may have minor errors).

At the other end of the scoring scale, an essay receiving a score of 1 suffers from the following difficulties:

- serious disorganization or underdevelopment;
- little or no detail, irrelevant specifics, or questionable responsiveness to the task;
- serious or frequent errors in sentence structure or usage.

An essay receiving a score of 0 is blank, is written in a foreign language, is identical to the prompt, or consists of random keystrokes.

What the Writing Scoring Guidelines Mean

Each of the first three scoring guidelines relates to one of the skills we've already studied in the Reading section. Here's how.

- **The essay effectively addresses the topic and the task.** This guideline corresponds to the work we've done on *finding the purpose.* An effective written response accomplishes a specific purpose. On the TOEFL, this means responding to one of the prompts. A weak essay has no clear purpose or doesn't achieve its purpose.
- **The essay is well organized and well developed, with clearly appropriate explanations, exemplifications, and/or details.** This guideline matches with the exercises we completed on understanding the *structure.* Good essays demonstrate strong structure, whereas weak essays frequently lack well-developed examples.
- **The essay displays unity, progression, and coherence.** This guideline corresponds to the work we've done on *finding the main idea* of a reading passage. Each paragraph should be connected to the main theme of the passage and contribute to the development of the passage's ideas or argument. An essay receiving a score of 5 stays on topic, whereas an essay receiving a lower score goes off the topic.

The fourth and final guideline will be addressed later in this chapter. However, it is worth noting that on the TOEFL, you don't have to write in perfect English to get a 5. It's acceptable to have some spelling and grammar mistakes in your essay.

Similarities in the Writing and Reading Guidelines

The skills you learned in the Reading section can also help you write a well-structured, organized essay. In fact, the reading passages in this text are great examples for the TOEFL essay! The following techniques from the Reading section are particularly useful:

1. Understand the structure of the passage. Remember, TOEFL passages are always made up of an introduction, several body paragraphs, and a conclusion. Make sure your essays also contain these three key elements and separate them into distinct paragraphs.
2. Use the first sentence of each paragraph to present the main idea. Remember, the first sentence (also known as the topic sentence) should clearly present the main idea of each paragraph.
3. Use the remaining sentences to provide details and examples. Be sure to support each of your points with a reason and a specific idea or an example.
4. Use direction markers to unify your ideas. Use transitions as markers to clearly identify continuations of same-direction ideas or to highlight contrasting ideas.

PART 1: EXPRESSING YOUR PURPOSE

Our first goal is to make sure your essays have a clear purpose. To do that, we need to look at the types of tasks the TOEFL will feature.

Purpose and the Writing Section

You need to clearly express your purpose in your introductory paragraph. If you recall our earlier discussion of introduction paragraphs (in the Reading and Speaking chapters), you may already have a good idea of how to express your purpose. In general, your introduction needs to accomplish the following tasks:

1. Introduce the topic of your discussion
2. Present your *thesis* statement

Writing an Effective Introduction Paragraph

Here's an example of a writing task similar to one you may encounter on the TOEFL. You would be asked to write an essay explaining whether you agree or disagree with the following topic:

> Parents should select their children's friends carefully to make sure those friends reflect proper values.

Although there are many ways of writing an introduction paragraph, the following strategy will help you write an effective introduction regardless of the topic. Following this strategy will help you write *quickly*.

Step 1: Pick a Side

If the goal of your writing is to have a clear purpose, you must know what that purpose is before you start writing. Otherwise, your essay will lack focus and coherence. On opinion questions, there is no right or wrong answer, as you saw in Core Concept: Speaking. You will be evaluated only on how well you defend your position. Remember that for an opinion essay, your purpose as an author is to convince the reader that your position is correct.

Step 2: State Your Position

Once you've chosen your position, your first job is to state it. Here's an example of a typical first sentence for this type of response.

> I do not believe that parents should select their children's friends.

As you saw in Chapter 4 (Core Concept: Speaking), it's best to make a clear, direct statement of your position. Try using some of the following phrases:

I believe	*I feel that*	*In my opinion*
In my view	*I think that*	*I do not believe*
I do not feel that	*My position is*	*It is my belief that*

Step 3: **State the Reason for Your Opinion**

Once you've stated your position, you've established for the reader *what* you believe. Now, you must explain *why* you believe your position is correct. Here's an example.

I do not believe that parents should select their children's friends. It would be harmful to children if they were not allowed to choose their own friends. Parents should be interested in their children's friends, but they should let their children pick their own friends.

When stating why you believe your position, it may be helpful to use some of the following phrases:

I believe this because	*I feel this way because*	*The reason I think this is*
This is because	*Since*	

Drill #1: Write an Introduction Paragraph

Write an introduction paragraph explaining whether you agree or disagree with each of the following prompts. Remember to follow the three steps described on the previous pages. Compare your introductions with those at the end of the drill.

1. It is the teacher's responsibility to make a student learn the material.

    _____

    _____

    _____

    _____

2. Material on the Internet should be censored or controlled to protect the public.

    _____

    _____

    _____

    _____

3. Colleges and universities should offer more distance learning courses to accommodate the needs of students.

    _____

    _____

    _____

    _____

4. When choosing a career, financial gain should be the most important consideration.

    _____

    _____

    _____

    _____

5. Schools should have mandatory testing each year to prove they are meeting minimum educational standards.

    _____

    _____

    _____

    _____

Sample Responses to Drill #1

The following are sample introduction paragraphs for the prompts. Compare your paragraphs with the ones below and see how well they match up. As always, they do not have to match exactly. As long as your format is similar, you have the right idea.

1. I believe that it is a teacher's responsibility to make a student learn the material. Many students are of a young age and do not realize the value of education. Therefore, it is up to the teacher to help them learn the lessons and realize the value of the material.

2. In my opinion, material on the Internet should not be censored. The Internet is a free zone and it would be wrong for this area to be controlled. Plus, what government or agency would be responsible for censoring the Internet, which is available worldwide?

3. In my view, colleges and universities should offer more distance learning courses. I believe this because in today's world, many people have a lot of demands on their time. Some students are parents or hold part-time jobs. This means that they don't have as much time for school. Distance learning courses would be a good solution to this problem.

4. I do not feel that financial considerations should be the most important ones when choosing a career. If a person is not happy in his or her job, then the money will not be important. A person's happiness should be the number one consideration when choosing a career.

5. I feel that it would be wrong for schools to have mandatory testing each year. I think that each school should be allowed to decide how best to educate its students. Some schools do not focus as much on testing as other schools and use other ways of grading their students, such as projects and final papers. These schools should not be forced to have tests.

These examples are not perfect, and that's acceptable on the TOEFL. But each one is simple, direct, and clearly states the purpose. That's all that is required of an introductory paragraph.

Summary: Expressing Your Purpose

The introduction is your first impression, so make it a good one! To craft an effective introduction, follow these steps.

1. **Decide what your purpose is:** Know what your task is. Are you trying to convince or inform? Are you picking one option over another?
2. **State the thesis:** Always include a simple and direct statement of the topic.
3. **State why:** This is your connection between the task and topic.

For an effective introduction, remember these don'ts.

• **Don't** go into detail about your examples in your introduction.
• **Don't** repeat the task or assignment word for word.

PART 2: ORGANIZING YOUR IDEAS

Now that we've taken care of the purpose, we need to focus on organization. Organization is one of the most important factors in your writing score. Disjointed or unfocused writing is easy for the graders to spot and will lead to a lower score.

On the TOEFL, each writing task should be organized as follows:

- **Introduction:** You've worked on this already. This is the part in which you state the topic and your purpose.
- **Body:** As with speaking, this is the part in which you should provide the details and examples important to your purpose. You'll examine body paragraphs next.
- **Conclusion:** This is the part in which you summarize your essay. You'll look at written conclusions later in this chapter.

Building the Body

One of the things TOEFL graders look for is your ability to thoroughly provide support for your purpose. The best way to do that is by writing an effective body paragraph.

Writing an Effective Body Paragraph

Good body paragraphs make your writing more effective and more organized, both of which are good things on the TOEFL. The first step in creating a good body paragraph is to write a topic sentence.

Step 1: Write a Topic Sentence

A good topic sentence does two things: it provides a *transition* between ideas and clearly states the main idea of the paragraph. To refresh your memory on how to compose a topic sentence, flip back to Core Concept: Speaking. For writing, you are going to use the same method. A topic sentence should introduce the main point of the paragraph.

Let's continue to work with a previous topic.

> Parents should carefully select their children's friends to make sure those friends reflect proper values.

In our introduction, we stated what our position was and why we believe our opinion was correct. Now, in the body paragraphs, we have to support our position. Here's our introduction.

I do not believe that parents should select their children's friends. It would be harmful to children if they were not allowed to choose their own friends. Parents should be interested in their children's friends, but they should let their children pick their own friends.

To make a clear transition statement, use the topic or thesis of the previous paragraph as a starting point. Look at the following transition:

> One reason I believe that **parents should let children pick their friends** is that children need to develop independence.

Notice how the bold portion repeats an idea found in the last sentence of the introduction. Using this technique makes your writing flow better and appear more organized.

Our next paragraph may say

> Another reason I think **parents should let children pick their friends** is that children may resent a parent who picks their friends.

And our final body paragraph may say

> In addition to the feelings of resentment a child may have, a final reason **parents shouldn't pick their children's friends** is that the children may not get along very well.

This paragraph also uses a link to the main idea of the preceding paragraph. As with the Speaking section, topic sentences and transitions will help your essay appear organized.

Step 2: Provide Examples

For many of the assignments on the TOEFL, your main goal in the body paragraphs will be to support your opinions. On others, your task will be to report facts stated in either a reading passage or a lecture.

In either case, your model is still the same.

- **State** the example or reason (what the example is).
- **Explain** its significance (why the example is important).

Remember that you've learned how to incorporate examples into your spoken and written responses. The key to making good use of examples is to make sure each example is:

- **specific,** not overly general or hypothetical (made up)
- **explained** in sufficient detail

Now let's look at three types of examples that will help make your essay more convincing: examples that *support* your main idea, examples that *summarize* your main idea, and examples that *evaluate* your main idea.

Supporting Examples

Supporting examples are the most common type of examples and perhaps the easiest to use. They are used to show the reader why you have a particular viewpoint or position. On the TOEFL, you may see similar tasks that ask the following:

- Do you agree or disagree with the following statement? It is better for students to gain real-world experience than to spend their time in a classroom.
- Describe a book you have read and why that book was important to you.
- Some teachers prefer to lecture to students, whereas others prefer to engage students in a dialogue. Which teaching style do you think is better and why?

For each of these tasks, your mission is to convince your readers that your view is correct by presenting them with facts and evidence.

Summarizing Examples

Some tasks require you to explain or summarize someone else's opinion. For these tasks, you are not trying to *convince* the reader of anything; instead, your purpose is to *report* what you've read or heard. On the TOEFL, summarizing tasks look like the following:

- The professor describes the controversy surrounding a new technique. Explain the technique and what the controversy is.
- In the conversation above, the man presented his opinion on the new budget proposal. State his opinion and explain the reasons he gives for holding that opinion.
- Using details and examples from the piece you just heard, explain how musicians have been influenced by cultural and intellectual movements.

Evaluating Examples

One of the more difficult tasks you may encounter on the TOEFL asks you to evaluate someone else's viewpoint. These tasks require you to judge how valid a position is. The purpose of your examples is to weaken the position. The following is an example of an evaluation task:

Explain how the points in the lecture you've just heard cast doubt on it.

Regardless of the type of example, the way you present your examples remains the same.

Effective Examples

As stated at the beginning of this chapter, you must provide details for each example and an explanation of the meaning or significance of each. The following is a sample response containing poorly used examples:

One reason I believe lecturing is a better teaching method is that teachers can control the content. Also, the teachers are able to organize things better. Finally, lectures let the students focus on only the important parts of the lesson.

This response contains several good ideas, but the problem is that the author failed to provide specific details for each example. You cannot assume that your reader understands exactly what point you are making and why; instead, you must explain each of your examples fully.

For each example you intend to use, ask yourself why the example is appropriate. What makes the example a convincing one?

Let's return to our previous examples and see how they can be made better. Here is the first example from the response above.

1.   Lectures allow teachers to control the content.

Now, we need to ask why this example should convince a reader that lecturing is a better teaching method. Here are some reasons.

Example: Lectures allow teachers to control the content.

Why?

1.   The teacher is the only one speaking, so there are no digressions.
2.   The teacher can plan the lecture beforehand, ensuring all the important information is addressed.

Example: Lectures allow teachers to organize better.

Why?

1.   Speaking without planned notes can be difficult.
2.   The teacher can practice the lecture numerous times, ensuring it is well organized.

Example: Lectures help students focus on important information.

Why?

1.   The teacher can emphasize important information more effectively in a lecture.
2.   Students can pay attention to the teacher, not other students.

Now, let's rewrite our earlier paragraph, using the examples more effectively.

One reason I believe lecturing is a better teaching method is that teachers can control the content. When a teacher lectures, all the information presented is supplied by the teacher. There are no digressions because the students are not interrupting the lesson or distracting the teacher. Also, a teacher has the opportunity to plan the lecture beforehand, meaning that the teacher can ensure all the important information is discussed. In a conversation or dialogue, a teacher may never get to some important points because the students may ask too many questions about a certain topic.

Another reason I prefer lecturing to a conversation or a dialogue is that a lecture is much more organized. It can be very difficult to speak without notes or a plan. During a dialogue,

For more reading and writing practice, be sure to check out *TOEFL Reading & Writing Workout.*

the subjects can change very rapidly and can be hard to follow. But a lecture is planned beforehand, so the topics are easier to follow. Also, the teacher can practice the lecture repeatedly and fix any problems in organization.

The final advantage of a lecture is that it helps the students focus on only the most important information. Because the teacher has planned the talk in advance, he or she can let the students know when an important point is being made. This will help the students focus. Additionally, when the students are engaged in a dialogue, a student may pay too much attention to another student's remarks or become distracted by a question or response. In a lecture, this problem is avoided because the student has to pay attention only to the teacher.

Note that when we use examples effectively, we end up having to use more paragraphs. This is necessary to keep our responses organized.

The Example Template

When you use an example in an essay, try to follow this template.

> Sentence 1: Introduce the example and tie it back to your thesis.
> Sentence 2: State one reason why your example is important or relevant to your thesis.
> Sentence 3: Add detail to reason #1.
> Sentence 4: State another reason why your example is important or relevant to your thesis.
> Sentence 5: Add detail to reason #2.
> Sentence 6 (optional): Provide a summary of your reasons, and relate them back to your thesis.

Here's an example of the template in action.

Task: Describe a book you have read and why that book was important to you.

(1) One book that is extremely important to me is *The Suffrage of Elvira* by V. S. Naipaul. (2) One reason I enjoy this book so much is that I like its subject matter. (3) The book provides a humorous look at local politics, and I find politics a fascinating subject. (4) Naipaul is skilled at critically examining his topics, and I think his depiction of politics is very interesting. (5) In this book, he presents a satire of the political process that is both witty and insightful. (6) Because of my interest in politics, *The Suffrage of Elvira* is an important book.

Drill #2: Write Body Paragraphs That Use Examples

Please use the blank spaces below to answer each of the questions presented. Then read the sample responses at the end of the drill to see how your writing compares.

1. Do you think success is more likely to result from a willingness to take risks or from careful planning

Example #1: _____

Why example #1 is important: _____

_____

_____

_____

Example #2: _____

Why example #2 is important: _____

_____

_____

Body paragraph #1: _____

_____

_____

_____

_____

_____

Body paragraph #2: _____

_____

_____

_____

_____

2. Is it more important to be able to work with a group of people on a team or to work independently?

Example #1: _____

Why example #1 is important: _____

_____

_____

_____

Example #2: _____

Why example #2 is important: _____

_____

_____

_____

Body paragraph #1: _____

_____

_____

_____

_____

_____

_____

Body paragraph #2: _____

_____

_____

_____

_____

_____

_____

_____

3.   Do you agree or disagree with the following statement?

Education should be free.

Example #1: _____

Why example #1 is important: _____

_____

_____

_____

Example #2: _____

Why example #2 is important: _____

_____

_____

Body paragraph #1: _____

_____

_____

_____
_____
_____
_____
_____

Body paragraph #2: _____
_____
_____
_____
_____
_____
_____
_____

4. Do you agree or disagree with the following statement?

    Technology has made the world a better place to live.

    Reason #1: _____
    Why reason #1 is important: _____
    _____
    _____
    _____

    Reason #2: _____
    Why reason #2 is important: _____
    _____
    _____

    Body paragraph #1: _____
    _____
    _____
    _____
    _____
    _____
    _____

    Body paragraph #2: _____
    _____
    _____
    _____

_____

_____

_____

5. Do you agree or disagree with the following statement?

Learning about the past has no value for the present.

Example #1: _____

Why example #1 is important: _____

_____

_____

_____

Example #2: _____

Why example #2 is important: _____

_____

_____

_____

Body paragraph #1: _____

_____

_____

_____

_____

_____

_____

_____

Body paragraph #2: _____

_____

_____

_____

_____

_____

_____

_____

6. Read the following passage about America's Independence:

Independence Day is the national holiday of the United States of America commemorating the signing of the Declaration of Independence by the Continental Congress in Philadelphia, Pennsylvania. The Declaration of Independence's purpose was to declare freedom and independence of the thirteen American colonies from England.

Under the rule of England's King George III, there was growing unrest in the colonies concerning the inordinately high taxes that had to be paid to England. After years of humiliation, the colonists had enough and the Continental Congress, a committee of colonists formed to defend the rights of the American colonists, discussed the general outline of the Declaration of Independence in early spring of 1776. Thomas Jefferson was chosen to write the first draft and on July 4, 1776, together with other discontented representatives from the thirteen colonies, Congress voted and approved the Declaration.

The Continental Congress met in the Pennsylvania State House, and in total, forty-two of the fifty-six delegates signed the Declaration of Independence on that significant day. John Hancock presumably signed first as President of Congress and other notable figures such as Benjamin Franklin and John Adams were among the signatories. So significant was this event that John Trumball's vast painting of all the signers gathering in Independence Hall's chamber room for the signing now hangs in our nation's Capitol building.

On that cool Philadelphia day, a child was posted on the street outside Independence Hall. Once he got confirmation that the Declaration was signed, he signaled the bell tower to ring the 2,000-pound Liberty Bell atop the Pennsylvania State House, signaling to the citizens that America was now free from British rule. As the powerful sound of the bell rang on July 4, echoing from all corners of the city, the people of Philadelphia knew that a new era of self-rule had begun in this new nation

Now read the following lecture on the same subject:

Professor: America's history is full of romantic myths, not the least of which is the story about America's Independence Day. Let's take a closer look at some of the inaccuracies surrounding this patriotic story. To start with, there is very little truth in the popular legend that the liberty bell was struck on July 4 1776 to announce the signing of the declaration. The liberty bell was and is still located in the city of Philadelphia, but it was not associated with Independence Day until almost 70 years later when a novelist made the dramatic story up to sell his work. He was the first person known to refer to the bell using the name Liberty Bell. The name stuck throughout subsequent history later reinforced by the anti-slavery movement during its attempts to end slavery in the new nation.

So how did the date July 4 gain its prominence? America actually declared independence on July 2, 1776 at a meeting of the congress and there are newspaper accounts of this on record. But, after congress approved the final wording of the declaration, a hand-written copy was sent to the publisher a few blocks away to be typed up and distributed to the people. It is likely the printer did not complete the job until a couple of days after and he stamped his work complete on July 4 so the typed-up copies of the declaration all had the date July 4 on them and that might be part of why this date became part of history.

Lastly, the famous scene of all the delegates gathering to sign the declaration never actually occurred. Congress ordered an official copy of the declaration be carefully handwritten onto parchment for the delegates to sign. Because transcribing the declaration onto parchment took almost a month, the official signing didn't begin until August 2 at a signing ceremony. Most of the delegates signed on that day while those who were not present gradually added their names later.

Another interesting note about Trumball's famous painting, since the declaration was debated and signed over the span of several months, many of the figures were never in the same room at the same time.

Summarize the points made in the lecture you just heard, explaining how they relate to the contents of the reading.

Point #1: _____

Why point #1 casts doubt on the reading: _____

_____

_____

_____

Point #2: _____

Why point #2 casts doubt on the reading: _____

_____

_____

_____

Body paragraph #1: _____

_____

_____

_____

_____

_____

_____

Body paragraph #2: _____

_____

_____

_____

_____

_____

_____

Sample Responses to Drill #2

Use the following sample responses as a guide to judge your work. Did your response contain strong topic sentences? Did you relate your examples back to your thesis? Did you explain why your examples are relevant?

1.   Do you think success is more likely to result from a willingness to take risks or from careful planning?

Careful planning is usually better than taking risks. Planning for success allows a person to take the steps they need to accomplish a goal. For example, doing well on a test can best be accomplished by setting aside time to study the topics of the test and practicing the skills needed. The surest way to get a good grade is to study.

In addition, careful planning helps a person overcome challenges in the way of a goal. Often, there can be unexpected difficulties, but planning will help a person anticipate a challenge and plan to beat it. At the end of the semester, most classes have tests.. Planning can help a student study for each test instead of running out of time trying to cram for several tests at once. Thus, careful planning will help a person succeed more often than taking risks.

2. Is it more important to work with a group of people on a team or to work independently?

Working with a team of people is a more important skill to have than working alone. It is important for people to work well with a group because many tasks can be completed better with several people rather than by a single person. For example, a group could make a presentation by assigning each member a task at which each excels. One member of a group might be better at designing the display while another member is better at speaking to an audience. By working together, they will make a better presentation than working alone.

In addition, groups can get more work done in a shorter amount of time than a single person can. Several mechanics can change the tires on a car faster than just one. They are each working together to accomplish a goal, and together they are more efficient. That is why it is more important to be able to work in groups.

3. Do you agree or disagree with the following statement? Education should be free.

I believe that education should be free for students. First, it is important for everyone in a country to be educated rather than to live in one in which they are not. A country with well educated people will have better jobs, and the people will better be able to communicate with one another.

Another reason I think education should be free is that education promotes equality and justice. If everyone has an equal ability to learn, everyone will have a more equal chance of getting a job. Free education increases diversity in schools, which also increases equality. Thus, education should be free.

4. Do you agree or disagree with the following statement? Technology has made the world a better place to live.

There are many reasons I agree with this statement. One reason is that technology and the internet have increased access to information so that more people can learn about current events. Before the internet, people had to rely on newspapers for their daily news, but now people can get news as it happens. This makes people more knowledgeable about their communities in real time.

Another reason technology has made the world a better place is that it allows people to see things from around the world. I can watch television shows from foreign countries from anywhere while I am traveling. This helps me learn about other places and languages. Without technology, this would not be possible, so technology has made the world a better place.

5. Do you agree or disagree with the following statement? Learning about the past has no value for the present.

I disagree with the statement that learning about the past has no value for the present. There is a saying that those who do not learn about their past will repeat it. Learning about big historical events can help a country avoid old problems. The events that led to world war II inspired countries of the world to come together and form the United Nations so they could work together to avoid another terrible war.

This is also true on a smaller scale too. A person can learn how to cook better by understanding mistakes from their past and a person may become a better gardener with experience. These are the reasons I think learning about the past has value for the present.

6. Summarize the points in the professor's lecture, and explain how the points cast doubt on the reading.

The first point that the professor makes that casts doubt on the reading is that the Liberty Bell was not actually involved with the signing of the declaration of independence. The reading states that the bell was struck to notify people of the signing of the declaration, but the professor says that this did not happen; this idea became popular seventy years after the signing of the declaration of independence.

Another point that the professor makes that casts doubt on the reading is that the declaration wasn't signed until August and that the painting of the signing didn't happen. The reading stated that most of the people signed the declaration on July 4, 1776, but the professor said that it took time to handwrite the declaration and that signing it happened over time instead of at one meeting. It is likely that the painting is more of an idea than something that actually happened.

Summary: Using Examples Effectively

Proper use of examples is important to your TOEFL score. When using examples, always remember to do the following:

1. **State** the example.
2. **Explain** how the example supports your position or achieves your purpose.

Avoid these common mistakes when using examples.

- **Don't** introduce an example without explaining how it relates to your purpose.
- **Don't** forget to provide specific details for each of your examples.
- **Don't** use more than one example per paragraph.

PART 3: WRITING THE PERFECT BODY PARAGRAPH

Now that you understand the proper structure and ways to use examples in your writing, let's work on writing a perfectly structured paragraph. Here's a body paragraph for our sample topic: parents should carefully select their children's friends to make sure those friends reflect proper values. As always, your essay does not need to match our example exactly. Just be sure you're using a structure similar to that of our example.

One reason I believe that parents should let children pick their friends is that children need to develop independence (**topic sentence**). It is very important for a child to become independent, and the early part of a child's life can affect the level of independence a child has (**statement of example**). For example, children who are not allowed to pick their friends may believe that their parents will always make important decisions for them (**explanation of significance**). This belief could make children dependent on their parents, which would have a negative effect on their development (**explanation of significance**).

That's all there is to it! Now, try to write some body paragraphs for the topics that follow.

Drill #3: Write Body Paragraphs

For each of the following tasks, write a body paragraph (or two). You've already written introductions for these, so it may help to read over what you've written. Before you write, think of one or two examples that support your view. Compare your paragraphs with those at the end of the drill.

1. It is the teacher's responsibility to make a student learn the material.

2. Material on the Internet should be censored or controlled to protect the public.

3. Colleges and universities should offer more distance learning courses to accommodate the needs of students.

4. When choosing a career, financial gain should be the most important consideration.

5. Schools should have mandatory testing each year to prove they are meeting minimum educational standards.

_____

_____

_____

_____

_____

_____

Sample Responses to Drill #3

The following are sample responses. Check your paragraphs against these models. Make sure your body paragraph includes both a topic sentence and an example or reason.

1. One reason I believe it is a teacher's responsibility to help students learn is that many students are of a young age (**topic sentence**). A first- or second-grade teacher works with children who are only six or seven years old (**statement of example**). At this age, a student is too young to recognize the value of education (**explanation of example**). Therefore, it should be the teacher's job to make sure the children learn.

This body paragraph ends by restating the author's main point, which also helps the reader stay focused on the thesis.

2. First of all, material on the Internet should not be censored because the Internet is a free zone (**topic sentence**). The Internet is not owned by any one government or company (**statement of example**). This means that no one should have the right to say what can or cannot be posted on it (**explanation of example**). Companies or governments can control what material shows up on their websites, but they cannot control what private citizens do (**explanation of example**).

    Second, technology makes it too difficult to censor material on the Internet (**topic sentence**). Every day, new computer programs are developed that make other programs obsolete (**statement of example**). As soon as someone figures out how to censor material on the Internet, someone else can figure out how to break the code (**explanation of example**). This means that a tremendous amount of money would have to be spent on developing new technology, and this expense would not be worth it (**explanation of example**).

This response includes two body paragraphs. Notice how the second paragraph logically connects to the first through the use of the transition word *second*. Try to make sure your body paragraphs are nicely connected both to the thesis and to each other.

3. One important reason that colleges should offer more distance learning courses is that people are busier than they used to be (**topic sentence**). In addition to work and hobbies, there are more parents going to college these days (**statement of example**). All these things make it difficult to attend college (**explanation of example**). However, education is a valuable thing, and everyone should have access to it (**explanation of example**). If universities offered more distance learning courses, more people could find time for an education (**explanation of example**).

Try to use some of the direction marker words and transitions you learned in the reading exercises in Core Concept: Reading and Core Concept: Speaking. For example, this paragraph uses "however" to emphasize the importance of education and how distance learning courses will allow more people to get their education.

4. The most important thing in choosing a career should be the happiness it brings, not the money (**topic sentence**). There is an old saying, "You can't buy happiness," and this statement is very true (**statement of example**). Many people who have lots of money also have strained relationships with their spouses and children (**explanation of example**). Often, they feel they can't trust whether people like them or their money (**explanation of example**). These strains can make a person very unhappy, no matter how much money they have (**explanation of example**).

You should also try to use some emphasis markers in your writing. Stating that something is the "most" important reason or something is "very true" gives your words more of an impact. However, don't overuse these words. Too many of them can distract the reader.

5. Schools should not have mandatory testing each year because tests are not always the best way of measuring education (**topic sentence**). Tests, especially standardized tests, can cover only a limited amount of skills (**statement of example**). There are some things in education that are not easy to test, such as writing and creative thinking (**explanation of example**). For this reason, schools should not be forced to have mandatory testing (**explanation of example**).

    In addition, not all students do well on tests (**topic sentence with statement of example**). Some students are better at writing essays or giving a speech (**explanation of example**). Not all students perform best on standardized tests (**explanation of example**). Therefore, it is unfair for those students to have to take these tests, and schools may not get an accurate view of how successful they are (**explanation of example**).

In the second paragraph, the topic sentence is combined with the statement of the example, which is acceptable.

Summary: Building the Body

The body provides the reader with the key points of your thesis. Build strong body paragraphs by doing the following:

1. **Begin with a topic sentence:** A good topic sentence references the subject you will discuss and also provides a transition to link your ideas together.
2. **Provide details:** The rest of the body should contain important details that help you achieve your purpose.

Build strong body paragraphs by avoiding the following:

*   **Don't** try to discuss more than one example per paragraph.
*   **Don't** present an example without providing specific details.

PART 4: CONCLUDING YOUR RESPONSE

As you've seen in Core Concepts: Reading, a conclusion is essential to summarizing any argument. In this section, you are going to follow the same approach and simply restate your purpose.

Here's a sample conclusion from our practice prompt.

In conclusion, there are many reasons why parents should not pick friends for their children. Children who are allowed to pick their own friends will be more independent and will get along better with friends they've selected.

Drill #4: Write Conclusion Paragraphs

For each of the following tasks, write a concluding paragraph (can be a sentence or 2 or 3). Remember everything we stated above.

1. It is the teacher's responsibility to make a student learn the material.

   _____

   _____

   _____

   _____

   _____

   _____

   _____

2. Material on the Internet should be censored or controlled to protect the public.

   _____

   _____

   _____

   _____

   _____

   _____

   _____

3. Colleges and universities should offer more distance learning courses to accommodate the needs of students.

   _____

   _____

   _____

   _____

   _____

   _____

4. When choosing a career, financial gain should be the most important consideration.

   _____

   _____

   _____

   _____

   _____

   _____

Sample Responses to Drill #4

1. Ultimately, it is the teacher's responsibility to make students learn the material. Education is too valuable to be left in the hands of students. A good teacher not only teaches the material but also gives students a love of learning.

This conclusion ends by making a general statement about the purpose. This is a good strategy if you don't want to repeat your examples or reasons again.

2. As this essay has demonstrated, material on the Internet should not be censored. The Internet is too big to be controlled, and the technology involved in censoring it would be too expensive.

This conclusion restates both the purpose and the examples.

3. In conclusion, it makes sense for colleges and universities to offer more distance learning courses. It is always better to make education more available, not less.

Here, we end with a strong statement about what we believe. The conclusion is a good time to emphasize a key point or idea, as the following examples show.

4. Clearly, there are many more important considerations than money when choosing a career. Happiness and family are much more important than money.

5. Thus, schools should not be required to have mandatory testing. Testing does not provide students with a fair assessment of their skills, and it makes schools focus more on the tests than on teaching important things.

Summary: Wrapping Things Up

The conclusion is essential to your responses on the TOEFL. It's easy to conclude an essay or speech. All you have to do is:

- **Restate:** Tell the reader once more what your purpose is and why you believe it.

Make sure to avoid the following:

- **Don't** introduce new examples or ideas.
- **Don't** leave out the thesis.

GRAMMAR REVIEW

This is a brief summary of the basics of English grammar. Become familiar with these terms so you can avoid common grammatical errors in your written and spoken responses.

Parts of speech

If you're interested in a more thorough review of grammar, look for The Princeton Review's *Grammar Smart* in most bookstores.

For an intensive vocabulary review, check out our *TOEFL Power Vocab*.

- **Noun**: person, place, or thing
  Example: I just remembered that I need to call my *mother*.

- **Pronoun**: stands in the place of a noun
  Example: *She* asked for a call last night.

- **Verb**: action word
  Example: I *dial* her home phone number.

- **Adverb**: modifies a verb
  Example: *Eagerly,* I wait for her to answer.

- **Adjective:** modifies a noun or pronoun
  Example: When she picks up, I can tell that she is *happy* to hear my voice.

- **Preposition:** links nouns or pronouns to other words
  Example: I excitedly share the details *of* my new job.

- **Conjunction:** connects words, clauses, or sentences
  Example: She is happy *and* invites me over for dinner.

- **Interjection:** abrupt remark
  Example: *"Oh dear!,"* she exclaimed when I said yes. "I guess I'll have to go to the store."

Tenses

- **Present:** an action that is currently happening
  Example: I *walk* to work every day.

- **Past:** an action that already happened
  Example: I *decided* that walking is better than driving.

- **Future:** an action that has not happened yet
  Example: I *will change* my mind later.

Agreement

- **Subject/Verb Agreement**: A singular subject needs a singular verb. A plural subject needs a plural verb.
  Example: The *window is* open.
  Example: The *windows are* closed.

- **Noun/Pronoun Agreement:** A singular noun takes a singular pronoun. A plural noun takes a plural pronoun.
  Example: The *student* wore *his/her* backpack.
  Example: The *students* wore *their* backpacks.

Spelling

- This is not really a point of grammar, but it is a common source of error on the TOEFL. Though it is not necessary for you to have perfect spelling to get a high score, it is important to know how to correctly spell as many words as possible. Many times, words with very simple meanings can be quite difficult to spell. You probably know the meaning of all the words in the following list, but we've included them as examples because they are commonly misspelled by native and non-native English speakers alike.

Commonly misspelled words:

accidentally	easily	hygiene	mathematics	quiet	usage
acknowledge	embarrass	illegal	natural	receipt	usually
average	existence	independent	neighbor	reference	vacuum
bachelor	experience	intelligence	nowadays	relevant	valuable
barbecue	February	khaki	office	rhythm	vicious
bureau	finally	knowledge	often	scissors	weather
celebrity	foreign	knee	original	separate	weird
children	generally	language	parallel	sincerely	whether
calendar	grammar	leisure	prejudice	technique	yacht
definitely	guarantee	luxurious	psychology	tongue	your
disease	happiness	magic	quantity	tragedy	you're
discipline	humorous	maintenance	quite	unfortunately	zoology

Parallelism

- All items in a list must have the same form.
  Example: The professor likes to *read books, grade papers,* and *play guitar.*

Complete sentences versus fragments

- A sentence must express a complete thought. It will always have a subject and a verb within it, in order to be a complete sentence. An incomplete sentence is known as a fragment and should not be used under any circumstances.
  Example of a fragment: The *student*, wearing a cap and gown. (This example has no verb.)
  Example of a complete sentence, The *student*, wearing a cap and gown, *attended* graduation.

Correct punctuation versus run-on sentences

- A run-on sentence is two or more sentences written together without proper punctuation separating them.

  Example of a correct sentence: The girls played volleyball all afternoon; it was not until later that they noticed someone had stolen their car.

  Example of a run-on sentence: The girls played volleyball all afternoon, it was not until later that they noticed someone had stolen their car.

Summary of All Core Concepts:
Reading, Listening, Speaking, and Writing

o   The TOEFL is a standardized test format that evaluates reading, listening, speaking, and writing. All the tasks on the TOEFL require you to work with and identify some basic features common to all of them. The more comfortable you are with these core concepts, the more comfortable you will be taking the TOEFL.

o   For each passage that you read, write on, speak about, or listen to on the TOEFL, you should focus on the purpose, examples, and conclusion. Practice identifying these parts in the sample drills in this book as well as other types of writing you encounter.

Chapter 6
Vocabulary

The TOEFL doesn't have a vocabulary specific section, but the fact remains that many of the questions, answer choices, and reading passages contain some difficult vocabulary. Part of your speaking and writing scores will also be based on your use of a variety of English words. This chapter will focus on ways to increase your vocabulary!

VOCAB, VOCAB, VOCAB

As you know, the TOEFL is an exam that measures four essential skills: reading, listening, speaking, and writing. Vocabulary is found in all of these areas, and having a strong vocabulary will benefit you throughout the TOEFL. In this chapter, we have assembled some crucial TOEFL vocabulary words along with pronunciation, definition, part of speech, an example sentence, and synonyms. It's a jackpot of useful words!

You can't improve your score substantially without increasing your vocabulary. You might think that studying vocabulary is the most boring part of preparing for the TOEFL, but it's one of the most important, and it's also one part of TOEFL preparation that's useful to you beyond the confines of the test itself. And the more words that you recognize (and know the meaning of) on the test, the easier it will be. So there's no avoiding the importance of vocabulary to your success on the TOEFL. Fortunately, one thing you have working in your favor is the fact that the same words tend to appear on the TOEFL year after year. The words we've collected for you in this chapter are the words that appear frequently on the TOEFL. So let's get started learning some new words!

Learn to Love the Dictionary

Get used to looking up words. If you see a word you don't know while studying for the TOEFL or elsewhere, it's probably a good TOEFL word. Look it up and make flashcards. Dictionaries will give you the pronunciation, while digital apps can provide quick, handy look-ups for new words. Looking up words is a habit. You may have to force yourself to do it in the beginning, but it becomes more natural over time. Many of the techniques in this book will help you on the TOEFL, but they don't have much relevance in day-to-day life. However, a great vocabulary and good vocabulary habits will add a tremendous amount of value to your career and beyond.

Learning New Words

How will you remember all the new words you should learn for the test? By developing a routine for learning new words. Here are some tips:

- To learn words that you find on your own, get into the habit of reading good books, magazines, and newspapers. Start paying attention to words you come across for which you don't know the definition. You might be tempted to just skip these, as usual, but train yourself to write them down and look them up.
- When you look up the word, say it out loud, being careful to pronounce it correctly. This will help you remember it.
- When you look up a word in the dictionary, don't assume that the first definition is the only one you need to know. The first definition may be an archaic one, or one that applies only in a particular context, so scan through all the definitions.
- Now that you've learned the dictionary's definition of a new word, restate it in your own words. You'll find it much easier to remember a word's meaning if you make it your own.

- Mnemonics—Use your imagination to create a mental image to fix the new word in your mind. For example, if you're trying to remember the word *voracious,* which means having an insatiable appetite for an activity or pursuit, picture an incredibly hungry boar eating huge piles of food. The voracious boar will help you to recall the meaning of the word. The crazier the image, the better.
- Keep a vocabulary notebook, or make a file with a list of new vocabulary words and put it on your desktop. Simply having a notebook with you will remind you to be on the lookout for new words, and using it will help you to remember the ones you encounter. Writing something down also makes it easier to memorize. Jot down the word when you find it, note its pronunciation and definition (in your own words) when you look it up, and jot down your mnemonic or mental image. You might also copy the sentence in which you originally found the word, to remind yourself of how the word looks in context.
- Do the same thing with flashcards. Write the word on one side and the pronunciation, the meaning, and perhaps a mental image on the other. Stick five or six of your flashcards in your pocket every morning and use them whenever you can. Stuck on a delayed subway train? Look at your flashcards. Standing in a long line at the bank? Look at your flashcards. Sick of engaging in small talk with boring acquaintances? Look at your flashcards. (Only kidding about that last one.)
- Use your new word every chance you get. Make it part of your life. Insert it into your speech at every opportunity. Developing a powerful vocabulary requires lots of exercise.
- Learn word roots. Many words share similar origins. By learning these common roots, you'll be better able to work with words you've never seen before. A good dictionary should list the origin and roots of the words in it.

Word	Pronunciation	Part of Speech	Definition	Sentence	Synonyms
absorb	ab SAWRB	verb	to take in or draw up	We are using a sponge to *absorb* most of the liquid that was spilled.	consume; soak up
abundant	uh BUHN duhnt	adjective	possessing a lot of something, often more than what is needed	The food was *abundant* at Thanksgiving dinner; we spent the next two weeks eating leftovers.	plentiful; full
accept	ak SEPT	verb	to receive with pleasure; to agree	The athlete was proud to *accept* his Olympic Gold Medal.	receive; approve
accumulate	uh KYOO myuh leyt	verb	to gather or collect	The geologist was hoping to *accumulate* more rock specimens on his trip out West.	acquire; gain; stockpile
adequate	AD i kwit	adjective	enough for a required purpose	She makes an *adequate* amount of money, but she still can't afford to go on fancy vacations.	unexceptional; acceptable
adjacent	uh JEY suhnt	adjective	located next to something; beside	Our house is *adjacent* to the corner grocery store.	neighboring; bordering
affect	uh FEKT	verb	to produce a change in; to move the emotions of someone	I hope your illness does not *affect* your ability to work.	change; move
analyzing	AN i lyz ing	verb	examining critically	The scientist spent hours *analyzing* the results of the experiment, and still he could not come up with an answer.	studying; investigating; evaluating
ancient	EYN shuhnt	adjective	very old; from the distant past	The *ancient* temple of Angkor Wat is almost 900 hundred years old.	antique; dated
appeal	uh PEEL	verb	to be attractive or pleasing	Eating snails is something that does not *appeal* to me.	attract; charm; interest

Word	Pronunciation	Part of Speech	Definition	Sentence	Synonyms
appropriate	uh PROH pree it	adjective	suitable or fitting to the situation at hand	A business suit is *appropriate* attire for a job interview.	correct; proper
artistic	ahr TIS tik	adjective	exhibiting visual taste or skill	She was so *artistic* that even her fruit bowl was arranged in a beautiful manner.	aesthetic; creative
assumptions	uh SUHMP shuhnz	noun	opinions which are taken for granted or presumed to be true	I made some *assumptions* about Dana's character without really knowing her.	beliefs; judgments
available	uh VEY luh buhl	adjective	able to be used, obtained, or accessed	The shoes I wanted to order from the store are, unfortunately, no longer *available*.	accessible; free
aware	uh WAIR	adjective	possessing knowledge	Soldiers need to be *aware* of potential danger at all times, even when they least expect it.	conscious; informed
beliefs	bih LEEFS	noun	things which are believed; convictions	Many *beliefs*, such as the idea that the world is flat, turn out to be wrong.	opinions; ideas
benefit	BEN uh fit	noun	a positive result or outcome	One *benefit* of exercise is that you will have more energy throughout the day.	advantage; gain
capable	KAY puh buhl	adjective	able to do something; good at a task	Having studied cooking in France for 10 years, she is a very *capable* chef.	skilled; accomplished
cast	kast	verb	threw	The fisherman *cast* his hook into the water, hoping for a bite.	flung; tossed
ceased	seest	verb	ended, stopped, or discontinued	When I lost my job, my expensive nights on the town *ceased*.	concluded; finished

Word	Pronunciation	Part of Speech	Definition	Sentence	Synonyms
certain	SUR tuhn	adjective	without doubt or reservation; particular	Since Rhonda answered only three of the ten questions, she was *certain* she had failed the exam.	confident; definite
circumstances	SUR kuhm stans iz	noun	the state of affairs	Given my financial *circumstances*, I am not sure I should be going on vacation right now.	situations; conditions
classified	KLAS uh fahyd	verb	arranged or organized according to type	The ornithologist *classified* his birds according to color, size, and beak type.	categorized; labeled
compare	kuhm PAIR	verb	to examine the differences and similarities between two things	If you *compare* Paris and New York, Paris is much cheaper.	contrast; evaluate
components	kuhm POH nuhnts	noun	parts of something	Her argument had several *components* I did not agree with.	elements; factors
compromise	KOM pruh mahyz	verb	to settle a disagreement by offering a concession	Since I am an early riser and my wife likes to sleep late, we decided to *compromise* and wake up at 10:00 A.M.	agree; meet halfway; negotiate
concerned	kuhn SURND	adjective	worried or upset	I was *concerned* when you did not show up for work at the usual time.	anxious; troubled; bothered
concrete	KON kreet	adjective	referring to an actual, material thing	Detectives look for *concrete* evidence, such as hairs and fingerprints, when solving a crime.	real; physical; solid
conform	kuhn FOHRM	verb	to act according to set standards	Teenagers often feel the pressure to *conform* in order to be popular.	adapt; follow; comply

Word	Pronunciation	Part of Speech	Definition	Sentence	Synonyms
connection	kuh NEK shuhn	noun	a joining of two things; a closeness or association with someone or something	There is a strong *connection* between wealth and education level.	relation; link; affiliation
considered	kuhn SID erd	adjective	thought of or viewed as	My *considered* opinion is that Bach is one of the greatest composers to have lived.	believed
consistent	kuhn SIS tuhnt	adjective	sticking to the same behavior or principles	Swimming has always been a *consistent* part of my life—I swim three days a week or more.	constant; regular
constant	KON stuhnt	adjective	not changing	Traffic jams are a *constant* source of irritation in modern life.	regular; reliable
constrained	kuhn STREYND	adjective	forced or confined	Being a raw-food vegetarian, she has a very *constrained* diet.	limited; restrained
convenient	kuhn VEEN yuhnt	adjective	easy to use or access	We live in a *convenient* location, right next to a 24-hour supermarket.	handy; advantageous
critical	KRIT i kuhl	adjective	tending to find flaws in something; judging harshly	He is a *critical* person with little patience for mistakes.	disapproving; demanding
crude	krood	adjective	rough or lacking refinement	He was a *crude* person who would frequently belch and tell dirty jokes.	unpolished; raw
decision	dih SIH zhuhn	noun	a choice made after considering something	The quarterback made a quick *decision* to go for a touchdown.	resolution; judgment
deepening	DEE puhn ing	adjective	becoming more intense or profound	There is an ever-*deepening* split forming between the rich and the poor.	increasing; growing

Word	Pronunciation	Part of Speech	Definition	Sentence	Synonyms
define	di FAHYN	verb	to describe precisely	Please *define* your duties as supervisor, so I have a better idea of what your job is.	specify; set
dense	dens	adjective	closely packed	The crowds at the game were so *dense* we could barely move.	thick; heavy
depict	di PIKT	verb	to represent, either in words or visually	In many of his novels, Charles Dickens would *depict* the struggles of poor children living in Victorian England.	show; illustrate
develop	dih VEL uhp	verb	to bring into being; to become affected by	After standing outside in the rain for three hours, it is likely that you will *develop* a cold.	grow; acquire
developing	dih VEL uh ping	adjective	in the process of growth or change, often used with reference to countries	Sudan is still a *developing* country, with few roads and little industry.	nonindustrial; primitive
directly	di REKT lee	adverb	in an honest, straightforward manner	The interrogator asked the witness to answer all questions as *directly* as possible.	candidly; openly
discover	dih SKUHV er	verb	to find out or acquire knowledge of	After Jim left, I was surprised to *discover* that he had left his cell phone at my house.	notice; realize
discuss	dih SKUHSS	verb	to talk over or write about	Janet liked to *discuss* politics with her friends, even though they often ended up in heated debates.	debate; consider
dominant	DOM uh nuhnt	adjective	being the most important force or component; commanding or controlling	For hundreds of years, the Romans were the *dominant* force in the Mediterranean.	chief; main; principal

Word	Pronunciation	Part of Speech	Definition	Sentence	Synonyms
eager	EE ger	adjective	excited to do something	We were surprised to find out that she was actually quite *eager* to mow the lawn.	excited; ready
eccentric	ik SEN trik	adjective	unusual; different from the normal standard	My aunt is quite an *eccentric* lady, with her bright hats adorned with birds and eggs.	bizarre; strange; weird
effect	i FEKT	noun	the result or end product of an action	Staying out in the sun for too long can have a damaging *effect* on the skin.	result; consequence
emerge	i MURJ	verb	to come into view, often from a hidden place	It is always exciting to watch a plane *emerge* from the clouds and head toward the landing strip.	appear; turn up; arise
engage	in GEYJ	verb	to attract the attention of	The rattle toy was able to *engage* the baby for hours.	interest; captivate
ensure	en SHOOR	verb	to guarantee or make certain	To *ensure* that I would not be late, I set my alarm clock an hour earlier than usual.	assure; secure
environment	en VAHY ruhn muhnt	noun	one's physical or psychological surroundings	Ferns grow best in an *environment* that is moist and full of light.	atmosphere; conditions
essential	uh SEN shuhl	adjective	absolutely necessary or required for something	Yeast is an *essential* ingredient in bread; without it, your dough will never rise.	basic; fundamental
establish	ih STAB lish	verb	to set up permanently; to show to be true	The wealthy industrialist wanted to *establish* a library that would be accessible to all.	create; found
evident	EV i dent	adjective	obvious or clear	It was *evident* that she had gone swimming, in spite of my orders against it.	apparent; plain

Word	Pronunciation	Part of Speech	Definition	Sentence	Synonyms
evolve	ee VOLV	verb	to develop or change gradually	We are hoping this poor neighborhood will *evolve* into a place that is safer.	advance; grow; mature
exist	ig ZIST	verb	to be alive or in existence; to be	Most Giant Pandas *exist* in the mountain regions of China.	live; survive
exposed	ik SPOHZD	adjective	without shelter or protection; laid open to view	In the desert, one is *exposed* to the Sun and heat all day long.	unprotected; open
familiar	fuh MIL yer	adjective	commonly known or experienced; acquainted with	I am not *familiar* with the book you are read-ing—is it good?	experienced; known
famous	FEY muhs	adjective	being very well known in the world	The inventor became *famous* for creating useful gadgets.	renowned; influential
function	FUHNGK shuhn	noun	the purpose or use for something	The *function* of the heart is to pump blood throughout the body.	task; role
fundamental	fuhn duh MEN tuhl	adjective	forming an essential part of something	Dribbling is a *fundamental* skill in basketball—every player must know how to do this.	basic; important
gradual	GRAJ oo uhl	adjective	taking place over a long range of time; little by little	Over the last cen-tury, there has been a *gradual* increase in the Earth's temperature.	steady; progressive
habitat	HAB i tat	noun	the natural surroundings of an organism	Snakes prefer a sunny and dry *habitat*.	environment; residence
illustrate	IL uh streyt	verb	to serve as an example of; to make clear	These diagrams *illustrate* the bad effects of smoking on one's health.	prove; demonstrate

Word	Pronunciation	Part of Speech	Definition	Sentence	Synonyms
immediately	i MEE dee it lee	adverb	occurring right away, without any delay	When I found out Maria was in the hospital, I called her *immediately*.	instantly; promptly
indicator	IN di kay ter	noun	something that acts as a sign	A high body temperature can be an *indicator* of illness.	sign; warning; clue
influence	IN floo uhns	verb	to contribute to, change, or modify; to exert power over	My father is a huge *influence* in my life—I have always admired him and sought his advice.	affect; sway
innovations	in uh VEY shunz	noun	new techniques or new things	Several *innovations* in Internet technology have made web surfing faster than ever.	changes; inventions
lack	LAK	verb	to not have; to be without	I am so busy with my new job that I *lack* the time to devote to my book club.	miss; need; want
limited	LIM i tid	adjective	restricted in number or amount; confined within physical boundaries	These days, you can take only a *limited* amount of baggage on airplanes.	fixed; definite
major	MEY jer	adjective	large or great in importance or amount	Fish is a *major* component in the Japanese diet.	big; main
materials	muh TEER ee uhlz	noun	substances which compose an object, or are used to build something	To build a tree house, you need the following *materials*: wood, nails, and glue.	supplies; components
mention	MEN shuhn	verb	to refer to briefly; to speak of	At lunch, Margot failed to *mention* that she had seen Tom the other day.	refer; bring up

Word	Pronunciation	Part of Speech	Definition	Sentence	Synonyms
necessary	NESS uh ser ee	adjective	being essential to or required of something	It's *necessary* to get a job if you want to be able to buy a house.	essential; needed
negative	NEG uh tiv	adjective	lacking positive characteristics; indicating opposition to something	She had a *negative* reaction when I suggested that we move out of the country.	bad; against; unfavorable
nowadays	NOW uh deyz	adverb	of or related to the present time	*Nowadays*, it is rare for a family to live without a television.	today; presently
objective	uhb JEK tiv	noun	the goal of a course of action	The *objective* of the United Nations is to maintain world peace.	aim; purpose
obvious	OB vee uhs	adjective	very clear	As she limped across the field, it was *obvious* that she had been injured.	apparent; evident
occasionally	uh KAY zhuh nuh lee	adverb	now and then; not often	Though I am a vegetarian, I *occasionally* eat fish.	sometimes; rarely
official	uh FISH uhl	adjective	of an office or position of authority	The *official* position of the apartment building is that no pets are allowed.	authorized; established
opinion	uh PIN yuhn	noun	a personal belief or judgment	After he was late several times, I did not have a good *opinion* of him.	view; estimation
option	OP shuhn	noun	the right to choose something	Prospective buyers have the *option* to buy the car with or without GPS.	choice; privilege
partial	PAHR shuhl	adjective	not complete	We have only a *partial* understanding of our galaxy.	halfway; unfinished
particular	per TIK yuh ler	adjective	related to or associated with a specific group or category	The child was very *particular* about the kinds of foods she ate.	exact; specific

Word	Pronunciation	Part of Speech	Definition	Sentence	Synonyms
pattern	PAT ern	noun	the design, often repeated, of something; a regular and consistent combination of qualities	The *pattern* of the wallpaper consists of flowers and trees.	arrangement; motif
periodic	peer ee OD ik	adjective	occurring at regular time intervals	At *periodic* times through the day, you need to take this medication.	alternate; intermittent
phenomenon	fi NOM uh non	noun	something unusual, significant, or impressive	A solar eclipse is a natural *phenomenon* that some people will never witness in their lifetimes.	wonder; marvel; miracle
physical	FIZ i kuhl	adjective	related to the body or material things	Of all sports, wrestling is the one that involves the most *physical* contact.	real; earthly
portray	pawr TREY	verb	to depict visually or describe in words	The painter always liked to *portray* his subjects next to a window.	represent; draw
possible	POSS uh buhl	adjective	able to exist or occur	Many years ago, people thought it wasn't *possible* for humans to travel to the Moon.	likely; achievable
potential	puh TEN shuhl	noun	possibility; an ability or skill that may be developed in the future	Long legs indicate great *potential* as a runner.	promise; aptitude
prefer	pri FUR	verb	to like something more than another thing	I *prefer* coffee to tea.	choose; favor
primary	PRAHY mer ee	adjective	the most important; the first in a series	The *primary* source of crime in major cities is drug use.	main; principal

Word	Pronunciation	Part of Speech	Definition	Sentence	Synonyms
principal	PRIN suh puhl	adjective	first or most important	My *principal* reason for leaving this job is the low pay.	chief; primary; main
profound	pruh FOUND	adjective	going beyond what is on the surface; deep	Aristotle gave us a *profound* understanding of human life.	thoughtful; weighty
promote	pruh MOHT	verb	to help or encourage	The treaty was designed to *promote* trade relations between the two nations.	boost; nurture; aid
prove	proov	verb	to establish the truth or validity of	There is little evidence to *prove* your claim that you were in the shower during the crime.	verify; confirm
published	PUHB lisht	verb	prepared and distributed a piece of writing for public sale	The writer finally *published* his first novel after years of rejection.	issued; released
qualities	KWOL i teez	noun	the traits or characteristics of someone or something	The house has many desirable *qualities*, including a large lawn and pool.	features; properties
rapid	RAP id	adjective	very fast; occurring with great speed	He is a *rapid* painter who can paint an entire house at record-setting speed.	speedy; quick
rate	reyt	verb	to rank or assess the value of	The study attempted to *rate* cars on the basis of affordability and reliability.	measure; judge
realistic	ree uh LIS tik	adjective	seeming close to reality; resembling what is true or practical	It is not *realistic* to assume that next year I will earn a million dollars.	reasonable; sensible

Word	Pronunciation	Part of Speech	Definition	Sentence	Synonyms
recent	REE suhnt	adjective	not long past; having occurred in the near past	*Recent* events in the Middle East have demonstrated that peace is unlikely.	current; modern
recommend	rek uh MEND	verb	to suggest as useful or good	I asked my friend to *recommend* a hairdresser to me.	advise; advocate
reflects	ri FLEKTS	verb	shows an image of; demonstrates	Giving money to that homeless person *reflects* how kind you are.	attests; manifests
relation	ri LEY shuhn	noun	a connection between two things, sometimes familial	Bob's facial features are just like mine, but he is no *relation* to me.	association; kinship
reliable	ri LAHY uh buhl	adjective	trustworthy and dependable	The Toyota is one of the most *reliable* cars on the market—it rarely breaks down.	constant; unfailing; predictable
rely	ri LAHY	verb	to depend on or put trust in	You can *rely* on me to pay you back in two weeks' time.	depend; trust
remain	ri MEYN	verb	to stay in the same position or state	If I *remain* at this job for another year, I will be eligible for a significant pay raise.	continue; last
require	ri KWAHYR	verb	to have need for; to demand or insist upon	A medical degree will *require* many courses of study in the sciences.	necessitate; ask
resistant	ri ZIS tuhnt	adjective	being opposed to or against something	The child was *resistant* to naptime.	contrary; rebellious
result	ri ZUHLT	noun	the outcome of an action or course of events	One *result* of the stock market crash is lower consumer spending.	consequence; outcome

Word	Pronunciation	Part of Speech	Definition	Sentence	Synonyms
ritual	RICH oo uhl	noun	a ceremony or procedure used in a tradition, often religious	One of the *rituals* of Passover is to abstain from eating bread for the week.	tradition; habit
routes	rootz	noun	roads or ways to travel	The map shows several *routes* that will take us from Chicago to Detroit.	paths; passages
sake	SEYK	noun	the purpose or reason for something	For the *sake* of your health, you must quit smoking.	benefit; motive
sense	sens	noun	a mode of perceiving the world; an intuition	Dogs have a very strong *sense* of smell.	feel; impression
significance	sig NIF i kuhns	noun	the meaning or importance of something	The *significance* of the computer is apparent in every aspect of our lives.	importance; meaning
solution	suh LOO shuhn	noun	the answer to a question or problem	If the physics problem is too hard, you can find the *solution* at the back of the book.	resolution; explanation
sophisticated	suh FIS ti kay tid	adjective	in possession of worldly knowledge; complex or advanced	It was such *sophisticated* math that only a skilled mathematician could understand it.	worldly; intricate
specific	spi SIF ik	adjective	clearly defined or exact	The doctor gave the patient *specific* instructions to take the medication only at night.	definite; particular
speculate	SPEK yuh leyt	verb	to think about or reflect on without necessary evidence	Since she refuses to answer my questions, we can only *speculate* as to what her true motives were.	guess; conjecture

Word	Pronunciation	Part of Speech	Definition	Sentence	Synonyms
stages	STEY jiz	noun	steps in a process	There are many *stages* involved in becoming a cop, including basic training and field experience.	degrees; levels
standards	STAN derdz	noun	a level of quality by which others are ranked	The school has such low *standards* that it is virtually impossible to fail.	guidelines; ideals; requirements
subsequent	SUHB si kwuhnt	adjective	occurring after something else	The defeat of Greece and its *subsequent* decline led to the birth of the Roman Empire.	following; succeeding
succeeding	suhk SEE ding	adjective	coming after or following	People today may resent these tax hikes, but *succeeding* generations will thank us for the debt relief.	subsequent; next
sufficient	suh FISH uhnt	adjective	enough for what is needed, but not going beyond that	Fortunately, we found *sufficient* food for the last remaining days of our camping trip.	adequate; decent
suggest	suhg JEST	verb	to mention, hint, or propose	She was hoping the waiter would *suggest* a good dish off the menu.	imply; advise
support	suh POHRT	verb	to encourage or to uphold; to bear weight or financial responsibility	Having known you for many years, I *support* your decision to run for president.	promote; help; back up
survive	ser VAHYV	verb	to stay alive	The stranded hikers were able to *survive* by eating berries and grass for several days.	live; remain; endure
technique	tek NEEK	noun	method of performance; technical skill	The famed chef had a secret *technique* for making great bread.	approach; procedure

Word	Pronunciation	Part of Speech	Definition	Sentence	Synonyms
technological	tek nuh LOJ i kuhl	adjective	related to science and industry	*Technological* innovations such as the vacuum and washing machine have made housework much easier.	industrial; mechanical
tend	tend	verb	to take care of or look after	I am happy to *tend* to your plants while you are away on vacation.	oversee; guard; watch over
topic	TOP ik	noun	a subject of study or discussion	The historian's favorite *topic* of conversation was the Trojan War.	matter; issue
tradition	truh DISH uhn	noun	a custom or belief that has been handed down throughout history	The Christmas *tradition* involves decorating a tree and leaving out cookies for Santa Claus.	convention; practice
traditional	truh DISH uh nuhl	adjective	based on an established custom or convention	In a *traditional* Italian meal, pasta is always served.	conventional; established
typically	TIP i kuh lee	adverb	conforming to regular behavior	In Seattle, it *typically* rains every day.	normally; usually
underneath	uhn der NEETH	preposition	below	I keep my slippers *underneath* my bed.	beneath; under
unifying	YOO nuh fahy ing	adjective	tending to bring together or unite	Attending sports events can have a *unifying* effect on a community.	joining; solidifying
unique	yoo NEEK	adjective	one of a kind; having no equal	New York City is a *unique* place—there is no place like it in the entire world.	unusual; not typical
unpredictable	uhn pri DIK tuh buhl	adjective	unable to be predicted or foreseen	Life as a musician is *unpredictable*—you never know when you'll get your next gig.	uncertain; unreliable

Word	Pronunciation	Part of Speech	Definition	Sentence	Synonyms
unusual	uhn YOO zhoo uhl	adjective	not ordinary or common	Marge's blue hair gave her an *unusual* appearance.	strange; remarkable
value	VAL yoo	verb	to place importance in; to calculate the monetary worth	Of all the traits that a friend could possess, honesty is the one I *value* most.	appreciate; prize
varied	VAIR eed	adjective	characterized by many different qualities	People in my school come from *varied* backgrounds—one student grew up in Kansas, another in Saudi Arabia.	assorted; diverse
vertical	VUR ti kuhl	adjective	in a direction from top to bottom (as opposed to left to right)	At the edge of the cliff was there was a 40-foot *vertical* drop.	upright; perpendicular
visual	VIZH oo uhl	adjective	pertaining to seeing	The film had great *visual* effects, such as fireballs and flying people.	observable; viewable
waste	WEYST	verb	to fail to use, or to use for no good reason	We *waste* electricity every time we leave a lamp on in an unoccupied room.	expend; squander

While the TOEFL does not explicitly test vocabulary, building your vocabulary of English words will help you in many ways. First, it will lessen the chance of seeing or hearing words you don't know in the Reading or Listening sections. Second, it will give you a broader choice of words to use in your Speaking and Writing responses. And third, possibly the most valuable way that learning more vocabulary will help you is to increase your comfort level when communicating with others in English overall.

ROOT WORDS

One of the easiest—and quickest!—ways to build your vocabulary is to learn common roots that are used to form words in the English language. As you may have already guessed, English has "borrowed" from Latin and Greek very heavily over the years. We can see these influences still showing up in our language today.

For example, the root "mal," from Latin, means "bad." So, if you see the word "malaria," you may not know that it describes a disease that is transmitted by mosquitoes. But you might be able to take a reasonable guess that it has a negative meaning because "mal" is contained in "malaria."

Now, just because you see "mal" in a word doesn't mean it *must* mean something bad. For example, "male" certainly doesn't have a negative meaning. But, when you're trying to learn a large amount of vocabulary in a reasonably short time (like when you're preparing for the TOEFL!), learning root words can be a great way to accomplish your goal.

Below you'll find a list of a large number of Latin and Greek roots. One of the best ways to study them is to create "Root Cards." (You'll need a couple packs of 3″ × 5″ cards for this exercise, using one card per root word.)

On the front of the card, write the root and its meaning:

> 'mal'
> means 'bad'

And on the back of the card, write as many words as you can think of that use that root.

> malaria
> malicious
> malice
> malignant

When you learn a new word, look at the etymology in the dictionary and see if the word uses one of the roots in the Master Root List (see the next page). If it does, add it to your card!

Then, review your cards every few days (or more frequently) so you can commit the roots and their meanings to memory.

Here is a list of many roots that show up in English words. We've also added a few words for each one to get you started.

Master Root List

Root	Meaning	Example(s)
ab	away from/negative prefix	abnormal, abnegate
ac/acr	sharp	acute, acrid, acrimonious
ad/at	to, toward	adduct, adhere
amb	go/walk	amble, ambulate
ambi	both/mixed	ambidextrous, ambivalent
ami/amo	love	amicable, amorous
an/anti	against	antifreeze, antibiotic
andr/anthr	human	anthropology, android
anim	life, spirit	animated, animal
ante	before	anteroom, anterior
apt/ept	skill, ability	aptitude, adept
arbo	tree	arbor, arboretum
arch	rule, over	archdiocese, archbishop
aud	sound	audible, audio
auto	self	automatic, autonomous
bell/belli	war	belligerent, bellicose
ben/bono	good	benefit, bonus
bi	two	biannual, bipartisan
bio/bios	life	biology, biography
bra	arm	embrace, bracelet
carn	meat, flesh	carnivore, incarnate
cent	hundred	century, centigrade
chron	time	chronology, chronograph
circ/circu	around	circle, circuit, circumference
cis/cise	cut	incisor, scissor, excise
cli	lean	incline, recliner
clu/clo/cla	close, shut	clasp, closure
co/com/con	with, together	community, cooperate
contr-	against	contradict, contrast
cred	believe	incredible, credibility, credo
culp	blame	culprit, exculpate
cur/cour	run (a course)	incur, discourse

Root	Meaning	Example(s)
de	away from/opposite, of	decline, deny
dec/deci	ten	decade, decimal
dent	teeth	dental, denture
derm	skin	dermatologist, dermatitis
desc	down	descent, descendant
dext	ability	ambidextrous, dexterity
di	two, apart, split	diode, dilute
dic/dict	say, tell	edict, dictionary
dign/dain	worth	dignity, disdain
dis	apart from, not	distant, dissipate
domi	rule over	dominant, domicile
dorm	sleep	dormitory, dormant
duc/dul	lead	duct, conductor
dys	faulty, bad	dysfunction, dyslexia
e/ex/ej	out, outward	exit, eject, emote
en/em	into	enter, embolden
epi	upon	epicenter, epilogue
equ/equi	equal	equidistant, equal
esce	becoming	coalesce, evanesce
eu	good, pleasant	euphoria, euphemism
extr	outside, beyond, additional	extraterrestrial, extraneous, extra
fac/fic/fig	do, make	factual, fictional, figurative
fid	faithful	confide, confidential, fidelity
fort	strong	fortify
fract	break, split	fraction, fracture
frat	brother	fraternal, fraternity
fren	highly energetic	frenzy, frenetic
gen	birth, creation, kind, type	gender, general
geo	earth	geography, geocentric
gno/kno	know	agnostic, knowledge
grand	big	grandeur, grandiose
graph	write	graphic, dysgraphia
grat	grateful	gratitude, ingrate
gress	step	progress, egress
gyn	female	gynecology, androgynous
her/hes	stick (on)	cohesive, adhere
herb	plant	herbal, herbicide
hetero	different, mixed	heterogeneous, heterodox
hex/sex	six	hexagon, sextuplet

More Great Books
Well, not books, but cards. The Princeton Review sells TOEFL flashcards to help you review the top key terms that you absolutely must know. Buy them wherever books are sold or online!

Root	Meaning	Example(s)
homo	same	homogenous, homophone
hyd/hydr	water	hydrate, hydrant
hyper	over, beyond	hyperactive, hyperventilate
hypo	under, insufficient	hypodermic, hypothermia
il	not	illicit, illegal
im	not, into	impotent (not), imported (into)
in	not, into	incapable (not), internal (into)
inter	between	interstate, interlock
intra	within	intramural
itis	inflammation, infection	arthritis, bronchitis, appendicitis
ium	place, building of	stadium, terrarium
jeu/ju	play, youthful	juvenile, junior
lab/labo	work	labor, laboratory
laud	praise	applaud, laudable
lav	wash	lave, lavish
lev	rise	levitate, elevate
loc/log/loqui	to speak	loquacious
lu/luc/lum	light	luminous, lucid
mag/magna	great	magnificent, magnanimous
mal	bad	malicious, malignant
man/manu	hand	manual, maneuver, manufacture
mar/mer	sea	marine, mermaid
matr	mother	matron, matriarch
met/meter	measure	metric, thermometer
meta	more, beyond	metaphysics, metaphor
mic/micro	tiny	microscope, microchip
mill	thousand	millimeter, millennium
mis	wrong, bad	mistake, misfortune
mit	send	transmit, emit
mob/mobi	moving	mobilize
mor/mort	death	immortal, mortify
morph	change (shape)	amorphous, morphology
mut	change, alter	mutate, transmute
nat/natu	natural, birth	natural, natal
neg	negative	negate, negligent
neo/nov	new	novel, neonatal
noct	night	nocturnal
nom/nym	name	pseudonym, nominal
non/not	negative prefix	nonfat, nonsense

Root	Meaning	Example(s)
nounce	call	announce, pronounce
nox/nec	harmful	noxious, necrosis
ob	against	obstruct, obnoxious
ology	study of	biology, theology
omni	all, every	omniscient, omnipresent
ory	place of	observatory, directory
pac/pax/plac	peace, pleasing	pacific, placid
pan	all, everywhere	pandemic
par	equal	parity, partner
para	beyond, beside	paranormal, paralegal
path	feeling, emotion	empathy, apathetic
patr	father	patron, paternal
pen/pend	weight	pendulum, penury
pent	five	pentagon
peri	around	periscope, peripheral
pet/pec	small	petite, peckish
phil	love, high regard	philanthropy, oenophile
phob	fear	agoraphobic
phon	sound	phonetic, euphonium
pod/ped	foot	pedal, podiatry
pon/pos	place, put	position, ponder
port	carry	transport, portable
post	after	posterity, posterior
poten	power, influence	potent, potential
pre	before	pre-existing, preclude
pro	for	promote, proponent
prox	near	proximity, approximate
pseudo	false	pseudonym
quad	four	quadriceps, quadrant
qui	quiet	acquiesce, quietude
quint	five	quintuple
re	again	restart, regain
sci/scien	knowledge	science, prescient
scop	see	microscope, telescopic
scrib/scrip	write	script, scribe
sec/sequ	follow, come after	sequence, second
sed/sid	sit, be still	sedate, sidle
solo	alone	solitary, soliloquy
son/soni	sound	sonorous, sonic

Root	Meaning	Example(s)
spec/spic	see, look	spectacle, inspect
sta/sti	still, unmoving	stationary, still
sua	smooth	suave, assuage
sub	under	submarine, suboptimal
super	beyond, greater than	supersonic, superficial
syn/sym	bring together	synonym, symbiotic
tact	touch	tactile, intact
tech/techn	tools	technical, technology
tele	at a distance	telephone, teleport
temp	time	temporary, tempo
ten/tend	hold	tender, attend
ter	earth, ground	terrain, territory
tox	harmful, poisonous	toxic, toxemia
tract	pull	traction, tractor
trans	across	transit, transmit
trep	fear, anxiety	intrepid, trepidation
tri	three	triad, trimester
un	not	uncooperative, uncommon
uni	one	unicorn, united
us/ut	use	utility, useful
val/vale	value, feel	valor, validate
vend	sell	vendor
ver/vera/veri	true	aver, veritable, veracity
verd	green	verdant, verdure
verge	boundary, together	converge
verse	turn	reverse, converse
vi/vit/viv	alive	vital, vivacious
vid/vis	see	visual, video
voc	call, talk	vocation, vocalize
vor	eat, consume	voracious, herbivore

If you find that root words are helping you get a better grasp of English vocabulary, here's another exercise that can be incredibly valuable: word webs!

Use the collections of words that we've included over the next few pages, like this one:

Synchronize	Chronicle	Anachronism	Amoral
Apathy	Apartheid	Amorphous	Metamorphosis
Sympathy	Empathy	Pathos	Antipathy
Parity	Disparate	Dissociate	Disparity
Disperse	Dissuade	Dissipate	Dignify
Deign	Disdain	Metacognitive	Dismiss

Start with any word right in the middle of your paper. Circle the roots you see in that word:

Then, look for another word in the group that uses one of the same roots as the one you started with. Write the new word on your paper, circle its roots, and connect the same roots together with a line:

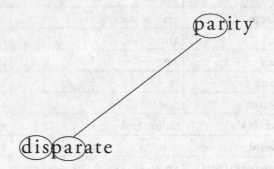

Continue this process until you have used all of the words in the set!

As you go along, make sure to look up the words you don't recognize so you can connect the root words' meanings to the meanings of the actual words.

Word Web #1

Miscreant	Misanthrope	Mistake	Anthropology
Philanthropy	Androgynous	Misogyny	Philosophy
Technophile	Technophobe	Technology	Technique

Word Web #2

Substantiate	Subterranean	Subordinate	Terrestrial
Terrarium	Subvert	Advertise	Extrovert
Traverse	Extraterrestrial	Extrapolate	Supervise
Superimpose	Supersede	Sediment	Sedate
Subside	Subservient	Introvert	

Word Web #3

Voracious	Devour	Carnivorous	Carnage
Incarceration	Infiltrate	Input	Inject
Ingratiate	Incarnate	Intractable	Protract
Tractor	Antecedent	Antebellum	Rebel
Belligerent	Bellicose	Enamored	Amorous
Amity	Amicable	Innate	Nascent
Naïve	Natal	Native	Renaissance
Omnivorous	Omniscient	Omnipotent	Potential
Potent	Potentate	Prescience	Preface
Prefix	Predestine		

These are examples of what your word webs might look like. You'll see that, in a couple of instances, the words don't all connect into the same web—and that's okay! What's important is that you recognize the roots and learn to guess the meanings of words based on their roots.

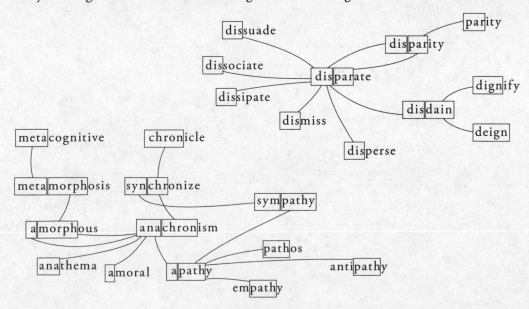

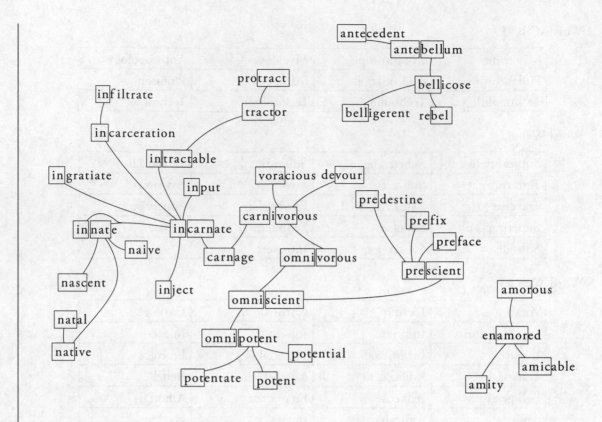

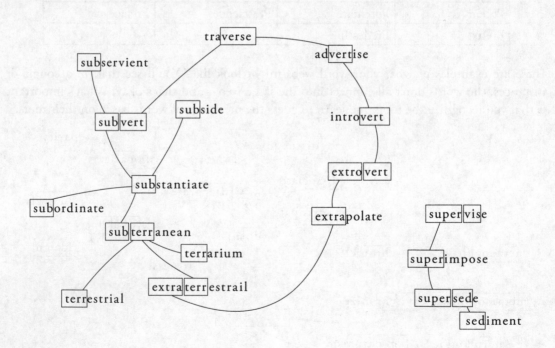

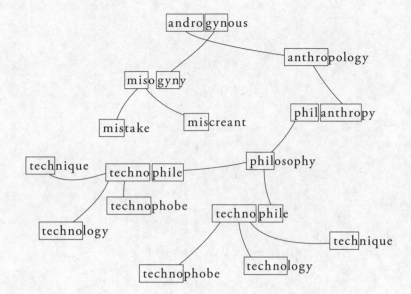

Part III:
Cracking Each
Section of the
TOEFL

Chapter 7
Cracking the
Reading Section

The TOEFL Reading section consists of these elements:

> Three to four **passages**, each approximately 700 words long
>
> - Each passage is followed by 10 questions.
> - You will have 54 to 72 minutes to complete the entire section.

As mentioned in the introduction, many of the questions are multiple choice and worth one point each, but some questions are worth two or more points. Typically, questions that are worth more appear at the end of the section.

Some of the words and phrases in the reading passages are underlined in blue on the screen; if you click on these phrases, a definition is provided. You can see what the screen will look like in the picture on the opposite page.

In this case, if you click on the words *uranium isotope* or *moniker*, you will see a definition of the word or phrase in question. You'll also notice that some of the words appear in gray boxes. These words have a special type of question associated with them, which we'll look at soon.

During the actual test, some very difficult words will appear underlined in the reading passages. The TOEFL will give you a definition of these words, so don't worry when you see them!

Remember, if you prefer, you are free to skip questions within this section; simply click on the "Next" button on the top right-hand side of the screen. You can return to questions you've skipped when you are ready. You can also click the "Review" button to see a display of all the questions you've answered and all those you've left blank. From this screen, you can return to any question. Remember to enter an answer for EVERY question. If you choose to skip one and come back to it, it's smart to choose an answer before you skip it. That way, you definitely have an answer in—and if you end up running out of time, at least you have an answer entered!

As we mentioned in the early part of this book, the Reading scores are subdivided into four sections:

Advanced (24–30). Students who score in the "Advanced" range are usually comfortable reading content that covers a wide range of difficulty and can fully understand connections among the information in a text. These students usually have a strong command of vocabulary and grammar, and can make inferences easily from the text.

High-Intermediate (18–23). Students who score in the "High-Intermediate" range are usually comfortable reading academic passages, but may have an incomplete understanding of complex texts. Generally, their ability to understand is sufficient in most texts, but these students may find harder texts challenging.

Low-Intermediate (4–17). Scores in the "Low-Intermediate" range indicate a limited ability to understand academic texts. Students in this range have a basic command of vocabulary, but have difficulty understanding concepts like main idea and author's purpose in more complex texts.

Below Low-Intermediate (0–3). Scores in the "Below Low-Intermediate" range indicate a very limited ability to comprehend academic texts and have an incorrect understanding of vocabulary and grammar.

Use your active reading skills and tackle the passage below

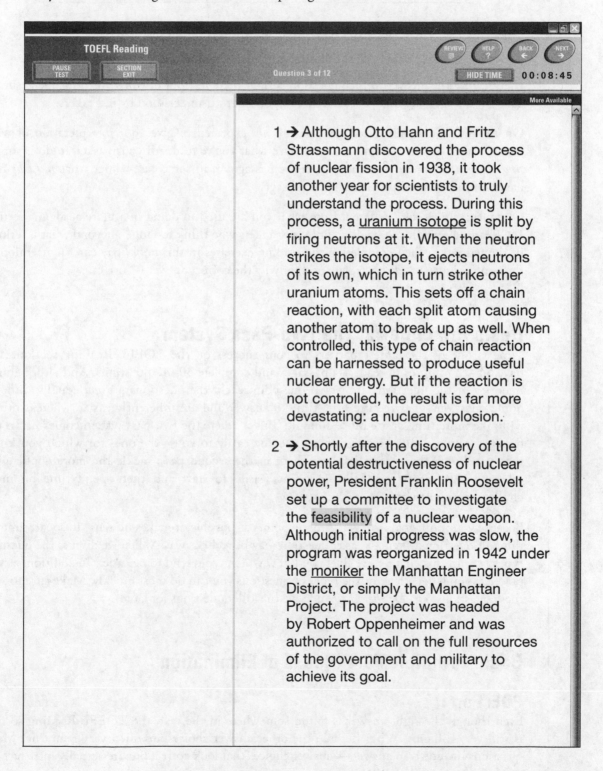

TOEFL Reading

Question 3 of 12

HIDE TIME   00:08:45

More Available

1 → Although Otto Hahn and Fritz Strassmann discovered the process of nuclear fission in 1938, it took another year for scientists to truly understand the process. During this process, a <u>uranium isotope</u> is split by firing neutrons at it. When the neutron strikes the isotope, it ejects neutrons of its own, which in turn strike other uranium atoms. This sets off a chain reaction, with each split atom causing another atom to break up as well. When controlled, this type of chain reaction can be harnessed to produce useful nuclear energy. But if the reaction is not controlled, the result is far more devastating: a nuclear explosion.

2 → Shortly after the discovery of the potential destructiveness of nuclear power, President Franklin Roosevelt set up a committee to investigate the feasibility of a nuclear weapon. Although initial progress was slow, the program was reorganized in 1942 under the <u>moniker</u> the Manhattan Engineer District, or simply the Manhattan Project. The project was headed by Robert Oppenheimer and was authorized to call on the full resources of the government and military to achieve its goal.

CRACKING THE READING SECTION: BASIC PRINCIPLES

Basic Principle #1: It's in There!
The first and most important principle of the Reading section is a simple one.

> **The answer to every single question is found in the passage!**

That's right. The answer to each question is right there in front of you. This principle is simple enough, but it is one that is often either forgotten or misunderstood by test takers.

On the TOEFL Reading section, you are *not* expected to give your interpretation of what you've read. You are *not* required to analyze what you've read. All you're asked to do is simply *find the best answer* to the question in the passage or, in some cases, infer what *must be true* based on information provided in the passage.

Of course, this is very different from what you are used to doing in a more academic setting. The Reading section can be difficult for test takers who think too much beyond what is written in the passage. When completing the reading exercises in this book, pay careful attention to the approach used and the explanation for why the correct answer is correct.

Basic Principle #2: The Two-Pass System
Time is one of the largest barriers to your success on the TOEFL Reading section. You have 54–72 minutes to read 3–4 passages and complete 30–40 questions. And although the majority of the questions are worth one point each, the questions are *not* equally difficult. Some question types require little time to answer and are inherently easier, whereas others will take more time or are more difficult. This is where the two-pass system comes in. In the first pass, knock out the questions that come easily to you—the ones for which you know that you know the correct answer. Then, in the second pass, tackle the more challenging questions. This way you tally up points easily to start and then spend time on more challenging questions.

Because your only goal is to get as many points as possible, it makes no sense to spend time on difficult questions when an easier question may be a click away. When we discuss the question types later in this chapter, we'll let you know which types tend to be easier. In addition, as you practice, you'll get a feel for the types of questions you can do most quickly. Make sure to seek these questions out. *Do them first* and save the killer questions for later.

Basic Principle #3: Process of Elimination

POE: Part I
Even though the right answer is found somewhere in the text, the TOEFL Reading section is still very difficult. Why? Because the other answer choices are often very tempting. Many questions include trap answers—answer choices that look correct but are actually incorrect.

To do well on the Reading section, you must use Process of Elimination, or POE. Simply put, POE involves comparing answer choices and finding reasons to eliminate one or more. POE requires you to be aggressive and get rid of many of the answer choices! Because the majority of the questions have only four choices, eliminating even one answer greatly increases your odds of getting a question correct if you are forced to guess. When using POE, make sure you examine each answer choice carefully. *Never* blindly pick the first answer that stands out or seems good, because it may be a trap!

Let's look at a sample question to see how to use POE. On the test, you won't see the answer choices as letters, but we'll use them in this book to make the explanations clearer.

1. The word feasibility as used in the passage is closest in meaning to:

    a. appropriateness
    b. reasonableness
    c. possibility
    d. viability

This question is based on an earlier reading passage, but that is actually not important right now. We are concerned only with the answer choices. When using POE, use your scratch paper to write "a," "b," "c," "d," and then make a mark next to each answer, based on your impression of it. Some possibilities are listed below.

Symbol	Meaning
✓	Good or okay answer
~	Weak answer
?	Unknown answer
✓✓	Best answer
X	Bad answer

Don't waste time writing down the whole question and complete answer choices. We have copied the whole question here for purposes of illustrating our point. On the actual test, you should try to write down a paraphrased version of the question and answer choices.

For the example above, we may mark our scrap paper in the following way:

1. The word feasibility as used in the passage is closest in meaning to:

   X a. appropriateness
   ~ b. reasonableness
   ✓ c. possibility
   ? d. viability

So in this case, even if we can't decide which answer is the "best" one, we can see that one of the choices is definitely out. And because we like the third answer, we may as well eliminate the "weak" answer too. That leaves us with the third and fourth answer choices. In this case, the third choice looks okay, whereas the fourth choice is a bit of a mystery.

On the TOEFL, there will be times when you're unsure of a choice. The answer may contain difficult vocabulary words or be hard to follow. Never eliminate an answer just because you don't understand it. Instead, mark it as "unknown," and check the other choices. If the remaining choices are no good, then the "unknown" choice must be correct. If one of the other choices seems more likely, then go with that one.

We'll talk more about what to do when you are stuck or down to two choices when we look at the different question types.

POE: Part II

The second part of POE is the ability to recognize the types of wrong answers found on the TOEFL. The wrong answers have to be tempting enough for you to want to pick them, but not right enough to be the best answer. In general, the wrong answers on the TOEFL Reading section fall into one of the following categories:

- **Not mentioned:** This category consists of information that is not found in the passage. Often, the answer makes common sense or may be true in the real world. However, on the TOEFL, every correct answer must be found in the passage.
- **Extreme:** These answer choices use wording that is too strong or absolute. These choices usually include words such as *all, always, impossible, must, never,* or *none.* Correct answers on the TOEFL usually do not contain such strong language.
- **Right answer, wrong question:** These choices contain information that is mentioned in the passage; however, the information doesn't answer the question.
- **Verbatim:** Many wrong answers repeat parts of the passage word for word. Unfortunately, the choices use these words in the wrong context or incorrectly. These answers can be especially tempting.
- **Beyond the information:** Choices in this category are based on information in the passage, but they go beyond the given information, meaning that they give more information than the passage provides. For example, if the passage states "some species of chimpanzees make crude tools out of branches," the answer choice may read "many animals can make tools." This answer goes beyond the information by changing "some species of chimpanzees" to "many animals."

When you are preparing for the TOEFL, make sure you review all the questions, even the ones you've gotten right. Read each wrong answer choice, and see if you can figure out what makes it wrong. Becoming familiar with the wrong answers is almost as important as finding the right answers. Also, while you are practicing, identify and note *why* certain answers are wrong. Make sure to mark each wrong answer with one of the five categories we discussed in POE: Part I.

CRACKING THE READING SECTION: BASIC APPROACH

When approaching the Reading section of the TOEFL, follow these steps.

> 1. **Actively read the passage,** looking for the purpose, structure, and main idea.
> 2. **Attack the questions** based on question type.
> 3. **Find the answer in the Passage and Use POE.**

Let's look at each of these steps in greater detail.

Step 1: Actively Read the Passage

One of the biggest mistakes you can make on the TOEFL is to attempt to read and understand every single word of the passage. There are many problems with this approach. One is that you simply do not have enough time to read the entire passage and accurately answer all of the questions. A second problem is that there is far more information in the passage than you will ever need to know to answer the questions. The more of the passage that you read, the more likely you are to become confused or distracted. Finally, remember that you get points for answering questions, not reading passages. You want to spend your time answering questions and earning points, not reading.

Instead of reading the entire passage, use the active reading strategies described in Chapter 2, Core Concept: Reading. Don't spend too much time on this step, and don't try to understand all the details in the passage. Read the passage, looking for the following major points:

1. The purpose
2. The structure
3. The main idea

On the TOEFL, you will see that paragraphs referred to in the questions are marked by a ➔; this will help you quickly locate the paragraphs. You may see black squares ■ in the passage, and some of the words will be shaded in gray, whereas others will be underlined. Try not to be distracted by these symbols, words, and phrases—there will be questions about them later, but don't get bogged down by them while you're reading.

Here's a passage similar to one you would find on the TOEFL. It should look familiar to you. We used it to introduce you to the look of the test in Chapter 1. Take a few moments to actively read it.

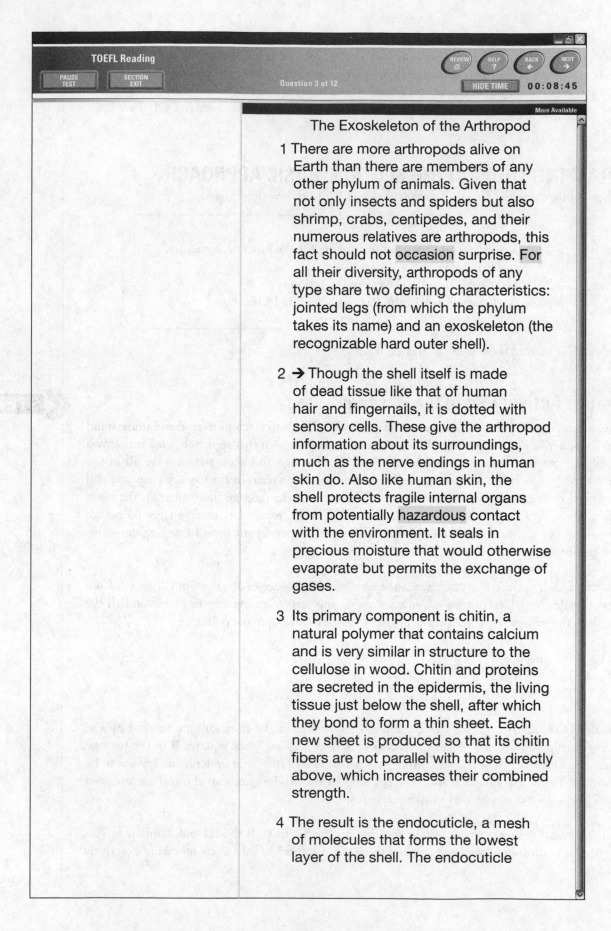

TOEFL Reading

PAUSE
TEST

SECTION
EXIT

Question 3 of 12

REVIEW

HELP
?

BACK
←

NEXT
→

HIDE TIME   00:08:45

More Available

The Exoskeleton of the Arthropod

1 There are more arthropods alive on Earth than there are members of any other phylum of animals. Given that not only insects and spiders but also shrimp, crabs, centipedes, and their numerous relatives are arthropods, this fact should not occasion surprise. For all their diversity, arthropods of any type share two defining characteristics: jointed legs (from which the phylum takes its name) and an exoskeleton (the recognizable hard outer shell).

2 → Though the shell itself is made of dead tissue like that of human hair and fingernails, it is dotted with sensory cells. These give the arthropod information about its surroundings, much as the nerve endings in human skin do. Also like human skin, the shell protects fragile internal organs from potentially hazardous contact with the environment. It seals in precious moisture that would otherwise evaporate but permits the exchange of gases.

3 Its primary component is chitin, a natural polymer that contains calcium and is very similar in structure to the cellulose in wood. Chitin and proteins are secreted in the epidermis, the living tissue just below the shell, after which they bond to form a thin sheet. Each new sheet is produced so that its chitin fibers are not parallel with those directly above, which increases their combined strength.

4 The result is the endocuticle, a mesh of molecules that forms the lowest layer of the shell. The endocuticle

TOEFL Reading

PAUSE TEST   SECTION EXIT

Question 3 of 12

REVIEW GT   HELP ?   BACK   NEXT

HIDE TIME   00:08:45

More Available

is not quite tough enough for daily wear and tear. Over time, however, its molecules continue to lock together. As the endocuticle is pushed upward by the formation of new sheets by the epidermis, it becomes the middle shell layer called the exocuticle. With its molecules bonded so tightly, the exocuticle is very durable. There are points on the body where it does not form, since flexibility is needed around joints. This arrangement allows supple movement but provides armor-like protection.

5 Though strong, the chitin and protein exocuticle itself would provide a poor barrier against moisture loss. Therefore, it must be coated with lipids, which are also secreted by the epidermis. These lipids, mostly fatty acids and waxes, form the third, outermost layer of the shell. They spread over the cuticles to form a waterproof seal even in dry weather. This lipid layer gives many arthropods their distinctive luster.

6 Combined, the endocuticle, exocuticle, and lipid coating form a shell that provides formidable protection. The external shell has other advantages. One is that, because it has far more surface area than the internal skeleton found in vertebrates, it provides more points at which muscles can be attached. This increased number of muscles permits many arthropods to be stronger and more agile for their body size than birds or mammals. The coloration and markings of the exoskeleton can be beneficial as well. Many species of scorpion, for instance, have cuticles that contain hyaline. The

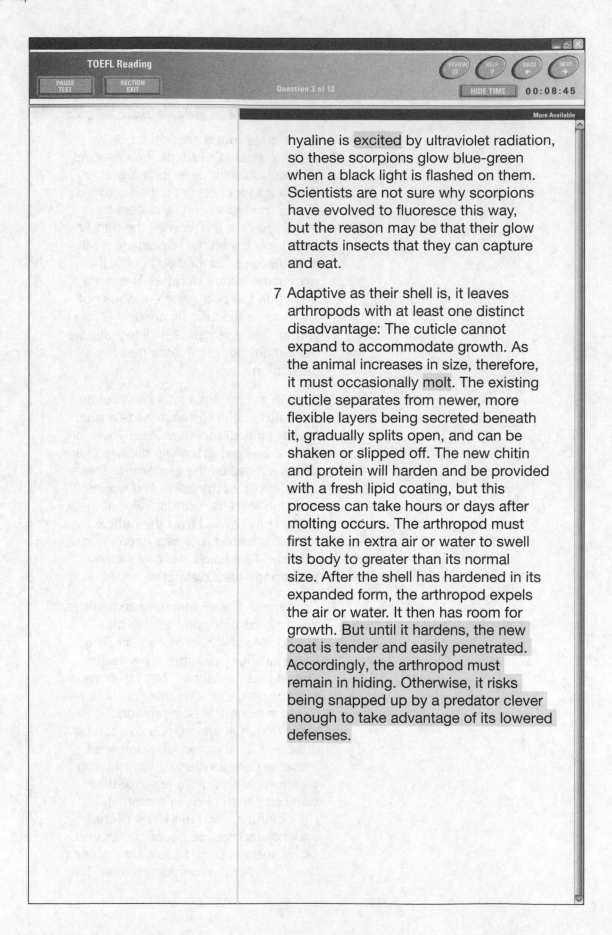

TOEFL Reading

Question 3 of 12

PAUSE TEST

SECTION EXIT

REVIEW

HELP ?

BACK

NEXT

HIDE TIME

00:08:45

More Available

hyaline is excited by ultraviolet radiation, so these scorpions glow blue-green when a black light is flashed on them. Scientists are not sure why scorpions have evolved to fluoresce this way, but the reason may be that their glow attracts insects that they can capture and eat.

7 Adaptive as their shell is, it leaves arthropods with at least one distinct disadvantage: The cuticle cannot expand to accommodate growth. As the animal increases in size, therefore, it must occasionally molt. The existing cuticle separates from newer, more flexible layers being secreted beneath it, gradually splits open, and can be shaken or slipped off. The new chitin and protein will harden and be provided with a fresh lipid coating, but this process can take hours or days after molting occurs. The arthropod must first take in extra air or water to swell its body to greater than its normal size. After the shell has hardened in its expanded form, the arthropod expels the air or water. It then has room for growth. But until it hardens, the new coat is tender and easily penetrated. Accordingly, the arthropod must remain in hiding. Otherwise, it risks being snapped up by a predator clever enough to take advantage of its lowered defenses.

Now that you've had a minute to look over this passage, state the main idea. What is the author's purpose, and how is the passage structured?

Main idea: _____

_____

Structure: _____

_____

Purpose: _____

_____

For this passage, the main idea is "arthropods have a tough outer shell that protects them and provides them with other advantages." The structure is fairly typical, with each of the body paragraphs describing some aspect of the shell. Paragraph 2 (the first body paragraph—remember, Paragraph 1 was your Introduction) describes the shell itself and its functions. Paragraphs 3 and 4 describe the endocuticle and the exocuticle, the first two layers of the shell. Paragraph 5 describes the outer lipid layer of the shell. Paragraphs 6 and 7 present the advantages and one disadvantage of the shell. Putting this all together, you can determine that the author's purpose is to inform.

If you had trouble coming up with these answers, be sure to review Chapter 2, Core Concept: Reading.

Step 2: Attack the Questions

After actively reading the passage, go to the questions.

Generally, the questions are arranged in rough chronological order. This means that early questions will be answered in the first few paragraphs, and later questions will be answered further down in the passage. The questions on the TOEFL come in a few different varieties.

Most of the questions are multiple choice, such as those shown below. Unless otherwise noted, questions will ask for the one "best" answer.

11. Why is an arthropod vulnerable after molting?

   a. It is far from sources of water.
   b. It is more visible to predators.
   c. Its shell is soft.
   d. The loss of energy makes it weak.

Other questions require you to click on part of the passage. These questions look like the following:

> 15. Look at the four squares [■] in the passage. Where would the following sentence best fit in the passage? Click on the [■] to add the sentence to the passage.

For these questions, you'll have to go back to the passage and click on one of the squares to answer it. Other questions of this variety may ask you to click on a word or phrase. Again, unless otherwise noted, questions will ask for the one "best" answer.

The final type of question is multiple-multiple-choice questions. These questions require you to choose several correct answers.

> 20. A brief summary of the passage is provided below. Click on the THREE sentences that best complete the summary. Some sentences are not part of the summary because they do not express the main idea. *This question is worth 2 points.*

These questions are followed by several sentences. To choose a sentence, click on it and then use the mouse to drag the sentences you select into the summary box. You can remove one of your choices by clicking on it again.

In general, the multiple-choice questions are the easiest. You should do them on your first pass. The summary questions—the multiple-multiple-choice ones—take the longest, so save them for last. (They usually turn up at the end anyway.) The passage-based questions fall somewhere in between these two.

Question Types

The questions on the Reading section of the TOEFL can be grouped into several different categories. Each question requires its own strategy, but remember that for each question, the answer is somewhere in the passage. Also, some questions are much more common than others, so you may not see all of the following types when you take the TOEFL.

The question types on the TOEFL are as follows:

1. **Vocabulary in context:** These are some of the most common questions on the TOEFL. You may be asked the meaning of a word or phrase. These questions are some of the easiest, so do them on your first pass.

2. **Reference:** These questions usually ask you what noun a pronoun connects to, though sometimes they may ask you about a noun, adverb, or adjective. Because these questions also direct you to a certain point in the passage, do these on your first pass.

3. **Lead words:** Some questions refer to a word highlighted in gray in the passage. Other questions may ask about a specific word or phrase, even if there is nothing highlighted in the passage. Also do these on your first pass.

4. **Paraphrase:** Paraphrase questions ask you to find the answer choice that means the same as a bolded sentence in the passage. Do these on your first pass.

5. **Definition:** This type of question asks you to find the part of the passage that defines a certain word or phrase. Do these on your first pass, too.

6. **Before/after:** These questions are rare. They ask you what kind of paragraph would likely precede or follow the passage. If you encounter one of these, you may want to do it on your second pass.

7. **Sentence insertion:** For this type of question, you'll see four black squares [■] placed throughout the passage. Your job is to figure out in which of these spots a given new sentence would best fit. Do these on the second pass.

8. **EXCEPT/NOT/LEAST:** These questions can be some of the most difficult on the test so save them for the second pass. For these, you are looking for the answer that is *not* supported by the passage.
   EXCEPT/NOT/LEAST questions also tend to take longer to answer than most multiple-choice questions.

9. **Inference:** This popular question type can be one of the trickiest types; therefore, you should save these questions for the second pass. Inference questions ask you to find the statement that is implied or suggested by the passage. Remember, the TOEFL uses a narrow interpretation of *inference*, and correct responses to these questions *must be true* based on the information provided in the passage.

10. **Main Point/Primary Purpose/Summary:** These questions ask you to find the main point(s) and idea(s) from the passage. Some questions ask you to find one main point or idea and are worth one point. Others may ask you to select two to four main points or ideas and are worth two points. Regardless of how many points you're asked to identify, they require knowledge of the passage as a whole. So, do them on your second pass.

Familiarize yourself with this list. As you'll see, being able to recognize the question types will aid you in both your approach to finding the answer and your POE strategy.

STEP 3 » Step 3: Find the Answer in the Passage and Use POE

As we've stated before—and it cannot be emphasized enough—the correct answer to each Reading question is *always* found in the passage. The trick on the TOEFL is, of course, finding that answer in an efficient manner. Fortunately, each question provides a clue, or hint, as to where we need to look for our answer.

Here is our general system for dealing with questions on the TOEFL.

Proven Techniques

1. **Read and rephrase the question.** You'll notice that many questions on the TOEFL are not written in a straightforward manner. Before you head back to the passage to find the answer, make sure you understand what the question is asking you to find.
2. **Go back to the passage and find the answer.** The question will usually direct you to the appropriate part of the passage. Go back to the passage and read 3 to 5 lines above and below the reference point to get the context of the text. Essentially, you are looking for a "window" in the passage where the answer will be. Never answer a question from memory alone because you're more likely to fall for a trap answer.
3. **Identify *exactly* what the passage says.** This is the most important step of all. After returning to the passage and reading the appropriate part of it, you should be able find exactly what the passage says. Sometimes, it's easier to put it into your own words, but make sure that your answer is as close as you can make it to what the passage says. If you can't find the answer or put it into your own words, you may be reading the wrong part of the passage or you may need to read more lines. If you are having a hard time doing this in the beginning, don't worry. Keep practicing it!
4. **Use POE.** Once you have an idea of what the passage says, return to the question and use POE: eliminate answers that don't match the passage.

Make sure to practice this system on each question until it becomes automatic. The best way to approach the TOEFL is to have a clear, consistent plan of attack.

PUTTING IT ALL TOGETHER

Now, let's return to our earlier passage and work through the questions, one of each type. We'll go through the steps and talk about the best way to find the correct response. Then you can try the process on your own with the drills in the next chapter.

The Exoskeleton of the Arthropod

1 There are more arthropods alive on Earth than there are members of any other phylum of animals. Given that not only insects and spiders but also shrimp, crabs, centipedes, and their numerous relatives are arthropods, this fact should not occasion surprise. For all their diversity, arthropods of any type share two defining characteristics: jointed legs (from which the phylum takes its name) and an exoskeleton (the recognizable hard outer shell).

2 Though the shell itself is made of dead tissue like that of human hair and fingernails, it is dotted with sensory cells. These give the arthropod information about its surroundings, much as the nerve endings in human skin do. Also like human skin, the shell protects fragile internal organs from

potentially hazardous contact with the environment. It seals in precious moisture that would otherwise evaporate but permits the exchange of gases.

3 Its primary component is chitin, a natural polymer that contains calcium and is very similar in structure to the cellulose in wood. Chitin and proteins are secreted in the epidermis, the living tissue just below the shell, after which they bond to form a thin sheet. Each new sheet is produced so that its chitin fibers are not parallel with those directly above, which increases their combined strength.

4 The result is the endocuticle, a mesh of molecules that forms the lowest layer of the shell. The endocuticle is not quite tough enough for daily wear and tear. Over time, however, its molecules continue to lock together. As the endocuticle is pushed upward by the formation of new sheets by the epidermis, it becomes the middle shell layer called the exocuticle. With its molecules bonded so tightly, the exocuticle is very durable. There are points on the body where it does not form, since flexibility is needed around joints. This arrangement allows supple movement but provides armor-like protection.

5 Though strong, the chitin and protein exocuticle itself would provide a poor barrier against moisture loss. Therefore, it must be coated with lipids, which are also secreted by the epidermis. These lipids, mostly fatty acids and waxes, form the third, outermost layer of the shell. They spread over the cuticles to form a waterproof seal even in dry weather. This lipid layer gives many arthropods their distinctive luster.

6 Combined, the endocuticle, exocuticle, and lipid coating form a shell that provides formidable protection. The external shell has other advantages. One is that, because it has far more surface area than the internal skeleton found in vertebrates, it provides more points at which muscles can be attached. This increased number of muscles permits many arthropods to be stronger and more agile for their body size than birds or mammals. The coloration and markings of the exoskeleton can be beneficial as well. Many species of scorpion, for instance, have cuticles that contain hyaline. The hyaline is excited by ultraviolet radiation, so these scorpions glow blue-green when a black light is flashed on them. Scientists are not sure why scorpions have evolved to fluoresce this way, but the reason may be that their glow attracts insects that they can capture and eat.

7 Adaptive as their shell is, it leaves arthropods with at least one distinct disadvantage: The cuticle cannot expand to accommodate growth. As the animal increases in size, therefore, it must occasionally molt. The existing cuticle separates from newer, more flexible layers being secreted beneath it, gradually splits open, and can be shaken or slipped off. The new chitin and protein will harden and be provided with a fresh lipid coating, but this process can take hours or days after molting occurs. The arthropod must first take in extra air or water to swell its body to greater than its normal size. After the shell has hardened in its expanded form, the arthropod expels the air or water. It then has room for growth. But until it hardens, the new coat is tender and easily penetrated. Accordingly, the arthropod must remain in hiding. Otherwise, it risks being snapped up by a predator clever enough to take advantage of its lowered defenses.

Remember, before going to the questions, take a moment to identify the main idea, purpose, and general structure. But don't spend too much time doing this (no more than two minutes)! If you're having trouble finding the main idea or purpose, go to the questions. Ready?

Question Type #1: Vocabulary in Context Questions

Here's our first question.

1. The word occasion in the passage is closest in meaning to:

    a. multiply
    b. cause
    c. demonstrate
    d. limit

First, identify the question type. This is a **vocabulary in context** question, one of the easiest and most common question types on the TOEFL. You can identify them because they ask for the meaning or definition of a word, typically shaded in gray, in the passage.

Now that we've identified what type of question it is, let's rephrase the question to make sure we know what it's asking. Generally, when rephrasing, try to rethink the question using the words *what* or *why*. For example, this question is basically asking us:

What does the word *occasion* mean in the passage?

You may want to jot down your rephrased version of the question on your scrap paper. Even if you don't, it is important to make sure you know exactly what it is you're looking for when you return to the passage.

For a vocabulary in context question, we'll first go back to the passage and read a few lines before and after the word in question. As you read, pretend that you crossed the word out in the passage.

There are more arthropods alive on Earth than there are members of any other phylum of animals. Given that not only insects and spiders but also shrimp, crabs, centipedes, and their numerous relatives are arthropods, this fact should not occasion surprise. For all their diversity, arthropods of any type share two defining characteristics: jointed legs (from which the phylum takes its name) and an exoskeleton (the recognizable hard outer shell).

Next look at the word in question and replace it with your own word. Usually, the sentence itself or the surrounding sentences will give you a clue as to the meaning of the word. In this case, the line says that the "fact should not _____ surprise." Look at the first sentence, which tells us that there are "more arthropods alive…than there are members of any other phylum." And after that, the passage states that "given that…are arthropods."

The context clues are that there a lot of these arthropods and that we shouldn't be surprised. So when answering in your own words, you may think that *occasion* means to "cause" or "lead to." Once we've come up with our own answer, we can return to the choices and use POE. We need a word that means "lead to" or "cause." Be sure to ask yourself "Who or what is the sentence talking about? What is it saying?" This will give you insight about what word you should put in the "blank" that you created when you pretended to cross the word out.

1. The word occasion in the passage is closest in meaning to:

    a. multiply
    b. cause
    c. demonstrate
    d. limit

> **Grammar point!**
> Whenever you see ellipses (…) in English, it can mean two things. If they are at the end of a sentence, the author has not finished her thought. If they are in the middle of a quote, they are used to represent the whole quote without having to write every word in the passage.

Let's evaluate our choices. Ask yourself whether the answer matches what the passage said or your paraphrase.

*   Does (A) mean "lead to" or "cause"? No. *Multiply* means to increase the amount of something. Cross it out.
*   Does (B) mean "lead to" or "cause"? Yes! Sometimes one of the answer choices will be exactly your word! But, just to be safe, check the other answers, too.
*   Does (C) mean "lead to" or "cause"? No —*demonstrate* means "to show" or "present."
*   Does (D) mean "lead to" or "cause"? No. *Limit* means "to confine" or "restrict."

POE Strategies for Vocabulary in Context Questions

The previous question may have been easy for you, or it may have been fairly difficult. If it was easy, chances are you were comfortable with the words. If you had a hard time, you probably didn't know all the words.

Even if you don't know all of the words in a vocabulary in context question, there are still some steps you can take to help increase your chances of getting the question correct. Let's look at the POE strategies we can use to answer this next question.

4. The word hazardous in the passage is closest in meaning to:

    a. frequent
    b. perilous
    c. outer
    d. unpredictable

Here's the text from the passage.

> These give the arthropod information about its surroundings, much as the nerve endings in human skin do. Also like human skin, the shell protects fragile internal organs from potentially hazardous contact with the environment. It seals in precious moisture that would otherwise evaporate but permits the exchange of gases.

A few things may affect your ability to answer this question. First, you may have trouble making sense of the lines in the passage. Second, you may not be confident about each of the words in the answer choices.

In either of these cases, your strategy is the same. Pick a word from the answers with which you are familiar. Let's start with "frequent," which means "happening often." If this is the correct answer, there should be a word or phrase in these lines that means something similar to "happening often." However, none of the words in the passage has anything to do with "frequent" or "happening often." Therefore, we can eliminate (A).

You can repeat this strategy for the other words with which you are confident. As we've said before, the right answer is supported by the passage. You should be able to match your answer to a word or phrase from the passage. If you can't, it's not the right answer.

For this question, the correct answer is (B). The sentence tells us that the "shell protects... organs...." Therefore, "hazardous" must mean "something to protect against." Neither (C) nor (D) is close to this meaning. One mistake many students make is eliminating answers just because they don't know what the words mean. Instead, be sure to put a '?'.

Vocabulary in Context Questions Summary

For vocabulary in context questions, do the following:

1. **Go back to the passage** and read a few lines before and after the word in question.
2. **Come up with your own word** for the shaded word based on the clues in the sentences.
3. **Return to the answer choices and eliminate** any choices that
   - are not supported by any words or phrases from the passage; and
   - are dictionary definitions of the word, but are incorrect in the context of the passage.

Question Type #2: Reference Questions

Now let's move on to the next type of question.

6. The phrase This arrangement in the passage refers to:

    a. the low number of joints on an arthropod
    b. the absence of the exocuticle on certain parts of the body
    c. the toughness of the exocuticle
    d. the composition of the lipid coating

This question looks similar to a vocabulary in context question. The difference, however, is that this question asks us not what the phrase *means,* but what it *refers to.* If we rephrase the question, it would look something like this:

What does the phrase *This arrangement* refer to?

If you want to write this down on your scratch paper, you might note: this arrangement refers to _____. This type of question is called a **reference** question. Our strategy for solving reference questions is similar to that for vocabulary in context questions. For reference questions, however, we want to focus on the lines *before* the phrase or word because the reference cannot be after the phrase.

Here are the lines we need to work with.

As the endocuticle is pushed upward by the formation of new sheets by the epidermis, it becomes the middle shell layer called the exocuticle. With its molecules bonded so tightly, the exocuticle is very durable. There are points on the body where it does not form, since flexibility is needed around joints. This arrangement allows supple movement but provides armor-like protection.

For a reference question, it is important to understand how authors use phrases in their writing to mean certain things. An author must fully explain a concept before he or she can then refer to that idea with a shorthand such as "this arrangement." Otherwise, the reader will have no idea what the author is writing about.

Thus, for a reference question, find the noun that appears before the reference. Look at the sentence before the reference.

There are points on the body where it does not form, since flexibility is needed around joints.

The answer to our question should be found in this sentence. What's the noun in this sentence? The most specific one is *points on the body where it does not form.* This is probably the one we're looking for. Let's return to the answer choices and use POE.

6. The phrase This arrangement in the passage refers to:

    a. the low number of joints on an arthropod
    b. the absence of the exocuticle on certain parts of the body
    c. the toughness of the exocuticle
    d. the composition of the lipid coating

We're looking for an answer that is close to *points on the body where it does not form*. By the way, because we're using POE, we are not especially concerned about what the thing is that we are looking for. We're just seeking to locate the item that "this arrangement" is shorthand for. We're also not going to worry about fancy terms such as *exocuticle*. So, let's look at the answer choices.

- Start with (A). This choice mentions the *low number of joints*. Does this match *points on the body where it does not form*? No.
- Choice (B) seems to match *points on the body where it does not form*. It mentions the *absence...on certain parts of the body*. Notice how that answer is very similar to "points on the *body* where it *does not form*." Still, check the remaining choices as well.
- Choice (C) may seem to match, but notice that the toughness is mentioned not in the sentence before the shaded phrase, but two sentences away. It is very rare for an author to place the referent so far away from the shorthand reference. Therefore, eliminate this choice.
- Finally we come to (D). Notice that (D) mentions the *lipid coating*. Does this match? Well, the lipid coating doesn't show up until later, so no. That means (D) can't be correct.

Therefore, (B) is the best answer.

POE Strategies for Reference Questions

Reference questions have clear POE guidelines. Eliminate answers that:

- mention words or phrases that show up only *after* the reference
- use words or phrases that are not mentioned at all in the two or three sentences before the reference

As long as you follow these two guidelines, reference questions should be fairly easy.

Question Type #3: Lead Word Questions

Here is the next question type.

5. The layer of the shell called the exocuticle is strong because:
    a. its molecules are closely bonded
    b. it is drier than the endocuticle
    c. its fibers are parallel
    d. it is water-resistant

Our first task is to rephrase the question. Remember to try to use "what" or "why." For this question, our rephrasing may say

Why is the exocuticle strong?

We call this a **lead word** question. A question of this sort has a word or phrase that will *lead* you to the right answer. For lead words, pick the most specific part of the question. Your lead word should also be something that you will have an easy time spotting in the passage. For this question, our lead word is *exocuticle*. It's easy to find in the passage, and it's the most specific part of the question. Once we find the lead word, we'll read a few lines before and after it.

Here's the text on which we need to focus.

> With its molecules bonded so tightly, the exocuticle is very durable. There are points on the body where it does not form, since flexibility is needed around joints. This arrangement allows supple movement but provides armor-like protection.

When looking for lead words, there are a couple of things to keep in mind. First, the questions are arranged in a rough chronological order. That means the early questions refer to earlier parts of the passage, whereas later questions refer to later parts. Use the question number to give yourself a rough idea of where to look for the lead word.

Second, when looking for lead words, always look for the first instance of the word. Some words may show up more than once in the passage. Start with the first appearance. If you are unable to answer the question in your own words, move on to the next mention of the lead word.

In this case, it looks like we're in the right section of the passage. Look for what the passage says about the exocuticle. According to the passage, the exocuticle is "durable" because "its molecules" are "bonded so tightly." This appears to be what we need. Let's look at the question again.

5. The layer of the shell called the exocuticle is strong because:
   a.   its molecules are closely bonded
   b.   it is drier than the endocuticle
   c.   its fibers are parallel
   d.   it is water-resistant

Now, let's consider each answer choice. Remember to eliminate answers that don't match up with "durable" or "bonded so tightly."

- Choice (A) seems to match very nicely. Still, we should check the remaining choices.
- Choice (B) states the reason the exocuticle is strong is because it is drier than the endocuticle. This does not match what is stated in the passage, so it must be wrong.
- Choice (C) states that the exocuticle's strength is due to parallel fibers. This is a trap answer. According to the passage, each sheet of the shell is formed so that its *chitin fibers are not parallel with those directly above*. If you fell for this choice, you probably tried to answer from memory. *Always* return to the passage to verify your answer.
- The same reasoning from (C) applies to (D). According to the passage, it is the lipids that are water-resistant, not the exocuticle.

Thus, our answer is (A).

POE Strategies for Lead Word Questions

You may have noticed that some of the wrong answers on lead word questions contain words or phrases found throughout the passage. There are a couple of reasons for this. First, if you are trying to answer the question from memory, you are likely to pick one of these choices because it contains words or phrases you may remember having read. Second, on the TOEFL, it is actually a *disadvantage* to try to read and understand everything in the passage. But many students still try to comprehend everything. This makes them more likely to become confused about what they've read and choose one of these trap answers.

Thus, on lead word questions, you should focus on only a small part of the passage, no more than four to five lines. Try to match words or phrases from the answer choices with the lines that you are studying. Eliminate any choices that

- contain words or phrases not mentioned in the lines close to the lead word or detail
- mention words or phrases that show up in the passage, but are beyond the four-to-five-line range

On the TOEFL, the correct answers to lead word and detail questions are generally within four to six lines of the lead word or detail, so if you're stuck, these are safe guidelines to follow.

Quick Review: Vocabulary in Context, Reference, and Lead Word Questions

These questions tend to be easier than the others. Make sure you find and do all of these questions in your first pass. As you may have noticed, there is a pattern. In each case, the question referred to a specific part of the passage. The answer to the question was found within four to five lines of the part of the passage referred to in the question. Thus, let's summarize our strategy:

1. Rephrase the question. Remember to ask What? or Why?
2. Use clues in the question to find the appropriate place in the passage.
3. Read a few lines before and after the lead word or reference.
4. Identify exactly what the passage says; if you can't, state the answer to the question in your own words.

The wrong answers to these questions also follow a very similar pattern. Make sure to eliminate answers that are

- not mentioned in the passage at all
- mentioned in the passage, but beyond the specific lines needed to answer the question

Let's continue our discussion of question types. Here's our passage again.

The Exoskeleton of the Arthropod

1 There are more arthropods alive on Earth than there are members of any other phylum of animals. Given that not only insects and spiders but also shrimp, crabs, centipedes, and their numerous relatives are arthropods, this fact should not occasion surprise. For all their diversity, arthropods of any type share two defining characteristics: jointed legs (from which the phylum takes its name) and an exoskeleton (the recognizable hard outer shell).

2 Though the shell itself is made of dead tissue like that of human hair and fingernails, it is dotted with sensory cells. **These give the arthropod information about its surroundings, much as the nerve endings in human skin do.** Also like human skin, the shell protects fragile internal organs from potentially hazardous contact with the environment. It seals in precious moisture that would otherwise evaporate but permits the exchange of gases.

3 **Its primary component is chitin, a natural polymer that contains calcium and is very similar in structure to the cellulose in wood.** Chitin and proteins are secreted in the epidermis, the living tissue just below the shell, after which they bond to form a thin sheet. Each new sheet is produced so that its chitin fibers are not parallel with those directly above, which increases their combined strength.

4 The result is the endocuticle, a mesh of molecules that forms the lowest layer of the shell. The endocuticle is not quite tough enough for daily wear and tear. Over time, however, its molecules continue to lock together. As the endocuticle is pushed upward by the formation of new sheets by the epidermis, it becomes the middle shell layer called the exocuticle. With its molecules bonded so tightly, the exocuticle is very durable. There are points on the body where it does not form, since flexibility is needed around joints. This arrangement allows supple movement but provides armor-like protection.

5 Though strong, the chitin and protein exocuticle itself would provide a poor barrier against moisture loss. Therefore, it must be coated with lipids, which are also secreted by the epidermis. These lipids, mostly fatty acids and waxes, form the third, outermost layer of the shell. They spread over the cuticles to form a waterproof seal even in dry weather. This lipid layer gives many arthropods their distinctive luster.

6 **Combined, the endocuticle, exocuticle, and lipid coating form a shell that provides formidable protection.** The external shell has other advantages. One is that, because it has far more surface area than the internal skeleton found in vertebrates, it provides more points at which muscles can be attached. This increased number of muscles permits many arthropods to be stronger and more agile for their body size than birds or mammals. The coloration and markings of the exoskeleton can be beneficial as well. **Many species of scorpion, for instance, have cuticles that contain hyaline.** The hyaline is excited by ultraviolet radiation, so these scorpions glow blue-green when a black light is flashed on them. Scientists are not sure why scorpions have evolved to fluoresce this way, but the reason may be that their glow attracts insects that they can capture and eat.

7 Adaptive as their shell is, it leaves arthropods with at least one distinct disadvantage: The cuticle cannot expand to accommodate growth. As the animal increases in size, therefore, it must occasionally molt. The existing cuticle separates from newer, more flexible layers being secreted beneath it, gradually splits open, and can be shaken or slipped off. The new chitin and protein will harden and be provided with a fresh lipid coating, but this process can take hours or days after molting occurs. The arthropod must first take in extra air or water to swell its body to greater than its normal size. After the shell has hardened in its expanded form, the arthropod expels the air or water. It then has room for growth. But until it hardens, the new coat is tender and easily penetrated. Accordingly, the arthropod must remain in hiding. Otherwise, it risks being snapped up by a predator clever enough to take advantage of its lowered defenses.

Question Type #4: Paraphrase Questions

Our next group of questions deals with the passage and its structure. Here's one example.

9. Which of the following choices best expresses the essential meaning of the highlighted sentences in paragraph 7? Incorrect choices will change the meaning or leave out important details.

 a. Arthropods are vulnerable to predators only during the period in which their shell is tender and easily penetrated.
 b. Predators typically prefer to eat arthropods that are waiting for their new coats to harden.
 c. While the arthropod's shell is hardening, the arthropod cannot rely on its shell to protect it from predators.
 d. When the arthropod's defenses are lowered, it will use many different strategies to avoid predators.

This type of question is a **paraphrase** question. We usually won't have to rephrase these questions. Instead, we have to worry more about rephrasing the shaded portion of the passage. Let's take a look at the lines in question to see what the passage says.

But until it hardens, the new coat is tender and easily penetrated. Accordingly, the arthropod must remain in hiding. Otherwise, it risks being snapped up by a predator clever enough to take advantage of its lowered defenses.

See our section on "Trim the fat!" on page 90.

When paraphrasing, you need to *find the essential information*. Thus, trim the fat. Get rid of unnecessary modifiers and descriptive phrases (remember, modifiers and descriptive phrases simply tell you more information about the subject). Look for the subject and the main verb of the sentence or sentences in question. For example, let's break down the sentences into their most basic parts.

1. ~~But until it hardens~~, the new coat is tender and easily penetrated.

The subject here is *new coat*, and the important thing about it is that it's *tender* and *easily penetrated*. Cut out the phrase *but until it hardens*, which is a modifier.

2. ~~Accordingly~~, the arthropod must remain in hiding.

The subject of this sentence is *arthropod*, and the verb is *must remain in hiding*. Cut the rest.

3. ~~Otherwise~~, it risks being snapped up by a predator ~~clever enough to take advantage of its lowered defenses~~.

The important parts here are *it* (the arthropod) *risks being snapped up by a predator*.

Now, our job is to find the answer choice that contains these elements and these elements only. Here are the choices again.

a. Arthropods are vulnerable to predators only during the period in which their shell is tender and easily penetrated.
b. Predators typically prefer to eat arthropods that are waiting for their new coats to harden.
c. While the arthropod's shell is hardening, the arthropod cannot rely on its shell to protect it from predators.
d. When the arthropod's defenses are lowered, it will use many different strategies to avoid predators.

Let's consider each choice.

- Start with (A). It does mention *arthropods* and *predators*, which is good. However, we are missing some information. There is no mention of *hiding*, one of our key elements. Also, (A) states that arthropods are "vulnerable...only during this period...." That is beyond the information in the passage. Eliminate (A).
- Choice (B) is problematic because it makes *predators* the subject. We should have something that talks about arthropods. Eliminate this choice.
- Now look at (C). It first mentions the weakened shell, which matches with sentence 1. Next, it says the arthropod "cannot rely on its shell." At first this doesn't seem to match, but sentence 2 states that the creature "must remain in hiding"—this is an example of "not relying on its shell." Finally, the choice mentions the predators from sentence 3. Everything matches, so keep this choice.
- Choice (D) is close, but it has one big problem. It mentions "many different strategies," whereas the passage mentions only one. We don't want any choice that adds information, so eliminate (D).

That leaves (C) as the best answer.

POE Strategies for Paraphrase Questions

If you're having trouble paraphrasing the sentence in question, the easiest POE strategy is to eliminate any answers that introduce new information. These choices will always be *wrong*. Another good strategy is to try to identify the subject of the sentence. One of the choices will usually have a different subject. Eliminate this choice.

Question Type #5: Definition Questions

Let's look at another type of question.

> 2. Click on the boldface sentence in the passage in which the author gives a definition.

This is a **definition** question. It's asking you to find the sentence in the passage that includes a definition of another word. Once again, we don't have to rephrase this type of question. Go to the passage and look for the four sentences in boldface. Here they are.

1. These give the arthropod information about its surroundings, much as the nerve endings in human skin do.
2. Its primary component is chitin, a natural polymer that contains calcium and is very similar in structure to the cellulose in wood.
3. Combined, the endocuticle, exocuticle, and lipid coating form a shell that provides formidable protection.
4. Many species of scorpion, for instance, have cuticles that contain hyaline.

We need to paraphrase each one, looking for the sentence that clarifies the meaning of a word or phrase. Unfortunately, these questions are mostly based on your comprehension. If you are comfortable with the words in the sentences, then go ahead and answer the question. If you are having trouble understanding the sentences, skip the question.

In Chapter 2, Core Concept: Reading, we discussed "trimming the fat"—cutting out the nonessential information from the sentence. In a definition question, the definition will usually turn up in the "fat" part of the sentence. Thus, we need to separate the sentence into its different parts and examine them. For definition questions, follow the procedure below.

1. Find the subject, verb, and object.
2. Look at the other parts of the sentence.
3. See if the remaining parts define or clarify the subject, verb, or object.

For example, in sentence 1, the subject is *These*, and the main verb is *give*. The object is *information*. So, the sentence basically reads: These give information.

Now, examine the remaining parts of the sentence. First, we have the phrase *the arthropod*—does this define anything from the basic sentence? No. It only clarifies what is receiving the information. The next phrase is *about its surroundings*. This is not a definition; it is a prepositional phrase. The final part is "much as the nerve endings in human skin do." Does this refer back to the main sentence, defining something from it? No, it does not. Instead, it makes a comparison. Eliminate this choice.

Do the same for the second sentence. The second sentence breaks down as follows: Its component is chitin.

The first word we cut out was *primary*. This is an adjective, a modifier. It doesn't define anything. The rest of the sentence states "a natural polymer that contains calcium and is very similar in structure to the cellulose in wood." Could this define one of the terms from the main sentence? In fact, it does. It provides a definition of *chitin*. Thus, this is our answer.

POE Strategies for Definition Questions

As stated previously, your success on definition questions will be largely based on your comfort level with the sentences. If you're having a hard time figuring out the meaning of a sentence, keep the following in mind:

- Definitions frequently are introduced using the words *which, that,* or *means*. Look for sentences in which the author uses these words.
- Trim away prepositional phrases. These are phrases beginning with words such as *of, on,* and *in*. A definition will *not* be a prepositional phrase.
- Watch out for sentences that merely list or introduce examples. Remember, you need a phrase that tells you what a word or concept means, *not an example* of the word or concept.

Question Type #6: Before/After Questions

It's time to look at yet another type of question.

8. The paragraph following the passage would most logically continue with a discussion of:

   a. different strategies used by predators to capture arthropods
   b. non-arthropods that have protective shells
   c. the defense mechanisms of other types of animals
   d. adaptations arthropods make to survive during molting

Some questions ask about a hypothetical paragraph before or after the passage; thus, we call these **before/after** questions (note that *before* questions are very rare on the TOEFL). First, rephrase the question.

What would a paragraph after the passage discuss?

Or in other words, What might come next? To answer this type of question, we need to concern ourselves with only the last paragraph. Here it is again.

Adaptive as their shell is, it leaves arthropods with at least one distinct disadvantage: The cuticle cannot expand to accommodate growth. As the animal increases in size, therefore, it must occasionally molt. The existing cuticle separates from newer, more flexible layers being secreted beneath it, gradually splits open, and can be shaken or slipped off. The new chitin and protein will harden and be provided with a fresh lipid coating, but this process can take hours or days after molting occurs. The arthropod must first take in extra air or water to swell its body to greater than its normal size. After the shell has hardened in its expanded form, the arthropod expels the air or water. It then has room for growth. But until it hardens, the new coat is tender and easily penetrated. Accordingly, the arthropod must remain in hiding. Otherwise, it risks being snapped up by a predator clever enough to take advantage of its lowered defenses.

Use active reading strategies to figure out the basic meaning of the paragraph. The first sentence tells us that we will discuss a "disadvantage" of the shell. The body of the paragraph proceeds to give details about the disadvantage but, once again, we don't need to worry too much about these details. The author ends the paragraph by discussing how the arthropod is at a disadvantage while its defenses are lowered.

The correct answer to a before/after question will be related to the *main idea* of the paragraph. In our own words, this final paragraph is about a disadvantage of the shell and the arthropod's vulnerability.

Now use POE on the answer choices. What matches the last few sentences best?

- Choice (A) discusses the strategies of predators. But the final paragraph—in fact, the entire passage—is about arthropods. Thus, our answer should also be about arthropods. Eliminate this choice since it doesn't match the passage.
- Choice (B) has the same problem; it discusses non-arthropods, but our paragraph is specifically about arthropods. Again, it doesn't match, so (B) is wrong.
- Choice (C) mentions defense mechanisms, but once again it discusses other animals, not arthropods. That doesn't match, which means (C) is wrong as well.
- Finally, we're left with (D). This choice discusses both arthropods and their defenses when they lack shells ("adaptations…during molting"). That matches exactly what we need.

Choice (D) is our answer.

POE Strategies for Before/After Questions

The key to these questions is to stay as close as possible to the main idea of the first or last paragraph, depending on whether you are doing a before or an after question. Eliminate answer choices that do the following:

- **Introduce new information:** The right answer will match the topic of the paragraph. Get rid of any choices that bring in information not mentioned in the paragraph.
- **Interrupt the structure:** Make sure the topic in the answer choice doesn't appear elsewhere in the passage. The ideas in the passage should follow a logical order—don't return to a topic that's been discussed previously (as in after questions) or will be discussed later (as in before questions).
- **Repeat information:** The correct answer will be based on the paragraph, but will not repeat information that has already been mentioned.

Question Type #7: Sentence Insertion Questions

Now we'll look at another structure-based question. Here's the passage again, but notice the placement of four black squares (■).

The Exoskeleton of the Arthropod

1 There are more arthropods alive on Earth than there are members of any other phylum of animals. Given that not only insects and spiders but also shrimp, crabs, centipedes, and their numerous relatives are arthropods, this fact should not occasion surprise. For all their diversity, arthropods of any type share two defining characteristics: jointed legs (from which the phylum takes its name) and an exoskeleton (the recognizable hard outer shell).

2 Though the shell itself is made of dead tissue like that of human hair and fingernails, it is dotted with sensory cells. These give the arthropod information about its surroundings, much as the nerve endings in human skin do. Also like human skin, the shell protects fragile internal organs from potentially hazardous contact with the environment. It seals in precious moisture that would otherwise evaporate but permits the exchange of gases.

3 Its primary component is chitin, a natural polymer that contains calcium and is very similar in structure to the cellulose in wood. Chitin and proteins are secreted in the epidermis, the living tissue just below the shell, after which they bond to form a thin sheet. Each new sheet is produced so that its chitin fibers are not parallel with those directly above, which increases their combined strength.

4 The result is the endocuticle, a mesh of molecules that forms the lowest layer of the shell. The endocuticle is not quite tough enough for daily wear and tear. ■ Over time, however, its molecules continue to lock together. ■

As the endocuticle is pushed upward by the formation of new sheets by the epidermis, it becomes the middle shell layer called the exocuticle. ■ With its molecules bonded so tightly, the exocuticle is very durable. ■ There are points on the body where it does not form, since flexibility is needed around joints. This arrangement allows supple movement but provides armor-like protection.

5 Though strong, the chitin and protein exocuticle itself would provide a poor barrier against moisture loss. Therefore, it must be coated with lipids, which are also secreted by the epidermis. These lipids, mostly fatty acids and waxes, form the third, outermost layer of the shell. They spread over the cuticles to form a waterproof seal even in dry weather. This lipid layer gives many arthropods their distinctive luster.

6 Combined, the endocuticle, exocuticle, and lipid coating form a shell that provides formidable protection. The external shell has other advantages. One is that, because it has far more surface area than the internal skeleton found in vertebrates, it provides more points at which muscles can be attached. This increased number of muscles permits many arthropods to be stronger and more agile for their body size than birds or mammals. The coloration and markings of the exoskeleton can be beneficial as well. Many species of scorpion, for instance, have cuticles that contain hyaline. The hyaline is excited by ultraviolet radiation, so these scorpions glow blue-green when a black light is flashed on them. Scientists are not sure why scorpions have evolved to fluoresce this way, but the reason may be that their glow attracts insects that they can capture and eat.

7 Adaptive as their shell is, it leaves arthropods with at least one distinct disadvantage: The cuticle cannot expand to accommodate growth. As the animal increases in size, therefore, it must occasionally molt. The existing cuticle separates from newer, more flexible layers being secreted beneath it, gradually splits open, and can be shaken or slipped off. The new chitin and protein will harden and be provided with a fresh lipid coating, but this process can take hours or days after molting occurs. The arthropod must first take in extra air or water to swell its body to greater than its normal size. After the shell has hardened in its expanded form, the arthropod expels the air or water. It then has room for growth. But until it hardens, the new coat is tender and easily penetrated. Accordingly, the arthropod must remain in hiding. Otherwise, it risks being snapped up by a predator clever enough to take advantage of its lowered defenses.

The black squares in the fourth paragraph are used for **sentence insertion** questions. Here's an example.

4. Look at the four squares [■] that indicate where the following sentence could be added.

While this process continues, the endocuticle is gradually shifted.

Where would the sentence best fit?

To answer this type of question correctly, we need to look at the sentences before and after each black square. The correct answer will join these two sentences together by mentioning an idea from each sentence. Here are the sentences before and after the first black square.

> The endocuticle is not quite tough enough for daily wear and tear. ■ Over time, however, its molecules continue to lock together.

Our task is to try to match the sentence in the question with the ideas in these two sentences. The answer choice mentions a "process." Does this match with anything in these two sentences? It doesn't appear to do so. Let's look at the rest of the sentence in the answer. It also states that the "endocuticle is gradually shifted." Does this match with the details in these two sentences? Although we can match the word *endocuticle*, neither of the sentences discusses a "shift." Therefore, we can't place the sentence here.

Now, let's look at the second pair of sentences:

> Over time, however, its molecules continue to lock together. ■ As the endocuticle is pushed upward by the formation of new sheets by the epidermis, it becomes the middle shell layer called the exocuticle.

Now, we'll try to match our sentence with ideas from this pair of sentences. We need to find something that corresponds to "this process." The first sentence in the pair refers to "molecules... lock together." This seems like a process. Next, we want to match up the part of the sentence that talks about the endocuticle gradually shifting. The second sentence in the pair says "as the endocuticle is pushed upward...." This matches nicely with the "gradually shifting" part in the question. This looks like a likely place to add the new sentence.

Check the other two sentence pairs. Here's the third.

> As the endocuticle is pushed upward by the formation of new sheets by the epidermis, it becomes the middle shell layer called the exocuticle. ■ With its molecules bonded so tightly, the exocuticle is very durable.

The first sentence in this pair is a good match for the sentence we have to add because it mentions the "formation of new sheets," which seems like a process. However, the problem is the second sentence in the pair. This sentence mentions the *durability* of the exocuticle, which doesn't match with the shifting in the sentence we have to add. That makes this choice incorrect.

Finally, here's the fourth pair.

> With its molecules bonded so tightly, the exocuticle is very durable. ■ There are points on the body where it does not form, since flexibility is needed around joints.

In this case, it is clear that this pair of sentences does not match at all. The first sentence refers to the *exocuticle,* whereas the sentence we need to add is about the *endocuticle.* Furthermore, the second sentence in the pair is about places where there is no shell because flexibility is needed. These ideas are not part of the sentence we have to add. It looks as if the second black square is the best place to add the sentence, so your answer should look like this.

> Over time, however, its molecules continue to lock together. While this process continues, the endocuticle is gradually shifted. As the endocuticle is pushed upward by the formation of new sheets by the epidermis, it becomes the middle shell layer called the exocuticle.

Keep in mind that when you click the black square on the TOEFL, the sentence will appear in the passage. This will make it easier to look for matches.

POE Strategies for Sentence Insertion Questions

Much like other questions in the Reading section of the TOEFL, these questions are all about matching information. The best answer is simply the one that is the closest match to the information in the passage. When doing a sentence insertion question, eliminate choices that don't match or are only half right.

- **Doesn't match:** The sentence you add should form a link between two sentences. If the ideas in the paragraph don't match the ideas in the added sentence, eliminate that choice.
- **Half-right:** Make sure the added sentence matches ideas with *both* the sentence before and the sentence after it. Wrong answers often are only partial matches.

We've looked at several different question types. Let's pause for a brief review before we continue.

Quick Review: Paraphrase, Definition, Before/After, and Sentence Insertion Questions

All of these question types refer you to a specific part of the passage, which is typically highlighted or marked. So there is no difficulty in figuring out where in the passage the answer lies. The difficulty lies in finding the right answer. In general, when answering questions of this type, focus on the following POE guidelines:

- **Doesn't match:** This is one of the easiest ways to eliminate an answer choice. If the information in the choice doesn't match the passage, it's wrong.
- **New information:** Be very suspicious of answer choices that introduce new information. These choices are usually wrong.
- **Half-right:** Read each choice carefully because wrong answers will typically match only half of the information in the passage or answer choice. Make sure *all* the information corresponds.

Questions of this type can be a little more challenging than the question types we've looked at already. Try these questions only after answering the vocabulary in context, reference, lead word, and detail questions.

Question Type #8: EXCEPT/NOT/LEAST Questions

EXCEPT/NOT/LEAST questions tend to be one of the most difficult types of questions in the Reading section. Let's look at these questions and figure out how to crack them.

Once again, here's our practice passage for reference.

The Exoskeleton of the Arthropod

1 There are more arthropods alive on Earth than there are members of any other phylum of animals. Given that not only insects and spiders but also shrimp, crabs, centipedes, and their numerous relatives are arthropods, this fact should not occasion surprise. For all their diversity, arthropods of any type share two defining characteristics: jointed legs (from which the phylum takes its name) and an exoskeleton (the recognizable hard outer shell).

2 Though the shell itself is made of dead tissue like that of human hair and fingernails, it is dotted with sensory cells. These give the arthropod information about its surroundings, much as the nerve endings in human skin do. Also like human skin, the shell protects fragile internal organs from potentially hazardous contact with the environment. It seals in precious moisture that would otherwise evaporate but permits the exchange of gases.

3 Its primary component is chitin, a natural polymer that contains calcium and is very similar in structure to the cellulose in wood. Chitin and proteins are secreted in the epidermis, the living tissue just below the shell, after which they bond to form a thin sheet. Each new sheet is produced so that its chitin fibers are not parallel with those directly above, which increases their combined strength.

4 The result is the endocuticle, a mesh of molecules that forms the lowest layer of the shell. The endocuticle is not quite tough enough for daily wear and tear. Over time, however, its molecules continue to lock together. As the endocuticle is pushed upward by the formation of new sheets by the epidermis, it becomes the middle shell layer called the exocuticle. With its molecules bonded so tightly, the exocuticle is very durable. There are points on the body where it does not form, since flexibility is needed around joints. This arrangement allows supple movement but provides armor-like protection.

5 Though strong, the chitin and protein exocuticle itself would provide a poor barrier against moisture loss. Therefore, it must be coated with lipids, which are also secreted by the epidermis. These lipids, mostly fatty acids and waxes, form the third, outermost layer of the shell. They spread over the cuticles to form a waterproof seal even in dry weather. This lipid layer gives many arthropods their distinctive luster.

6 Combined, the endocuticle, exocuticle, and lipid coating form a shell that provides formidable protection. The external shell has other advantages. One is that, because it has far more surface area than the internal skeleton found in vertebrates, it provides more points at which muscles can be attached. This increased number of muscles permits many arthropods to be stronger and more agile for their body size than birds or mammals. The coloration

and markings of the exoskeleton can be beneficial as well. Many species of scorpion, for instance, have cuticles that contain hyaline. The hyaline is excited by ultraviolet radiation, so these scorpions glow blue-green when a black light is flashed on them. Scientists are not sure why scorpions have evolved to fluoresce this way, but the reason may be that their glow attracts insects that they can capture and eat.

7 Adaptive as their shell is, it leaves arthropods with at least one distinct disadvantage: The cuticle cannot expand to accommodate growth. As the animal increases in size, therefore, it must occasionally molt. The existing cuticle separates from newer, more flexible layers being secreted beneath it, gradually splits open, and can be shaken or slipped off. The new chitin and protein will harden and be provided with a fresh lipid coating, but this process can take hours or days after molting occurs. The arthropod must first take in extra air or water to swell its body to greater than its normal size. After the shell has hardened in its expanded form, the arthropod expels the air or water. It then has room for growth. But until it hardens, the new coat is tender and easily penetrated. Accordingly, the arthropod must remain in hiding. Otherwise, it risks being snapped up by a predator clever enough to take advantage of its lowered defenses.

Now, take a look at a new type of question.

6. All of the following are mentioned as benefits of the exoskeleton EXCEPT:

   a. protection against water loss
   b. distinctive coloration and markings
   c. ability to take in extra air or water
   d. armor-like protection

You'll notice this question has the word EXCEPT written in capital letters. Yet, test takers still often look for the "right" answer. For EXCEPT/NOT/LEAST questions, your task is to find the answer that is *not* mentioned. Here's how:

1. Rephrase the question, eliminating the EXCEPT/NOT/LEAST part.
2. Use the answer choices like a checklist, returning to the passage to find each one.
3. Mark each answer choice as either TRUE or FALSE based on the passage.
4. Choose the answer that's different from the other three.

Here's how it works. First, we'll rephrase the question, removing the EXCEPT part. Our new question asks

What are the benefits of an exoskeleton?

Now, we'll go through each choice, looking for evidence in the passage. Think of each choice as a lead word—scan the passage for the word or phrase, and read a few lines before and after to see if it answers the questions.

- The first choice is "protection against water loss." Go back to the passage and try to find the part that talks about "water loss." This topic appears in paragraph 5. It states that the shell forms a "waterproof seal." This means that (A) is true. Mark that on your scratch paper.

  (A)   True

- Next, check (B). Our lead phrase for this choice is "coloration and markings." Scan through the passage. Where does it mention this topic? Paragraph 6 says that "coloration and markings of the exoskeleton can be beneficial...." So this answer is true as well. Mark it down on your scrap paper.

  (A)   True
  (B)   True

- The third choice is "ability to take in extra air or water." Let's look through the passage for these lead words. Find them? These words show up in the final paragraph, but that paragraph is about the *disadvantages* of the shell. So this choice is false. Note this on your scrap paper.

  (A)   True
  (B)   True
  (C)   False

- Finally, let's verify our answer by checking the fourth choice, which is "armor-like protection." A quick scan of our passage reveals this phrase in the fourth paragraph. This statement is true as well. Thus, we're left with the following:

  (A)   True
  (B)   True
  (C)   False
  (D)   True

- Now all we do is pick the answer choice that is different: (C). It is very important to check all of the choices when doing EXCEPT/NOT/LEAST questions. Many test takers go through the choices too quickly and end up picking the answer that *is* in the passage instead of the one that *isn't*.

POE Strategies for EXCEPT/NOT/LEAST Questions

These questions are similar to detail and lead word questions. However, they are the *opposite* because you are going to *eliminate* answers that are:

- **Supported by the passage:** Remember, we want the choice that is *not* supported by the passage.

Additionally, the correct answer may:

- **Contain information not mentioned:** Information not found in the passage makes a good answer for these questions.
- **Use extreme language:** Extreme language is usually bad; but for these questions, it's acceptable.

EXCEPT/NOT/LEAST questions can take a little more time to answer than other types of detail or lead word questions, so make sure to do them in your second pass.

Question Type #9: Inference Questions

Here's our next question type.

7. It can be inferred from the passage that molting:

   a. happens regularly during the life of the arthropod
   b. always takes days to complete
   c. leaves the arthropod without its normal defense
   d. causes the arthropod to grow larger

Inference questions ask for a very specific type of answer. An inference is a conclusion reached based on the available evidence. For example, if a friend of yours walks in and has wet hair, you may infer that it is raining outside. That inference may or may not be true. Perhaps your friend just washed his hair or was sprayed with a hose. However, on the TOEFL, the correct inference is the answer that *must be true* based on the information in the passage.

Our approach to these questions remains the same as many other types. First, restate the question.

What does the passage suggest about molting?

Next, use a lead word to locate the appropriate part of the passage. For this question, we'll use the word *molting*. This word shows up in the final paragraph as the word *molt*. As we've seen with detail and lead word questions, the correct answer should be within four or five lines of the reference. However, for inference questions, you should not attempt to answer in your own words first; this is because you can't be sure which inference will be the correct response, and the answer you predict may not be close to the answer choice.

Instead, we'll follow a process similar to the one we used for EXCEPT/NOT/LEAST questions. We'll look at each answer choice and see if it is true based on the lines about molting. Here's the question again.

7. It can be inferred from the passage that molting:

   a. happens regularly during the life of the arthropod
   b. always takes days to complete
   c. leaves the arthropod without its normal defense
   d. causes the arthropod to grow larger

- Let's start with the first choice. Go back to the paragraph about molting, and look for any information regarding how regularly it takes place. Remember to read only the lines around our lead word. Because there is no information on the regularity of molting, (A) must be wrong. Eliminate it.
- Now move on to the next choice. Go back to the passage, and look for evidence that molting "always takes days to complete." There is some information about time, but make sure you read carefully. The passage states that "this process can take hours or days...." But that doesn't mean that molting "always" takes days. So, eliminate (B).
- For the third choice, there is some indication that it is true. If you read toward the end of the paragraph, it states that the "new coat is tender and easily penetrated. Accordingly, the arthropod must remain in hiding." It took a little searching, but this is the answer we need.
- Of course, we should still look at the final answer. The fourth choice suggests that molting "causes the arthropod to grow larger." Is there any evidence for this in the passage? Choice (D) is supported in the passage ("As the animal increases in size, therefore, it must occasionally molt."), but the passage doesn't say that molting *causes* growth.

So (C) is the best answer.

POE Strategies for Inference Questions

Inference questions require a very careful reading of the passage because the wrong answers can be very attractive. When eliminating answers, you should carefully look for the following:

- **Could be true:** Some answers may be true. However, this is not good enough on the TOEFL. You must be able to support the truth of the answer with the passage. In other words, the correct answer *must* be true.
- **Extreme:** The wrong answer on inference questions will often use extreme wording. Watch out for answers that contain the following words:

always   *never*   *impossible*   *all*   *none*   *best*   *worst*

- **Beyond the information:** The wrong answer on an inference question may contain some information found in the passage but make a claim or connection that is not found in the passage.

Inference questions require careful reading of both the passage and the answer choices. The right answer is usually a clever paraphrase of information in the passage. Because these questions can be very tricky, you may want to do them during your second pass.

Question Type #10: Main Idea/Primary Purpose/Summary Questions

The final question type on the TOEFL is the **main idea/primary purpose/summary** question. These questions are typically worth two points and require you to find multiple correct answers.

Here's an example of one.

10.   **Directions:** An introductory sentence for a brief summary of the passage is provided below. Complete the summary by selecting the THREE answer choices that express the most important ideas in the passage. Some sentences do not belong in the summary because they express ideas that are not presented in the passage or are minor ideas in the passage. ***This question is worth 2 points.***

> **Animals in the phylum called arthropods have shells or exoskeletons with distinctive characteristics.**
>
> -
> -
> -

Answer Choices	
Insects, spiders, shrimp, crabs, and centipedes are all arthropods.	The chitin in the exoskeleton is similar in chemical composition to the cellulose in wood.
The shell has three layers that protect an arthropod from injury and water loss.	Because the shell is hard, it must be discarded and replaced as the arthropod grows.
The hyaline in a scorpion's shell glows under black light because it is excited by ultraviolet radiation.	The large surface area of the shell makes possible a high number of muscles and a variety of adaptive colorations.

For this type of question, you will click and drag answer choices to add them to the summary. Fortunately, these questions always show up at the end of the section, so by the time you attack a summary question, you should have a pretty good idea of the passage's main points.

Your main task for this question is to separate *details* from *main ideas*. Use your understanding of the structure of a passage to figure out which choice is a detail and which choice is a main point. In general, details will appear in the middle of paragraphs and are often mentioned only once. Main ideas will appear at the beginning or end of paragraphs and show up throughout the passage.

Let's go through each choice and decide if it's a detail or a main idea.

- The first choice is as follows:

    Insects, spiders, shrimp, crabs, and centipedes are all arthropods.

    Is this one of the main ideas of the passage? It's certainly mentioned in the first paragraph, but what is the majority of the passage about? If you said the exoskeleton, you are correct. Our answers should be about the exoskeleton, so let's eliminate this choice.

- Here's the second choice.

    The shell has three layers that protect an arthropod from injury and water loss.

    This choice is more in line with what we need. The passage described the shell, and this answer summarizes the structure of the shell. Let's add it to our summary.

    - **The shell has three layers that protect an arthropod from injury and water loss.**

    ○

    ○

- The next choice says

    The hyaline in a scorpion's shell glows under black light because it is excited by ultraviolet radiation.

    Is this a main idea or a detail? Where does this fact appear in the passage? Notice how it shows up in a paragraph about the benefits of the shell. That means that this fact is likely just an example of a benefit. The passage even uses the phrase "for instance" when discussing this fact. Plus, the entire passage is not about scorpions. Thus, it's a detail, not a main idea.

- Here's the next choice.

> The chitin in the exoskeleton is similar in chemical composition to the cellulose in wood.

Although it does talk about the exoskeleton, this choice provides a *very specific* detail about the chitin. We're looking for a *more general* description. Let's look at the other choices to see if they are better answers.

- The next choice reads

> Because the shell is hard, it must be discarded and replaced as the arthropod grows.

This choice talks about the shell as well. It gives a good summary of the final paragraph of the passage, which talked about the disadvantages of the exoskeleton. Because the entire passage gave information on the benefits and disadvantages of the exoskeleton, we should add this choice to our list.

  - The shell has three layers that protect an arthropod from injury and water loss.

  - Because the shell is hard, it must be discarded and replaced as the arthropod grows.

  -

- Here's our final option.

> The large surface area of the shell makes possible a high number of muscles and a variety of adaptive colorations.

This choice is also part of the main idea. Notice how it differs from the previous choice about the scorpion's markings. This choice mentions two benefits, not just one. And it doesn't mention just one type of arthropod. Therefore, it belongs in the summary.

- Here are our final choices.

    - The shell has three layers that protect an arthropod from injury and water loss.

    - Because the shell is hard, it must be discarded and replaced as the arthropod grows.

    - The large surface area of the shell makes possible a high number of muscles and a variety of adaptive colorations.

Notice how this summary matches the summaries we practiced in Chapter 2, Core Concept: Reading. We've mentioned each of the important points from the topic sentences of the passage. On a passage that describes two different categories, you might also see a question that asks you to pair characteristics with each category. Approach these the same way!

POE Strategies for Main Idea/Primary Purpose/Summary Questions

For these questions, eliminate answers that don't show up as key points during your initial reading of the passage. Use the structure of the passage to help eliminate answers. Remove choices that are:

- **Too specific:** Watch out for choices that contain specific facts or details. Make sure you don't include examples! Remember, examples only support the main point; they don't state it.
- **Not mentioned:** Make sure the information in the choice is actually found in the passage. Some answer choices are cleverly worded to distract you.

These questions can be very difficult, but if you've been practicing the active reading strategies in this book, they should be much easier. Still, save these questions for last.

Reading Summary

Congratulations! You've just cracked an entire section of the TOEFL. Before we give you a drill to practice your new skills, let's review some of the key ideas from this chapter.

Basic Ideas

o **It's in there:** No matter how difficult the question may seem, remember that the answer is somewhere in the passage.

o **Two-pass system:** Not all questions are created equal. Do all the questions that you find easier first, and save the killer questions for last. This system is what we call your Personal Order of Difficulty—wherein you get to choose to tackle the questions that feel the easiest to you first and tally those points and then come back around for the more challenging questions.

o **POE:** Sometimes it's easier to find the wrong answer than the right answer. Make sure you know the POE guidelines for the test.

The Approach

o **Actively read the passage,** looking for the purpose, structure, and main idea.

o **Attack the questions** based on question type.

o **Find the answer** to the question in the passage.

o **Use POE** to eliminate bad answers.

Timing Tips

- ○ For the first few passages, time yourself to see how long it takes you to complete the passage.

- ○ Once you have a good idea of how long it takes you, time yourself to work a little bit faster each time.

- ○ Try to maintain your accuracy.

Reading Personal Order of Difficulty (POOD)

- ○ Which question types do you feel most confident about? _____

- ○ Which questions have you determined aren't worth your investment of time on test day? _____

- ○ Remember to decide whether you want to select the first, second, third, or fourth answer as your "guess" for any question that you decide not to do.

Chapter 8
Reading Practice
Drills

Here are some practice reading passages. Remember to use the two-pass approach you just learned in the previous chapter. At this point, don't worry about time—just focus on getting the right answers and understanding the process. After you've completed these drills, be sure to read through the explanations of the right and wrong answers in the next chapter.

Reading Practice Drill #1

Impeachment

1 Under the Constitution, the House of Representatives has the power to impeach a government official, in effect serving as prosecutor. The Senate then holds the impeachment trial, essentially serving as jury and judge, except in the impeachment of a president when the chief justice presides. The president, vice president, and all civil officers of the United States are subject to impeachment; conviction means automatic removal from office.

2 ➜ The concept of impeachment originated in England and was adopted by many of the American colonial governments and state constitutions. At the Constitutional Convention, the framers considered several possible models before deciding that the Senate should try impeachments. Since 1789, only 20 federal officers have been impeached by the House, 16 of which were tried by the Senate. Four were dismissed before trial because the individual had left office, 8 ended in acquittal and 8 in conviction. All of those convicted were federal judges.

3 ➜ Impeachment is a very serious affair. It is perhaps the most awesome power of Congress, the ultimate weapon it wields against officials of the federal government. The House of Representatives is the prosecutor. The Senate chamber is the courtroom. The Senate is the jury and also the judge, except in the case of a presidential impeachment trial when the chief justice presides. The final penalty is removal from office. There is no appeal.

4 ➜ So grave is this power of impeachment, and so conscious is the Congress of this solemn power, that impeachment proceedings have been initiated in the House only sixty-six times since 1789. Only twenty federal officers have been impeached: three presidents, one cabinet officer, one senator and fifteen federal judges. Nineteen cases have reached the Senate. Of these, three were dismissed before trial because the individuals had left office, eight ended in acquittal, and eight in conviction. Each of the eight Senate convictions has involved a federal judge.

5 The American colonial governments and early state constitutions followed the British pattern of trial before the upper legislative body on charges brought by the lower house. Despite these precedents, a major controversy arose at the Constitutional Convention about whether the Senate should act as the court of impeachment. Opposing that role for the Senate, James Madison and Charles Cotesworth Pinckney asserted that it would make the president too dependent on the legislative branch. They suggested, as alternative trial bodies, the Supreme Court or the chief justices of the state supreme courts. Hamilton and others argued, however, that such bodies would be too small and susceptible to corruption. In the end, after much wrangling, the framers selected the Senate as the trial forum.

6 There was also considerable debate at the convention in Philadelphia over the definition of impeachable crimes. In the original proposals, the president was to be removed on impeachment and conviction "for mal or corrupt conduct," or for "malpractice or neglect of duty." Later, the wording was changed to "treason, bribery, or corruption," then to "treason or bribery" alone. A final revision defined impeachable crimes as "treason, bribery, or other high crimes and misdemeanors."

7 In the Constitution, the House is given the "sole power of impeachment." To the Senate is given "the sole power to try all impeachments." Impeachments may be brought against "the President, Vice President, and all civil officers of the United States." Conviction is automatically followed by "removal from office."

8 While the framers very clearly envisaged the occasional necessity of initiating impeachment proceedings, they put in place only a very general framework. ■ They left many questions open to differences of opinion and many details to be filled in. ■ Despite the open-endedness, as Peter Charles Hoffer and N.E.H. Hull note in their book *Impeachment in America 1635–1805*, thanks to the framers, a tool used in Parliament to curb kings and punish placemen was molded into an efficient legislative check upon executive and judicial wrongdoing. ■ The power of the English House of Commons to impeach anyone, for almost any alleged offense, was restrained; the threat of death and forfeiture upon conviction was lifted; and the interference of the Commons and the House of Lords with the regular courts of justice was limited. ■ American impeachment law shifted, at first inadvertently and then deliberately, from the orbit of English precedent to a native republican course. Federal constitutional provisions for impeachment reflected indigenous experience and revolutionary tenets instead of English tradition.

1. The word power in the passage is closest in meaning to:

   a. motivation
   b. desire
   c. bearing
   d. authority

2. According to paragraph 3, what three roles do the House of Representatives and Senate play in the impeachment process?

   a. Government official, jury, judge
   b. Prosecutor, jury, judge
   c. President, prosecutor, judge
   d. Civil officers, jury, prosecutor

   Paragraph 3 is marked with an arrow [➜]

3. What can be inferred from paragraph 2 about the decision to impeach a government official?

   a. The decision is made in the Senate.
   b. Impeachment results in removal from office.
   c. Impeachment occurs often.
   d. Impeachment rarely occurs.

   Paragraph 2 is marked with an arrow [➜]

4. The word wields in the passage is closest in meaning to:

    a. uses
    b. maintains
    c. formulates
    d. shapes

5. According to paragraph 4, how many impeachment proceedings have been initiated since 1789?

    a. Twenty
    b. Three
    c. Sixty-six
    d. Nineteen

    Paragraph 4 is marked with an arrow [➜]

6. According to the passage, the impeachment process incorporates:

    a. the House of Representatives and the Senate
    b. the Senate and the President
    c. a Chief Justice and the House of Representatives
    d. a Chief Justice and the Senate

7. Which of the sentences below best expresses the essential information in the highlighted sentence in the passage? Incorrect choices change the meaning in important ways or leave out essential information.

    There was also considerable debate at the convention in Philadelphia over the definition of impeachable crimes.

    a. Philadelphians debated considerably over the definition of impeachable crimes.
    b. Formidable debate occurred at the convention in Philadelphia concerning the meaning of impeachable crimes.
    c. Impeachable crimes were debated at the convention in Philadelphia.
    d. The classification of impeachable crimes was a significant debate at the Philadelphia convention.

8. ALL of the following are mentioned as part of the final definition of impeachment EXCEPT:

    a. corruption
    b. misdemeanors
    c. bribery
    d. treason

9. Look at the four squares [■] that indicate where the following sentence could be added to the passage.

Consequently, the American version of impeachment was clearly quite different than the English version upon which it was based.

Where would the sentence best fit?

Click on a square [■] to add the sentence to the passage.

10. Directions: An introductory sentence for a brief summary of the passage is provided below. Complete the summary by selecting the THREE answer choices that express the most important ideas in the passage. Some sentences do not belong in the summary because they express ideas that are not presented in the passage or are minor ideas in the passage.

The power of impeachment was initiated during the Constitutional Convention as a means to try government officials who do not act according to the law.

-
-
-

Answer Choices	
Sixty-two trials of impeachment have occurred since 1789.	The impeachment process is initially brought forth by the House of Representatives, and it is tried before the Senate.
A chief justice presides over the hearing of presidential impeachment, and this is the only instance in which the Senate is not the judge.	If a government official is convicted subsequent to impeachment, he/she is automatically removed from office.
The power to impeach is taken very seriously by Congress and very few government officials have been impeached.	The definition of impeachable crimes was an important component of the Constitutional Convention; nevertheless, the language defining it remains decidedly vague.

Reading Practice Drill #2

Fire Tornadoes

1 ➔ Fire tornadoes—also known as fire whirls, firenados, or fire twisters—look like tornadoes but are made up of fire. Therefore, they aren't really tornadoes at all. Tornadoes are formed when just the right weather elements combine: moist, warm air lying close to the ground; an unstable atmosphere; and air fronts that collide and propel moist air vertically into the sky.

2 A fire tornado has two parts: the core, which is actually on fire, and an invisible, rotating air pocket. It can reach temperatures of nearly 2,000°F, which is hot enough to even reignite ashes that have been sucked into the vortex from the ground. While real tornadoes occur as a result of atmospheric conditions high above, fire tornadoes result from hot, dry air rising quickly away from the ground. When hot, strong winds come into contact with an already burning brushfire, updrafts of hot air catch the fire and surrounding winds and send it whirling into the air. This whirling air forms columns; as more and more hot air is pulled into a column, the column begins to swirl, very much like a real tornado.

3 A fire twister's spinning column creates a vortex thanks to angular momentum. The law of angular momentum states that when an object is inside a spinning column, it will move faster and faster the closer it gets to the center of rotation. The fire tornado picks up flaming embers, combustible gases, burning debris, and ash. When sucked up by the firenado, unburned gases travel up the core until they reach an area where there is enough oxygen to ignite them. This ultimately creates a spinning fire tower that can be hundreds of feet tall.

4 While fire whirls move pretty slowly, they can cause significant damage. Anything—or anyone!— unfortunate enough to be in a fire whirl's path will likely either be set ablaze or flung vigorously from its location. But it's not just the fire that's dangerous—the winds it generates can create wind speeds of more than 100 mph, which is strong enough to knock down trees. Fire whirls also typically don't last very long, but when they do, they can wreak havoc and leave disaster in their wakes.

5 ➔ There have been numerous major firenados in the last 150 years, many of which have proved lethal. In 1871, the great Peshtigo Fire in Northeastern Wisconsin and Upper Michigan resulted from inauspicious conditions: dry weather during the summer, slash-and-burn farming practices, and a vigorous cold front that brought strong winds. Together, these three contributing factors created firenados that turned a few small prairie fires into a furious conflagration. The town of Peshtigo, with hundreds of wooden structures and lumberyards, sat in the middle of a forest of pine and hardwood. When the fire reached the town, it found abundant fuel. In just minutes, 100-mph winds and ambient temperatures of more than 700°F caused what is still recognized as the worst fire disaster in the history of the United States. As best as anyone could tell, nearly 2,000 people lost their lives.

6 More recently, a fire twister was recorded in January 2003 on Mount Taylor in Canberra, Australia. It had a diameter of almost 1,600 feet and winds of more than 160 mph. In April 2016, a fire tornado nearly claimed the life of a firefighter in Alberta, Canada. His team was fighting a blaze that started as an out-of-control campfire. The firefighter's teammate yelled at him to watch out. Without thinking, he jumped into the nearby river, saving his own life.

7 Unfortunately, we still don't know much about fire twisters. Because they can arise in any part of a fire, there is no way to predict where one might appear. And because they don't usually last very long, it's reasonable to consider that even firefighters can't identify where a fire twister has touched ground. Even with that information, we would still be left with the question of whether the fire caused the vortex or whether the vortex was helped by the fire. Perhaps someday we'll find out!

1. It can be inferred from paragraph 1 of the passage that fire tornadoes:

   a.   are truly tornadoes
   b.   form easily
   c.   look like tornadoes
   d.   result only from an unstable atmosphere

   Paragraph 1 is marked with an arrow [➔]

2. The word whirling in the passage is closest in meaning to:

   a.   spinning
   b.   working
   c.   flying
   d.   jumping

3. The word it in the passage refers to:

   a.   the fire
   b.   the air pocket
   c.   the fire tornado
   d.   the ashes

4. Which of the following is NOT mentioned as a characteristic of a fire tornado?

   a.   Column
   b.   Core
   c.   Air pocket
   d.   Angular momentum

5. Which of the following is an example of angular momentum?

    a.   A runner running faster the further she runs
    b.   A tennis player hitting harder earlier in the game
    c.   An ice skater spinning faster as she pulls her arms in to her body
    d.   A swimmer swimming faster at a higher altitude

6. The author implies that:

    a.   fire whirls don't move quickly
    b.   fire whirls don't cause damage
    c.   fire whirls can't knock down trees
    d.   fire whirls can last for days

7. The phrase wreak havoc in the passage is closest in meaning to :

    a.   start sizeable fires
    b.   last forever
    c.   move quickly
    d.   cause significant damage

8. According to paragraph 5 of the passage, firenados:

    a.   have happened more than once
    b.   have never been documented
    c.   first occurred in Peshtigo
    d.   are always lethal

Paragraph 5 is marked with an arrow [➔]

9. The word inauspicious in the passage is closest in meaning to:

    a.   lucky
    b.   fortunate
    c.   unlucky
    d.   dangerous

10. Directions: An introductory sentence for a brief summary of the passage is provided below. Complete the summary by selecting the THREE answer choices that express the most important ideas in the passage. Some sentences do not belong in the summary because they express ideas that are not presented in the passage or are minor ideas in the passage. This question is worth 2 points.

A firenado is one example of a natural phenomenon that is as uncommon as it is dangerous.

-
-
-

Answer Choices	
Firenados require a unique combination of conditions in order to occur.	A firefighter escaped a firenado by jumping into a river.
Firenados suck up ashes and gases into their core.	Scientists don't know much about firenados because it is hard to predict where or when they will occur.
Firenados can cause significant damage.	The firenado in Peshtigo was the first firenado on record.

Reading Practice Drill #3

Periodical Cicadas

1 ➤ Certain cicadas spend most of their lives about 2 feet underground, feeding on fluids from the roots of trees in forests across the eastern United States. These particular species, called periodical cicadas, are developmentally synchronized, meaning they develop into adults all at the same time. There are seven distinct species of periodical cicadas, four of which have 13-year lifecycles and three of which have 17-year lifecycles. After the respective 13 or 17 years of subterranean lifestyle, the almost-mature cicada nymphs emerge at a given place and time in astounding numbers— as many as 1.5 million cicadas per acre. The nymphs wait for a spring evening when the soil temperature about 8 inches below the surface is above 64°F. For the four 13-year-cycle species, which tend to be further to the south and west of the eastern United States, this may be as early as late April or early May. But for the three 17-year-cycle species, which are generally found more toward the northern end of the eastern United States, this may not happen until late May or early June.

2 Once they emerge they have only about 4–6 weeks to live. First, they find a new home on plants near their emergence location where they complete their transition into full adult cicadas. Next, they molt a final time and then remain in the leaves, where they are protected from most predators, to wait for their exoskeletons to completely harden. Within two months of their emergence, they have laid their eggs and their lifecycle has been completed. Once the mature cicadas die, there will be no more cicadas of that brood for another 13 or 17 years.

3 Periodical cicadas are divided into groups called broods; these broods are based on the calendar year in which they emerge. In 1898, entomologist C. L. Marlatt identified as many as 30 broods, although not all of them have actually been observed since then. He identified 17 broods with a 17-year lifecycle and 13 broods with a 13-year lifecycle. Brood VI, for example, has a 17-year lifecycle. It is typically found in Eastern Ohio, Western Maryland, Southwestern Pennsylvania, Northwestern Virginia, and West Virginia. Brood VI's last emergence was 2017, so it will emerge again in 2034.

4 Adult periodical cicadas are small, roughly one inch long, with males growing slightly larger than females. Cicadas do not have specific defense mechanisms: While their mouths are designed to pierce plants and suck out the plants' sap, they don't bite or sting. **Their sole purpose during their adult lives is to reproduce. Male cicadas form "aggregations," or choruses, and "sing" a mating song that is specific to their species in order to attract females to mate.** They don't create sound with vocal cords, like humans do, though. Instead, they produce sounds with their tymbals, corrugated exoskeletal structures that are specifically used to produce sounds. **On the male cicada, the pair of tymbals is located on the sides of the abdomen.** The membranes across the "ribs" of the tymbal vibrate quickly, and the cicada's body functions like a resonance chamber and magnifies the sound. The cicadas can adjust the "volume" of their sound by turning their bodies in different directions.

5 ■ **Periodical cicada populations grow to astounding numbers, not only because the only purpose of their adult lives is to reproduce, but also because they tend to escape natural population control by predators.** ■ Because they emerge only once every 13 or 17 years, predators cannot rely upon them as a regular part of the food cycle. ■ As a result, when the cicadas do become prey, their predators can seemingly eat their fill without making a significant impact on the cicada population. ■

6 Periodical cicadas are fascinating creatures, largely because they don't play a regular role in their environments' ecosystems. In fact, they are so fascinating that scientists named their genus Magicicada. Most interesting, though, is how they keep track of time and know when 13 or 17 years have passed. Alas, researchers don't actually know how they do it, other than knowing that it's some kind of molecular clock. The insects themselves make for difficult research, since researchers have to wait at least 13 years for a brood to reemerge!

1. The word nymphs in the passage is closest in meaning to:

   a.   immature cicadas
   b.   different species
   c.   roots of trees
   d.   water creatures

2. According to paragraph 1, periodical cicadas can be found:

   a.   around the world
   b.   throughout the western hemisphere
   c.   across the eastern United States
   d.   in the southeastern United States

   Paragraph 1 is marked with an arrow [➜]

3. The word they in the passage refers to:

   a.   southeastern United States
   b.   periodical cicadas
   c.   plants
   d.   predators

4. The cicadas are organized into broods according to:

   a.   the year in which they emerge
   b.   the length of their lifecycles
   c.   the length of their development cycle
   d.   Marlatt's preferences

5. The word magnifies in the passage is closest in meaning to:

   a.   makes louder
   b.   produces
   c.   makes worse
   d.   degrades

6. Click on the sentence (in bold text in the passage and repeated below) where the author describes how periodical cicadas attract mates.

   a.   Their sole purpose during their adult lives is to reproduce.
   b.   Male cicadas form "aggregations," or choruses, and "sing" a mating song that is specific to their species in order to attract females to mate.
   c.   On the male cicada, the pair of tymbals is located on the sides of the abdomen.
   d.   Periodical cicada populations grow to astounding numbers, not only because the only purpose of their adult lives is to reproduce, but also because they tend to escape natural population control by predators.

7. The word their in the passage refers to:

   a.   broods
   b.   cicada populations
   c.   cicada predators
   d.   cicada prey

8. Look at the four squares [■] that indicate where the following sentence can be added to the passage.

   This phenomenon is known as "predator satiation," a situation in which prey occur at an incredibly high population, drastically reducing the probability that an individual organism be eaten.

   Where would the sentence best fit?

   Click on a square [■] to add the sentence to the passage.

   (Here, on this practice test, circle your answer below.)

   a.   Square 1
   b.   Square 2
   c.   Square 3
   d.   Square 4

9. How do periodical cicadas know when to emerge?

   a.   They have calendars.
   b.   They can track the seasons.
   c.   They have a molecular clock.
   d.   Scientists don't have any ideas.

10. Directions: An introductory sentence for a brief summary of the passage is provided below. Complete the summary by selecting the THREE answer choices that express the most important ideas in the passage. Some sentences do not belong in the summary because they express ideas that are not presented in the passage or are minor ideas in the passage. This question is worth 2 points.

Periodical cicadas are unique creatures because of their unusual lifecycles and their lack of significant predators.

-
-
-

Answer Choices	
Periodical cicadas have a significant maturation process, emerging only when they are almost ready to lay eggs.	Four species have 13-year lifecycles.
Periodical cicadas do not have many natural predators because they emerge only once every 13 or 17 years, so their lifespan is too short for predators to rely upon them.	Once periodical cicadas emerge, they live only 4 to 6 weeks.
Periodical cicadas use their tymbals to make sounds during mating.	The soil temperature must be 64°F before the periodical cicadas will emerge.

Reading Practice Drill #4

Mandala Art

1 "Mandala" is a Sanskrit word meaning "circle." While it originated as a spiritual symbol in many Indian religions, the mandala has come to be known generically as a term for any diagram, chart, or geometric pattern that is intended to symbolically or metaphorically represent the cosmos. The typical "circle with a center" pattern represents the foundational structure of life and creation. This pattern is found in many places in our world, including biology, geology, physics, astronomy, and chemistry. For example, even atoms are circular in nature, with evenly balanced protons, neutrons, and electrons. Every cell has a nucleus, which also has a circle at the center. Even the Milky Way galaxy is circular, with our circular solar system within it. One could argue that each of these is a mandala in and of itself.

2 Carl Jung, the founder of analytical psychology, held that "a mandala is the psychological expression of the totality of the self." He sketched a small circular drawing every morning, and felt that whatever came to life in his mandala corresponded to his inner experience at the time. ■ He believed that he could track his internal transformations by looking at the differences in his drawings. ■ Fundamentally, Jung believed that if humans could harness the power of their subconscious—or, as he called it, the Self—then they could grow toward fulfilling their potential for wholeness, and live fully expressed lives. ■ He found that during periods of significant trial and tribulation many of his clients felt compelled to create mandalas. He found that people felt drawn to drawing or painting mandalas simply because it felt right to do so—it seemed that they instinctively turned to creating a mandala as a way to express their experience. ■

3 Why might humans have this instinct? Research into the fields of psychology and child development may shed some light on the subject. It would seem that circles are part of the basic creation of a personal identity. Studies conducted with babies show that as early as one week old, infants prefer to look at curved lines rather than straight lines. Additional research shows that two-month-old infants can discern shapes that look like faces from scrambled patterns. Psychologically, it is believed that simple, closed forms—like circles—are identified more quickly and recognized as meaningful, known, and familiar. Even the shape of an eye is spherical—simply put, it's a three-dimensional circle—and our field of vision is thus also circular.

4 Circles also appear very early in children's art. What begins as random scribbling progresses into drawing circles as early as age two. **By three or four years old, their drawings become more intricate, and without any input from adults, they begin drawing suns, flowers, and people whose arms and legs connect to large circular heads.**

5 As adults, when we draw circles—in particular, mandalas—we connect with our inner child. Some might say that we connect with our primary sense of self. **Researchers believe that mandalas give us a bridge to our home base, allowing us to recreate our sense of who we are.** Professionals also believe that mandalas help us center psychologically, and they are still used in psychotherapy practice. Drawing a mandala is an organic process—what's most important is the process itself, not the final product. **It may include flowers, shapes, lines, or totally abstract designs. Many therapists believe, as Jung did, that whatever emerges in a mandala matches whatever may be going on in the artist's life; further, if the artist allows their unconscious to come out through the mandala, psychologists believe he or she can align their conscious actions and decisions accordingly.**

1. Atoms, cells, and the Milky Way are mentioned as examples of:

   a.   circles in nature
   b.   patterns
   c.   symbols
   d.   the cosmos

2. The word held in the passage is closest in meaning to:

   a.   kept in hand
   b.   occupied
   c.   believed
   d.   guarded

3. The phrase trial and tribulation in the passage is closest in meaning to:

   a.   ease
   b.   difficulty
   c.   fun
   d.   happiness

4. Look at the four squares [■] that indicate where the following sentence can be added to the passage.

   Based on this belief and his recognition of his own internal evolution through the use of mandalas, he began to use them as a tool in his psychology practice.

   Where would the sentence best fit?

   Click on a square [■] to add the sentence to the passage.

   (Here, on this practice test, circle your answer below.)

   a.   Square 1
   b.   Square 2
   c.   Square 3
   d.   Square 4

5. What kinds of shapes are recognized more easily by the human eye?

   a. Circles
   b. Straight lines
   c. Squares
   d. Squiggly lines

6. The word their in the passage refers to:

   a. Jung
   b. Jung's clients
   c. children
   d. adults

7. By what age do children begin drawing more detailed and representative pictures?

   a. One week
   b. One year
   c. Two years
   d. Three to four years

8. Click on the sentence (in bold text in the passage and repeated below) where the author describes how drawing a mandala allows an adult to reestablish a connection with her subconscious.

   a. By three or four years old, their drawings become more intricate, and without any input from adults, they begin drawing suns, flowers, and people whose arms and legs connect to large circular heads.
   b. Researchers believe that mandalas give us a bridge to our home base, allowing us to recreate our sense of who we are.
   c. It may include flowers, shapes, lines, or totally abstract designs.
   d. Many therapists believe, as Jung did, that whatever emerges in a mandala matches whatever may be going on in the artist's life; further, if the artist allows their unconscious to come out through the mandala, psychologists believe he or she can align their conscious actions and decisions accordingly.

9. Which of the following is NOT mentioned in the passage?

   a.   The origin of the word "mandala"
   b.   Examples of mandalas in nature
   c.   Scientists who value mandalas
   d.   Friends of people who draw mandalas

10. Directions: An introductory sentence for a brief summary of the passage is provided below. Complete the summary by selecting the THREE answer choices that express the most important ideas in the passage. Some sentences do not belong in the summary because they express ideas that are not presented in the passage or are minor ideas in the passage. This question is worth 2 points.

    Mandala art has ancient roots and can play a therapeutic role for humans.

    •

    •

    •

Answer Choices	
The term "mandala" comes from an ancient language and has been passed on for generations.	Many ancient traditions and religions used mandalas in their ceremonies.
Children learn to draw circles before they learn to draw any other shapes.	Carl Jung, the founder of analytical psychology, found value in using mandalas with his patients.
Circles appear in artwork of peoples around the world.	Our solar system is a mandala.

Reading Practice Drill #5

Early Women Aviators

1 Aviation was an important element of the evolution in women's status in the early twentieth century. It seemed that no sooner had the first male aviators returned to Earth than women, too, were taken by an urge to fly. Women went from watching men take thrilling risks to becoming willing passengers and finally pilots in their own right.

2 The risks were great. Airplane technology progressed through trial and error, so engines frequently failed in flight. There were no standard radio beacons until 1929, so early pilots had to navigate by sight, and their only outside source of information was from communication with ground personnel. Because sight was so critical to the operation of the planes, poor visibility on cloudy or rainy days was a frequent cause of crashes. Despite the numerous hazards, women aviators were soon taking to the air. In doing so, they earned hard fought recognition for competence and achievement, and contributed richly to the progress of mechanical flight.

3 → Conventional wisdom that women were unsuited for flying made it difficult for them to raise money for the up-to-date equipment they needed to contend on an equal basis with men. Yet they still found ways to compete and often triumphed despite the odds against them. Ruth Law, for example, in 1916 flew 590 miles from Chicago to New York and set a new nonstop distance record. She was so successful that in 1917 she earned as much as $9,000 per week for exhibition and stunt flights. Ruth Law, as much as any woman of her day, exemplified the resourcefulness and determination demanded of a woman who wanted to fly. When she addressed the Aero Club of America after completing her historic journey, her plainspoken words testified to a motivation that was independent of gender. She had, she said, undertaken the flight strictly for the love of accomplishment and had "no expectation of reward."

4 → Recognition of women aviators' abilities did not always come easily. "Men do not believe us capable," the famed aviator Amelia Earhart once remarked to a friend. "Because we are women, seldom are we trusted to do an efficient job." Indeed, old attitudes died hard. ■ Charles and Anne Lindbergh, both famous, record-setting pilots, visited the Soviet Union in 1938. There they were astonished to discover both men and women flying in the Soviet Air Force, a phenomenon that was still unthinkable in America. Women had been grudgingly accepted as commercial pilots, but they were deemed unfit to fly in a military capacity. ■

5 Earlier, in 1917, Ruth Law had actually been the first woman authorized to wear an NCO military uniform, but despite her manifest talent, she had been denied permission to fly in combat. ■ The military informed her that she could do more good by teaching others to fly. In competitions with male pilots, Law had always insisted on equal and non-preferential treatment, so she was incensed by the army's refusal to let her fly. Indignant, she wrote a famous article for the magazine *Air Travel* entitled "Let Women Fly!" that has served as inspiration for many subsequent generations of female pilots. ■

6 → Ironically, when Ruth Law, one of the early twentieth century's most recognized symbols of female independence, announced her sudden retirement from flight in 1922, she cited traditional concerns: she wanted to settle down and have a family. Additionally, and perhaps just as importantly, her husband and promoter Charles Oliver had grown so anxious about the dangers of her flying that he lost weight every time she took to the air. In this way, a worried husband's concerns for his wife's welfare put an end to the illustrious career of America's foremost female aviator of the time.

1. Which of the sentences below best expresses the essential information in the highlighted sentence in the passage? Incorrect choices change the meaning in important ways or leave out essential information.

   a. Male pilots eventually allowed female pilots to rightfully fly their planes.
   b. After years of watching male pilots and joining them on plane rides, women were finally able to fly on their own.
   c. Men took thrilling risks by being passengers on commercial flights that women piloted on their own.
   d. Even though women started off as spectators, they eventually were able to become passengers.

2. Which of the following is NOT mentioned as a danger experienced by early pilots?

   a. Bad weather's effects on visibility
   b. Faulty equipment on planes
   c. Inability to communicate with ground personnel
   d. Lack of radio beacons on the ground

3. The word contend in the passage is closest in meaning to:

   a. cooperate
   b. accept
   c. vie
   d. revolt

4. Paragraph 3 implies that early women pilots had difficulty in:

   a. generating publicity
   b. taking lessons
   c. setting records
   d. getting aviation gear

   Paragraph 3 is marked with an arrow [➔]

5. According to paragraph 3 of the passage, Ruth Law set a record in 1916 for which of the following?

   a. The longest nonstop flight
   b. Flying across the ocean
   c. Amount of money earned by a female pilot
   d. Exhibitions and stunt flights

6. The word strictly in the passage is closest in meaning to:

   a. famously
   b. solely
   c. with discipline
   d. without help

7. The author mentions in paragraph 4 that old attitudes died hard to indicate that:

   a. many women pilots were killed in plane crashes
   b. changing beliefs about women pilots took time
   c. few women were interested in flying
   d. most early flight records were set by women

   Paragraph 4 is marked with an arrow [➔]

8. According to paragraph 6, what can be reasonably inferred about Ruth Law's retirement from flying?

   a. Domestic concerns about her husband's well-being largely influenced her decision to retire.
   b. She later grew resentful of her husband for forcing her to stop flying.
   c. After retirement, she never piloted a plane again.
   d. Had she not retired, Ruth Law would have continued to break even more flight records.

   Paragraph 6 is marked with an arrow [➔]

9. Look at the four squares [■] that indicate where the following sentence could be added to the passage.

   Stung by rejection, she wanted to use her published work to let others know that her success in aviation should prove that a woman was fit to participate in that industry.

   Where would the sentence best fit?

   Click on a square [■] to add the sentence to the passage.

   (Here, on this practice test, circle your answer below.)

   a. Square 1
   b. Square 2
   c. Square 3
   d. Square 4

10. Directions: An introductory sentence for a brief summary of the passage is provided below. Complete the summary by selecting the THREE answer choices that express the most important ideas in the passage. Some sentences do not belong in the summary because they express ideas that are not presented in the passage or are minor details in the passage.

Early women pilots faced many obstacles and challenges to achievement.

-
-
-

Answer Choices	
The number of famous women pilots increased greatly after the 1930s.	Female aviators had difficulty raising money for flight equipment; however, because of their resourcefulness, some did, in fact, succeed.
In the United States, women were not regarded as fit to fly in military combat despite having proven themselves as skilled pilots.	Concern about her family caused at least one famous aviator to give up flying.
Recognition of the achievements of female pilots was hard to come by, since prevailing attitudes maintained that women were inferior to men.	Charles and Anne Lindbergh flew to the Soviet Union and saw fewer female pilots than in the United States.

Reading Practice Drill #6

The Formation of the Rocky Mountains

1 ➔ The Rocky Mountains of North America extend 5,000 kilometers from New Mexico all the way up through Canada. Elevations along the range are about 1,500 meters along the lower plains to 4,399 meters at the highest peak, and widths range from 120 to 650 kilometers. The natural beauty, abundant wildlife, and fresh water of the ranges have attracted human inhabitants for the last 10,000 to 12,000 years.

2 The history of the Rocky Mountains begins in the pre-Cambrian era, a half-billion years ago. While this is long before the Rocky Mountains themselves began forming, their hard core rocks—consisting of granites, schists, gneisses, quartzites, and slates—were produced in ancient ranges. Erosion eventually leveled these mountain ranges, and during the Paleozoic and Mesozoic Eras, about 75 to 540 million years ago, the ocean invaded the land and deposited sediments some 20,000 feet deep. They included layers of sandstones, shales, and limestones.

3 At the close of the Mesozoic Era, during the Cretaceous period about 75 million years ago, the growth of the Rockies began. There was a tremendous squeezing that uplifted the region in a great series of folds, like wrinkles in a carpet. After the arching, erosion carved away at the mountains. ■ Some 10,000 feet of sedimentary rock were washed off the top of the arch, exposing the hard rock core. The erosional resistance of these hard, crystalline rocks led to the formation of the high peaks that still exist today. On the flanks of the core the sedimentary beds sloped outward. ■ Great quantities of sand and clay were spread out on the bordering plains and plateaus. This was only one of the cycles of upheaval and erosion that occurred in the region. ■

4 Near the end of the Eocene period, about 40 million years ago, the Rockies again rose several thousand feet. Volcanoes erupted, most extensively in the Yellowstone Plateau and the Absaroka Range. As the mountains were formed, streams eroded their sides, and thousands of feet of sediment spread out on plains and plateaus. Just before the Pleistocene period, about one million years ago, the region again uplifted. ■ Streams flowed faster and began to cut canyons, and rivers ate deep gorges through the ranges. The most recent geological event of note was the "Ice Age" during the Pleistocene Epoch, 1 million to 10,000 years ago. The high peaks of the Sangre de Cristo Mountains supported numerous small glaciers and snows accumulated on the sides of the mountains. These glaciers carved a typical collection of alpine landforms, such as cirques, horns, arêtes, and cols. Lower down in the glaciated valleys, various kinds of till and stratified sediments accumulated to form Moraines. Most of the glacial deposits and landforms present today date from the last glacial phase, known in the Rocky Mountains as the Pinedale Glaciation or Pinedale Stage. During this stage, over 90% of the Yellowstone National Park was covered in ice. The glaciated terrains formed in this era are among the most picturesque in the high alpine Rockies today, as glaciers formed and moved down the valleys, thereby further eroding the mountains into bold and dramatic forms.

5 There was even a "little ice age" from about 1550 to 1860—a few centuries of glacial advance—that made its mark on the mountains recently. For example, the Agassiz and Jackson glaciers in Glacier National Park reached their most forward positions by around 1860. The incessant sculpturing of the Rockies by rain, wind, and ice continues even today.

1. The purpose of paragraph 1 is to demonstrate that:

    a. the Rocky Mountains have not been fully explored until recently
    b. most of the Rocky Mountains are not very high
    c. there are many types of mountains in the Rocky Mountains
    d. human inhabitants are destroying the natural beauty of the Rocky Mountains

    Paragraph 1 is marked with an arrow [➔]

2. The word They in the passage refers to:

    a. sediments
    b. eras
    c. years
    d. mountain ranges

3. According to the passage, all of the following types of rock would be found at the core of the Rocky Mountains EXCEPT:

    a. gneiss
    b. cirque
    c. slate
    d. granite

4. The phrase only one of implies that the process just described in the passage:

    a. was completely unique
    b. was a single example among many
    c. was the most dramatic one
    d. was like a wrinkle in the carpet

5. The word ate in the passage is closest in meaning to:

    a. raised
    b. buried
    c. erased
    d. dug

6. The plains and plateaus that surround the Rocky Mountains were covered with:

   a. material washed down from the mountains
   b. hard core rocks such as slate
   c. densely packed volcanic deposits
   d. soil rich in organic matter

7. The passage indicates that some of the most dramatic-looking parts of the Rocky Mountains were formed by:

   a. volcanic eruptions
   b. rivers
   c. glaciers
   d. the ocean

8. Which of the following best describes the organization of the passage as a whole?

   a. A mountain range serves to illustrate a widespread geological process.
   b. The history of a geological feature is discussed in chronological order.
   c. Two time periods in the history of a mountain range are contrasted.
   d. The effects of a number of geological periods on North America are compared.

9. The phrase of note in the passage is closest in meaning to:

   a. catastrophic
   b. distinct
   c. important
   d. ancient

10. Look at the four squares [■] that indicate where the following sentence could be added to the passage.

But once again, the mountains began to be worn away as soon as they rose.

Where would the sentence best fit?

Click on a square [■] to add the sentence to the passage.

(Here, on this practice test, circle your answer below.)

a.   Square 1
b.   Square 2
c.   Square 3
d.   Square 4

Reading Practice Drill #7

Suburbanization in the United States

1 The term *suburb* commonly refers to a residential district on the outskirts of a city that grows more rapidly than its interior. The process of suburbanization began within the second quarter of the nineteenth century. The emergence of the industrial city at that time was spurred largely by developments in transportation. Until then the typical city had been a compact cluster of small buildings. People traveled primarily on foot, and goods were moved by horse and cart.

2 The early factories of the industrial age, built in the 1830s and 1840s, were located along waterways and near railheads at the edges of cities. Housing was needed for the thousands of people drawn by the prospect of employment, so within a short time, the factories were surrounded by mill towns of apartments and row houses that abutted the older, central cities. In response, many cities annexed these suburbs. In 1854, for example, the city of Philadelphia legally took over most of the county around it, and the governments of Chicago and New York followed suit. Indeed, most great cities of the United States grew as they did only by incorporating the suburban communities along their borders.

3 ➔ With the acceleration of industrial growth came crowding and social stresses. When the first commercially successful electric traction line was developed in Boston, it revolutionized urban transportation by alleviating these problems. Transportation had previously been provided by a large network of horse-drawn lines that had many disadvantages. First, caring for the horses was expensive and labor-intensive. Additionally, the large amounts of waste left on the roads were a public health hazard. The benefits of a new form of transportation based not on horsepower but electric power were immediately obvious.

4 Not only were electric streetcars cleaner, cheaper, and more efficient, but they were also much faster than horse-drawn cars, averaging 10–15 miles per hour (compared to 5–6 miles per hour). Moreover, cities were able to offer cheap fares, since each car was capable of holding more people than a horse-drawn car. Finally, businesses were quick to support local lines in their area because of increased business prospects; and local governments were eager to support the development of such lines, because long-term maintenance costs were very low once the initial expenditures had been made. Within a few years every major urban area had an electric streetcar network, which made quick, easy movement between distant points possible for large numbers of people. This new mobility encouraged people to look for housing farther out from the crowded urban core.

5 By the end of the 1950s, the American landscape had been completely transformed. The development of suburban tract houses had brought even more former city-dwellers outward into the suburbs. Like the streets of identical row houses that went up as cities expanded, suburban tract houses tended to be similar in design. This standardization made the houses low in cost. However, unlike city row houses, suburban tract houses were detached, often with sizable yards and on winding streets.

6 The post-war prosperity of the 1950s had given the urban middle class the desire and means to own single-family houses, and detached, suburban tract houses met this desire nicely. Most also had garages. Storage space for the family automobile had become a necessity as the car rapidly became the primary mode of transportation. Both because of and as a result of this shift towards private transportation, public facilities were built farther from each other and from public transportation. In an ironic twist of fate, the suburbs, which had originally been spawned by advances in public transportation, effectively killed it off in many major cities as people became almost entirely reliant on the private car to get around.

1. With which factor in suburbanization is the passage primarily concerned?

   a.   Manufacturing
   b.   Transportation
   c.   Job markets
   d.   Economic problems

2. Areas along the edges of cities have grown in response to:

   a.   the building of factories
   b.   new goods
   c.   new building materials
   d.   city policies

3. The word emergence in the passage is closest in meaning to:

   a.   spreading
   b.   history
   c.   problems
   d.   formation

4. Which of the following is NOT mentioned in the passage as a factor in nineteenth-century suburbanization?

   a.   Cheaper housing
   b.   Urban crowding
   c.   The advent of an urban middle class
   d.   The invention of the electric streetcar

5. The traction line mentioned in paragraph 3 enabled travel by:

   a.   automobile
   b.   cart
   c.   horse-drawn trolley
   d.   electric streetcar

   Paragraph 3 is marked with an arrow [➜]

6. The word mobility in the passage refers to the ability to:

    a.   travel
    b.   buy a house
    c.   find work
    d.   enjoy life

7. The phrase went up in the passage is closest in meaning to:

    a.   were built
    b.   were bought
    c.   increased in size
    d.   attracted interest

8. The word Most in the passage refers to:

    a.   city row houses
    b.   suburban tract houses
    c.   sizable yards
    d.   winding streets

9. The passage implies that before the electric streetcar:

    a.   only a few major urban areas had horse-drawn cars
    b.   few mill towns were incorporated into cities
    c.   city transportation was slow and difficult
    d.   city crowding was not a problem

10 . Directions: An introductory sentence for a brief summary of the passage is provided below. Complete the summary by selecting the THREE answer choices that express the most important ideas in the passage. Some sentences do not belong in the summary because they express ideas that are not presented in the passage or are minor details in the passage. This question is worth 2 points.

Suburbanization, the phenomenon of rapid growth from the edges of a city outward, has been helped by several factors.

-
-
-

Answer Choices	
The introduction of electric rail lines made it easier for people to travel long distances between work and home.	Open land outside urban cores allowed for the development of affordable and attractive tract housing.
Some suburbs were incorporated into the cities they adjoined as they grew.	The automobile has made it possible for people to travel quickly even without relying on public transportation networks.
Some cities are experiencing a movement back toward their centers.	Some suburbs have public facilities that are superior to those in cities.

Reading Practice Drill #8

Langston Hughes, The Heart of Harlem

1 In a very real sense, Langston Hughes was the poet laureate of Harlem during its famous Renaissance; having come there after living in cities such as Paris, he was able to view Harlem against a backdrop of broad experience. His signal contribution to the Harlem Renaissance was to further the development of a poetic language that recorded the voices he heard around him in all their variety. He was concerned with the Black metropolis—that is, with those elements that unified Black urban communities despite the differences in the specific places they were found. Returning to this theme again and again, he wrote about Harlem more often and more fully than any other poet. As Hughes wrote about himself, "I live in the heart of Harlem." He said of its people, "I love the color of their language and, being a Harlemite myself, their problems and interests are my problems and interests." Despite the many places he had lived, Hughes came to be associated almost exclusively with Harlem as his career developed.

2 ➔ When Hughes's first publication, *The Weary Blues* (1926), appeared, the New Negro Movement was in full swing; Harlem, as the intellectual center of the movement, had become the Mecca of all aspiring young Black writers and artists. In the early 1920s, Harlem was a newly created Manhattan suburb north of Central Park where thousands of African American families had settled. Settlements there had originally been founded by the Dutch, but a real estate bust there created openings for new residents just as a huge black population was migrating from the South. By 1925 there were around 200,000 African Americans living in Harlem. Black political organizations and churches opened next door to black theaters and dance halls, which led to a fantastic melting pot of poets, musicians, intellectuals, and entrepreneurs, a development that in turn gave rise to the Harlem Renaissance. This so-called Renaissance not only encouraged and inspired the Black creative artist, but it served also to focus as never before the attention of America upon the Black artist and scholar. As a result of this new interest, Harlem became a gathering place for downtown intellectuals and bohemians—many of them honestly seeking knowledge of Black art and culture.

3 ➔ For a period of about ten years, the most obvious and sensational aspect of the New Negro Movement for downtown New York was the nightlife of Harlem, and in particular the cabaret scene. In fact, Langston Hughes was first drawn to New York by the massive success of the first all-black musical, *Shuffle Along*, composed by Eubie Blake and Noble Sissle. One of Hughes's favorite methods of composition—whether in New York, Washington, DC, or Paris—was to write poetry while sitting in a club listening to jazz or the blues. In Washington in 1925, he wrote, "I tried to write poems like the songs they sang on Seventh Street...(these songs) had the pulse beat of the people who keep on going." The 1925 Renaissance, of course, was not just a cabaret boom, and it would be decidedly unfair to give the impression that it was. But the Harlem cabaret life of the period was definitely an important by-product of the new interest in Afro-American culture created by the movement, and this life strongly influenced the early poetry of Langston Hughes.

4 Langston Hughes died in 1967 at the end of a prolific career that saw the publication of sixteen books of poems, two novels, three collections of short stories, four volumes of "editorial" and "documentary" fiction, twenty plays, children's poetry, musicals and operas, three autobiographies, a dozen radio and television scripts, and dozens of magazine articles, in addition to seven anthologies of poetry that he edited.

1. Which of the sentences below best expresses the essential information in the highlighted sentence in the passage? *Incorrect* choices change the meaning in important ways or leave out essential information.

   a. Hughes was an important poet of his time, partly because he had a wide array of experiences that helped him better understand Harlem.
   b. Hughes lived in many places before he moved to Harlem.
   c. Harlem was of particular interest to Hughes because he had lived in many other cities prior to moving there.
   d. Hughes was an important poet of this time, partly because he lived in Harlem during the Harlem Renaissance.

2. The word signal in the passage is closest in meaning to:

   a. streetlight
   b. major
   c. indication
   d. action

3. Why does the author mention that Hughes wrote, "I love the color of their language and, being a Harlemite myself, their problems and interests are my problems and interests"?

   a. To give an example of Hughes's writing style
   b. To show that he understood the struggles that African Americans faced
   c. To emphasize that he was interested in the Black Metropolis
   d. To explain why Hughes wrote about Harlem so frequently

4. What can be inferred about the New Negro Movement mentioned in paragraph 2?

   a. It was solely a movement among poets and authors.
   b. It was caused by an influx of African Americans moving to the area from the South.
   c. It began before Hughes published his first book.
   d. It started in 1926.

   Paragraph 2 is marked with an arrow [➔]

5. The word Mecca in the passage is closest in meaning to:

   a. a city in Saudi Arabia
   b. an ancient city
   c. an area of Harlem
   d. somewhere that artists wanted to visit

6. Select the sentence from paragraph 3 that describes the people or culture of downtown Harlem.

   Paragraph 3 is marked with an arrow [➜]

7. It can be inferred from the passage that Langston Hughes was first attracted to New York by:

   a. New York's cabaret scene
   b. a successful musical
   c. other African American families settling there
   d. a desire to write poetry at cabarets

8. According to the passage, Langston Hughes:

   a. was the most successful African American author of his time
   b. attained massive amounts of wealth from his poetry
   c. achieved recognition only after his death
   d. wrote several different types of publications

9. The word it in the passage refers to:

   a. Harlem
   b. a cabaret room
   c. the 1925 Renaissance
   d. Seventh Street

10. The word prolific in the passage is closest in meaning to:

    a. productive
    b. argumentative
    c. chaotic
    d. verbose

Chapter 9
Reading Practice
Answers and
Explanations

READING PRACTICE DRILL #1

1.   **D**   This is a *vocabulary in context* question. Look at the lines from the passage. Try to predict your own word for the shaded word based on the clues in the sentence. Eliminate answer choices that either are not supported by the words or phrases in the passage or are dictionary definitions of the word but are incorrect in the context of the sentence.

> Under the Constitution, the House of Representatives has the power to impeach a government official, in effect serving as prosecutor. The Senate then holds the impeachment trial, essentially serving as jury and judge, except in the impeachment of a president when the chief justice presides.

Based on what you've read, this part of the passage is talking about the House of Representatives and its ability to impeach a government official. Choice (A), *motivation*, would mean the House has a drive or need to impeach, which is not correct in this context. Choice (B), *desire*, would mean the House wants to impeach, which is similarly incorrect. Choice (C), *bearing*, refers here to the ability to bring forth something, which is not the right connotation. The word *authority* would fit well with the ability to impeach someone. Therefore, (D) is the correct response.

2.   **B**   This is a *lead word* question. The question is asking for what paragraph 3 says about the roles of the House of Representatives and the Senate in impeachment. Use the lead words "House of Representatives" and "Senate" to find the answer in the passage.

> The House of Representatives is the prosecutor. The Senate chamber is the courtroom. The Senate is the jury and also the judge, except in the case of a presidential impeachment trial when the chief justice presides.

The passage clearly states that the House of Representatives and Senate are the prosecutor, jury, and judge. Therefore, the correct answer is (B). Choice (A) is incorrect because a government official is someone who can be impeached. Similarly, (C) is incorrect because the President can be impeached. And similarly, (D), is incorrect because civil officers can also be impeached.

3.   **D**   This is an *inference* question. Inference questions ask you to find what information must be true based on the information in the passage. Use lead words or references to find the information in the passage. Based on paragraph 2, what does the passage say about the decision to impeach a government official?

> Since 1789, only 20 federal officers have been impeached by the House, 16 of which were tried by the Senate. Four were dismissed before trial because the individual had left office, 8 ended in acquittal and 8 in conviction. All of those convicted were federal judges.

In short, in more than 200 years, only 20 federal officers have been impeached. Choice (D) is the correct answer—impeachment rarely occurs. Choice (A) is incorrect because the Senate conducts the impeachment trial. Choice (B) is incorrect because this part of the passage (paragraph 2, as specified by the question) does not discuss the removal from office. Choice (C) is incorrect because the passage states the opposite of this—impeachment does NOT occur often.

4. **A** This is a *vocabulary in context* question. Read a few lines above and below the word in question. Try to predict your own word for the shaded word based on the clues in the sentence. Eliminate answer choices that either are not supported by the words or phrases in the passage or are dictionary definitions of the word but are incorrect in the context of the sentence. Look at the sentence surrounding the word "wields."

> Impeachment is a very serious affair. It is perhaps the most awesome power of Congress, the ultimate weapon it wields against officials of the federal government.

The sentence is talking about the awesome power of Congress and how it is used as a weapon against the federal government. The correct response is (A). Choice (B), *maintains*, implies that this has been going on for a while and will continue. Choice (C), *formulates*, suggests that Congress creates this weapon. Choice (D), *shapes*, suggests that Congress gives physical form to this weapon.

5. **C** This is a *lead word* question. Don't be thrown off by the information in paragraph 2—this question specifically asks for data from paragraph 4—the question is about how many times impeachment proceedings have been initiated, not completed. Each answer choice contains numbers that have been mentioned in the passage in other contexts. Don't fall for the trap answer (A) that seems familiar. Choice (B), *three*, refers to the number of impeached presidents. The correct answer is (C), *sixty-six*. Choice (D), *nineteen*, refers to the number of cases that have reached the Senate.

6. **A** This is a *lead word* question. Because the question does not tell us where to look, use the lead words provided by the question. The lead words for this question are "the impeachment process incorporates."

> The House of Representatives is the prosecutor. The Senate chamber is the courtroom. The Senate is the jury and also the judge, except in the case of a presidential impeachment trial when the chief justice presides. The final penalty is removal from office. There is no appeal.

The information for this can be found in the third paragraph. This part of the paragraph states that both the Senate and the House of Representatives play a role, so (A) is the correct answer. Choice (B), correctly names the Senate but incorrectly includes the President. Be careful that you don't fall for (C), which is a sneaky trap answer. The only time the chief justice is involved is in the case of a presidential impeachment process. This question doesn't ask about a presidential impeachment specifically, so this answer is not correct. Choice (D) incorrectly includes the Chief Justice with the Senate.

7. **D** This is a *paraphrase* question. It asks you to paraphrase a sentence from the passage, finding the essential information in the original sentence and then matching it to each of the answer choices, eliminating any answers that do not contain all the essential information or ones that introduce new information. Look at the sentence and see how you can put it into your own words.

> There was also considerable debate at the convention in Philadelphia over the definition of impeachable crimes.

This sentence is talking about a debate regarding the definition of impeachable crimes and you need to find a version that expresses the "essential information." The best choice is (D). Choice (A) is incorrect because it was not the Philadelphians—people who are from or live in Philadelphia—who debated. Choice (B) is incorrect because "formidable" means "inspiring fear or respect through being impressively large." The word *formidable* is too extreme to replace "considerable." Choice (C) is incorrect because it does not discuss the size of the debate.

8. **A** This is an EXCEPT question. Rephrase the question, eliminating the EXCEPT, go back to the passage and look for each answer choice, marking each choice as TRUE OR FALSE. Choose the answer that is different from the other three. The correct response is (A) because it is the only one that is NOT mentioned in the passage. Choices (B), *misdemeanors*, (C), *bribery*, and (D), *treason*, can be found in the passage, so they are wrong. Be careful with EXCEPT questions—they're tricky!

9. This is a *sentence insertion* question. Remember to make sure the ideas in the new sentence match up with the sentences before and after the black square. Eliminate answers that do not match or only partially match. Look at the first square:

> While the framers very clearly envisaged the occasional necessity of initiating impeachment proceedings, they put in place only a very general framework.

This sentence doesn't work because the original sentence starts off with the transitional word *Consequently* and then discusses the American version. Therefore, the correct location of this question is going to be after something that can be compared to the American version.

The second square:

> They left many questions open to differences of opinion and many details to be filled in.

This sentence won't work either for similar reasons.

Third box:

> Despite the open-endedness, as Peter Charles Hoffer and N.E.H. Hull note in their book *Impeachment in America 1635–1805,* thanks to the framers, a tool used in Parliament to curb kings and punish placemen was molded into an efficient legislative check upon executive and judicial wrongdoing.

This sentence continues to discuss the English model of impeachment. The next sentence continues to discuss the English model of Impeachment. There is no transition needed between these sentences.

Fourth box:

> The power of the English House of Commons to impeach anyone, for almost any alleged offense, was restrained; the threat of death and forfeiture upon conviction was lifted; and the interference of the Commons and the House of Lords with the regular courts of justice was limited.

This is the correct response as the added sentence is a consequence of this sentence and transitions well into the next.

10.   This is a *summary* question. Remember to separate main ideas from details. Use your understanding of passage structure to help. Make sure to eliminate answers that are too specific or not mentioned in the text. The correct answer is as follows:

The power of impeachment was initiated during the Constitutional Convention as a means to try government officials who do not act according to the law.

These three statements appropriately summarize the passage:

- The power to impeach is taken very seriously by Congress and very few government officials have been impeached.

- The impeachment process is initially brought forth by the House of Representatives, and it is tried before the Senate.

- The definition of impeachable crimes was an important component of the Constitutional Convention; nevertheless, the language defining it remains decidedly vague.

These are the reasons why the other choices are incorrect:

- Sixty-two trials of impeachment have occurred since 1789.

    This statement is a detail and does not contribute to the main idea of the passage.

- A chief justice presides over the hearing of presidential impeachment, and this is the only instance in which the Senate is not the judge.

    This statement discusses the proceedings, but this is not the main point of the passage.

- If a government official is convicted subsequent to impeachment, he/she is automatically removed from office.

    This is another detail statement.

READING PRACTICE DRILL #2

1.   **C** This is an *inference* question. Inference questions ask you to find what information must be true based on the information in the passage. Use lead words or references to find the information in the passage. Based on paragraph 1, what does it say about fire tornadoes?

Fire tornadoes—also known as fire whirls, firenados, or fire twisters—look like tornadoes but are made up of fire. Therefore, they aren't really tornadoes at all. Tornadoes are formed when just the right weather elements combine: moist, warm air lying close to the ground; an unstable atmosphere; and air fronts that collide and propel moist air vertically into the sky.

The first sentence says that fire tornadoes look like tornadoes but are made up of fire, which supports (C). Choice (A) is wrong because the passage says they aren't really tornadoes. Choice (B) can be eliminated because the passage says that fire tornadoes form when "just the right weather elements combine," meaning that circumstances have to be exactly right or the fire tornadoes won't form at all. Choice (D) is incorrect: an unstable atmosphere is *one* contributing factor, but it is not the only one.

2. **A** This is a *vocabulary in context* question. Read a few lines above and below the word in question. Try to predict your own word for the shaded word based on the clues in the sentence. Eliminate answer choices that either are not supported by the words or phrases in the passage or are dictionary definitions of the word but are incorrect in the context of the sentence. Look at the lines from the passage.

> When hot, strong winds come into contact with an already burning brushfire, updrafts of hot air catch the fire and surrounding winds and send it _____ into the air. This whirling air forms columns; as more and more hot air is pulled into a column, the column swirls, very much like a real tornado.

In this case, the description of the column as it pulls more hot air inside is the key: the column swirls, supporting (A), *spinning*. Choice (B), *working*, does not make sense in this context. Choice (C), *flying*, does not capture the direction of the action. Choice (D), *jumping*, incorrectly suggests an up and down motion.

3. **C** This is a *reference* question: it's asking what noun the pronoun *it* replaces. Look at the passage.

> A fire tornado has two parts: the core, which is actually on fire, and an invisible, rotating air pocket. It can reach temperatures of nearly 2,000°F, which is hot enough to even reignite ashes that have been sucked into the vortex from the ground.

The passage is asking *what can reach temperatures of nearly 2,000°F?* That would be the fire tornado, or its core. Now do some POE: Choice (A), *fire*, (B), *air pocket*, and (D) *ashes*, are all mentioned in the passage, but they don't match "fire tornado," so get rid of them.

4. **D** This is a NOT question, which is a variation on an EXCEPT question. Rephrase the question, eliminating the NOT, go back to the passage and look for each answer choice, marking each choice as TRUE OR FALSE. Choose the answer that is different from the other three. Look at the second paragraph, where the fire tornado is described:

> A fire tornado has two parts: the core, which is actually on fire, and an invisible, rotating air pocket. It can reach temperatures of nearly 2,000°F, which is hot enough to even reignite ashes that have been sucked into the vortex from the ground. While real tornadoes occur as a result of atmospheric conditions high above, fire tornadoes result from hot, dry air rising quickly away from the ground. When hot, strong winds come into contact with an already burning brushfire, updrafts of hot air catch the fire and surrounding winds and send it whirling into the air. This whirling air forms columns; as more and more hot air is pulled into a column, the column swirls, very much like a real tornado.

Choices (A) *column*, (B), *core*, and (C), *air pocket*, are all mentioned in the paragraph, leaving you with (D), *angular momentum* as the correct answer.

5. **C** This is a *lead word* question. This question asks you to understand what the passage says about angular momentum and then find an example that matches that description. Look at the passage.

> The law of angular momentum states that when an object is inside a spinning column, it will move faster and faster the closer it gets to the center of rotation.

With that description, go to POE and eliminate answers that don't describe a spinning motion. Choices (A) describes running a further distance. Choice (B) describes hitting a tennis ball harder. Choice (C) describes an ice skater spinning, which matches the spinning column in the passage. Choice (D) describes swimming faster. Only (C) mentions spinning and is therefore the correct answer.

6.   **A**   This is an *inference* question. Inference questions ask you to find what information must be true based on the information in the passage. Use lead words or references to find the information in the passage. Remember that most questions on TOEFL Reading passages are arranged chronologically within the passage, so you're probably pretty close to the answer for this question by looking at where you found the previous answer. Take a look at that same paragraph.

> While fire whirls move pretty slowly, they can cause significant damage. Anything—or anyone!—unfortunate enough to be in a fire whirl's path will likely either be set ablaze or flung vigorously from its location. But it's not just the fire that's dangerous—the winds it generates can create wind speeds of more than 100 mph, which is strong enough to knock down trees. Fire whirls also typically don't last very long, but when they do, they can wreak havoc and leave disaster in their wakes.

Now, look at the answers to see what you can eliminate. Is there anything in the passage that matches what (A) says? Choice (A) suggests fire whirls don't move quickly, which matches "move pretty slowly" so keep (A) but check the other answers. Choice (B), *don't cause damage*, does not match since the passage mentions knocking down trees and wreaking havoc. Choice (C), *can't knock down trees*, is the opposite of what the passage says. Choice (D), *can last for days*, is the opposite of what the passage says—that fire whirls don't last very long. Choice (A) is correct.

7.   **D**   This is a *vocabulary in context* question. Read a few lines above and below the word in question. Try to predict your own word for the shaded word based on the clues in the sentence. Eliminate answer choices that either are not supported by the words or phrases in the passage or are dictionary definitions of the word but are incorrect in the context of the sentence. Look at the lines from the passage.

> But it's not just the fire that's dangerous—the winds it generates can create wind speeds of more than 100 mph, which is strong enough to knock down trees. Fire whirls also typically don't last very long, but when they do, they can _____ and leave disaster in their wakes.

"Wreak havoc" is linked to the word "and," which tells us that the phrase in question will be along the lines of "leave disaster in their wakes," the second part of that sentence. Choice (A), *start sizeable fires*, refers to a specific disaster. Choice (B), *last forever*, refers to duration rather than creating a disaster. Choice (C), *move quickly*, similarly does not refer to creating a disaster. Choice (D), *cause significant damage*, refers to creating unspecified damage, which would leave disaster in their wakes. If you were torn between (A) and (D), note that (A) is too specific for this context. Choice (D) is correct.

8.   **A**   This is an *inference* question. Inference questions ask you to find what information must be true based on the information in the passage, using lead words or references to find the materials. This question guides you to paragraph 5.

> There have been numerous major firenados in the last 150 years, many of which have proved lethal. In 1871, the great Peshtigo Fire in Northeastern Wisconsin and Upper Michigan resulted from inauspicious conditions: dry weather during the summer, slash-and-burn farming practices, and a vigorous cold front that brought strong winds. Together, these three contributing factors created firenados that turned a few small prairie fires into a furious conflagration. The town of Peshtigo, with hundreds of wooden structures and lumberyards, sat in the middle of a forest of pine and hardwood. When the fire reached the town, it found abundant fuel. In just minutes, 100-mph winds and ambient temperatures of more than 700°F caused what is still recognized as the worst fire disaster in the history of the United States. As best as anyone could tell, nearly 2,000 people lost their lives.

Once you've reviewed the paragraph, it's all about POE. Choice (A) is a reasonable match because the passage says there have been "numerous major firenados in the last 150 years." Choice (B) is out because they *have* been documented—after all, you know they happened long before anyone who's alive today was even born. Choice (C) can be eliminated because nothing says that the fire in Peshtigo was the *first* known occurrence of a firenado. Choice (D) is suspicious because it says "*always* lethal," which you can't prove from the passage. Therefore, (A) is the correct answer.

9.   **C**   This is a *vocabulary in context* question. Read a few lines above and below the word in question. Try to predict your own word for the shaded word based on the clues in the sentence. Eliminate answer choices that either are not supported by the words or phrases in the passage or are dictionary definitions of the word but are incorrect in the context of the sentence. Look at the lines from the passage.

> There have been numerous major firenados in the last 150 years, many of which have proved lethal. In 1871, the great Peshtigo Fire in Northeastern Wisconsin and Upper Michigan resulted from inauspicious conditions: dry weather during the summer, slash-and-burn farming practices, and a vigorous cold front that brought strong winds. Together, these three contributing factors created firenados that turned a few small prairie fires into a furious conflagration.

Looking at the sentence after the word in question, you see terms like "vigorous" and "strong" that describe the conditions from which the fire resulted. Together, these tell you that "inauspicious" means something negative. Try using POE. Choice (A), *lucky*, is a positive term. Choice (B), *fortunate*, is similar to lucky. Choice (C), *unlucky*, would describe this combination of negative influences, so keep it. Choice (D), *dangerous*, is negative, but it does not capture the sentence's meaning of the chances of all of these happening together. Therefore, (C), is correct.

10. This is a *summary* question. Remember to separate main ideas from details. Use your understanding of passage structure to help. Make sure to eliminate answers that are too specific or not mentioned in the text. This passage has discussed how firenadoes are created and the damage they can cause.

Therefore, the three points that show that "A firenado is one example of a natural phenomenon that is as uncommon as it is dangerous" are as follows:

- **Firenados require a unique combination of conditions in order to occur.**
  This answer shows that they are uncommon because they require a "unique combination" of conditions.

- **Firenados can cause significant damage.**
  This answer shows that firenados are dangerous.

- **Scientists don't know much about firenados because it is hard to predict where or when they will occur.**
  This answer supports the idea that firenados are uncommon.

The three incorrect answers are:

- **Firenados suck up ashes and gases into their core.**
  This answer is a detail describing how they are fueled.

- **A firefighter escaped a firenado by jumping into a river.**
  This answer is a detail describing what happened in a specific incident of a firenado in Canada.

- **The firenado in Peshtigo was the first firenado on record**
  This answer is a specific example.

READING PRACTICE DRILL #3

1. **A** This is a *vocabulary in context* question. Read a few lines above and below the word in question. Try to predict your own word for the shaded word based on the clues in the sentence. Eliminate answer choices that either are not supported by the words or phrases in the passage or are dictionary definitions of the word but are incorrect in the context of the sentence. Take a look at the lines in the passage.

    After the respective 13 or 17 years of subterranean lifestyle, the almost-mature cicada **nymphs** emerge at a given place and time in astounding numbers—as many as 1.5 million cicadas per acre.

    Ask yourself what the surrounding words say about the cicada, which are almost mature. Take the idea of "almost-mature" to the answers. Choice (A), *immature cicadas*, is an almost exact match, so keep it for now. There's no indication in the passage of a *different species*, so get rid of (B). The cicadas eat fluids from *roots of trees*, which makes (C) sound like a good answer, but it doesn't match in meaning, so it is incorrect. Choice (D), *water creatures*, is not mentioned at all, so eliminate it. Choice (A) is correct.

2. **C** This is a *lead word* question, asking what the passage says about where periodical cicadas can be found. Go look in the passage for the lines that discuss *periodical cicadas*.

> For the four 13-year-cycle species, which tend to be further to the south and west of the eastern United Sates, this may be as early as late April or early May. But for the three 17-year-cycle species, which are generally found more toward the northern end of the eastern United States, this may not happen until late May or early June.

Choice (A) says they are found *around the world*, but only the United States is mentioned, so eliminate it. Choice (B) says they are found *throughout the western hemisphere*, but again, only the United States is mentioned, so eliminate it. Choice (C) says the *across the eastern United States*, which matches the passage where it says, "to the south and west of the eastern United States," and "the northern end of the eastern United States" so keep (C). Choice (D) says *in the southeastern United States*, which is too narrow as the passage says they are in the north as well, so (D) is eliminated and (C) is correct.

3. **B** This is a *reference* question: it's asking what noun the pronoun *they* replaces. Look at the passage.

> Once they emerge they have only about 4–6 weeks to live. First, they find a new home on plants near their emergence location where they complete their transition into full adult cicadas.

This question requires you to look back into the previous paragraph, because there is no noun earlier in the same sentence or same paragraph. What was the passage discussing in the preceding paragraph? The cicadas that had emerged. Take that to the answers. Choice (A) references the *southeastern United States*, where some of the cicadas emerge, but that's not what the pronoun is referring to, so get rid of it. Choice (B), *periodical cicadas*, is exactly what we'd predicted. Choice (C), *plants*, was not mentioned. Choice (D), *predators*, was also not mentioned, so (B) is correct.

4. **A** This is a *lead word* question, so go back to the passage and look for the word *broods*.

> Periodical cicadas are divided into groups called broods; these broods are based on the calendar year in which they emerge. In 1898, entomologist C. L. Marlatt identified as many as 30 broods, although not all of them have actually been observed since then.

Using the first part of the first sentence, compare the answer choices. Choice (A), *the year in which they emerge*, is an almost identical match to the passage, so keep it. Choice (B), *the length of their lifecycles*, doesn't match—the passage doesn't discuss the cicadas' lifecycles as the determining factor of their brood organization. Choice (C), *the length of their development cycle*, is also not mentioned as an organizing factor. Choice (D), *Marlatt's preferences*, refers to the person who identified them but is not about the way they are organized, so eliminate everything except (A).

5. **A** This is a *vocabulary in context* question. Read a few lines above and below the word in question. Try to predict your own word for the shaded word based on the clues in the sentence. Eliminate answer choices that either are not supported by the words or phrases in the passage or are dictionary definitions of the word but are incorrect in the context of the sentence.

> The membranes across the "ribs" of the tymbal vibrate quickly, and the cicada's body functions like a resonance chamber and _____ the sound. The cicadas can adjust the "volume" of their sound by turning their bodies in different directions.

If you're not sure what exact word to use, ask yourself what the word relates to. It has something to do with the sound that the cicadas make, and the next sentence says that the cicadas can adjust the "volume" of their sound. So it probably has something to do with adjusting the volume. Take a look at the answers. Would it make sense to "make louder" the sound, as in (A)? Well, the meaning makes sense, so keep it. Choice (B) refers to producing sound, which is not specifically about the volume, so eliminate it. Choice (C) refers to making the sound worse, which also does not refer to volume, so get rid of (C). Similarly, (D) refers to degrading the sound, which again does not refer to volume. Choice (A) is correct.

6. **B** This question asks you to find the sentence in the passage that serves a particular purpose, namely to describe how periodical cicadas attract mates. Go directly to the answers and use POE. Choice (A) discusses the purpose of cicadas' adult lives, not their mating habits, so get rid of it. Choice (B) talks about the males forming choruses to attract mates, so keep it. Choice (C) discusses the males' tymbals, not mating habits, so eliminate it. Choice (D) talks about the cicadas' populations, not mating habits, so get rid of that too. Choice (B) is correct.

7. **C** This is a *reference* question: it's asking which noun the pronoun *their* refers to. Look at the passage.

> As a result, when the cicadas do become prey, their predators can seemingly eat their fill without making a significant impact on the cicada population.

Ask yourself, who is eating? The predators. Now go take a look at the answers, and eliminate any that don't match. Choice (A), *broods*, refers to the cicadas, not the predators. Choice (B), *cicada populations*, also refers to the cicadas rather than the predators. Choice (C), *cicada predators*, are indeed the predators, so keep it. Choice (D), *cicada prey*, refers to what cicadas prey on. Choice (C) is correct.

8. **D** This is a *sentence insertion* question. Remember to make sure the ideas in the new sentence match up with the sentences before and after the black square. Eliminate answers that do not match or only half-match. Here's the sentence we are going to add:

> This phenomenon is known as "predator satiation," a situation in which prey occur at an incredibly high population, drastically reducing the probability that an individual organism be eaten.

The "this" at the beginning of the sentence has to refer to something else before it, so it can't be inserted at the beginning of the paragraph—eliminate (A). The first and second sentences don't describe an event or phenomenon, so there's nothing for "this" in the inserted sentence to reference in either one. Eliminate (B) and (C). The last sentence, as the paragraph is currently written, describes predators being able to eat their fill without impacting cicada populations, which "this" could definitely reference. Putting the new sentence at the end of the paragraph, therefore, makes the most sense. Choice (D) is correct.

9. **C** This is a *lead word* question, so go back to the passage for information. Look for the part of the passage that discusses emergence, more or less in the same area where you've already been working. Look at what it says:

> Most interesting, though, is how they keep track of time and know when 13 or 17 years have passed. Alas, researchers don't actually know how they do it, other than knowing that it's some kind of molecular clock. The insects themselves make for difficult research, since researchers have to wait at least 13 years for a brood to reemerge!

With that information, take a look at the answers and see what matches. It's highly doubtful that insects have calendars, so eliminate (A). There is no evidence in the passage that the cicadas can track seasons, so eliminate (B). There is proof that scientists believe the cicadas have "some kind of molecular clock," which supports (C) and invalidates (D). Choice (C) is correct.

10. This is a *summary* question. Remember to separate main ideas from details. Use your understanding of passage structure to help. Make sure to eliminate answers that are too specific or not mentioned in the text. The question asks you to find three points that support the following idea:

Periodical cicadas are unique creatures because of their unusual lifecycles and their lack of significant predators.

The following three statements appropriately summarize the passage:
- Four species have 13-year lifecycles.

    This answer supports the idea that these insects have unusual lifecycles.

- Periodical cicadas do not have many natural predators because they emerge only once every 13 or 17 years, so their lifespan is too short for predators to rely upon them.

    This answer supports the idea that these insects have no significant predators.

- Once periodical cicadas emerge, they live only 4 to 6 weeks.

    This answer supports the idea that these insects have unusual lifecycles.

The incorrect answers are:
- Periodical cicadas use their tymbals to make sounds during mating.

    This answer doesn't show the stated reasons why the periodical cicadas are unique.

- Periodical cicadas have a significant maturation process, emerging only when they are almost ready to lay eggs.

    This answer does not show how periodical cicadas are unique.

- The soil temperature must by 64° F before the periodical cicadas will emerge.

    This answer tells us about periodical cicadas but not why they are unique.

READING PRACTICE DRILL #4

1. **A** This is a *lead word* question, so go back to see what the passage says about *atoms*, *cells*, and the *Milky Way*.

> This pattern is found in many places in our world, including biology, geology, physics, astronomy, and chemistry. For example, even atoms are circular in nature, with evenly balanced protons, neutrons, and electrons. Every cell has a nucleus, which also has a circle at the center. Even the Milky Way galaxy is circular, with our circular solar system within it. One could argue that each of these is a mandala in and of itself.

The "for example" and the last sentence give us the key: "…each of these is a mandala in and of itself." That means the author has listed them as examples of mandalas, or circles in our world. Using POE, (A) is a close match, so keep it. Choice (B) may be appealing, but it's not as precise as (A), so get rid of it. There is no mention of (C), *symbols*, or (D), *the cosmos*, in the passage, so eliminate (C) and (D). Choice (A) is correct.

2. **C** This is a *vocabulary in context* question. Read a few lines above and below the word in question. Try to predict your own word for the shaded word based on the clues in the sentence. Eliminate answer choices that either are not supported by the words or phrases in the passage or are dictionary definitions of the word but are incorrect in the context of the sentence.

> Carl Jung, the founder of analytical psychology, _____ that "a mandala is the psychological expression of the totality of the self." He sketched a small circular drawing every morning, and felt that whatever came to life in his mandala corresponded to his inner experience at the time.

A reasonable word to replace the word in question might be "believed" or "thought." Choice (A), *kept in hand*, is too literal a definition of held. Choice (B), *occupied*, does not work in the context of the passage. Choice (C), *believed*, fits our prediction. Choice (D), *guarded*, also does not work in the context of the passage. Choice (C) is correct.

3. **B** This is a *vocabulary in context* question. Read a few lines above and below the words in question. Try to predict your own word for the shaded words based on the clues in the sentence. Eliminate answer choices that either are not supported by the words or phrases in the passage or are dictionary definitions of the words but are incorrect in the context of the sentence.

> He found that during periods of significant _____ many of his clients felt compelled to create mandalas. He found that people felt drawn to drawing or painting mandalas simply because it felt right to do so—it seemed that they instinctively turned to creating a mandala as a way to express their experience.

The passage indicates that people felt compelled to create mandalas as a way to express their experience. So, replacing the words in question with "challenging experiences" could work. Now try some POE. Choice (A), *ease*, is the opposite of our prediction. Choice (B), *difficulty*, is a good match. Choice (C), *fun*, is also the opposite of our prediction, as is (D), *happiness*. Choice (B) is correct.

4. **C** This is a *sentence insertion* question. Remember to make sure the ideas in the new sentence match up with the sentences before and after the black square. Eliminate answers that do not match or only half-match. Here's the sentence we are going to add:

> Based on this belief and his recognition of his own internal evolution through the use of mandalas, he began to use them as a tool in his psychology practice.

This sentence uses pronouns like "this," "his," and "them," so ask yourself what these might refer back to. "His" likely refers to Carl Jung, and "them" refers to mandalas. Since the sentence describes how Jung used mandalas in his practice, which isn't mentioned until after the second square, eliminate (A) and (B). The last sentence describes the results of using mandalas in his practice, so it doesn't make sense to put this sentence at the end of the paragraph. Eliminate (D). Only (C), the correct answer, remains.

5. **A** This is a *lead word* question, so go back to the paragraph in the passage discussing shapes recognized by the human eye. Here's what it says:

> Why might humans have this instinct? Research into the fields of psychology and child development may shed some light on the subject. It would seem that circles are part of the basic creation of a personal identity. Studies conducted with babies show that, as early as one week old, infants prefer to look at curved lines rather than straight lines. Additional research shows that two-month-old infants can discern shapes that look like faces from scrambled patterns. Psychologically, it is believed that simple, closed forms—like circles—are identified more quickly and recognized as meaningful, known, and familiar. Even the shape of an eye is spherical—simply put, it's a three-dimensional circle—and our field of vision is thus also circular.

The second to last sentence says "…closed forms—like circles—are identified more quickly." As you use POE, eliminate any answers that are not "closed forms." Choice (A), *circles*, are closed forms—like circles, so keep (A). Choice (B), *straight lines*, are open forms. Choice (C), *squares*, are closed forms, but not circles. Choice (D), *squiggly lines*, are open forms. Choice (A) is correct.

6. **B** This is a *reference* question: it's asking what noun the pronoun *their* replaces. Look at the passage.

> He found that during periods of significant trial and tribulation many of his clients felt compelled to create mandalas. He found that people felt drawn to drawing or painting mandalas simply because it felt right to do so—it seemed that they instinctively turned to creating a mandala as a way to express their experience.

Ask yourself "whose challenging experiences is the author discussing?" It makes sense that the author is discussing the people who are drawing the mandalas, or his clients. Use POE. Choice (A), *Jung*, does not match our prediction. Choice (B), *Jung's clients*, is a good match, so keep it. Choice (C) discusses children generally. Choice (D) discusses adults generally. Choice (B) is correct.

7. **D** This is a *lead word* question, so go back to the passage to find what the passage says about children's drawings becoming more detailed. Here's what it says.

> Circles also appear very early in children's art. What begins as random scribbling progresses into drawing circles as early as age two. By three or four years old, their drawings become more intricate, and without any input from adults, they begin drawing suns, flowers, and people whose arms and legs connect to large circular heads.

The passage indicates that the detailed, representative pictures—suns, flowers, and people whose arms and legs connect to large circular heads—come about when children are three to four years old. Using POE allows you to eliminate (A), *one week*, (B), *one year*, and (C), *two years*. Choice (D), *three to four years*, is correct.

8. **D** This question asks you to find a sentence that serves a particular purpose. In this case, it's asking you to find a sentence that "describes how drawing a mandala allows an adult to reestablish a connection with her subconscious." Go straight to POE and eliminate answers that don't serve that purpose.

    Choice (A) discusses children's drawing, so eliminate it. Choice (B) discusses researchers' perspectives, so get rid of it. Choice (C) doesn't clearly state what it's describing, so get rid of it. Choice (D) discusses therapists' beliefs that mandalas are representative of internal issues and allow patients to align their conscious and unconscious actions and decisions, which matches the goal set forth by the question.

9. **D** This is a NOT question, which is a variation on an EXCEPT question. Rephrase the question, eliminating the NOT, go back to the passage and look for each answer choice, marking each choice as TRUE OR FALSE. Choose the answer that is different from the other three.

    Choice (A) is mentioned in the beginning of the first paragraph, so get rid of it. Choice (B) is mentioned at the end of the first paragraph, so it can also be eliminated. Choice (C) is discussed in the second and third paragraphs. Choice (D), however, is never mentioned. Choice (D) is thus correct.

10. This is a *summary* question. Remember to separate main ideas from details. Use your understanding of passage structure to help. Make sure to eliminate answers that are too specific or not mentioned. The question asks you to find three points that support the following idea:

    Mandala art has ancient roots and can play a therapeutic role for humans.

    The following three statements appropriately summarize the passage:
    - The term "mandala" comes from an ancient language and has been passed on for generations.
        This answer shows that mandala art has ancient roots.
    - Many ancient traditions and religions used mandalas in their ceremonies.
        This answer shows that mandala art has ancient roots.
    - Carl Jung, the founder of analytical psychology, found value in using mandalas with his patients.
        This answer shows that mandala art can play a therapeutic role for humans.

The incorrect answers are as follows:

- **Children learn to draw circles before they learn to draw any other shapes.**

    This answer does not specifically show the ancient roots of mandalas or their role in therapy.

- **Circles appear in artwork of peoples around the world.**

    This answer is too general.

- **Our solar system is a mandala.**

    This answer is a specific example of a mandala, showing neither its ancient roots nor its role in therapy.

READING PRACTICE DRILL #5

1. **B** This is a *paraphrase* question. It asks you to paraphrase a sentence from the passage, finding the essential information in the original sentences and then matching it to each of the answer choices, eliminating any answers that do not contain all the essential information or ones that introduce new information. Start by reading the highlighted sentence:

    > Women went from watching men take thrilling risks to becoming willing passengers and finally pilots in their own right.

    This sentence indicates the path women took in aviation, first as spectators, then as passengers, and finally as pilots. Choice (A) focuses on men rather than women. Choice (B) matches this sequence of events. Choice (C) similarly focuses on men rather than the women who are the focus of the original sentence. Choice (D) omits the important detail that women became pilots.

2. **C** This is a NOT question. Rephrase the question, eliminating the NOT, go back to the passage and look for each answer choice, marking each choice as TRUE OR FALSE. Choose the answer that is different from the other three. The question is looking for what is not mentioned as a danger for early pilots. Choice (A), *bad weather*, is mentioned in the second paragraph. Choice (B), *faulty equipment*, is also mentioned in the second paragraph. Choice (C), the *inability to communicate with ground personnel*, is not mentioned anywhere in the text. Choice (D), the *lack of radio beacons*, is also mentioned in the second paragraph. Choice (C) is the exception and thus correct.

3. **C** This is a *vocabulary in context* question. Read a few lines above and below the word in question. Try to predict your own word for the shaded word based on the clues in the sentence. Eliminate answer choices that either are not supported by the words or phrases in the passage or are dictionary definitions of the word but are incorrect in the context of the sentence.

    > Conventional wisdom that women were unsuited for flying made it difficult for them to raise money for the up-to-date equipment they needed to _____ on an equal basis with men.

The women's difficulty in getting good enough equipment and the phrase "on an equal basis with men" imply that women struggled to do as well as men. A good prediction for this blank might be "compete." Choice (A), *cooperate*, implies working together, not against each other. Choice (B), *accept*, does not match the prediction. Choice (C), *vie*, is a good match for this prediction. Choice (D), *revolt*, is too extreme.

4. **D** This is an *inference* question. Inference questions ask you to find what information must be true based on the information in the passage, using lead words or references to find the materials. For this question, read Paragraph 3.

> Conventional wisdom that women were unsuited for flying made it difficult for them to raise money for the up-to-date equipment they needed to contend on an equal basis with men. Yet they still found ways to compete and often triumphed despite the odds against them. Ruth Law, for example, in 1916 flew 590 miles from Chicago to New York and set a new nonstop distance record. She was so successful that in 1917 she earned as much as $9,000 per week for exhibition and stunt flights. Ruth Law, as much as any woman of her day, exemplified the resourcefulness and determination demanded of a woman who wanted to fly. When she addressed the Aero Club of America after completing her historic journey, her plainspoken words testified to a motivation that was independent of gender. She had, she said, undertaken the flight strictly for the love of accomplishment and had "no expectation of reward."

The first sentence of the paragraph states that it was "difficult for them to raise money for the up-to-date equipment they needed" so we know they struggled to get the gear they needed to fly. Choice (A), *generating publicity*, was not discussed as an issue. Choice (B), *taking lessons*, was also not discussed. Choice (C), *setting records*, was mentioned in the paragraph as something Ruth Law did, not something she struggled to do. Choice (D), *getting aviation gear*, matches our prediction and thus is the correct answer.

5. **A** This is a *detail* question. It asks for information about Ruth Law's records. Paragraph 3 states *Ruth Law, for example, in 1916 flew 590 miles from Chicago to New York and set a new nonstop distance record* so we know her record was for a nonstop flight. Choice (A) matches the prediction, so keep it. There is no mention of her flying across the ocean, so cross off (B). While the passage does mention Law's earnings, (C), and exhibition flights, (D), it does not say that she set records for those things, so (C) and (D) are incorrect. Choice (A) is the correct response.

6. **B** This is a *vocabulary in context* question. Read a few lines above and below the word in question. Try to predict your own word for the shaded word based on the clues in the sentence. Eliminate answer choices that either are not supported by the words or phrases in the passage or are dictionary definitions of the word but are incorrect in the context of the sentence.

> She had, she said, undertaken the flight _____ for the love of accomplishment and had "no expectation of reward."

The structure of the sentence indicates that Law wanted only one thing: accomplishment. Law wanted accomplishment, not fame, so eliminate (A). Choice (B) fits that definition, so keep it. Choice (C), *with discipline*, and (D), *without help*, do not fit with "love of accomplishment," so eliminate these choices, too. Choice (B) is correct.

7. **B** This is a *detail* question, so read paragraph 4 again.

> Recognition of women aviators' abilities did not always come easily. "Men do not believe us capable," the famed aviator Amelia Earhart once remarked to a friend. "Because we are women, seldom are we trusted to do an efficient job." Indeed, old attitudes died hard.

The old attitudes referred to in the passage are those against women's abilities as pilots. To say these beliefs "died hard" indicates that such erroneous attitudes did not change quickly. Choice (A), that *many women were killed in plane crashes*, is not mentioned. Choice (B), which refers to changing beliefs, matches our prediction, so keep it. Choice (C), which says that *few women were interested in flying*, is not mentioned. Choice (D), that *most early flight records were set by women*, was also not mentioned, so (B) is the correct answer.

8. **A** This is an *inference* question. Inference questions ask you to find what information must be true based on the information in the passage. Use lead words or references to find the information in the passage. Here's the paragraph:

> Ironically, when Ruth Law, one of the early twentieth century's most recognized symbols of female independence, announced her sudden retirement from flight in 1922, she cited traditional concerns: she wanted to settle down and have a family. Additionally, and perhaps just as importantly, her husband and promoter Charles Oliver had grown so anxious about the dangers of her flying that he lost weight every time she took to the air. In this way, a worried husband's concerns for his wife's welfare put an end to the illustrious career of America's foremost female aviator of the time.

The passage states that Law's husband lost weight each time she flew, and that his worries "put an end" to her career so it can be reasonably inferred that concerns about his health were a major factor in her early retirement. Choice (A) matches this prediction, so keep it. The passage does not provide information to support claims that she was resentful of her husband, so eliminate (B). Since the passage only states that she ended her career as a pilot, we do not know if she flew again, so eliminate (C). The paragraph also does not describe what her career could have been had she continued working as a pilot, so cross off (D).

9. **D** This is a *sentence insertion* question. Remember to make sure the ideas in the new sentence match up with the sentences before and after the black square. Eliminate answers that do not match or only half-match. Since the new sentence begins with "stung by rejection," we can infer that a previous sentence discusses how a woman was rejected for work in a particular industry and how that woman wished to write about her rejection. The first sentence of paragraph 5 shows how Law was rejected as a military pilot, and the last sentence explains that she wrote an article to express her anger, so (D) is the correct answer. Rejection is not discussed in the other three sentences preceding squares, so eliminate (A), (B), and (C).

10. This is a *summary* question. Remember to separate main ideas from details. Use your understanding of passage structure to help. Make sure to eliminate answers that are too specific or not mentioned in the text.

The following three statements appropriately summarize the passage:
- In the United States, women were not regarded as fit to fly in military combat despite having proven themselves as skilled pilots.

  This is an important point in the third and fourth paragraphs.

- Recognition of the achievements of female pilots was hard to come by, since prevailing attitudes maintained that women were inferior to men.

  This is the main topic of the fourth paragraph.

- Female aviators had difficulty raising money for flight equipment, but some still succeeded because of their resourcefulness.

  This is the main topic of the third paragraph.

The following answers are incorrect:
- The number of famous women pilots increased greatly after the 1930s.

  The passage does not mention aviation after the 1930s.

- Concern about her family caused at least one famous aviator to give up flying.

  While the passage does mention the reasons Law stopped flying professionally, it is not a main topic of the passage.

- Charles and Anne Lindbergh flew to the Soviet Union and saw fewer female pilots than in the United States.

  The passage states that Charles and Anne Lindbergh saw more female pilots in Russia than in the United States, so that choice contradicts the passage.

READING PRACTICE DRILL #6

1. **C** This is a *lead word/detail* question. It's asking what the first paragraph demonstrates or what it tells the reader. This paragraph describes the geographical dimensions of the Rocky Mountains: *Elevations along the range are…and widths range from 120 to 650 kilometers.* It does not discuss how fully the mountains have been explored until recently, so eliminate (A). We don't know how high *most* of the Rocky Mountains are, so eliminate (B). Choice (C) is reasonable because it addresses the different geographical characteristics presented in the passage. Since paragraph 1 doesn't discuss human inhabitants or their impacts on the mountains at all, eliminate (D). The correct answer is (C).

2. **A** This is a *reference* question: it asks what noun a particular pronoun refers to, or replaces. To help you identify this word, look for the last noun before the pronoun. In this case, the last noun before the pronoun is *sediments*, which matches (A). Choice (B), *eras*, appears earlier in the paragraph. Choice (C), *years*, also appears earlier, as does (D), *mountain ranges*. Thus, (A) is correct.

3.   **B**   This is an EXCEPT question. Rephrase the question, eliminating the EXCEPT, go back to the passage and look for each answer choice, marking each choice as TRUE OR FALSE. Choose the answer that is different from the other three. Paragraph 2 lists several types of rocks that are found in the mountains: granites, schists, gneisses, quartzites, and slates. Choices (A), (C), and (D) are included in this list of rock types, but (B) is not. Therefore, (B) is correct.

4.   **B**   This is an *inference* question. Inference questions ask you to find what information must be true based on the information in the passage, using lead words or references to find the materials. It asks what the phrase *only one of* implies. Read about the process that was just described in the passage: it describes how the Rocky Mountains were formed. The sentence continues to describe *cycles of upheaval,* indicating that there was more than one cycle. Choice (A) is wrong because we have no support for the idea that this upheaval was different from others. Choice (B) matches our prediction because the text says that the process was *one of the cycles,* implying that there were others. Choice (C) is wrong because the passage doesn't support the idea that this upheaval was *the most dramatic* one. You may think (D) is appealing because you remember seeing the phrase *wrinkle in a carpet* in the passage. However, that's not what the phrase in the question means in the context of the passage, so eliminate (D). Choice (B) is correct.

5.   **D**   This is a *vocabulary in context* question. Read a few lines above and below the word in question. Try to predict your own word for the shaded word based on the clues in the sentence. Eliminate answer choices that either are not supported by the words or phrases in the passage or are dictionary definitions of the word but are incorrect in the context of the sentence. It's asking what the word *ate* means in the passage. You might put something like "cut" or "carved" into the imaginary blank, because the previous phrase talks about how *Streams flowed faster and began to cut canyons….* Choice (A), *raised,* doesn't match the prediction. Choice (B), *buried,* also doesn't match. Choice (C), *erased,* similarly doesn't work in context. Choice (D), *dug,* matches our prediction best and is thus correct.

6.   **A**   This is another *lead word/detail* question. It asks for information about the plains and plateaus that surround the Rocky Mountains. If you scan the passage for *plains and plateaus,* you'll find them mentioned in paragraph 4: *As the mountains were formed, streams eroded their sides, and thousands of feet of sediment spread out on plains and plateaus.* Choice (A) says *materials washed down from the mountains,* which matches our prediction. Choice (B), which refers to *hard core rocks,* is not mentioned in the paragraph. Choice (C), *densely packed volcanic deposits,* and (D), *soil rich in organic matter,* are also not mentioned. Choice (A) is correct.

7.   **C**   This is a *lead word/detail* question that asks what the passage says about how some of the most dramatic-looking parts of the Rocky Mountains were formed. Paragraph 4 states that *The glaciated terrains… are among the most picturesque.* The rest of this sentence indicates that these were formed by glaciers. This matches (C) perfectly. Choice (A), *volcanic eruptions,* is not supported by the text. Similarly, (B), *rivers,* is not supported. Choice (C), *glaciers,* matches our prediction above. Choice (D), *the ocean,* is also not supported by the passage. Choice (C) is correct.

8.　**B**　This question asks how the entire passage is organized. Revisit the main points of the paragraphs: Paragraph 1 introduces the Rocky Mountains; Paragraph 2 discusses what happened a half-billion years ago during the Paleozoic and Mesozoic Eras; Paragraph 3 continues into the Cretaceous period, about 75 million years ago; Paragraph 4 discusses the end of the Eocene period about 40 million years ago; and Paragraph 5 discusses just a few hundred years ago. Choice (A) does not match the structure. Choice (B) fits this description, so keep it. Choice (C) describes a contrast of two periods, which is not supported by the text. Choice (D) compares the effects of various geological periods on North America, also does not match the text. Choice (B) is correct.

9.　**C**　This is a *vocabulary in context* question. Read a few lines above and below the word in question. Try to predict your own word for the shaded word based on the clues in the sentence. Eliminate answer choices that either are not supported by the words or phrases in the passage or are dictionary definitions of the word but are incorrect in the context of the sentence. The meaning you might use to replace *of note* could be "worth talking about." With this, evaluate the answers. You should find that (A), *catastrophic*, does not work in context. Neither does (B), *distinct*. Choice (C), *important*, could be "worth talking about" so keep it. Choice (D), *ancient*, does not match the context. The correct answer is (C).

10.　**D**　This is a *sentence insertion* question. Remember to make sure the ideas in the new sentence match up with the sentences before and after the black square. Eliminate answers that do not match or only half-match. In this case, *as soon as they rose* tells us that something happened as soon as the mountains started rising, so look in the passage. The only place in the passage near a square that talks about the mountains rising is just before the fourth square: *…the region again uplifted*. This idea is not mentioned near the other three squares, so (A), (B), and (C) are out. Choice (D) is correct.

READING PRACTICE DRILL #7

1.　**B**　This *lead word/detail* question asks you to identify the main factor that contributes to suburbanization. You should do this question on your second pass, once you have a better sense of the passage as a whole. Paragraph 1 discusses travel by foot and horse and cart; Paragraph 3 discusses how the electric traction line revolutionized urban transportation; Paragraph 4 continues to talk about electric streetcars; Paragraph 6 discusses storage space for the automobile and how rapidly the car became the primary mode of transportation. All of these points together support (B), *transportation*. Choice (A), *manufacturing*, is not supported by the text. Choice (B), *transportation*, matches our prediction above. Choice (C), *job markets*, is not supported by the passage. Neither is (D), *economic problems*. Choice (B) is therefore correct.

2.   **D**   This is a *lead word/detail* question. Scan the early paragraphs for *edges of cities,* which can be found in paragraph 2. Read several lines before and after *edges of cities* to identify what has influenced these areas. Further, paragraph 2 indicates that *many cities annexed these suburbs.* Therefore, the answer will have something to do with action taken by the cities themselves. Choices (A), *the building of factories,* (B), *new goods,* and (C), *new building materials,* do not address cities directly, while (D), *city policies,* does talk about the policies the cities enact. Choice (D) is correct.

3.   **D**   This is a *vocabulary in context* question. Read a few lines above and below the word in question. Try to predict your own word for the shaded word based on the clues in the sentence. Eliminate answer choices that either are not supported by the words or phrases in the passage or are dictionary definitions of the word but are incorrect in the context of the sentence. The line after "emergence" talks about the growth of the city beyond the *compact cluster of small buildings,* so your word might be *growth* or *arrival.* Choice (A), *spreading,* might seem like a reasonable match, so keep it. Choices (B), *history,* and (C), *problems,* do not match, so eliminate them. Choice (D), *formation,* matches very closely, so keep it. Between (A) and (D), (D) is a closer match to the initial meaning, so eliminate (A). Choice (D) is correct.

4.   **C**   This is a NOT question, which is a variation on an EXCEPT question. Rephrase the question, eliminating the NOT, go back to the passage and look for each answer choice, marking each choice as TRUE OR FALSE. Choose the answer that is different from the other three. You're looking for the one choice that is *NOT* indicated as a factor in nineteenth-century suburbanization. Choice (A), *cheaper housing,* is referenced in paragraph 5; (B), *urban crowding,* can be found in paragraph 3; (D), *the invention of the streetcar,* is mentioned in paragraphs 3 and 4. That leaves (C), *advent of an urban middle class,* as the answer that is not supported by the passage. Choice (C) is correct.

5.   **D**   This is another *lead word/detail* question. Find *traction line* in paragraph 3, and read a few lines before and after. Immediately before *traction line,* you'll see the word *electric,* so you know it must describe something that operates on electricity. Choice (A), *automobile,* (B), *cart,* and (C), *horse-drawn trolley,* do not require electricity to operate, so eliminate them. Choice (D), *the electric streetcar,* clearly uses electricity, since the word *electric* is in the answer choice. Choice (D) is correct.

6.   **A**   This *reference* question asks what *mobility* refers to in the passage. You'll find the word at the end of paragraph 4. The phrase *This new mobility* refers to something that came immediately before, so look at the previous sentence. The preceding sentence discusses the electric streetcar network that could be found in every major urban area, *which made quick, easy movement between distant points possible....* This is exactly what the word *mobility* is referring to. Choice (A), *travel,* matches in meaning, but (B), *buy a house,* (C), *find work,* and (D), *enjoy life,* do not, so eliminate them. Choice (A) is correct.

7. **A** This is a *vocabulary in context* question. Read a few lines above and below the word in question. Try to predict your own word for the shaded word based on the clues in the sentence. Eliminate answer choices that either are not supported by the words or phrases in the passage or are dictionary definitions of the word but are incorrect in the context of the sentence. The question is asking for the meaning of the phrase "went up." You might say something like developed or were built, since the preceding sentences in paragraph 5 talk about the development of suburban tract houses. Choice (A), *were built*, matches our prediction, so keep it. Choices (B), *were bought*, (C), *increased in size*, and (D), *attracted interest*, do not match the meaning of developed or were built, so eliminate them. Choice (A) is correct.

8. **B** This *reference* question asks what the word *Most* replaces. Look for the word in question; then look for the most recent noun mentioned. In this case, the most recent noun is *suburban tract houses*. Choice (A), *city row house*, does not match the prediction. Choice (B), *suburban tract houses*, matches exactly so keep it. Choice (C), *sizable yards*, and (D), *winding streets*, don't match, so eliminate them. Choice (B) is correct.

9. **C** This is an *inference* question. Inference questions ask you to find what information must be true based on the information in the passage, using lead words or references to find the materials. Paragraph 4 discusses some of the benefits the electric streetcar provided, including being clean, cheaper, more efficient, and faster. So if the electric streetcar was faster, city transportation before it was slower. Be careful with process of elimination. *Only a few* in (A) is extreme: the passage never indicates how many cities had horse-drawn cars. Choice (B) is similarly extreme: the passage doesn't specify how many mill towns were incorporated into cities, but the answer says *few* were. Choice (C), *city transportation was slow and difficult*, matches the predication. Choice (D) actually indicates the opposite of what's said in paragraph 3. Choice (C) is correct.

10. This *summary* question asks you to find three answers that express the most important ideas presented in the passage.

    The following three statements appropriately summarize the passage:

    - **The introduction of the electric rail lines made it easier for people to travel long distances between work and home.**

      This *is* a major point of the passage.

    - **Open land outside urban cores allowed for the development of affordable and attractive tract housing.**

      This *is* a major contributing factor to suburbanization and a major point made by the passage.

    - **The automobile has made it possible for people to travel quickly even without relying on public transportation networks.**

      The entire last paragraph discusses how the addition of a garage—storage for a car— was a huge bonus because the car had become the primary mode of transportation.

These are the reasons why the other choices are incorrect:

- **Some suburbs were incorporated into the cities they adjoined as they grew.**

  This is mentioned in the passage, but only as a contributing factor to the growth of the suburbs. It is not a major point made in the passage.

- **Some cities are experiencing a movement back toward their centers.**

  This is presented in present tense as something that is happening *now*. The passage doesn't give any insight about what is happening currently, so this answer should be eliminated.

- **Some suburbs have public facilities that are superior to those in cities.**

  The passage does not expressly state that facilities in suburbs are *superior* to facilities in cities.

READING PRACTICE DRILL #8

1. **A** This is a *paraphrase* question. It asks you to paraphrase a sentence from the passage, finding the essential information in the original sentences and then matching it to each of the answer choices, eliminating any answers that do not contain all the essential information or ones that introduce new information. The essential information here is that Hughes was important, lived in Harlem during its Renaissance, and had a broad range of international experience. Choice (A) seems to match both of these. Choice (B) addresses only the second half of the important information. Choice (C) isn't supported: we don't know that Hughes's other living experiences caused him to think Harlem was particularly interesting. Choice (D) matches only the first half of the important information.

2. **B** This is a *vocabulary in context* question. Read a few lines above and below the word in question. Try to predict your own word for the shaded word based on the clues in the sentence. Eliminate answer choices that either are not supported by the words or phrases in the passage or are dictionary definitions of the word but are incorrect in the context of the sentence. The question is asking for the meaning of the word "signal." You might say *main* or *most important*. Choice (A), *streetlight*, is incorrect in this context. Choice (B), *major*, matches with our prediction, so keep it. Choice (C), *indication*, also does not match. Neither does Choice (D), *action*, so eliminate them. Choice (B) is correct.

3. **D** This *lead word/detail* questions asks you why Hughes wrote, *I love the color of their language and, being a Harlemite myself, their problems and interests are my problems and interests.* You'll find this sentence in paragraph 1, so read a few lines above and below it. The paragraph states *Returning to this theme again and again...* and then provides examples of what he wrote and how he felt. This does not describe anything about his writing style, so (A) should be eliminated. These points were not made to show that he understood the struggles of African Americans, so (B) is not a good match. Choice (C) takes some of the points in the passage too far: we don't know that he was interested in the Black Metropolis, only that he was fascinated by Harlem. Choice (D), that Hughes frequently wrote about Harlem, however, does have support in the passage: *Returning to this theme again and again, he wrote about Harlem more often and more fully than any other poet.*

4. **C** This is an *inference* question. Inference questions ask you to find what information must be true based on the information in the passage, using lead words or references to find the materials. Read paragraph 2 for information about the New Negro Movement. The first sentence tells us the New Negro Movement was in full swing when Hughes's first publication appeared. Choice (A) is an extreme answer because of the word *solely*. Choice (B), referring to the influx of African Americans moving to the area from the South, is not supported in the passage. Choice (C), that it began before Hughes published his book, is a good match with our prediction. Choice (D) is a good trap answer because 1926 is mentioned in the passage, but that's when Hughes's book was published, not when the New Negro Movement began. Choice (C) is correct.

5. **D** This is a *vocabulary in context* question. Read a few lines above and below the word in question. Try to predict your own word for the shaded word based on the clues in the sentence. Eliminate answer choices that either are not supported by the words or phrases in the passage or are dictionary definitions of the word but are incorrect in the context of the sentence. Before the word Mecca, you'll see Harlem described as the *intellectual center of the movement,* and in the following sentence we learn that *thousands of African American families had settled* there. Together, these tell us that African Americans wanted to be in Harlem. Your phrase might be *somewhere African Americans want to be.* Choice (A) is a trap—Mecca is actually *a city in Saudi Arabia*, but that fact has nothing to do with the material in this passage. Choice (B), *an ancient city*, is also a trap. Choice (C), *an area of Harlem*, is a trap, too, because it mentions Harlem. Choice (D), *somewhere that artists wanted to visit*, is the best match to our answer.

6. This question asks you to select a sentence that describes the people or culture of downtown Harlem. Paragraph 3 observes that, *But the Harlem cabaret life of the period was definitely an important by-product...early poetry of Langston Hughes.* This is the only sentence in the paragraph that fulfills the question task.

7. **B** This is an *inference* question. Inference questions ask you to find what information must be true based on the information in the passage, using lead words or references to find the materials. Look in the passage for insight about what Hughes liked about Harlem initially. Paragraph 3 states that … *Langston Hughes was first drawn to New York by the massive success of the first all-black musical, Shuffle Along....* Choice (A), *New York's cabaret scene*, is a trap because a lot of the passage discusses the cabaret scene, but nothing supports the fact that this is what attracted Hughes to the city in the first place. Choice (B), *a successful musical*, matches our prediction. Choice (C), referring to *other African American families settling there*, would be logical but is not supported by the passage. Choice (D), *a desire to write poetry at cabarets*, may be tempting if you're simply looking for an answer that uses words from the passage, but it doesn't say the same thing that the passage says.

8. **D** This *lead word/detail* question is toward the end of the question set, so its answer is likely to show up later in the passage. This question is asking for a true statement about Langston Hughes. Read the last paragraph; then take a look at the answers. Choice (A) is extreme, saying he was the *most* successful African American author of his time. Choice (B) is not supported—there is no indication of his accumulation of wealth during his lifetime. Choice (C) is also not supported—we don't know when he achieved recognition. Choice (D) is supported by the last paragraph, which tells us about the variety of publications he wrote and edited. Choice (D) is correct.

9. **C** This *reference* question asks what *it* refers to in paragraph 3. Look for the most recent noun, which is *The 1925 Renaissance*. Choice (A), *Harlem*, does not match, nor does (B), *a cabaret room*. Choice (C), *the 1925 Renaissance*, is an exact match, so keep it. Choice (D), *Seventh Street*, also does not match our prediction. Choice (C) is correct.

10. **A** This is a *vocabulary in context* question. Read a few lines above and below the word in question. Try to predict your own word for the shaded word based on the clues in the sentence. Eliminate answer choices that either are not supported by the words or phrases in the passage or are dictionary definitions of the word but are incorrect in the context of the sentence. This question is asking for the meaning of *prolific*. Paragraph 4 talks about all the publications he wrote and edited, so your word might be *extensive* or *varied*. Choice (A), *productive*, works with our prediction, so keep it. Choice (B), *argumentative*, does not match. Choice (C), *chaotic*, also does not work in this context. Similarly, (D) does not make sense in this context. Choice (A) is correct.

Chapter 10
Cracking the
Listening Section

The Listening section of the TOEFL consists of the following tasks:

- Three to four **academic lectures,** at least two of which contain classroom dialogue
  - Each lecture is three to five minutes long.
  - A lecture may involve one speaker or multiple speakers.
  - Each lecture is followed by six questions.
- Two to three **conversations** involving two or more speakers
  - Each conversation is three to four minutes long.
  - A conversation has 12–25 exchanges.
  - Each conversation is followed by five questions.
- You will have 41–57 minutes to complete the entire Listening section.

The Listening section measures your ability to follow and understand lectures and conversations that are typical of an American educational setting. You will hear each lecture or conversation only once, but you are allowed to take notes while you are listening.

As we mentioned in the early part of this book, the Listening scores are subdivided into four sections:

Advanced (22–30). Students who score in the "Advanced" range can understand a wide variety of conversation and lecture topics in both formal and informal settings. They are able to identify the most important concepts in a conversation or lecture, and understand how speakers use figurative language. These students can also combine information and make inferences from statements in a lecture, even when they are presented out of order.

High-Intermediate (17–21). Students who score in the "High-Intermediate" range are able to understand most lectures and everyday conversations, but can find complex grammatical structures occasionally confusing. These students can generally identify important points, but have difficulty combining information that is presented out of order

Low-Intermediate (9–16). Scores in the "Low-Intermediate" range indicate basic ability to understand conversations and lectures, but will find abstract/complex topics and conversations with complex vocabulary or grammatical structures more difficult. These students are able to identify clearly stated main ideas, but may have difficulty connecting the dots on less obvious points.

Below Low-Intermediate (0–8). Scores in the "Below Low-Intermediate" range indicate a very limited ability to understand conversations and will be unable to identify main ideas or draw inferences from facts presented in a lecture.

At the beginning of the Listening section, you'll be instructed to put on your headset. An example of the screen is shown on the next page.

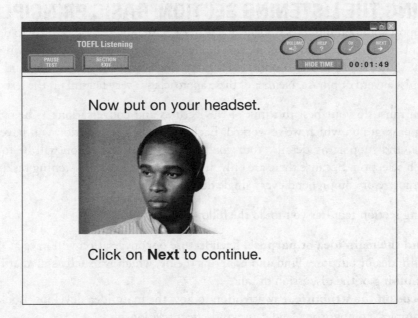

You'll also receive instructions on how to adjust the volume of the headset. Make sure the volume is at a comfortable level before the section begins.

LISTENING SECTION DIRECTIONS

You should be aware of a few special aspects of the Listening section before you take the TOEFL. First, unlike the Reading section, you are not allowed to skip questions and return to them later. *You must answer each question before you can proceed to the next one.* Second, some of the questions in the Listening section are heard, not read. These questions are indicated by a special headset icon, similar to what you've seen in this book.

It is important to be prepared for these audio questions. In this book, we use the headset icon to indicate when you should listen to the audio tracks in your Student Tools online. On the actual test, you will only hear this material; it will *not* appear on your screen.

CRACKING THE LISTENING SECTION: BASIC PRINCIPLES

One of the most common mistakes students make in the Listening section is to try to do too much. Some students try to take notes on every detail offered, and they end up not hearing important information. Other students try to understand every single word in the lecture, and they panic when they miss a word or phrase. Neither of these approaches is very helpful on the test.

Instead, you must do your best to think of the lectures and conversations as being similar to the reading passages on which we've worked. Each lecture or conversation will have a purpose, a main idea, and supporting details. Your goal for the Listening section will be to find these items in each selection. Because there are only five or six questions per listening task, there is no need to memorize or comprehend every single detail.

The Listening section requires you to do the following:

1. **Find the main idea or purpose.** Each lecture or conversation will have a main idea or purpose. Find and note this theme, which is usually stated at the beginning of the discussion or talk.
2. **Focus on the structure.** Pay attention to how the main idea develops. Look for examples, comparisons, and cause-and-effect relationships.
3. **Listen for tone and attitude.** Try to figure out if the speakers are positive, negative, or neutral toward the topic.
4. **Pay attention to transitions.** Make sure you are listening for transition words and phrases. These help you follow the logic of the lecture or conversation.

We'll look at all of these points in more detail in a moment, but there are two other important things to keep in mind when you approach the Listening section.

*   **Don't memorize.** As we said earlier, there is far too much information to try to memorize or retain. So, don't even bother trying. Keep in mind that the TOEFL is testing you on your ability to follow a logical flow of ideas, not on your ability to memorize information. Just relax and try to focus on the big issues, not the minor ones.

*   **Don't take too many notes.** One easy way to get sidetracked on the Listening section is to write down too many notes. Writing requires your concentration, and if you're concentrating on writing, you're probably not concentrating on listening. Focus on listening; in fact, if you are not comfortable taking notes, don't take any at all.

Basic Principle #1: Find the Main Idea or Purpose

We've spent a lot of time practicing this step with reading passages. Now we will apply our understanding of the main idea or purpose to a listening task. Fortunately, the patterns in the Listening section are very similar to the patterns in the Reading section. Lectures are designed around a main idea, whereas conversations are centered on a purpose.

In **lectures,** the speaker will typically introduce the main idea at the very beginning of the talk. Listen for phrases similar to the following:

- "Okay, today I want to talk about...."
- "What we're going to talk about today is...."
- "Today, we're going to look at...."
- "The topic for today's class is..."

The professor will then follow with the topic of discussion. If you're taking notes, you should write the topic down. Once you have the main topic, you can expect the lecturer to provide a purpose, explanation, or more information.

In a **conversation,** the beginning sentences will reveal the speaker's purpose. Listen for the purpose to appear after an initial greeting, as in the following examples:

- "Hi, what can I do for you?"
- "Hello, how can I help you?"
- "What can I do for you today?"
- "Is there something I can do for you?"

After this initial question, the other speaker will state his or her purpose. Usually this involves asking for some sort of help or assistance. If you are taking notes, you should write down what the purpose of the conversation is.

Basic Principle #2: Focus on the Structure

After finding the main idea or purpose, focus on the structure of the talk. Lectures and conversations each have standard structures. Listen for them as you take the TOEFL.

Types of Lecture Structures

Most lectures will have one of the following basic structures.

Lecture Structure #1: Compare/Contrast This type of lecture involves finding similarities and differences between two or more things. Listen for the speaker to introduce this framework by using one of the following phrases:

- several theories
- possible explanations
- many different views

After the framework is introduced, the speaker will list each item to be discussed and mention its characteristics. Listen for words that indicate compare/contrast, such as the following:

- in contrast
- on the other hand
- similarly
- however
- additionally
- also

Lecture Structure #2: Cause-and-Effect Relationships Some lectures attempt to explain why a certain situation occurs. Listen for the speaker to introduce this type of framework with the following phrases:

- Why would this happen?
- What is the reason for this?
- How could this happen?
- What leads to this?

If it seems that the speaker is describing a cause-and-effect situation, listen for the cause. A speaker will often use the following phrases to introduce the cause:

- x causes y
- x results in y
- x produces y
- x leads to y
- x brings about y
- x is responsible for y

After identifying the cause, look for the speaker to detail the effects with a phrase similar to the following:

- y is caused by x
- y results from x
- y is due to x
- y can be blamed on x
- y is attributable to x
- y happens because of x

Lecture Structure #3: Abstract Category/Specific Examples Another common lecture structure involves moving from an abstract category to a specific example. A lecture may also sometimes begin with specific examples and end with a more general interpretation of the examples. A speaker may introduce an abstract concept with one of the following phrases:

- one approach...
- one theory...
- the idea is...
- the concept...
- the basic premise is...

Next, the speaker will move to the examples, typically using the following phrases:

- for example...
- one instance of this is...
- consider...
- we see this in/with...
- this is illustrated by/with...

Even if you have difficulty understanding the abstract idea, you can usually figure it out by paying close attention to the examples used.

Lecture Structure #4: Sequences   A lecture may present a series of steps or stages. Listen for the lecturer to mention the following clues:

- process
- development
- stages
- transition

The steps or parts will typically be introduced with clear transitions, such as

- first...second...third...
- next...
- then...
- initially...
- finally...

Types of Conversation Structures
Conversations on the TOEFL also fall into some predictable patterns. Try to identify the pattern when listening to the people speak.

Conversation Structure #1: Problem/Solution   This is a typical conversation type on the TOEFL. One student has a problem, and another student offers advice or a possible solution. Listen for the first student to introduce the problem by mentioning one of the following:

- problem
- issue
- difficulty
- trouble

After describing the problem, the other person will offer some sort of advice or solution. Listen for the following phrases:

- why don't you...
- if I were you, I'd...
- maybe you should...
- have you tried/thought of...

For this structure, it is important to listen for what the problem is and what steps or solutions the speaker may take to solve it.

Conversation Structure #2: Service Encounter Another common conversation on the TOEFL is the service encounter. In this encounter, a student will discuss a problem with a professional—usually a professor, a librarian, or an office worker. The problem will be introduced in the same way as in the previous conversation type, but the response may differ. The service professional will usually explain *exactly* what the student needs to do to solve the problem. The solution may involve several parts. If so, listen for the following words to indicate the steps the student must take:

- requirement
- application
- form
- recommendation
- prohibited

Conversation Structure #3: Significant Event Some conversations on the TOEFL revolve around a significant event. This could be a meeting, an announcement, or a social event. Usually, the first speaker will introduce the event with one of the following phrases:

- have you heard about...
- did you see...
- let you know about...
- program/event/opportunity/chance

After noting the event, listen to any details about it. Also note what the speaker's plans are concerning the event. Listen for the following key words:

- participate
- plans
- open to
- free or busy

Basic Principle #3: Listen for Tone and Attitude

Although you are unlikely to be asked a tone question in the Listening section, an understanding of the speaker's tone or attitude is helpful on many types of questions. Speakers on the TOEFL often use phrases or words that can have more than one interpretation. However, if you are aware of the speaker's tone, you are less likely to misinterpret the phrase.

For example, lecturers on the TOEFL often say something like the following:

> "...and after the war, the country experienced a prolonged period of economic growth, right?"

Even though the speaker *appears* to be asking a question, he or she is actually just *emphasizing his or her point*. Being aware of the tone will help you interpret statements such as this one.

The tone of most lectures is fairly straightforward. Because the speaker is teaching a class, the tone will usually be similar to one of the following types:

- **Objective:** The speaker is simply listing facts or providing information. The speaker is an authority on his or her subject and so will not be unsure or uncertain about the topic. This type of tone can appear in any of the four common lecture types.
- **Subjective:** In some cases, the speaker will be presenting a position or making an argument. The speaker will try to convince the listeners about a certain view. This type of tone is more likely to appear in *compare/contrast* and *cause-and-effect* lectures.
- **Inquisitive:** There are also classroom discussions on the TOEFL. During a discussion, the professor leads the class through a number of questions, so the tone is inquisitive. The professor considers and responds to the students' questions as the lecture progresses. *Abstract category/specific example* lectures typically involve discussion, although other lecture types may as well.

Conversations tend to have slightly more personal tones. You can expect the tone to be similar to one of the following types:

- **Excited:** This tone is typical of the *significant event* conversation. The speaker is interested in the event and may be trying to influence others about it.
- **Disappointed/upset:** In this case, the speaker is not happy about the situation. He or she may express dissatisfaction with things or events. This usually occurs during the *problem/solution* encounter, although it can appear in other conversations too.
- **Uncertain or confused:** Sometimes the speaker is uncertain or confused, especially in *service encounters*. The speaker will be unsure of what action to take or how to proceed.

Of course, you don't have to spend valuable time during your test trying to figure out the exact tone. However, having a basic idea of the tone—as well as of the purpose of the lecture or conversation—will aid you when you are eliminating answers.

Basic Principle #4: Pay Attention to Transitions

From your work on the Reading section of the TOEFL, you should have a pretty good understanding of the common transitions used in writing. These transitions show up in lectures and conversations as well, and it is good to note them. However, two other types of transitions to be especially alert for are *reversals* and *negations*.

Reversal Transitions

Often, speakers on the TOEFL will reverse the direction or logic of the conversation or lecture. If you're not listening carefully, you may misunderstand the speaker. For example, look at the following lines:

"First, I want to look at the mechanism by which single-celled organisms reproduce...um, actually, let's come back to that in a moment. We need to talk about..."

In this situation, the speaker abruptly changes the topic. These reversals happen occasionally during lectures and somewhat more frequently during conversations. Here are some phrases to listen for.

- you know what?
- we'll come back to that in a moment
- actually, let's
- instead
- better yet
- I don't want to get into that now

Negation Transitions

Also, speakers will sometimes use a positive word to indicate a negation. Look for phrases like the following, where the negation words are italicized:

- I don't have to explain that, *right*?
- You guys are okay with this, *correct*?
- We don't need to go into that now, *okay*?

In each case, the speaker uses a positive word to express a negative statement. When used in this way, the positive words indicate that the speaker assumes the listener knows what the speaker is talking about and no further discussion or explanation is needed.

Reversals and negations can be tricky, but if you're on the lookout for them, they'll be easier to handle.

CRACKING THE LISTENING SECTION: BASIC APPROACH

Now we're ready to crack the Listening section. Here are the steps.

1. **Actively listen to the selection,** noting the main idea or purpose, structure, and tone.
2. **Attack the questions.** There's no skipping in the Listening section, so you'll have to do each question as it appears.
3. **Use POE aggressively,** using your understanding of the main idea, previous questions, and any notes you've taken to help you.

Let's try the steps on a practice passage. Use your online audio files to follow along.

Step 1: Actively Listen to the Selection

If you intend to take notes, take a moment to organize your scrap paper. Remember, don't try to write down everything. Instead, as we've discussed, focus on the main topic, structure, and tone. Listen carefully for these parts and be sure to write them down.

Keep in mind the basic principles you have learned throughout this book. You should expect to hear the main idea or purpose at the very beginning of the speech and the majority of the details and supporting examples throughout the rest. A lecture or conversation usually will have a conclusion as well. Screens similar to the ones that follow will introduce each passage.

Headphones On!

When you are ready, play Track 3 on your audio files online. After you are finished listening to the lecture and questions that follow, try to answer the questions below. If you are having difficulty answering the questions, replay the selection. A transcript of the lecture follows for your reference. (But don't cheat and read along as you listen to the track!)

What is the *main idea* of the lecture?

_____
_____
_____

What is the *structure* of the lecture?

_____
_____
_____
_____

What is the lecturer's *tone*?

_____
_____
_____

Let's look at a transcript of the lecture and find the important points.

Narrator: Listen to a biology professor give a talk on an environmental issue.

Professor: There's been a lot of talk over the last few decades about greenhouse gases—those gases in the atmosphere that trap radiation from the Sun so that after it passes into the atmosphere it doesn't pass out. People are increasingly conscious of the environmental effects of their daily activities, which is a good thing. But all the publicity can be confusing too. I think writing for the general public about science is a real service, but...well, it's not nice to say, but...I wish some of these people would verify things with real scientists more often. They'd save themselves some embarrassment.

With that in mind, I'd like to clear up some things about that hot topic: carbon dioxide. Carbon dioxide is a greenhouse gas; it absorbs energy from the Sun. In that respect, it's like water vapor and methane, two other naturally occurring greenhouse gases. You all know that carbon dioxide is produced when we burn fossil fuels—coal, petroleum products, natural gas—and that those fuels run a lot of the machines and manufacturing processes that drive modern life.

Those are the sources that get all the public attention, but, of course, we produce carbon dioxide as a waste product too. It's one of the by-products of respiration. We breathe in air, use up some of the oxygen, and breathe out air that contains carbon dioxide. So do other animals. Because carbon dioxide is part of the natural life cycle, nature has a way of dealing with it. How does nature control the amount of carbon dioxide floating around in the atmosphere?

Male Student: I thought the ocean soaked it up.

Professor: Yes, that's one way. Carbon dioxide is very soluble in water. Soluble...uh, I don't have to explain that one to you because the root's related to the word *dissolve,* right? So carbon dioxide is pulled readily out of the air and into the water. Now, the oceans also release some of their carbon dioxide, but on balance, they absorb more; so that means that, if we produce artificially more than would naturally be emitted through life processes, the ocean could, as Jason put it, soak it up.

Unfortunately, if we're looking for a solution to carbon dioxide pollution, the ocean isn't it, and that's because the ocean absorbs gases from the atmosphere very, very slowly. If we suddenly increased the amount of carbon dioxide we produced, current models suggest that it would take 1,000 years for it to mix into seawater. And even then, there would still be a small amount left. So over the short and medium term, we can't rely on the ocean to take up the slack for us.

Okay, so that's one way nature deals with carbon dioxide. What's the other?

Female Student: Plants, isn't it? I mean, plants breathe carbon dioxide the way we breathe air.

Professor: Sure—I was actually kind of surprised that wasn't the one mentioned first. Yes, plants require carbon dioxide for photosynthesis. The more dense the growth of large plants, the more carbon dioxide is absorbed. Such an area—including forests of large, old-growth trees, and also the ocean—where carbon dioxide is absorbed in large quantities, is called a carbon sink. The carbon dioxide gas is sucked in kind of the way water is sucked down the drain in your sink after you wash the dishes. In fact, in the ocean, there are algae, seaweed...um, other kinds of marine plants too that rely on carbon dioxide to perform photosynthesis, just like the green plants on land. It's just that algae are far, far smaller.

Now, here's something interesting: Like the ocean, green plants release carbon dioxide into the atmosphere as well as absorb it—uh, when a plant dies...you know, if it burns in a forest fire or just dies of old age and decays, then its carbon dioxide is back in the air. So it only holds it in over its lifetime. However—this is the interesting part—unlike the ocean, green plants soak up carbon dioxide to use it—to make the energy they need to live and grow. So what they've found in some regions...populated, industrialized regions...is that increased levels of carbon dioxide can stimulate plant growth. There's more of the fuel the plants need for energy, so they grow more green and dense and lush and use more of it—in other words, the amount of carbon dioxide used up by plants can increase quickly in response to the environment. Some people have suggested that we can use that natural phenomenon to help deal with increased levels of greenhouse gases in the atmosphere.

Narrator: What is the discussion mainly about?

What is the problem with relying on the oceans to solve the problem of excess amounts of carbon dioxide? Why does the professor mention that carbon dioxide is a by-product of respiration? What did the professor call areas where carbon dioxide is absorbed in large quantities? What did the professor mean by this?

As stated earlier, expect the main idea to show up early in the lecture. The very first sentence of the lecture gives us the topic.

"There's been a lot of talk over the last few decades about greenhouse gases—those gases in the atmosphere that trap radiation from the Sun so that after it passes into the atmosphere it doesn't pass out."

A little later on, the professor specifies exactly what aspect of greenhouse gases the lecture will discuss.

"With that in mind, I'd like to clear up some things about that hot topic: carbon dioxide."

From these lines, we have the *basic purpose* of the lecture. Hopefully, you are now on the lookout for the things the professor wants to clear up. The professor continues to talk about two major areas. The first is in the following lines:

> **Professor:** How does nature control the amount of carbon dioxide floating around in the atmosphere?
>
> **Male Student:** I thought the ocean soaked it up.
>
> **Professor:** Yes, that's one way.

This is the first important *detail* in the lecture. You may have noticed that the professor also mentioned the following:

> "Unfortunately, if we're looking for a solution to carbon dioxide pollution, the ocean isn't it, and that's because the ocean absorbs gases from the atmosphere very, very slowly."

These lines have a good *tone* indicator ("unfortunately") and a good *transition* ("and that's because"). You should also note that the professor repeats the fact about the ocean not being suitable for absorbing carbon dioxide in the next four lines as well, so you have a few opportunities to pick up this important point.

The next major detail occurs here.

> **Professor:** Okay, so that's one way nature deals with carbon dioxide. What's the other?
>
> **Female Student:** Plants, isn't it? I mean, plants breathe carbon dioxide the way we breathe air.

The professor continues with the following, which you may have noted:

> However—this is the interesting part—unlike the ocean, green plants soak up carbon dioxide to use it—to make the energy they need to live and grow.

Once again, the lecturer uses strong *transitions,* such as "however," and *tone* words, such as "interesting part," to alert you to important details. If you were able to pick up on these parts of the lecture, chances are you'll be in pretty good shape for the Listening section. As we've mentioned before, you're *not* expected to memorize or comprehend every detail of the lecture.

Here are some possible responses to the earlier questions.

- What is the *main idea* of the lecture? <u>Oceans and plants are nature's way of controlling carbon dioxide.</u>
- What is the *structure* of the lecture? <u>It's mostly compare and contrast. Two methods are looked at.</u>
- What is the lecturer's *tone*? <u>Mostly neutral, with occasional positive ("here's the interesting part") and negative ("unfortunately") digressions.</u>

You'll find that a basic understanding of these major points will help you to answer most of the questions following the lecture or conversation. The important thing is not to become stressed or worried that you didn't understand every single part of the talk.

Step 2: Attack the Questions

The questions in the Listening section are very similar to the questions in the Reading section. Of course, the major differences are that you will hear the lecture or conversation only *once* and that you will *not* be able to skip questions and come back to them later.

The following types of questions appear most often in the Listening section:

1. **Main idea questions:** The first question of the set will typically be a main idea question. Considering the work you've done up to this point, the main idea question shouldn't be too difficult for you to answer. However, we'll go over some POE strategies just in case.

2. **Detail questions:** The majority of the questions following the lectures or conversations will ask about facts from the selections. The details will not be about minor points, but rather about major points.

3. **Purpose questions:** Some questions will ask you *why* the speaker mentioned a particular detail or fact. For these questions, it is helpful to think about the overall structure of the selection.

4. **Definition questions:** Often, during a lecture (definitions rarely, if ever, show up in conversations), the lecturer will define a particular term for his or her students. Pay attention if you hear the speaker signal a definition with one of the following expressions:
   - A *caucus* **is** a secret party meeting.
   - A *caucus* **is defined as** a secret party meeting.
   - A *caucus* **is the word used for** a secret party meeting.
   Sometimes the speaker will reverse the order of the term and the definition.
   - A secret party meeting **is known as** a *caucus*.
   - A secret party meeting **is called** a *caucus*.
   - A secret party meeting **is referred to as** a *caucus*.
   Finally the definition may be placed in the middle of a larger phrase.
   - A *caucus*—a secret party meeting—is usually held in emergencies.
   - A *caucus*, **that is,** a secret party meeting, is usually held in emergencies.
   - A *caucus*, **or** a secret party meeting, is usually held in emergencies.

5. **Inference or suggestion questions:** The TOEFL will often test your ability to "read between the lines" (or more precisely, "listen between the lines"). There will often be questions asking what the speaker is suggesting or what he or she really means by a particular phrase. A person will often suggest something by using one of the following phrases:
   - **Why not** come back later?
   - **How about** coming back later?
   - **What about** coming back later?
   - **Why don't you** come back later?
   - **If I were you, I'd** come back later.
   - **You should** come back later.
   - **You could always** come back later.
   - **Maybe you could** come back later.
   - **It may not be a bad idea** to come back later.
   Each of these constructions is a way of expressing the same basic idea that someone may return later.

6. **Multiple-multiple-choice questions:** Some questions in the Listening section require you to select more than one example. Many times, these questions ask you to list the main details or points made in the lecture.

Step 3: Use POE Aggressively

Because you are unable to listen to the lecture or conversation more than once, you'll have to focus on using good POE strategies when answering the questions. If you've missed a key point of the lecture or conversation, you can still increase your chances of getting a question correct by eliminating answers that aren't likely to be correct.

Before we go through the question types and the POE strategies, you may want to listen to Track 3 online one more time. We'll identify the question types and apply test-taking techniques to work through the questions that follow.

Main Idea Questions

Question 1 is a typical main idea question on the TOEFL.

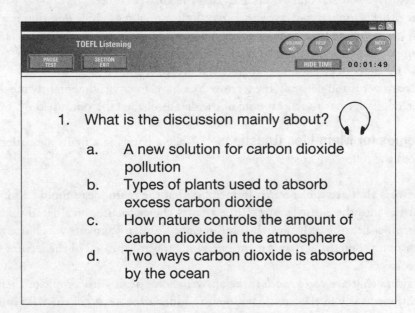

As we saw earlier in our active listening section, the speaker began by talking about carbon dioxide and mentioned two major ways that carbon dioxide is absorbed by nature—by oceans and by plants. Thus, (C) is the best answer.

Here's why the other answer choices are incorrect.

- For main idea questions, wrong answer choices may be *too specific*. For example, (B) talks only about plants. Even if you weren't sure exactly what the lecture was about, you may have noticed that plants did not appear until the end of the lecture. Any details that you hear mentioned only toward the *end* of the lecture will *never* be the main idea.

- Of course, some answers will contain information that is *not mentioned* at all. Choice (A) states that the lecture was about a "solution" for pollution. But no solution was offered. Even if you feel that you missed something important during the lecture, be aggressive. The lecture mentioned two key points: the ocean and plants. Choice (A) states there is "a new solution"—that is, only one. The great thing about a multiple-choice test is that there are usually a few ways to look at wrong answers.

- Questions on the TOEFL will also typically contain a *trap* answer, which uses words or phrases from the lecture or conversation in a deceptive manner. Choice (D) is a good example of a trap answer. The first part of the choice talks about "two ways." This matches up with the two key examples used in the lecture. Next, the choice talks about "carbon dioxide," which obviously is part of the lecture also. Finally, the choice contains "the ocean," a match with one of the examples in the lecture. Unfortunately, the lecture is about two ways *nature* absorbs carbon dioxide, not two ways the ocean absorbs it. The lesson here is that if you are uncertain of the right answer, and if one of the choices seems too good to be true, it's a trap. Still, be careful to use this advice only when you're stuck; otherwise, you'll drive yourself crazy over-analyzing the answer choices.

- One other wrong answer type that may appear on a main idea question is a choice that is *too broad*. This is the opposite of an overly specific answer choice. For example, suppose there had been the following answer choice:
  (E) The effect of environmental issues on everyday life
  This answer is too general. The lecture does have an environmental theme, but the correct answer has to reflect more of the details of the talk, not just the basic idea.

POE Strategies for Main Idea Questions
When answering a main idea question, make sure you avoid the following answer types:

- **Answers that are *too specific*:** Remember that the main idea should be something that ties into the entire lecture. If the answer choice focuses on a detail that you remember hearing only once, it is too specific. Similarly, an answer choice that focuses on something that is mentioned only toward the end of the lecture will not be correct.

- **Answers that are *too broad*:** If the answer choice deals with a topic or theme mentioned early in the lecture but doesn't address the *details* of the talk, it is too broad and therefore incorrect.

- **Answers that are *not mentioned*:** The TOEFL is not a memorization test. If you don't recall hearing anything about the focus of a particular answer choice, then that choice is most likely incorrect. The selections on the TOEFL are centered on a topic and continually refer back to it; thus, it is unlikely that you somehow missed the main idea.

- **Answers that are *traps*:** Use this only as a last resort. If you are really stuck on a question, avoid answers that seem too good to be true.

Once you've answered the main idea question, keep the answer you've selected in mind. It can help you on some of the other questions.

Detail Questions

As you know from the Reading section, detail questions ask you about specific facts from the discussion. Fortunately, the wrong answers to detail questions in the Listening section tend to be a little more obviously wrong. Question 2 is a typical detail question.

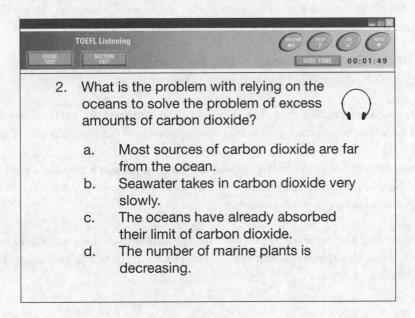

The answer to this question was one of the key points in the lecture. Recall that the professor alerted us to an important point by saying the following:

> "Unfortunately, if we're looking for a solution to carbon dioxide pollution, the ocean isn't it, and that's because the ocean absorbs gases from the atmosphere very, very slowly."

We noted this because of the speaker's use of the important tone indicator word *unfortunately*. Thus, the correct answer is (B).

If you are having trouble identifying the incorrect answers, you may still be able to eliminate some answers. *Extreme* answers, for example, are usually incorrect. You've seen these answers in the Reading section, and they appear in the Listening section as well. Choice (C) is a good example of an extreme choice. It makes a pretty absolute statement: that oceans have "absorbed their limit" of carbon dioxide. Many extreme answers use words such as the following:

always	*never*	*all*
none	*every*	*everything*
nothing	*only*	*impossible*

Another way of eliminating answers on detail questions is to cross off choices that are *contrary to the main idea*. For example, in this lecture, if you were able to figure out that the speaker gave oceans and plants as the two main examples, you should eliminate (D) because that focuses on marine plants, which was a separate example in the lecture.

If you keep your eyes out for these two common types of wrong answers, you will have a 50 percent chance of getting the question right; those odds aren't so bad!

POE Strategies for Detail Questions   When you are stumped on a detail question, don't give up. Look for the following types of answers and eliminate them:

- *Extreme* **answers:** Compare the answers. Eliminate any with extreme wording and go with the safe answer. Correct answers on the TOEFL often use fairly bland language.
- **Answers that are *contrary to the main idea*:** Even if you are uncertain of a specific detail from the selection, you may be able to use your understanding of the main idea to eliminate choices.

Detail questions may also have *trap answers*. Unfortunately, these answers are harder to identify than those on main idea questions. But again, if all else fails, try not to pick answers that seem too obvious or easy.

Purpose Questions

It is important to try to pay attention to the structure of the selection as you listen. If you grasp the structure, it will make purpose questions, like the following one, easier.

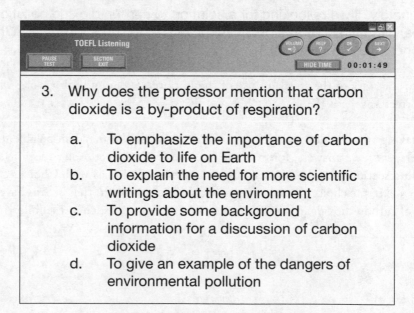

Before trying to answer this question, think about the structure of the lecture. We saw earlier that the professor looks at two key examples (oceans and plants) and compares and contrasts them. Although the lectures on the TOEFL may have some minor digressions, most of the information should in some way relate to the big picture. That means you can safely eliminate answers that seem to introduce *new ideas*. For example, (B) should be eliminated. The lecture is not about scientific writings (although they are mentioned once, they never appear again). Similarly, (D) can be eliminated as well: the lecture doesn't focus on environmental pollution or its dangers.

That leaves (A) and (C). Once again, think about the big picture and look for the answer containing information that is *contrary to the main idea*. Choice (A) talks about "life on Earth." But half of the lecture is about the ocean, which is not alive, so eliminate (A). That leaves us with (C) as the correct answer.

POE Strategies for Purpose Questions   Keep the main idea in mind as you attack purpose questions. Get rid of answers that contain the following:

- **New ideas:** The purpose of examples and details is to support the main idea. Answer choices that contain new information not related to the main idea are wrong.

- **Information contrary to the main idea:** You should also eliminate any answers that seem to go against the main idea of the lecture.

Definition Questions
Definition questions require you to recall a very specific part of the lecture. Thus, they can be very difficult. Question 4 is an example of one.

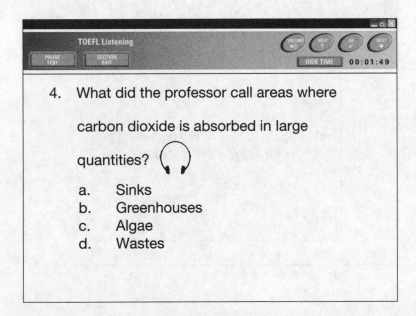

Unfortunately, if you didn't catch this part of the lecture, POE won't help you much. You can use your knowledge of the words and common sense to eliminate choices, but if you're unsure of the words, you'll have to take a blind guess.

The professor defined the word at this point in the lecture:

"Such an area—including forests of large, old-growth trees, and also the ocean—where carbon dioxide is absorbed in large quantities, is called a carbon sink. The carbon dioxide gas is sucked in kind of the way water is sucked down the drain in your sink after you wash the dishes."

Therefore, the correct answer is (A).

POE Strategies for Definition Questions Your best option when trying to use POE on definition questions is to

- **Use your vocabulary:** If you happen to know one or more of the words in the answer choices, see if any of the words will work. It is unlikely that the correct definition for a question on the TOEFL will be radically different from the standard definition of the word.

Inference/Suggestion Questions

For inference and suggestion questions, you will often hear a portion of the speech replayed before you answer the questions. When a portion of the lecture is going to be repeated, you will always see a screen similar to the one below.

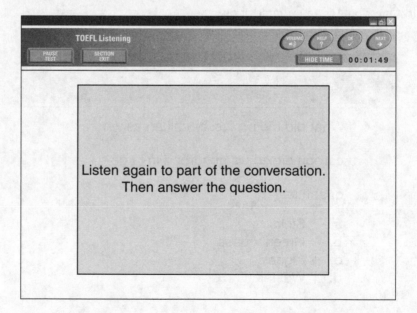

On the actual test, the excerpt from the selection will not appear on the screen; you will only hear it.

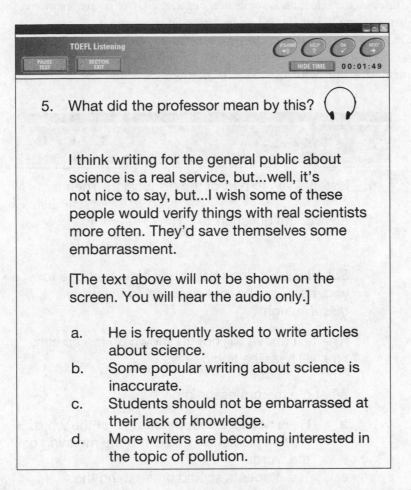

For these types of questions, we have to figure out what the speaker is *really* saying.

The phrase in question contains a suggestion.

"I wish some of these people would verify things with real scientists more often."

Thus, the speaker is indicating that he thinks the writers need to verify their work. The next part of the selection clarifies this suggestion further.

"They'd save themselves some embarrassment."

Let's start eliminating some answers.

- Choice (A) is on the *wrong topic*. The speaker is stating his wish for other people's writing, not making a suggestion to himself; that wouldn't make sense. Eliminate it.
- Choice (C) has the same problem. The professor is talking about *writers,* not students.

- Choice (D) has the *wrong tone*. Even if you're not exactly sure what the speaker is trying to say, you may be able to identify the selection as positive or negative. In this case, the selection is somewhat negative ("They'd save themselves some embarrassment"), but (D) is fairly *positive*. So eliminate it.
- We're left with (B) as the correct answer.

Let's try it again, this time with an inference question.

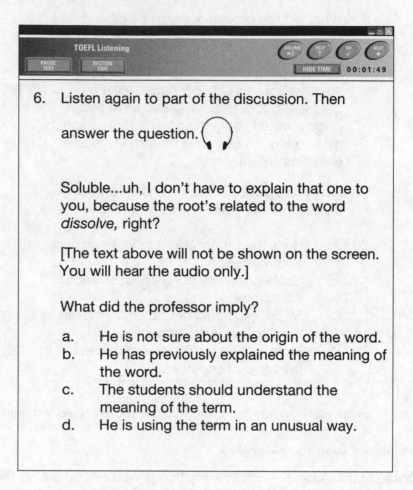

This selection contains a good example of the negations we mentioned earlier when discussing transitions. As used in this context, the word *right* means that the speaker assumes the students understand the topic without needing any further explanation. We also have some POE options on this question.

- Choice (A) is on the *wrong topic*. The professor is addressing the students, not himself. Eliminate this choice.
- Choice (D) has the *wrong tone*. The professor is indicating that he doesn't "have to explain" the term, so it doesn't make sense for him to use the term in an unusual way and not explain it.
- That leaves (B) and (C). Choice (B) is tempting, but we have no way of knowing whether it's true; remember that on the TOEFL, we should be able to support our inferences.
- Therefore, (C) is the best answer.

POE Strategies for Inference or Suggestion Questions The three most important POE strategies for these questions are to pay attention to the following types of answers:

- **Wrong topic:** Stick to the topic. Think about the main idea, and eliminate answers that don't relate to it. Also, eliminate answers that don't make sense based on your understanding of the selection.
- **Wrong tone:** Even if you're unsure of what the speaker is saying, you may be able to figure out the tone. Decide if the speaker views the subject as positive or negative, and eliminate answers that don't work.
- **Extreme:** Inference and suggestion questions often have extreme answer choices as well. If you see one, eliminate it.

Multiple-Multiple-Choice Questions

These questions ask you to select more than one answer. You must rely on your knowledge of the main idea and the structure of the selection to answer them correctly. Question 7 is an example of this type.

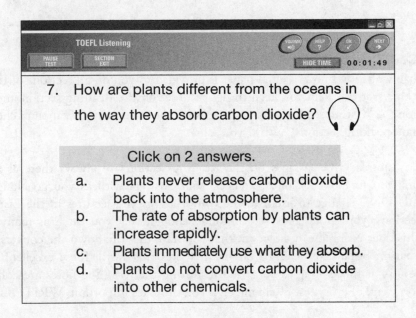

As you can see, it's important while you're listening to try to understand the structure of the lecture. This lecture involved a *comparison and contrast* between two ways in which carbon dioxide is absorbed by nature. You may remember that the professor hinted that some important information was about to come when he made the following statement:

"However—this is the interesting part—unlike the ocean, green plants soak up carbon dioxide to use it—to make the energy they need to live and grow."

Thus, we know that plants use the carbon dioxide they absorb. Now, let's use POE. You may have noticed that both (A) and (C) contain *extreme* language: the words "never" and "immediately." Thus, in this instance as well as with other questions on the TOEFL, they're wrong. So, even if you didn't remember the exact differences mentioned in the talk, you can still get the question right. In this case, the correct answers are (B) and (D).

POE Strategies for Multiple-Multiple-Choice Questions Multiple-multiple-choice questions are typically either *detail* questions or *main idea* questions, so use the same POE strategies provided earlier in this chapter.

FINAL TIPS FOR THE LISTENING SECTION

Tip 1: Know the Test, and You're Halfway There!

Because the TOEFL iBT is given on such a grand scale, just like any standardized test, appropriations have been made so that every official ETS iBT you take essentially looks the same. This includes everything from the instructions on the screen to test day procedures. And, since ETS has done its utmost to make sure there are no major changes made to the test to throw you off or trip you up, knowing the test will only help YOU save precious moments on the test. Remember, "Knowing is half the battle."

Tip 2: Scratch Paper—Use It WISELY

As you probably already know, scratch paper is provided to you on all sections of the TOEFL iBT. While this fact can help you keep things in order on the Reading section and help you brainstorm on the Writing section, scratch paper should be your staple weapon of choice on the Listening and Speaking sections. "Why," you ask?

The answer is simple. The passages on the Reading section are always there as a veritable safety net for you to fall back on and check your answers with as you go along. Because you have only ONE chance to listen to the conversations and lectures in the Listening and Speaking sections, your notes must be thorough enough that you catch as many details as possible. (This does NOT mean, however, that you have to write down the conversations and lectures verbatim, because NO ONE on Earth writes that fast!) These excellent notes will be yours to look at for as long as you need to during the test (The notes are collected and destroyed at the end of every test.) Remember, if you think it's important, WRITE IT DOWN!

Tip 3: Know Your Vocabulary!

The English language is vast, and while the exact number of words in the English language is a hotly debated topic, it never hurts to know more vocabulary words. Because the topics covered on the TOEFL iBT do not range out of a certain scope of academic topics, knowing the jargon used in those fields will benefit you greatly. Since seeing a word in context is the fastest way to improve your working vocabulary—a vocabulary that you can readily use—read as much as you can and watch your vocabulary soar to new heights! Check out Chapter 6 for a helpful vocabulary list with terms, definitions, pronunciation, and more.

Tip 4: Do What You Can To Prepare

Tip 3 told you to read as much as you can as a way to improve your working vocabulary. However, doing this alone will not improve your English ability. You also need to hear how the words are spoken. In English, as in other languages, HOW something is said is just as important as WHAT is said. Thus, intonation plays a role in how what you say gets received. You should not only listen to English, but REPEAT what you hear, as well. If imitation is the best form of flattery, then why not imitate NATIVE speakers of English?

NOTE TAKING

The Ten Commandments of Note Taking

1. Don't write everything you hear. When listening, be alert and attentive. Pay attention to the main points. Concentrate on the meat of the material, not the fat.
2. USE KEY WORDS! Notes should NEVER be in full sentences.
3. Take accurate notes. Paraphrase what the speaker says using your own words, but do not change the meaning. If you are going to quote directly, quote correctly.
4. Think BEFORE you start writing. Write down only things that are important. Do not take notes just to take notes.
5. Have a uniform system of abbreviations or shortcuts that make sense to you. Use an outline with indentations to show importance. Leave space for additional notes.
6. BE CONCISE! Keep your notes short and to the point.
7. Don't worry if you miss a point.
8. Don't keep notes on oddly shaped pieces of paper. You don't want to take notes on a napkin and accidentally throw your notes away!
9. Shortly after finishing your notes, go back and fill in spots you missed and spell out words you wrote only parts of the first time.
10. Review your notes regularly.

THE FIVE R'S OF NOTE TAKING

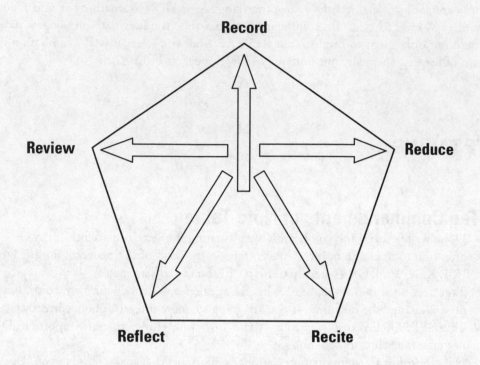

Record	During the lecture, write down as many meaningful facts as possible. Write legibly.
Reduce	Don't try to write everything. Listen to part of the lecture and paraphrase what the speaker has said. Summarizing clarifies meaning, strengthens relationships between ideas, and strengthens memory.
Recite	Cover the details of your notes and attempt to summarize what you have just heard using only the keywords. This will help you internalize the material faster.
Reflect	The best students will look back on their notes and categorize them in their mind. Putting things into categories, outlines, or other structures will help when you are trying to access the information at a later date.
Review	Skim over your notes anytime you feel a bit lost of confused within the listening section.

6 HABITS OF BAD LISTENERS

1. Thinking the Subject Matter Is Boring

Everyone has subjects they don't like. Most people have a favorite subject in school. Have you noticed that you pay more attention in the classes you like?

All you have to do is remember one tiny word and you'll be okay: USE. Good listeners will try to find SOMETHING practical in what the speaker is saying so the listener may use it later on.

2. Criticizing the Speaker

Have you also noticed that school subjects and whether or not you like them also affects what you think about the teacher? Many students feel the teachers of the classes they like are prettier or more handsome, smile more, and are nicer! This is WRONG!

Since you will not be tested on HOW the speaker speaks, whether he or she speaks with an accent, or how fast he or she speaks, DO NOT CRITICIZE these things!

Even though the speaker's style might be annoying, good listeners soon become oblivious to the speaker's mannerisms and pay attention to the speaker's content. Good listeners know that WHAT the speaker is saying is ten times more important than HOW he or she says it.

3. Pay Attention

Too many times, we let little things about a speaker bother us. Sometimes it can be as simple as how a certain word is said, or the speaker's accent. Either way, if we pay attention to these kinds of things and not to what the speaker is saying, we will miss the important points the speaker is trying to make.

Sometimes, the problem is that what the speaker is saying comes in conflict with our own opinions and because that bothers us, we tune the speaker out because we don't like hearing about things we don't agree with. This can be especially dangerous, because whether or not we agree with what is being said, we should be paying attention. After all, it could be on the test!

4. Organization

We mentioned earlier that organization while taking notes is very important. While your personal organization is very important, understanding the speaker's organization is equally, if not more, important. If you know what the speaker's main purpose is and you are able to figure out the organization (sometimes this is given in the opening statements of the speaker's lecture), you will be better able to anticipate what the speaker is going to say. Expecting someone to say something is one of the tactics of successful active listeners.

5. Main Ideas vs. Details

The more things you listen to, as well as the more often you are required to take notes, the better you will get at each of these practices. You must be able to distinguish between main ideas and minor details quickly. The quicker you are able to do this well, the better organized your notes will be. This will allow you to find information easier when the time comes to access your notes.

6. Take Notes While You Listen

While you are listening, make sure you are writing things down, not getting lost in the speaker's lecture. Sometimes what the speaker is saying can be overwhelming, but just as Rome wasn't built in a day, you won't get better at note taking unless you practice a lot. The more often you take notes while you listen to something, the more information you will retain.

Listening Summary

Good job! You are halfway through your TOEFL preparation. Here are some important points to remember that will help you crack the Listening section.

- o **Don't memorize; understand!** The most common mistake on the Listening section is to try to do too much. Look for the big picture: main idea, structure, and tone. Don't get lost in the details.

- o **Taking notes is optional:** If taking notes interferes with your ability to comprehend what you're listening to, then don't do it. Take notes only if you are able to write and maintain your focus on the selection.

- o **If you do choose to take notes, remember the Five R's of note taking:** record, reduce, recite, reflect, review.

- o **Know what bad answers look like:** Make sure you're familiar with the kinds of bad answers that appear most frequently on the TOEFL.

- o **Stay aggressive!** If you don't catch an important detail, don't panic. Stay aggressive and eliminate answers based on your knowledge of the main idea, structure, tone, and previous questions.

Now that you've worked with the passages and lectures on the TOEFL, practice the Listening section with the drills that follow. Then move on to the Speaking and Writing sections, where you will create some passages and speeches of your own.

Chapter 11
Listening Practice Drills

You're now ready to crack the Listening section. Remember to use the strategies and guidelines you learned in the previous chapter. Pay special attention to POE (Process of Elimination). If you're stuck, get rid of as many bad answers as you can. After you've finished, check your answers and look over the explanations provided in the next chapter. Good luck!

Listening Practice Drill #1: A Conversation

On the TOEFL you will see screens similar to the ones shown below and on the pages that follow. Listen to Track 4 in your Student Tools. Then answer the following questions.

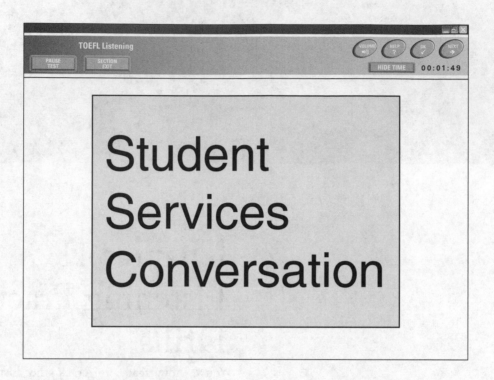

1. What are the speakers mainly discussing?

   a. An increase in student services fees
   b. Helping Kamah figure out why she's feeling down
   c. Majoring in psychology
   d. The difference between professionals and amateurs

2. Why does Julia encourage Kamah to go to the student counseling center?

   a. She feels it was a helpful resource for her.
   b. It's off-campus, so no one will know she's going.
   c. She won't need a referral to go.
   d. She will be judged by the professionals.

3. What is Kamah's initial reaction to going to the student counseling center?

   a. She is afraid of being judged.
   b. She doesn't think it will help.
   c. She has already gone and found it unhelpful.
   d. She didn't know it was an option.

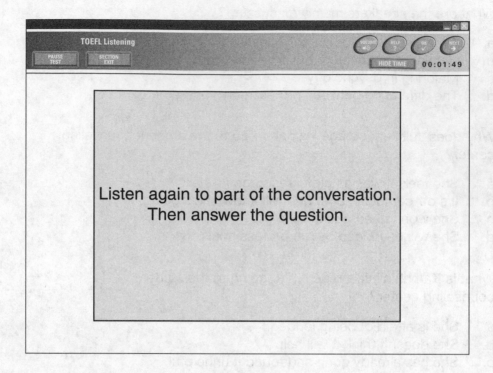

Listen again to part of the conversation.
Then answer the question.

4. Listen again to part of the conversation. Then answer the question.

K: Yeah, I guess. But I bet it costs a lot. I just don't have much to spend these days.

J: Actually, it's one of the resources we pay for with our student services fees every semester. I mean, there's a limit as to how often you can go in a semester, but at least you can get some kind of help at no extra cost.

What does Julia imply about the student counseling center?

a. She no longer needs the support of the center.
b. She thinks Kamah will be fine without going.
c. It will not cost Kamah anything to start getting help.
d. It is an underused resource on campus.

5. What does Kamah say are her primary symptoms?

Click on 2 answers.

a. She feels down a lot.
b. She has thought about transferring schools.
c. She has not been sleeping well.
d. She is losing weight.

Listening Practice Drill #2: A Conversation

Listen to Track 5 in your Student Tools. Then answer the following questions.

1. Why does the professor want to talk with the student?

   a. She has exciting news to share.
   b. She wants to offer him an internship.
   c. She is concerned about his grades.
   d. She wants to recognize him for his achievements.

2. What explanation does the student offer in response to the professor's concern?

   a. He has been spending too much time with friends.
   b. He was up late playing video games.
   c. He doesn't care about his grades.
   d. He has been working more than usual.

3. What does the professor offer as the first step in a plan to help the student?

   a. Attend a different section of the class
   b. Read anything he missed already
   c. Attend office hours
   d. Write an extra paper

4. What else does the student commit to in order to ensure he passes the class?

   a. Doing extra credit projects outside of class
   b. Reading any material he missed
   c. Reading extra material
   d. Conducting additional online research on the topics covered

5. Listen again to part of the conversation.

   "Plus, if you're not in class, I'm afraid you won't learn the material well enough to get a good enough grade on the final to pass the class."

   What does the professor imply?

   a. The student hasn't learned anything this semester.
   b. The student will pass the class without difficulty.
   c. The student can take the class online.
   d. The student is in danger of failing the class.

Listening Practice Drill #3: A Lecture

Listen to Track 6 in your Student Tools. Then answer the following questions.

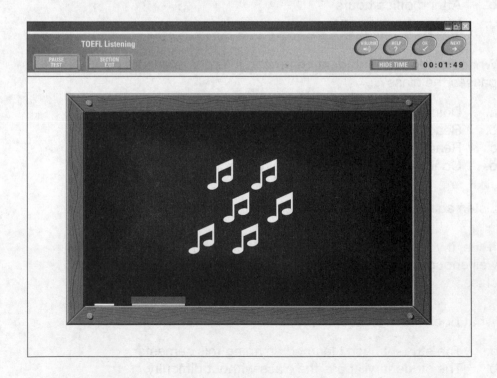

1. What is the lecture mainly about?

   a. How composers express their political beliefs in their music
   b. Why composers write their music in particular styles
   c. How two composers incorporated nationalistic themes in their music
   d. Why Louis Armstrong was a popular musician

2. According to the professor, which of the following did composers include in their music to represent their national identities?

   a. Folk songs
   b. Non-European ideals
   c. Mazurkas
   d. African music

3. Why does the professor believe that African Americans were interested in purchasing recordings of slave spirituals?

   a. They expressed African Americans' desires to be recognized as equals.
   b. They represented music similar to that of African Americans' ancestors.
   c. They represented music with which former slaves and their early descendants could identify.
   d. They identified feelings that were common across all African Americans.

4. Listen again to part of the lecture.

   "So, what do I mean by saying that the nationalism in jazz is split along ethnic lines? Well, check this out: jazz originally came out of spiritual songs slaves would sing."

   What did the professor mean by this?

   "Check this out."

   a. He's going to answer his own question.
   b. He needs to confirm some facts.
   c. He is going to check out some jazz from the library.
   d. He is going to write a check.

5. Why did the professor think it was interesting that Louis Armstrong was popular among both White Americans and African Americans?

Click on 2 answers.

   a. He was African American.
   b. He was an accomplished musician.
   c. He ignored elements of the slave spirituals.
   d. He embraced self-sufficiency as a personal ideal.

6. Why does the professor believe that Chopin incorporated folk rhythms in his music?

   a. He wanted to help the Polish people maintain a sense of identity.
   b. He disliked the folk rhythms.
   c. He wanted to create modern dance music.
   d. He wanted to honor the Mazovia region of Poland.

Listening Practice Drill #4: A Lecture

Listen to Track 7 in your Student Tools. Then answer the following questions.

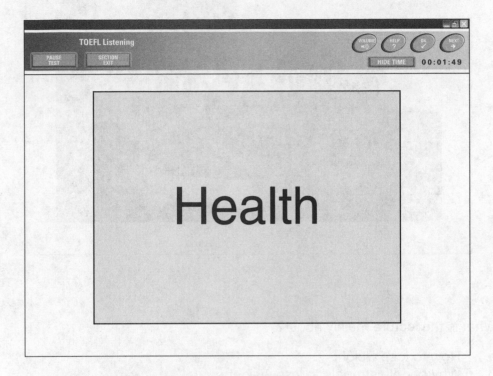

1. What is the lecture mainly about?

   a. How to lose weight
   b. Why people struggle to lose weight
   c. Why America's obesity problem is worse than that in other countries
   d. The impact that fast food has had on Americans' health

2. Which of the following is true, according to the professor?

   a. It's easy to lose weight.
   b. Walking to work is better than driving.
   c. Portion sizes have shrunk in the last 50 years.
   d. There can be more than one factor that contributes to weight gain.

3. Listen again to part of the lecture.

   "One consideration is that for some folks, the system that sends signals back and forth between organs such as the stomach and the brain is out of whack. So what can happen is that when the stomach sends a signal to the brain to stop taking in food, the brain doesn't recognize it and so the person just keeps eating."

   What did the professor mean by this?

   "Out of whack"

   a. The system may be unemployed.
   b. The system may be overused.
   c. The system may not function properly.
   d. The system may cause overeating.

4. What does the professor suggest as a viable weight loss solution?

   a. Dieting
   b. Exercise
   c. Protein shakes
   d. Using a scale

5. Which one of the following factors is a possible contributor to the obesity epidemic?

   a. Stress
   b. Massage
   c. Salt intake
   d. Increased movement

6. What does the professor believe contribute to the likelihood to overeat?

   Click on 2 answers.

   a. Watching television
   b. Reward system
   c. Nausea
   d. Broken feedback system

Listening Practice Drill #5: A Lecture

Listen to Track 8 in your Student Tools. Then answer the following questions.

1. According to the professor, why was trade with nonessential goods difficult?

    a.   Poor societies cannot devote resources to making nonessential goods.
    b.   Nonessential goods are often large and heavy to carry.
    c.   Different societies have different systems of value.
    d.   The decorations used by early societies were too simple to be valuable.

2. Why did people begin relying on gold and gold specialists?

    Click on 3 answers.

    a.   Gold was difficult to transport.
    b.   Travelers were in danger from thieves.
    c.   Only specialists could determine its value.
    d.   Gold doesn't spoil.

3. How did gold specialists indicate the value of the gold they received?

    a.   They recorded where it had been mined.
    b.   They recorded its purity and density.
    c.   They lent out only the highest-quality gold.
    d.   They issued receipts in different colors.

4. Listen again to part of the lecture. Then answer the question.

Male Student: So if you were storing 500 ounces of gold of whatever percent purity, you'd give the receipt back, and get your 500 ounces of gold back? They kept it for you in your own little drawer or something?

Male Professor: Whoops! I guess I did make it sound that way—thanks for catching that!

What did the professor mean by this?

"Whoops! I guess I did make it sound that way—thanks for catching that!"

    a.   The professor was not sure what the student said.
    b.   The professor's statement was misleading.
    c.   The professor wanted to emphasize a different point.
    d.   The student's interpretation is correct.

5. Why did the professor say the receipts issued by gold shops were the first ancestors of money?

    a.   All gold shops used the same standard format.
    b.   They were written on small slips of paper.
    c.   They represented the value of something else.
    d.   They were used in societies where bartering was still practiced.

6. What is an ingot?

    a.   A piece of gold
    b.   A gold specialist's shop
    c.   A receipt
    d.   A cultural object

Chapter 12
Listening Practice
Answers and
Explanations

LISTENING PRACTICE DRILL #1: A CONVERSATION

Here is the transcript for Drill #1. Read through it and pay attention to the structure and purpose of the talk.

J: Hi Kamah, how ya doing?

K: Oh, hi, Julia. Um, I guess I'm okay.

J: Oh? What's going on? Is everything alright?

K: Yeah, I guess. It's just…I don't know. I'm having a hard time caring about much these days. I just feel down, but I don't know why. I haven't been sleeping well, and I just feel kind of down.

J: Have you thought about going to the student counseling center? They're incredibly helpful. Last year I was having a hard time with some family stuff that came up, and it was really nice to be able to talk to someone to help sort out what was going on in my head.

K: No, I don't like sharing my problems. I don't want people to think I can't handle life, or something.

J: Yeah, I understand. But the cool thing about the folks there is that they're professionals—they're not the people you're going to see walking around campus. And they know that we ALL have stuff going on, and sometimes just need some help to figure it out and get through it.

K: Yeah, I guess. But I bet it costs a lot. I just don't have much to spend these days.

J: Actually, it's one of the resources we pay for with our student services fees every semester. I mean, there's a limit as to how often you can go in a semester, but at least you can get some kind of help at no extra cost.

K: Hmm… I just feel like I'm lost and that no one will be able to help me. Do you really feel like it helped you?

J: I felt exactly the same way, and yes, I do believe that they were able to help. You'll never know if they can if you don't at least give it a shot.

> K: I suppose you're right. Okay, I'll at least go check them out. I guess it can't really hurt.

This conversation falls into the students discussing a problem category, a very typical pattern on the TOEFL. Our first goal with a conversation is to identify the purpose of the interaction. Like the main idea, the purpose appears early in the conversation. In this case, the following lines reveal the purpose:

> K: Oh, hi, Julia. Um, I guess I'm okay.

> J: Oh? What's going on? Everything alright?

> K: Yeah, I guess. It's just…I don't know. I'm having a hard time caring about much these days. I just feel down, but I don't know why. I haven't been sleeping well, and I just feel kind of blah.

Once you identify a problem, your next goal is to try to listen for the solutions offered. In many cases, one listener will offer a solution, only to have the other speaker reject it. The listener will then advise another possible solution. In this case, the listener offers the following advice:

> J: Have you thought about going to the student counseling center? They're incredibly helpful. Last year I was having a really hard time with some family stuff that came up, and it was really nice to be able to talk to someone to help sort out what was going on in my head.

After the speaker says she doesn't like to share her problems because she doesn't want to be judged, the listener responds by showing the speaker won't be judged:

> J: Yeah, I understand. But the cool thing about the folks there is that they're professionals—they're not the kids you're going to see walking around campus. And they know that we ALL have stuff going on, and sometimes just need some help to figure it out and get through it.

The speaker then proposes another reason not to go to the counseling center:

> K: Yeah, I guess. But I bet it costs a lot. I just don't have much to go around these days.

The listener again challenges this objection:

> J: Actually, it's one of the resources we pay for with our student services fees every semester. I mean, there's a limit as to how often you can go in a semester, but at least you can get some kind of help at no extra cost.

It is also very important to pay attention to tone when listening to conversations. Does the speaker accept the solutions or reject them? Was the problem solved by the end of the conversation or will it still be an issue? Paying attention to the tone will help you with POE.

Look at some of Kamah's responses. What is her tone?

> *K:* No, I don't like sharing my problems. I don't want people to think I can't handle life, or something.

> *K:* Yeah, I guess. But I bet it costs a lot. I just don't have much to go around these days.

> *K:* I suppose you're right. Okay, I'll at least go check them out. I guess it can't really hurt.

It seems as if she's initially against the idea, but eventually comes around to being willing to consider the solution of going to the counseling center.

Now, let's take a look at the questions.

1. **B** This question asks about the overall purpose of the selection. As we've discussed, the two are talking about helping Kamah find a resource to help deal with feeling down. Eliminate (A) because although fees are mentioned, this is not the primary point of the selection. Choice (B) is the correct answer, because it focuses on Kamah's emotional state. Choice (C) is out because the speakers are not talking about what either student should major in. Choice (D) is never mentioned.

2. **A** This is a detail question. When Julia first suggests that Kamah should go to the counseling center, she says she had gone, herself, and found it helpful, which directly relates to (A).

3. **A** This is another detail question. Kamah's initial response to Julia's suggestion was as follows:

> *K:* No, I don't like sharing my problems. I don't want people to think I can't handle life, or something.

When she says she doesn't want people to think she can't handle life, that's another way of saying she doesn't want to be judged by others, which matches (A).

4. **C** This questions asks us the purpose of something one speaker says.

> *K:* Yeah, I guess. But I bet it costs a lot. I just don't have much to go around these days.

J: Actually, it's one of the resources we pay for with our student services fees every semester. I mean, there's a limit as to how often you can go in a semester, but at least you can get some kind of help at no extra cost.

In this part of the conversation, Julia is telling Kamah that the cost of the counseling center is already included in their student fees, so she won't have any additional out-of-pocket expenses, which is exactly what (C) says.

5. **A, C** This questions asks for two details out of the passage. Within the first two statements Kamah makes, she says the following:

K: Yeah, I guess. It's just…I don't know. I'm having a hard time caring about much these days. I just feel down, but I don't know why. I haven't been sleeping well, and I just feel kind of blah.

This statement corresponds to (A) and (C).

LISTENING PRACTICE DRILL #2: A CONVERSATION

Here is a transcript of the conversation played for these questions.

Make sure to read through the transcript below to familiarize yourself with the types of structures you will see on the TOEFL.

M: Um, excuse me, Professor? You wanted to speak with me?

P: Yes, Matthew. Please, come in and have a seat.

M: Thank you. I got the note in my mailbox. Is everything okay?

P: Well, Matthew, I wanted to talk with you about your grade in my class.

M: Oh?

P: I'm concerned. I haven't seen you in class much lately, and you know that participation is a significant portion of your final grade. Plus, if you're not in class, I'm afraid you won't learn the material well enough to get a good enough grade on the final to pass the class.

M: Yes, ma'am, I understand. It's just…I've had to pick up more shifts at work because my dad lost his job and I'm trying to help pay the bills.

P: That's a tough position to be in. Let me ask, are evenings easier for you to attend class? If so, you can come to my Thursday evening class section for the rest of the semester. But I need you to commit to being there every week through the end of the term.

M: Oh, yes, that would work much better for me! I can absolutely be there for all of the remaining classes. Thank you so much!

P: Well, I also need to know that you'll learn the material that you've missed in the last few classes. Can you make my Friday afternoon office hours? I'm willing to meet with you to review the material if you're willing to catch up on the reading you've missed.

M: Yes, I can definitely make the Friday afternoon office hours. If we can start next week, I promise I'll get all of the reading done from the classes I missed.

P: Very well, then. I'll see you in class this Thursday evening and next, and then I'll see you in office hours next Friday, with all of the reading under your belt.

Once again, our first challenge during a conversation on the TOEFL is to identify the purpose. The purpose should appear within the first two to four exchanges between the speakers.

In this conversation, the purpose is stated in the following lines:

P: Well, Matthew, I wanted to talk with you about your grade in my class.

M: Oh?

P: I'm concerned. I haven't seen you in class much lately, and you know that participation is a significant portion of your final grade. Plus, if you're not in class, I'm afraid you won't learn the material well enough to get a good enough grade on the final to pass the class.

This conversation is about what we'd call a "service encounter." Matthew has been summoned to his professor's office to discuss his grade in her class. After identifying a conversation as a service encounter, listen for any problems the student may have encountered and any actions the professional recommends to the student. The first problem occurs at the following point in the conversation:

> *P:* I'm concerned. I haven't seen you in class much lately, and you know that participation is a significant portion of your final grade. Plus, if you're not in class, I'm afraid you won't learn the material well enough to get a good enough grade on the final to pass the class.

The student gives an explanation for his absences:

> *M:* Yes, ma'am, I understand. It's just…I've had to pick up more shifts at work because my dad lost his job and I'm trying to help pay the bills.

The professor then offers two solutions:

> *P:* That's a tough position to be in. Let me ask, are evenings easier for you to attend class? If so, you can come to my Thursday evening class section for the rest of the semester. But I need you to commit to being there every week through the end of the term.

> *M:* Oh, yes, that would work much better for me! I can absolutely be there for all of the remaining classes. Thank you so much!

> *P:* Well, I also need to know that you'll learn the material that you've missed in the last few classes. Can you make my Friday afternoon office hours? I'm willing to meet with you to review the material if you're willing to catch up on the reading you've missed.

Now let's take a look at the questions.

1. **C** The professor clearly states that her concern is about the student's grades, especially since he has missed several classes. This most closely matches (C).

2. **D** In response to the professor's concern, the student replies that he's working more to help pay the bills since his dad lost his job. This matches up nicely with (D).

3. **A** The tricky part of this question is that the professor offered two possible solutions and the question is asking for the first of those two. At the very least, make sure to eliminate anything that wasn't mentioned at all, like (D). Then, think about which one was the bigger step, the more important step, or the one that would logically come first. In this case, the first step she offered was to allow the student to sit in on a different section of the class that meets in the evenings instead of during the day. This most closely matches (A).

4. **B** The second part of the solution the professor offered was office hours on Fridays, but she included the expectation that the student would do all of the necessary reading before coming to office hours. So, the part that the student explicitly committed to was catching up on all of his reading, or (B).

5. **D** Remember that inference questions are supported by the content of the conversation just as much as detail questions are. When the professor says "I'm afraid you won't learn the material well enough to get a good enough grade on the final to pass the class," she's implying that if it's not good enough to pass, then he will fail. This matches (D).

LISTENING PRACTICE DRILL #3: A LECTURE

Read the following transcript of the first lecture. Ask yourself how the lecture compares with reading selections with which you've worked.

Professor: One of the most interesting aspects of history is the exploration of how artists expressed their political opinions in their art, particularly when people didn't feel they could speak their minds without recrimination. Among those expressions were music composers who incorporated ideas and motifs of a nationalistic style into their compositions. These themes, such as folk songs, can be associated with particular countries or regions of countries and are therefore part of a country's identity.

Frederic Chopin was one of the earliest composers to incorporate nationalistic ideas into his music, which was written primarily for solo piano. Born in Poland in 1810, Chopin grew up in a country that found itself controlled politically by Russia, Austria, and Prussia. As a result, he felt compelled to incorporate many elements of traditional Polish music in his compositions, in essence in an effort to maintain the Polish identity despite non-Polish rule.

A particularly remarkable example of his use of folk music elements is in his mazurkas, of which he wrote at least 69 for piano. These are a variation of their original structure, which was a folk dance from Poland's Mazovia region. These folk dances were traditionally played on bagpipe and fiddle. Chopin "borrowed" the same rhythmic structures employed in the folk dances and used those as the basis for his mazurkas. The end results are not really intended as music for dancing and are definitely more technically sophisticated, but the underlying rhythms and melodies are clearly identifiable.

Closer to home, we also see obvious nationalistic tendencies in 20th century jazz music. Interestingly, though, these tendencies are split along ethnic lines: the White American influence and the African American influence. Particularly intriguing is the fact that this divide came about in a country that for so long has prided itself on welcoming people of all backgrounds, going so far as to call itself a "melting pot."

So, what do I mean by saying that the nationalism in jazz is split along ethnic lines? Well, check this out: jazz originally came out of spiritual songs slaves would sing. In the 1920s, what was really the heart of the Jazz Age, so to speak, these spirituals were recorded and marketed directly as "race music," and were directly marketed toward members of the African Americans. So, this begs the question: why would an art form that was reminiscent of slavery be marketed toward African Americans decades after the abolition of slavery? I think it's because that's part of the "national" identity that former slaves and their first couple generations of descendants could identify as their own.

Interestingly, Louis Armstrong, himself an African American, was a popular jazz artist among both African Americans and White Americans—but his form of jazz totally ignored any musical elements of the slave spiritual! He crossed the "divide," so to speak! As jazz evolved, it continued to establish and support the desires of the African American community, especially during a time when segregation was still common and racism widespread. At the pinnacle of the free jazz movement, for example, ideals such as self-sufficiency and a non-European "ideal" underscored the efforts of many independent recording facilities, not just those of the musicians themselves.

Just as with a reading passage, a lecture will state its main purpose first. However, since the lectures are spoken, you will probably hear a brief introduction or greeting before the main idea is introduced. Here's an example.

One of the most interesting aspects of history is the exploration of how artists expressed their political opinions in their art, particularly when people didn't feel they could speak their minds without recrimination. Among those expressions were music composers who incorporated ideas and motifs of a nationalistic style into their compositions.

The first part of the excerpt is a brief introduction ("One of the most interesting...recrimination"), after which the professor states the main purpose—"Among those expressions were music composers who incorporated ideas and motifs of a nationalistic style into their compositions."

Based on this statement, the lecture is most likely going to fit into the Abstract Category/Specific Examples category of lectures. That means we have to look for specific examples of composers incorporating nationalistic ideas into their compositions. Here's the first.

> Frederic Chopin was one of the earliest composers to incorporate nationalistic ideas into his music, which was written primarily for solo piano.

As you listen to the rest of the lecture, listen for the other example given:

> Closer to home, we also see obvious nationalistic tendencies in 20th century jazz music.

With this understanding of the two examples, let's look at the questions.

1. **C** Knowing that this passage fits into the Abstract Category/Specific Example structure helps significantly on the main idea questions: use Process of Elimination to get rid of answers that don't address the entire passage. Choice (A) is too broad—this lecture didn't discuss ALL composers; (B) brings in the question of musical styles, which are not discussed; and (D) is too narrow—while the professor discussed Louis Armstrong, that's not the main point of the lecture. Choice (C) is correct because the lecture discusses both Chopin and Louis Armstrong, two musicians who incorporated nationalistic themes into their music.

2. **A** Be careful to categorize details that are mentioned to the best of your ability. In this case, the question is asking about a general characteristic that composers included in their works, which would have been mentioned earlier in the lecture, like (A). Choice (B) was mentioned closer to the end of the lecture, when discussing jazz music. Choice (C) was a type of composition that Chopin wrote, and (D) was never mentioned in the lecture.

3. **C** Think about the common theme of this passage: ethnic/national identity. Even if you don't remember exactly what the professor said, choose the answer that comes closest to the overall ideas expressed. In this case, (C) is the only option that comes close to matching ethnic/national identity.

4. **A** As with any colloquial expression, pay attention to the way the ideas are connected: the first sentence presents a question, and the second one includes an answer to that question. Find the answer that comes closest to describing that relationship, like (A).

5. **A, C** Hopefully this is in your recent memory, because Louis Armstrong was the last major topic discussed. Use Process of Elimination as effectively as you can, and you should at least be able to get rid of

(D). Bringing in a bit of common sense, you could likely get rid of (B): yes, he was an accomplished musician, but that doesn't necessarily address why he appealed to both White American and African American audiences. This would leave you with (A) and (C).

6. **A** Once again, keep the main idea of the lecture in mind: ethnic/national identity. Eliminate answers that aren't in line with that idea. This will lead you directly to (A), since it's the only choice that deals with identity.

LISTENING PRACTICE DRILL #4: A LECTURE

Here is a transcript of the second lecture. Try to use the active reading strategies you learned to identify the key parts.

Professor: Obesity. Pretty much everyone recognizes it's a serious problem. Recent statistics indicate that nearly 78 million adults and 13 million children in the United States alone deal with the physical and emotional effects of obesity every day. It would seem like the solution is easy, wouldn't it? Eat less and move more. Or in other words, consume fewer calories and increase the number of calories burned through physical activity. And yet, more than 90 million Americans continue to battle the bulge. What makes it so difficult to lose weight? Experts believe there are a number of contributing factors.

One consideration is that for some folks, the system that sends signals back and forth between organs such as the stomach and the brain is out of whack. So what can happen is that when the stomach sends a signal to the brain to stop taking in food, the brain doesn't recognize it and so the person just keeps eating. And as if that alone wasn't bad enough, at the end of a meal the "reward system" can come into play. How so? Well, think about the last time you were at a restaurant and you were convinced that you were absolutely stuffed, and then the waitress brought over the dessert tray. Those desserts looked pretty tempting, didn't they? Turns out that's because of your "reward system." It can make you want to eat whether you're hungry or not when you see or smell appetizing food. No wonder reducing the number of calories consumed can be so challenging!

So, we're eating too much. But, experts also believe we're eating too much of the wrong foods, too. Most folks eat more than they should of red meat, unhealthy fats, refined grains, and processed food—never mind fast food options! What that ends up meaning is that we're eating fewer healthy foods, like fruits and vegetables, whole grains and nuts. Without these foods in our diets, we're not getting all of the nutrition our body needs. Some experts believe this causes us to eat even more of those same unhealthy foods in a desperate attempt to get all of the nutrients it craves.

Experts also believe that societal factors may contribute to difficulty losing weight. Think back to that last dinner at a restaurant again. Think about the size of your meal. Would you be surprised to learn that in the last 50 years restaurant portions have quadrupled in size?! And we haven't even talked about the increase in the size of beverages. Serving sizes of beverages have actually increased by a factor of 6 in the same time frame!

But wait, there's more! It's not all about calories in—it's also about calories out. Today's Americans move a whole lot less than those of 50 years ago did. Our jobs require us to sit behind desks more. We spend more of our 'down time' behind a screen of some variety—surfing the web or streaming a show on a laptop or tablet, watching TV, or playing games on a phone. We meet friends for coffee instead of going for a hike. We commute to work and school in cars, rather than on bicycles or by using our own two feet.

And then there's also speculation that our lifestyles, themselves, are contributing to our weight gain. Our stress levels are higher than ever before, so we're not sleeping, which knocks more than just our eating systems off course. We're tired, so we reach for sugary, caffeinated drinks. Then we race through our fast food lunches because we have to get back to our desks. We have to spend extra time at our desks doing our work because we're not as productive as we'd like to be. And we're not as productive as we'd like to be because we're tired…and so it begins all over again.

So what's the solution? Well, experts disagree there, too. From my experience, it starts with small changes that can help knock you out of your rut. Something as simple as committing to walking 15 minutes a day at lunchtime or drinking a full glass of water for every glass of soda you drink can be the starting point. For some folks, that's all it takes. For others, there's more involved to ultimately regain a healthy weight. But one thing's for sure: there's no single formula that works for everyone.

Just as with a reading passage, a lecture will state its main purpose first. However, since the lectures are spoken, you will probably hear a brief introduction or greeting before the main idea is introduced. Here's an example:

> Obesity. Pretty much everyone recognizes it's a serious problem. Recent statistics indicate that nearly 78 million adults and 13 million children in the United States alone deal with the physical and emotional effects of obesity every day. It would seem like the solution is easy, wouldn't it? Eat less and move more. Or in other words, consume fewer calories and increase the number of calories burned through physical activity. And yet, more than 90 million Americans continue to battle the bulge. What makes it so difficult to lose weight? Experts believe there are a number of contributing factors.

The first part of the excerpt is a brief introduction ("Obesity…battle the bulge."), after which the professor states the main purpose—"What makes it so difficult to lose weight? Experts believe there are a number of contributing factors."

Based on this statement, the lecture is most likely going to fit into the cause-and-effect category of lectures. That means we have to look for the causes of obesity mentioned in the lecture. Here's the first.

> One consideration is that for some folks, the system that sends signals back and forth between organs such as the stomach and the brain is out of whack.

Other potential causes are also mentioned:

> But, experts also believe we're eating too much of the wrong foods, too.

> Experts also believe that societal factors may contribute to difficulty losing weight.

> But wait, there's more! It's not all about calories in—it's also about calories out. Today's Americans move a whole lot less than those of 50 years ago did.

> And then there's also speculation that our lifestyles, themselves, are contributing to our weight gain.

So those are the main points the professor is making. Now let's take a look at the questions.

1. **B** While there is a bit of commentary toward the end about potential solutions to the issue of obesity, the passage as a whole is primarily dedicated to discussing the factors that contribute to obesity, or why people have a hard time losing weight. This matches (B).

2. **D** It's certainly challenging to remember all the details about every point the professor made, so use your understanding of the structure of the passage and a bit of common sense to at least eliminate answers that you're fairly certain don't match the professor's thinking. Choice (A) is certainly not in line with what the professor believes—after all, we just said in the previous question that the passage is about the difficulty of losing weight, not the ease of doing so! Choice (B) might be a "maybe" at first glance, so if you're not sure, leave it for now. Choice (C) is definitely out—the professor was clear that portion sizes have increased, not decreased, in the last half century. Choice (D), though, is pretty close to what the entire passage was about: multiple causes that affect weight gain. If you still have (B) in, it's easily eliminated because (D) is much more in line with the content of the passage.

3. **C** A common question topic on the TOEFL Listening section is the use of colloquial phrases, like this one. Use the context of the passage to determine the intended meaning of phrases like these.

> One consideration is that for some folks, the system that sends signals back and forth between organs such as the stomach and the brain is out of whack. So what can happen is that when the stomach sends a signal to the brain to stop taking in food, the brain doesn't recognize it and so the person just keeps eating.

The professor is describing a system that isn't working correctly, which matches (C).

4. **B** When the professor discusses a problem, be sure to pay attention to possible solutions. The only one mentioned by the professor is exercise, (B). If you don't recall the details, eliminate anything you don't remember hearing about and guess!

5. **A** When a lecture is about cause and effect, definitely remember to at least note the primary causes and primary effects. Of the answer choices presented, the only one that is close to anything the professor discussed is (A) *stress*, which is mentioned in the next to last paragraph. Also remember to keep a bit of common sense involved: (B) doesn't have anything to do with weight gain, and (D) is commonly accepted as a way to decrease weight gain. That means you should at least be able to eliminate two answers and then guess between (A) and (C).

6. **B, D** On multiple answer questions, remember that Process of Elimination is key to choosing the right answers. While (A) might make sense as a contributing factor, it was never mentioned by the professor. Choice (C) is also not likely to be a cause of overeating. That leaves you with the two causes the professor did identify, (B) and (D).

LISTENING PRACTICE DRILL #5: A LECTURE

Read the transcript of the lecture, noting the main idea, structure, and tone. How do the students' questions relate to the main idea?

Male Professor: Since yesterday's brief introduction on the origin of banking confused some of you, today I would like to review it a little bit. Banking the way we know it today is a convenience. The money used in banking represents a certain amount of value, but the money itself isn't valuable; it's just paper. To see how we got here...suppose we think about a society far, far back in history—what would it have used before the paper money we have today?

Female Student: Didn't they trade with the goods themselves?

MP: Sure. The system of exchanging one good for another of equal value is called *bartering*. Bartering was common in early societies, first with essential goods, then with nonessential goods. By nonessential, I mean, for example, art or cultural objects. You might trade a curtain that had been dyed in a decorative pattern for some wheat. The curtain's decorative value isn't essential to survival the way the food value of the grain is. That's the first step toward a money economy: recognizing trade-worthy value in something that isn't essential to survival.

Of course, you may see a hitch. Different cultures don't value the same decorations, so something could be worth a lot to one tribe and nothing to another. With food, that's not a problem—everyone has to eat—but with nonessential items, you're going to use something with cross-cultural value. Can anyone think of anything that would work?

Male Student: How about gold? It's durable...easy to shape...and it's beautiful. Is that why cultures started using it as money?

MP: Well, you can't refer to the earliest trade with gold as a money economy, but yes. Gold is a perfect example. As societies grew more stable and trade flourished, gold, usually molded into small ingots, gradually replaced the system of bartering. There were problems with gold, though.

FS: Yeah, I was going to say, gold is heavy, isn't it? How did people carry enough of it around to buy things? And wasn't it dangerous—like, you'd get robbed if people knew you had money with you?

MP: Definitely. Hauling all your gold around was a real risk in early societies, when there were bandits roaming around and no police to help you. And as you say, gold is heavy and unwieldy. One advantage it has, though, is that, unlike livestock or food, it doesn't go bad, so you don't have to use it up immediately.

That combination of characteristics gave people an idea. They started leaving their gold ingots with gold specialists for safekeeping. The specialists stored the gold for a small fee, and they gave their customers receipts, the way you'd get today. So you'd get something that said that, you know, you were the owner of such-and-such an amount of gold stored at this particular shop. The quality of gold from different mines varies, so the purity and density of your gold ingots—you know, how heavy they were for their size—determined their value and would also be recorded.

Then, when you wanted to use it, you just went back, gave the shopkeeper the receipt, and he gave you your gold.

MS: So if you were storing 500 ounces of gold of whatever percent purity, you'd give the receipt back, and get your 500 ounces of gold back? They kept it for you in your own little drawer or something?

MP: Whoops! I guess I did make it sound that way—thanks for catching that! No, you'd get 500 ounces of gold of the same purity back. They would have equal value, but would not necessarily be the exact same pile of ingots that you originally gave to the shopkeeper.

FS: The shopkeeper would use the gold or lend it out while you were storing it?

MP: Sure, and you can see how that's another of the beginnings of banking as we know it. You wouldn't get back your very own pile of gold; you'd get back a pile of equal value. It was the value itself that was important.

MS: So how did it become like money? I mean, we're still talking about big, heavy stacks of things, and—

MP: Well, that's the last point. Eventually, people figured out that they could use their receipts from storing gold to trade with one another. If they wanted to buy something, instead of running to the gold shop, withdrawing gold, and bringing it to another shop to pay for food or clay pots or whatever, they just gave the food merchant a receipt for the appropriate amount of gold. The merchant could then cash it in for gold, and the trade would be complete. And that's the last major step: the receipts became the first real ancestor of the money we use today because they stood for value actually attached to goods somewhere else.

Some of the academic lectures will include questions from the students and other forms of discussion. While this may appear to make the lectures more confusing, the student questions actually help you to follow the lecture and figure out the main idea.

First, let's figure out what the main topic is. As always, the professor mentions it at the very beginning of the lecture.

> MP: Banking the way we know it today is a convenience. The money used in banking represents a certain amount of value, but the money itself isn't valuable; it's just paper. To see how we got here...suppose we think about a society far, far back in history—what would it have used before the paper money we have today?

Now that we know the lecture will be about the beginnings of banking, we should look for a sequence of ideas. The first student question introduces a key point.

> FS: Didn't they trade with the goods themselves?

As we said earlier, the students' comments and questions provide an easy way to follow the development of the lecture. Now the professor will explain the important idea below.

> MP: Sure. The system of exchanging one good for another of equal value is called *bartering*. Bartering was common in early societies, first with essential goods, then with nonessential goods....Of course, you may see a hitch. Different cultures don't value the same decorations, so something could be worth a lot to one tribe and nothing to another.

A student now asks a question, which again helps us understand the progression of ideas in the lecture.

> MS: How about gold? It's durable...easy to shape...and it's beautiful. Is that why cultures started using it as money?

> MP: Well, you can't refer to the earliest trade with gold as a money economy, but yes. Gold is a perfect example. As societies grew more stable and trade flourished, gold, usually molded into small ingots, gradually replaced the system of bartering. There were problems with gold, though.

This exchange brings us to another key part of the lecture. The professor details the problems.

> MP: Definitely. Hauling all your gold around was a real risk in early societies, when there were bandits roaming around and no police to help you. And as you say, gold is heavy and unwieldy. One advantage it has, though, is that, unlike livestock or food, it doesn't go bad, so you don't have to use it up immediately.

The lecture then continues with a longer explanation of how the problems with gold led to a new idea. But even if you missed some of that discussion, notice how the next student comment helps you figure out the key point.

> MS: So if you were storing 500 ounces of gold of whatever percent purity, you'd give the receipt back, and get your 500 ounces of gold back? They kept it for you in your own little drawer or something?

This comment gives us some clue as to what the professor was talking about before—the ability to store gold. Now the professor continues with the sequence.

> MP: Sure, and you can see how that's another of the beginnings of banking as we know it.

> MS: So how did it become like money? I mean, we're still talking about big, heavy stacks of things, and—

> MP: Well, that's the last point. Eventually, people figured out that they could use their receipts from storing gold to trade with one another.

As you can see, in each case the discussion between student and professor helped to clarify the major points of the lecture. So, make sure to be aware of this when dealing with an academic discussion on the TOEFL.

Now let's take care of the questions.

1. **C** This question was answered when the professor talked about bartering and the point was introduced with the use of a direction marker: "of course...." The answer choices in this question are very good candidates for POE. Choice (A) is extreme. It says that societies "cannot" devote resources. This is an absolute statement and should be eliminated. Choice (D) is another type of extreme answer, one that shows up every once in a while. The problem with this answer is that it can be seen as somewhat offensive. It judges the decorations as "too simple." The TOEFL will never have a correct answer that makes a negative value judgment. The characteristics in (B) refer to gold, but the question is asking about goods. Therefore, (C) is the best answer as the professor specifically said, "Different cultures don't value the same decorations."

2. **A, B, D** Get rid of (C), which is extreme because it states that "only" specialists could determine the value of gold.

3. **B** Once again, (C) is extreme, so eliminate it. Choice (D) never appears in the lecture, so eliminate it as well. Choice (A) is certainly tempting, but the lecture said that "the quality of gold from different mines varies, so the purity and density of your gold ingots—you know, how heavy they were for their size—determined their value and would also be recorded." Thus, (B) is best.

4. **B** Here's a transcription of the excerpt to which you're asked to listen for this question.

> *MS:* So if you were storing 500 ounces of gold of whatever percent purity, you'd give the receipt back, and get your 500 ounces of gold back? They kept it for you in your own little drawer or something?

> *MP:* Whoops! I guess I did make it sound that way—thanks for catching that!

The professor's use of the word *whoops* indicates a mistake of some sort. Eliminate (A) because the student is confused about what the professor said, not the other way around. Eliminate (D) because the line in question is about the professor ("I guess....") ("I guess I did make it sound that way...."), not the student. And no *different point* is introduced in this line, so (C) is incorrect.

5. **C** The professor mentions the answer to this question at the end of the lecture when he says, "the receipts became the first real ancestor of the money we use today because they stood for the value actually attached to goods somewhere else." Alternatively, use POE. Choice (A) is extreme; it says "all" gold shops used the same format. Choice (D) refers to bartering, which was mentioned in the beginning of the sequence as something that came before money. Eliminate it. Although the receipts may have been on "small slips of paper," the passage does not mention that. Therefore (B) is incorrect.

6. **A** This is a definition question. This type of question can be tough because if you miss the definition during the lecture it's hard to use POE. If you recalled that the word *ingot* appeared during the discussion of gold, you may be able to eliminate (C) and (D) because they don't refer to gold. The professor gives a sufficient clue as to the definition of the term here.

> *MP:* The quality of gold from different mines varies, so the purity and density of your gold ingots—you know, how heavy they were for their size—determined their value and would also be recorded.

Chapter 13
Cracking the
Speaking Section

Of all the sections on the TOEFL, the Speaking section often causes the most anxiety in test takers. Of course, we're going to talk about some ways to help you crack this section, but first let's look at what you can expect in the Speaking section.

- **One Independent Task:** You will be asked to choose between two options. You'll have
  - 15 seconds preparation time
  - 45 seconds speaking time
- **Two Reading, Listening, and Speaking Integrated Tasks:** You will read a passage, listen to a conversation or lecture, and respond. For each task, you'll have
  - 45 seconds reading time
  - 60- to 90-second conversation/lecture
  - 30 seconds preparation time
  - 60 seconds speaking time
- **One Listening and Speaking Integrated Task:** You will listen to a lecture and respond. You'll have
  - 1- to 2-minute conversation/lecture
  - 20 seconds preparation time
  - 60 seconds speaking time
- The entire Speaking section will take about 17 minutes.

As you can see, one of the challenges of the Speaking section is the way in which the questions require you to apply a variety of different skills—reading, listening, and, of course, speaking.

The Speaking section is scored on a scale from 0 to 30. As we mentioned in the early part of this book, the Speaking scores are subdivided into five sections:

Advanced (25–30). A score in the "Advanced" range tells schools you can speak fluently on a wide range of topics using an appropriate variety of vocabulary and grammar.

High-Intermediate (20–24). A score in the "High-Intermediate" range tells schools that you can speak comfortably about personal experiences and about content you've read and listened to. Your speech is fairly fluid, pronunciation is clear, and vocabulary is used appropriately.

Low-Intermediate (16–19). A "Low-Intermediate" score tells schools that you can generally speak about personal experiences and about content you've read and listened to. However, you may have some challenges when it comes to pronunciation and intonation, which makes it more challenging for a listener to understand what you're trying to say. You also may have some difficulty with grammatical structures and vocabulary.

Basic (10–15). A "Basic" score indicates to schools that you can handle basic conversations in English, but may have difficulty with grammatical structures. You can offer broad responses, but may lack the vocabulary to present well-developed responses to questions.

Below Basic (0–9). A "Below-Basic" score indicates that you didn't finish your responses, or that your speech is difficult for listeners to understand.

SPEAKING SECTION DIRECTIONS

The Speaking section has a fairly unique format, so it is helpful to familiarize yourself with the directions before you take the test. That way, you'll feel prepared and more comfortable when you actually take the TOEFL.

The Speaking section begins with a microphone test. At the beginning of the section, you'll be asked to answer a sample question. **This question does not affect your TOEFL score, so don't worry about it**. Your response is used simply to adjust the microphone volume, which will be done automatically at the conclusion of your response. The microphone test screen will look similar to the one shown below.

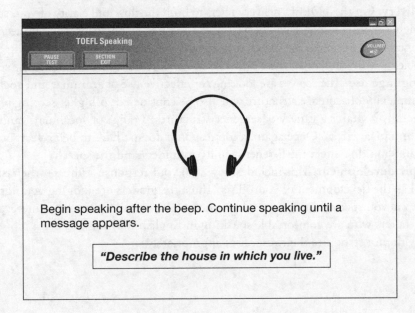

As you speak, the computer will adjust the volume of the microphone. When a message appears on the screen that tells you to stop speaking, the adjustment has finished.

After the adjustment is finished, the directions appear.

The first question will ask you to respond to familiar topics—you will be asked to choose between two options. You will have 15 seconds to organize your thoughts and then 45 seconds to respond.

The next two questions will give you 45 seconds to read a short text after which the text is removed from the screen and the audio will begin immediately. You will listen to a talk on the same topic as the reading and combine information from both the talk and the reading in your spoken response.

The final question asks you to listen to a lecture that lasts between 1 and 2 minutes and then respond to it. After you hear the lecture you will have 20 seconds to prepare your response and then 60 seconds to speak.

You can take notes during all readings, conversations, and lectures, if you find that doing so is helpful. However, the directions for each question will not appear on the screen; you'll be able to listen to them only once, so be sure to listen carefully.

> Remember, it is much more important to speak clearly than quickly. You have only a short time. You will not lose points for having an accent, but the graders must be able to easily understand what you are saying in your answer.

HOW THE SPEAKING SECTION IS SCORED

Each of your spoken responses will be evaluated on a scale of 0–4 by 3–6 different graders. The average of all six scores is then converted to the 0–30 scaled score. The graders consider three major areas when judging the quality of your response—let's look at each in detail.

1. **Delivery:** On the TOEFL, delivery refers to both the flow and clarity of your speech. A higher-scoring response will be well-paced and free of long pauses and unnecessary interjections. Although the speech may contain minor pronunciation errors or problems with intonation, these errors do not detract from understanding the speech.

2. **Language use:** The scorers are looking for effective use of grammar and vocabulary. Complexity of sentence structure will also be considered. A higher-scoring response generally contains a variety of sentence structures, a range of vocabulary, and few grammatical errors. Once again, a top response doesn't have to be perfect, but the errors shouldn't affect the listener's ability to understand the speech.

3. **Topic development:** This includes how well your response addresses the task as well as the development of your ideas. Thus, the graders are judging you not only on *how* you speak, but also on *what* you say. This is an important point because test takers who are comfortable speaking in English may not achieve a top score if they do not structure their responses appropriately.

CRACKING THE SPEAKING SECTION: BASIC PRINCIPLES

The Speaking section of the TOEFL can be very intimidating, but it doesn't have to be. The first important point about the Speaking section is that although there are four different questions, the *types* of responses you will give are all fairly similar. Basically, your goal is to use the skills you've learned throughout the Reading and Listening sections, and use them together with standard templates for responses on the Speaking section. If you are comfortable with the work you've done in the Reading and Listening sections, then your primary focus will be on learning the templates for each Speaking task.

Another important point to consider is the *score range* of the programs to which you're applying. The top score on the Speaking section is 30 (although there are only six questions and the top score on each is a 4, the TOEFL converts your 0–24 points to a 0–30 scaled score); however, many programs are looking for scores far lower than 30. So before you devote too much time to worrying about this section, check the requirements of the schools in which you're interested.

Finally, realize that you *do not* have to sound like a native speaker to score well. It is perfectly acceptable to speak with an accent and make some mistakes in grammar and word use. What ultimately matters is how *understandable* your speech is.

Thus, cracking the Speaking section requires you to be aware of the following:

1. **How you sound.** When speaking, you must try to avoid unnecessary pauses and try to speak at an even pace.
2. **Your command of English grammar and vocabulary.** A top-scoring response uses a variety of words and contains some complex sentence structures.
3. **What you say.** Good responses have a clear flow of ideas and use appropriate transitions to link topics.

Let's examine each of these requirements in more detail.

Basic Principle #1: How You Sound

As mentioned earlier, this does NOT mean you have to sound like a native speaker. It means that you should speak confidently and clearly. The three biggest mistakes you can make are:

- pausing often and breaking up the flow of your speech with unnecessary words such as *um* and *uh*—take a deep breath, instead!
- delivering your speech in a mechanical "robot" voice, as if you were reading the response from a page
- speaking too quickly and, as a result, the listener can't understand what you say

The best way to avoid the first challenge is to use the speaking templates you'll learn in this chapter. These are basic patterns that you can use to organize your response. If you master these templates, you'll know exactly what you need to say for each task, which should help you avoid too many pauses in your speech.

As for the second issue, the best way to avoid a mechanical delivery is to practice. Once you familiarize yourself with the templates, practice using them with a variety of different topics. The more you practice using the templates, the more natural your speech will sound. It's also a good idea to remind yourself to smile when you respond, because it makes your response more pleasant to listen to, which is certainly not going to hurt your score! Practice smiling when you speak on the phone or to your friends, and see how they react! The best way to reduce your speed will help with nerves, too—breathe! Deep breaths in between sentences and thinking about a relaxed exhale will help you slow down your delivery.

Basic Principle #2: Your Command of English Grammar and Vocabulary

This book is not intended to be a comprehensive grammar handbook; however, we will give you some basic grammatical structures to follow, and you should make sure to memorize the Grammar Review at the end of Chapter 5. (Check out The Princeton Review's *Grammar Smart* if you need more work with grammar.) Similarly, although working on your vocabulary is a worthwhile goal, we're going to focus on only some of the words that will be useful to you on the TOEFL. The Princeton Review also publishes *TOEFL Power Vocab* for additional vocabulary practice.

Improving and Varying Sentence Structure

Let's start with some common sentence structures. Here is the most basic type of sentence.

> Ichiro hit the ball.

This sentence has a simple pattern: *subject* (Ichiro), *verb* (hit), *object* (the ball). Although many of your constructions will follow this simple pattern, you'll have to vary your sentence structure somewhat to achieve a higher score on the TOEFL. For example, here's another way we can express the same idea.

> The ball was hit by Ichiro.

This sentence moves the words around and creates a different emphasis. By using "the ball" as the *subject,* we give it more emphasis. Furthermore, by moving "Ichiro" to the *object* of the sentence, we de-emphasize him. If we add some more information to the sentence, we can use the following construction:

> After hitting the ball, Ichiro ran to first base.

This sentence structure allows us to express two different actions, "hitting the ball" and "ran." And as you've seen, we can use *transitions* to make our sentences even more complex.

> Although Ichiro hit the ball, he was unable to reach first base safely.
> Ichiro hit the ball, but he was unable to reach first base safely.
> Ichiro hit the ball and reached first base safely.

All of these are types of sentences that you can use to increase your TOEFL Speaking score. Let's practice some of them.

PRACTICE USING COMPLEX SENTENCE STRUCTURES

Rewrite each of the following sentences by first switching the subject and the object. Next, add in the new information by using one of the complex structures discussed earlier. Don't forget to use transitions.

Here's an example:

> Maria bought a picture frame.
> Rewrite: <u>A picture frame was bought by Maria.</u>

Now add in this new information: "She needed it for her house."

Combine and rewrite: <u>Needing a picture frame for her house, Maria bought one. Also: A picture frame was bought by Maria because she needed it for her house.</u>

Now try it. Then compare your answers with those given at the end of the drill.

1. Steve attended class.
   Rewrite: _____
   Add new information: "Steve did not do his homework."
   Combine and rewrite: _____

2. Ellen chose the black shirt.
   Rewrite: _____
   Add new information: "Ellen prefers the color black."
   Combine and rewrite: _____

3. The professor gave two reasons for the behavior.
   Rewrite: _____
   Add new information: "The professor described the behavior first."
   Combine and rewrite: _____

4. The class required both a midterm and final exam.
   Rewrite: _____
   Add new information: "A student cannot pass the class without passing the midterm and final exam."
   Combine and rewrite: _____

5. The firm hired Ivan.
   Rewrite: _____
   Add new information: "Ivan was the most qualified candidate."
   Combine and rewrite: _____

6. Soccer is Andrew's favorite sport.
   Rewrite: _____
   Add new information: "Andrew started playing soccer when he was very young."
   Combine and rewrite: _____

7. Jaime asked a question.
   Rewrite: _____
   Add new information: "Jaime needed directions to the student center."
   Combine and rewrite: _____

8. Guillermo read the book.
   Rewrite: _____
   Add new information: "Guillermo wrote a paper on the book."
   Combine and rewrite: _____

9. Heather forgot her book.
Rewrite: _____
Add new information: "She needed it for class."
Combine and rewrite: _____

10. Dennis plays the guitar.
Rewrite: _____
Add new information: "Dennis is learning to play the piano."
Combine and rewrite: _____

ANSWERS TO PRACTICE USING COMPLEX SENTENCE STRUCTURES

Here are the rewritten versions of the sentence and some suggested ways of combining the sentences with the new information provided.

1. Steve attended class.
   Rewrite: _The class was attended by Steve._
   Add new information: "Steve did not do his homework."
   Possible responses: _Although he did not do his homework, Steve attended the class._

   Despite not doing his homework, Steve attended the class.

   Steve attended the class even though he did not do his homework.

2. Ellen chose the black shirt.
   Rewrite: _The black shirt was chosen by Ellen._
   Add new information: "Ellen prefers black."
   Possible responses: _Preferring black, Ellen chose that shirt._

   Because she preferred black, Ellen chose that shirt.

   Ellen chose that shirt because she prefers black.

3. The professor gave two reasons for the behavior.
   Rewrite: _Two reasons for the behavior were given by the professor._
   Add new information: "The professor described the behavior first."
   Possible responses: _After describing the behavior first, the professor gave two reasons for it._

   The professor first described the behavior and gave two reasons for it.

   The professor gave two reasons for the behavior after first describing it.

4. The class required both a midterm and final exam.
   Rewrite: Both a midterm and final exam were required by the class.
   Add new information: "A student cannot pass the class without passing the midterm and final exam."
   Possible responses: Because the class requires both a midterm and final exam, a student cannot pass the class without passing both exams.

   Requiring a midterm and final exam, the class cannot be passed unless a student passes the exams.

   The class requires a midterm and final exam, and a student cannot pass the class unless he or she passes both exams.

5. The firm hired Ivan.
   Rewrite: Ivan was hired by the firm.
   Add new information: "Ivan was the most qualified candidate."
   Possible responses: Being the most qualified candidate, Ivan was hired by the firm.

   Because he was the most qualified candidate, Ivan was hired by the firm.

   The firm hired Ivan because he was the most qualified candidate.

6. Soccer is Andrew's favorite sport.
   Rewrite: Andrew's favorite sport is soccer.
   Add new information: "Andrew started playing soccer when he was very young."
   Possible responses: Andrew's favorite sport is soccer because he started playing it when he was very young.

   Because he started playing it when he was very young, Andrew's favorite sport is soccer.

   Having played since he was very young, Andrew's favorite sport is soccer.

7. Jaime asked a question.
   Rewrite: A question was asked by Jaime.
   Add new information: "Jaime needed directions to the student center."
   Possible responses: Needing directions to the student center, Jaime asked a question.

   Jaime asked a question because she needed directions to the student center.

   Because she needed directions to the student center, Jaime asked a question.

8.   Guillermo read the book.
     Rewrite: The book was read by Guillermo.
     Add new information: "Guillermo wrote a paper on the book."
     Possible responses: Guillermo read the book and also wrote a paper on it.

                                 Guillermo read the book because he had to write a
                                 paper on it.

                                 The book was read by Guillermo so that he could
                                 write a paper on it.

9.   Heather forgot her book.
     Rewrite: The book was forgotten by Heather.
     Add new information: "She needed it for class."
     Possible responses: Although she needed it for class, Heather forgot her
                                 book.

                                 Heather forgot her book although she needed it for
                                 class.

                                 Heather forgot her book even though she needed it
                                 for class.

10. Dennis plays the guitar.
     Rewrite: The guitar was played by Dennis.
     Add new information: "Dennis is learning to play the piano."
     Possible responses: Dennis plays the guitar and is also learning to play
                                 the piano.

                                 Dennis is learning to play the piano, although he can
                                 play the guitar already.

                                 Although he plays the guitar, Dennis is learning to
                                 play the piano.

The important lesson to learn from this exercise is to see that there are many ways of expressing the same idea. You'll need to use a variety of sentence structures to score well on the TOEFL. You can practice this exercise on your own also. Take sentences from a book, magazine, or newspaper article and practice rewriting them in a variety of different ways.

Improving and Building Your Vocabulary

The Speaking section asks to you do the following tasks:

- Describe
- Summarize
- Contrast

Let's look at each task and the types of words and phrases that are appropriate to fulfill each one.

Descriptions   Some tasks ask you to describe a problem, an opinion, or a personal preference. If you are describing details, you can use the following phrases:

- one **aspect** of...
- one **characteristic** of...
- one **quality** of...
- one **issue** (for describing a problem)...
- one **feature**...
- one **attribute**...
- one **element**...
- one **thing**...

For example, you may be asked to do the following on the TOEFL:

Describe a friend of yours, and explain why you consider this person a friend. Use details and examples to support your view.

For this task, you are asked to describe your friend. Your response may look like the sample below (note the descriptions are in boldface type).

One of my best friends is Joel. He is my friend for many reasons. One **characteristic** of Joel's that I really admire is his honesty. He always tells the truth to me. Another **quality** of Joel's that I like is his optimistic attitude. Joel always has a positive word for everyone. Joel's sense of humor is a final **aspect** of his personality that I admire. He is always able to make me laugh. For these reasons, I consider Joel a great friend.

As you can see, each word above can be used when describing a specific detail. Now it's your turn to answer the question above, using as many of the descriptive phrases as possible.

_____

_____

_____

_____

_____

Summaries   Another common task on the TOEFL Speaking section involves summarizing a reading or lecture. When summarizing, try using some of the following phrases:

- **according to** the reading/lecture/speaker...
- the reading/lecture/speaker **states that**...
- the reading/lecture/speaker **argues that**...
- the reading/lecture/speaker **holds that**...
- the reading/lecture/speaker **asserts that**...
- one reason/explanation **presented by** the reading/lecture/speaker...
- the reading/lecture/speaker **claims that**...
- the reading/lecture/speaker **expresses** the point/reason/opinion...
- the reading/lecture/speaker **indicates that...**
- the reading/lecture/speaker **believes...**

Here's an example of a reading passage that you will be asked to summarize.

Read the following passage and then summarize the points made by the author.

New research in the field of neuroscience is leading some researchers to change their beliefs about how the brain forms. An early view of the brain held that intelligence was primarily determined by genes. Now, however, a new study casts doubt on that view. Researchers have discovered that the neurons in the brain develop in the early stages of infancy. The more stimulation these neurons receive, the more connections the neurons make with other neurons. Cognitive scientists believe that intelligence is partly based on the number of connections between neurons in the brain.

Now, summarize the important parts of the passage. One response might look like this (again, with the summarizing terms shown in boldface):

According to the reading, some scientists have to change their views about the brain. The reading **states that** the early view of the brain is wrong. One reason given, according to the reading, is that there is a new study. The reading **claims that** the new study shows that brain development occurs during childhood. It also **argues that** the amount of stimulation a child receives leads to a higher intelligence.

Now try your own summary of this same paragraph. In addition, practice summarizing by using parts of some of the other reading passages in this book.

_____

_____

_____

_____

_____

Contrasts   The final type of speaking task asks you to contrast ideas. Here are some helpful phrases to use when contrasting ideas.

- in **contrast to**...
- one **difference between**...
- **unlike**...
- one **distinction between**...
- **dissimilarly**...
- one **disagreement between**...
- one **inconsistency between**...
- one point at **issue** is...
- one point of **disagreement** is...

Let's look at a task that requires you to contrast two things.

Read the following passage:

For more than three hundred years, the world understood physics as a predictable system. Isaac Newton's three laws of motion allowed physicists to predict the motion of not just falling apples and thrown balls, but comets, planets, and stars as well. The amazing degree of accuracy of these predictions had convinced scientists that the universe obeyed precise laws, a belief that in many ways was reassuring because it was comforting to think of the universe as an orderly, predictable place.

Now read the following lecture on the same topic:

What would you guys think if I told you I could walk right through that wall over there? You probably wouldn't believe me. As you all know from, uh, basic physics, two solid objects cannot occupy the same space. But the truth is that...is that neither I nor the wall is really solid. That's right...I am mostly made up of empty space. I know it's weird, but think about it. I'm made of atoms, and atoms are mostly empty space. And it was in the early um, early twentieth century when the discovery was made that atoms can pass through other objects. If you shoot a number of atoms...I think it was Niels Bohr who did this experiment...at a sheet of metal, some of them will pass right through it. And although the probability is extremely unlikely...because I have so many atoms in my body...if I walked into that wall an infinite number of times, at some point I would pass right through it. So our world isn't as nice and predictable as we may believe.

Explain how the lecture casts doubt on or otherwise relates to the reading.

This asks us to contrast the information presented in both selections. (To "cast doubt" means "to cause something to be doubted.") Here's a sample response, with the contrasting terms shown in boldface.

One **difference between** the two is the predictable nature of physics. The reading states that the universe is predictable. In **contrast to** this idea, the professor says the world isn't always predictable. **Unlike** the reading, the lecture gives some information on how atoms can be unpredictable. This is **inconsistent with** the reading, which talks about larger objects, such as planets. However, the biggest point at **issue between** the two is whether or not we can predict events in the universe.

Can you find other contrasting ideas in the lecture? Use the contrasting phrases listed above in your response. You can also practice on your own. A good place to look for contrasting ideas is in the editorial pages of your local newspaper. Find two articles or opinions on the same topic and try to contrast them.

Basic Principle #3: What You Say

One key to scoring well on the Speaking section is to make sure the ideas about which you are talking are clearly connected to one another. You should use transitions to relate certain parts of your speech to other parts.

Here are some of the common transition words you will need to use on the TOEFL.

Words that indicate a *sequence* or progression					
First	*Second*	*Third*	*Next*	*After*	*Lastly*
Then	*Previously*	*Before*	*Following*	*Finally*	

Words that indicate a *connection* between ideas			
Because	*Therefore*	*Thus*	*And*
Also	*Furthermore*	*Additionally*	*So*

Words that indicate a *contradiction* between ideas			
However	*Despite*	*Yet*	*Although*
But	*In contrast to*	*On the other hand*	

Now practice using these transitions in the exercise that follows.

PRACTICE: USING TRANSITIONS

Read the following sentences aloud, connecting them with the appropriate transition word or words. Compare your answers with those given after the drill.

1. Jane would like to go home during the holiday break, _____ she doesn't have enough money.
2. Sasha intends to major in mathematics _____ it is her favorite subject.
3. First, you must mix the two chemicals together. _____, wait for the reaction to occur.
4. One of the main reasons Jose took the job was the salary; _____, the location was a factor.
5. _____ Ming had never met Anna before, they acted like old friends.
6. The professor is known for his harsh grading scale; _____, students say that he is one of the best teachers at the school.
7. The class requires students to write a 20-page research paper. _____, the students have to complete a group project.
8. Marco had _____ believed that he wanted to go to business school, but now he plans to attend law school.
9. It is very difficult to do well in this class without doing the required reading. _____, I recommend keeping up with the assignments.
10. Neela was sure that she had failed the exam, _____ she received a passing grade.

ANSWERS AND EXPLANATIONS FOR PRACTICE: USING TRANSITIONS

Here are the appropriate transitions.

1. Jane would like to go home during the holiday break, **but** she doesn't have enough money.

This sentence *contrasts* two ideas. You also could have used *although*.

2. Sasha intends to major in mathematics **because** it is her favorite subject.

Here, we need to *connect* the two ideas. The first part is explained by the second part of the sentence.

3. First, you must mix the two chemicals together. **Then,** wait for the reaction to occur.

There is a *progression* of ideas in this sentence. You also may have used *next* or *second*.

4.   One of the main reasons Jose took the job was the salary; **additionally,** the location was a factor.

We need to *connect* both of the reasons together. Other possible responses include *furthermore* and *also*.

5.   **Although** Ming had never met Anna before, they acted like old friends.

There is a *contrast* between the first idea and the second one.

6.   The professor is known for his harsh grading scale; **however,** students say that he is one of the best teachers at the school.

Another *contrasting* set of ideas. The first part says something negative, whereas the second part expresses something positive.

7.   The class requires students to write a 20-page research paper. **Furthermore,** the students have to complete a group project.

Both of the requirements need to be *connected*. You could have used *also* or *additionally* as well.

8.   Marco had **previously** believed that he wanted to go to business school, but now he plans to attend law school.

This sentence shows a *progression* of ideas.

9.   It is very difficult to do well in this class without doing the required reading. **Therefore,** I recommend keeping up with the assignments.

The first part and the second part are *connected* to each other. You could have also used *thus*.

10.   Neela was sure that she had failed the exam, **yet** she received a passing grade.

These two ideas *contrast* with one another. You also could have used *but*.

You can practice this drill on your own. Try making statements that require using each of the transitions presented on page 380.

CRACKING THE SPEAKING SECTION: BASIC APPROACH

Now that we've gone over the basic principles, we're ready to think about strategic ways to approach the Speaking section. To do so, complete the following:

1. **Learn the appropriate template for each task,** and use it for your response.

2. **Use the appropriate vocabulary for each task.** Remember to use words that describe, contrast, and summarize, as well as words that show preferences. Transitions are also important to help the grader follow your train of thought.

3. **Listen to and practice speaking English as often as possible.** There's no better way to improve your speaking ability than to actually practice speaking. You can even use the recording app on your phone to record your responses so you can listen to them yourself! This will help you get a better sense of what it's like to be a listener!

Let's spend some time on the first step because it is one of the keys to doing well on this section.

Step 1: Learn the Appropriate Templates

Remember the three qualities that the graders are listening for? How you sound, your use of language, and what you say. The best way to attack all three aspects on a regular basis is to have a structured plan of attack for each task. The following templates provide exactly that—a strategic plan for each individual assignment. Memorize them! Then all you have to do on test day is adapt them a little bit to respond to the actual questions you are asked.

As we mentioned earlier in this chapter, the first item that you will see in the speaking section of the TOEFL is one Independent task. Let's prepare for that with a handy template.

Template #1: Choose an Option Question

The first type of task on the TOEFL presents you with two options. You'll have to decide which one you believe is better and support your decision.

Here's the template:

> State better option
> Reason #1
> Detail for Reason #1
> Reason #2
> Detail for Reason #2

Here's a sample prompt:

> Some universities give financial aid in the form of grants, which don't have to be paid back, whereas others provide financial assistance in the form of loans, which must be paid back. Which option do you think is better and why? Support your decision with reasons and examples.

The following would have been an acceptable response:

State better option	I think it is better to offer student loans.
Reason #1	I **prefer** loans because they make the student responsible.
Specific detail for reason #1	A student who has to pay back a loan becomes personally responsible for his or her education.
Reason #2	**Furthermore,** loans are safer for the school.
Specific detail for reason #2	Grants require the school to give away large amounts of money, and there is no guarantee that the school will get the money back.
Reason #3	**Lastly,** a student with a loan is probably more likely to stay in school.
Specific detail for reason #3	If the student doesn't complete the degree, it will be harder to pay back the money.

Did you remember to read the sample response aloud? If not, go for it!

Now, practice this template. Remember to use the descriptive words that you've learned. As before, keep track of your time: you'll have 15 seconds to prepare and 45 seconds to respond.

> Some people believe that universities should require students to take classes on ethics, whereas others believe a school should focus only on academic issues. Which do you think is better? Support your decision with reasons and examples.

State better option	
Reason #1	
Specific detail for reason #1	
Reason #2	
Specific detail for reason #2	
Reason #3	
Specific detail for reason #3	

As we also mentioned earlier in this chapter, the second items that you will encounter in the speaking section of the TOEFL are two reading, listening, and speaking integrated tasks. As before, let's prepare with another template.

Template #2: Summarize an Opinion Question

The second task requires you to read a brief passage and listen to a conversation about it. Then you'll have to summarize the opinion or position given in the conversation.

Reading: You'll have 45 seconds to read the passage, which will usually discuss some sort of campus life issue. Most likely, you won't need to take notes while you read the passage.

Listening: The conversation will start automatically, so be ready to listen! During the 60–90 seconds you're listening, pay attention to the speaker's opinion or attitude about the reading, and pay close attention to the *reasons* the speaker gives for his or her position. Write them down if you can.

Here's the template you should keep in mind as you read and listen:

    State the requested opinion
    Reason #1 for opinion
    Detail for Reason #1
    Reason #2 for opinion
    Detail for Reason #2

Once again, the template looks similar to Template #1, focusing not only on the answer to the question (in this case, the speaker's opinion), but also on the reasons behind the answer.

Here's an example.

Read the following announcement from the university president:

Because of recent budget constraints, the university has decided to close the computer labs during weekends and reduce their operating hours during the week from 8:00 A.M. to 10:00 P.M. to 9:00 A.M. to 8:00 P.M. These changes are necessary in order to compensate for an unexpected budget shortfall. Without these cutbacks, the school would be forced to reduce service in other important areas, such as the library and the cafeteria.

Headphones On!

Play Track 9 in your Student Tools. Transcripts of all the audio tracks in this chapter begin on page 395.

The woman offers her opinion of the announcement. State what her opinion is and what reasons she gives for having that view.

You'll have 30 seconds to prepare and 60 seconds to respond.

Here's the template for our response.

State opinion	The woman **believes** that the decision to reduce the hours of the computer lab is a **bad** idea.
Reason #1	Her first **reason for claiming this** is that she needs a computer for her class work.
Detail for reason #1	The woman **states that** she doesn't have a computer and that some of her classes require her to use one.
Reason #2	**Also,** the woman **claims** it will be harder to complete all of her work.
Detail for reason #2	**According** to the woman, the best time to do work is on the weekends. Now she fears that the labs will be too full during the week.

Did you practice reading the response aloud?

As you can see, all you have to do is basically repeat the reasons given by the speaker. You won't be required to do anything else. Now, it's your turn to try the template with the following example.

You'll have 45 seconds to read the passage.

Read the following announcement from the president of a university:

Effective immediately, the university is instituting a new policy on off-campus visitors. Any guests are now required to register with campus security and obtain a guest pass which must be worn at all times. This new policy is necessary in order to keep all the students safe and to increase campus safety's knowledge of who is on campus.

Play Track 10 in your Student Tools.

The man gives his opinion on the announcement. State the man's opinion and provide the reasons he gives for holding it.

Headphones On!

Give yourself 30 seconds to prepare and 60 seconds to respond.

State requested opinion	
Reason #1	
Detail for reason #1	
Reason #2	
Detail for reason #2	

Template #3: Summarize/Contrast Question

The third task will begin with a reading passage and then be followed by an academic lecture that will either agree or disagree with the reading. Your job is to show how the lecture relates to or contrasts with the reading. Both the lecture and the reading will present some characteristics of a given topic.

Reading: Once again, you'll have 45 seconds to read the passage. While you read, take brief notes about the characteristics mentioned—typically there will be three to five characteristics to track.

Listening: The lecture will start automatically, so be ready to listen! You will be able to tell within the first couple sentences whether the lecture agrees or disagrees with the reading passage. While you listen to the lecture, listen for the characteristics mentioned and jot them down if you can. Think about how the characteristics in the lecture agree or disagree with the information in the reading.

Here's the template you should keep in mind as you read and listen:

Main Response
Characteristic #1 from reading
Detail #1 from lecture
Characteristic #2 from reading
Detail #2 from lecture
Characteristic #3 from reading
Detail #3 from lecture

Since this task asks you to compare or contrast the reading with the lecture, you should think about how you take your notes. Your most efficient approach will likely be to create two columns, one for your notes about the reading and one for your notes about the listening. Then, as you take notes on the characteristics, you can line them up to be better able to compare them. Try it out with the sample below, and compare your notes to our suggestions on the next page.

Here's a sample. You'll have 45 seconds to read a passage like this.

Read the following passage about captive breeding:

Both environmentalists and animal rights activists consider captive breeding a solution to the threat of extinction of certain endangered species. In captive breeding, endangered animals are caught and bred, and the offspring is then released back into the wild. Unfortunately, the results of this program have been mixed. In many cases, the animals that are released back into the wild are unable to survive. The time spent in human captivity makes it more difficult for them to acquire food and to fit in with other members of their species.

Play Track 11 in your Student Tools.

> The professor describes the results of a captive breeding experiment. Explain how the results of the experiment relate to the reading on the topic.

Headphones On!

Here's what your notes might look like:

Reading
Captive breeding
    breed in captivity, set babies free
Mixed results
    Many released animals can't survive

Listening
Problems re: reintroduce
    animal into wild
"Working out"
1st time—Lynx died
Taught them to hunt
Kept together so they
    can get along

Notice that we can easily see that the reading says there are "mixed results," but just to the right of that we noted that there's been a situation in which reintroducing animals into the wild is "working out." This can be helpful in crafting your response to the prompt.

Once the lecture is finished, you'll have 30 seconds to prepare and then 60 seconds to speak.

Here's a possible response to the prompt:

Main response	The experiment with the lynx shows that captive breeding can be successful.
Characteristic #1 from reading	**One problem** with captive breeding, **according to** the reading, is that animals do not always survive when reintroduced into the wild.
Detail #1 from lecture	**But** the scientists seemed to be having good luck reintroducing the lynx into the wild.
Characteristic #2 from reading	The reading **states that** a major problem is that the animals don't know how to hunt.
Detail #2 from lecture	**However,** for the experiment, biologists first taught the animals how to hunt before releasing them.
Characteristic #3 from reading	**Another** problem in the reading is that the animals don't know how to interact with other members of the species.
Detail #3 from lecture	Scientists were able to get around this, **however,** by keeping the lynx together in a group.

Did you read this one aloud? If not, go back and do so—it's great practice!

For this type of question, it's acceptable if you run out of time before you list all of the characteristics. Your goal while speaking is to be as clear as possible, so don't rush through the details because it may make you harder to understand.

Try this template with the following example. You have 30 seconds to prepare and 60 seconds to respond.

Read the following passage about methane:

Methane is a colorless, odorless gas that occurs naturally as a result of the decomposition of plant and animal matters. Methane is a hydrocarbon like coal and oil, and it's all that remains of long-dead plants, dinosaurs, and other prehistoric animals. Although methane can be produced by volcanic activity, scientists usually connect the presence of methane with the presence of biological life. Many microorganisms excrete methane as a waste product, and scientists often infer the presence of these creatures by measuring the amount of methane in the air.

Headphones On!

Play Track 12 in your Student Tools.

The professor presents some facts about Mars. Explain how these facts may indicate life.

You have 30 seconds to prepare and 60 seconds to respond.

Main response	
Characteristic #1 from reading	
Detail #1 from lecture	
Characteristic #2 from reading	
Detail #2 from lecture	
Characteristic #3 from reading	
Detail #3 from lecture	

As we also mentioned earlier in this chapter, the final item that you will encounter in the speaking section of the TOEFL is one listening and speaking integrated task. As before, let's prepare with another template.

Template #4: Summarize Question

The final task asks you to listen to a 1- to 2-minute lecture and show how the speaker's points support his or her main idea.

Listening: While listening to the lecture, focus on identifying the main idea. Don't worry about identifying every detail—you need only enough details so that you can talk for a minute.

Keep this template in mind as you listen:

> State the main idea
> State Reason #1
> Detail for reason #1
> Link between reason #1 and main idea
> State Reason #2
> Detail for reason #2
> Link between reason #2 and main idea

Notice that this template is a little bit different: you have to do more than just list the reasons and details. You also have to take the final step to explain how the reasons support the main idea. When you respond, make sure you state the main idea right away. If you focus too much on the details, you'll lose points.

Here's an example.

Play Track 13 in your Student Tools.

> **Using points and examples from the talk, explain how the Internet has contributed to censorship.**

You have 20 seconds to organize your thoughts and 60 seconds to respond.

Headphones On!

Here is a sample response.

State main idea	The professor **argues that** the Internet actually promotes censorship, rather than fights it.
Reason #1	The **first** reason given by the professor is that the Internet has so much information on it.
Detail for reason #1	The Internet contains information from a wide variety of sources, including the government and companies.
Link between reason #1 and main idea	This censors information **because** the huge amount of information means that some views will never be heard.
Reason #2	**Furthermore,** the Internet makes it harder to find information.
Detail for reason #2	**For example,** the professor **states that** search engines show only the most popular websites.
Link between reason #2 and main idea	This contributes to censorship by leading users to a very small number of websites and hiding the other sites from them.

Now practice using the template on the following example.

Play Track 14 in your Student Tools.

Headphones On!

Using points and examples from the talk, explain how the participants and items in a ritual represent other things.

You have 20 seconds to prepare and 60 seconds to respond.

State main idea	
Reason #1	
Detail for reason #1	
Link between reason #1 and main idea	
Reason #2	
Detail for reason #2	
Link between reason #2 and main idea	

Step 2: Learn the Appropriate Vocabulary

Throughout this lesson, certain words and phrases have appeared in **bold.** These words and phrases are particularly important on the Speaking section of the TOEFL. Go through this chapter and any other passages in the book and study the types of vocabulary words used.

For the Speaking section, you should use three major categories of words. They are as follows:

- **Words that indicate preference.** This category includes words such as **favorite, best, most, better, superior,** and **favorable.** These are types of words that are helpful when explaining your opinion or preference. You'll also use these words on one of your Writing tasks. This category would also include the opposites of the above words, such as **worse, less, inferior, worst,** and **least.** Try to find other examples of preference words in this book.

Preferred	Not Preferred
Best	Worst
Better	Worse
Most	Least
More	Less
Superior	Inferior
Preferable	Not preferable
Preferably	Not preferably
Like	Dislike
Approve	Reject
Favored	Not favored

- **Words that describe, summarize,** and **contrast.** These words are useful when you are describing someone else's speech or conversation. These are the words that were discussed in the "Basic Principles" section at the beginning of this chapter. Make sure to review them frequently.
- **Transition words.** Be certain to familiarize yourself with the words in this category. Pay particular attention to the direction of your response so you can identify which transition you need. See page 380 for a refresher.

 ## Step 3: Listen and Practice Spoken English

This book has shown you how to construct responses, but you'll have to continue practicing by speaking aloud. One of the best ways to increase your speaking ability is to listen to spoken English as often as possible. If you don't live in an English-speaking country, you can still hear English spoken in movies or on the Internet. But you need to do more than just listen—you need to actually practice speaking aloud.

Here are some suggestions for practicing your speaking on your own:

- Stand in front of a mirror and speak to your reflection.
- Use the microphone on your computer or on your phone to record yourself speaking. Then listen to the recording and see what you can identify that can be improved. Or, ask a friend or teacher who is a native English speaker to listen to it and give you some feedback.
- Read newspaper or magazine stories out loud.
- Find videos online and then listen to and repeat short excerpts.
- Find textbooks that have questions at the end of each chapter and answer the questions out loud.
- Do a search for "Toastmaster Table Topics" and practice answering some of the questions you'll find there.

Here are some ideas for practicing speaking with a friend:

- Ask your friend a question and give her 15 seconds to think of a response and then 45 seconds to speak. Then have her do the same for you.
- Find a newsworthy story online or in the paper and ask your friend his opinion on the situation. Then have him do the same.
- Look for scenes from plays that require only two speakers and practice saying the lines out loud together.
- Go to a movie and then discuss it afterward. Include the characters, the plot, the scenery, your favorite part, the best-looking actor, and more in your conversation!

APPENDIX: TRANSCRIPTS TO AUDIO TRACKS

Listen to these audio tracks without reading the transcripts. Then go back and read them aloud for the practice!

Track 9

Now listen to two students discuss the announcement.

Woman: Did you hear the announcement? They're cutting back the computer lab hours!

Man: Yeah, but it's better that they cut down there than at the library or the cafeteria.

W: Maybe for you, but I don't have a computer. I use the computer lab a lot. Plus, I need to have access to a computer for my economics class.

M: Well, they'll still be open during the week.

W: I know. But I get most of my work done during the weekend. The labs are usually empty then. They'll probably be filled with students now. It's going to make it really hard for me to get all my class work done.

M: Hmm. I didn't really think of that.

Track 10

Now listen to the following conversation about the announcement:

Man: I think the university's new policy is great.

Woman: Really? I think it's going to be annoying. I have some friends visiting, and they're going to have to spend all this time registering. And what if they lose their passes?

M: True. But that's a minor inconvenience. It's worth it if the campus is safer. Remember that vandalism that took place at the library was done by someone from off-campus.

W: I still think the school is overreacting. One bad thing happens, and they go and change the policy.

M: No, there have been other incidents. A couple months ago, there were some things stolen from one of the dorms. And the students reported seeing a suspicious figure.

W: I guess you're right.

Track 11

Now listen to a professor give a talk about the same topic.

Okay, so we've been talking about some problems faced by biologists when they try to reintroduce species into the wild. As we've um...ah, talked about, sometimes the animals aren't ready or able to go...to fit into their native habitats. But there have been some new strategies used which seem to be, uh, working out. For example, biologists recently reintroduced four lynx—you guys know what a lynx is, right?—into the wild. The first time they tried it, the cats died of starvation—they didn't know how or where to hunt. This time, they kept the animals longer and let them mature. They also forced the animals to hunt for food instead of giving them the food directly. And finally, they kept the lynx together in a big pen so they know how to get along with other members of their species.

Track 12

Now listen to a professor give a talk about the same topic.

So, there's been some interesting news for those of you who dream of life on other planets. It turns out that Mars has a pretty high concentration of methane in its atmosphere. Now, usually when we think of life, we associate it with oxygen, right? But that's because we're kind of prejudiced. A whole host of creatures need no oxygen whatsoever.

The reason that this is important is that it looks like Mars has very little geologic activity. Methane can be produced without life, but as far as we know, there are no active volcanoes on Mars. Plus, here's another interesting point—methane only lasts about 300 years in the atmosphere. So that means the methane we're seeing now is fairly new...and it's being replenished somehow.

Track 13

Listen to a lecture given in a sociology class.

Now oftentimes, when we think of the Internet, we think of it as the ultimate expression of free speech. There is no regulation of content on the Internet. People and organizations can put anything they want on the Web. Also, the Internet allows access to a huge amount of information. You can find almost anything you want there, but social scientists have argued that the Internet is actually responsible for a new type of censorship. In most cases, censorship involves a suppression of ideas. But the Internet censors material in a different way.

According to these sociologists, the censorship found on the Internet is subtle, but just as bad as any form of censorship. Basically, the Internet censors viewpoints by having too much information. That's right. Because the Internet contains information from companies, organizations, individuals, and even the government, any one viewpoint or idea can easily be buried under the tide, meaning that no one is exposed to it. Another way the Internet increases censorship is that because it is so vast, information becomes harder to find. Popular search engines direct users to the most popular websites and very seldom do people take the time to look at any more than the first two or three sites listed. Thus, these search engines are practicing an electronic form of censorship—unpopular ideas are hidden and inaccessible to the average user.

Track 14

Listen to a talk given in an anthropology class.

All cultures partake in certain rituals and ceremonies. Although these rituals and ceremonies may sometimes seem hard to decipher, the essence of these actions is representation—the motions and the items used in the ceremony or ritual stand in for, or symbolize, something else. Usually, the members of the ritual are trying to control or affect something that lies outside their power, such as the weather or the gods, so they must use symbols to stand in for it.

For example, the Dieri people of central Australia use a very symbolic rainmaking ceremony. First, the rainmakers are bled. Their blood drips into a hole in the ground, which represents rain dropping from the sky. Next, the rainmakers take two rounded stones, which stand for clouds, and carry them some distance away. They then place the stones high up in a tree, which symbolizes the height of the clouds in the sky. Or, for another example, there is the fairly common ceremony in which a victim is chosen to symbolize all the sins and wrongdoings of a culture. The victim is then cleansed, either through a ritual bath or through death, in order to wash away the sins of the people. In fact, this is where the term "scapegoat" comes from, because one culture used a goat as its ceremonial symbol.

Speaking Summary

All right, only one more section to crack before you're ready to take the TOEFL! First, let's review what you should do on the Speaking tasks.

o **Know what the graders want.** Remember that graders are looking for the following: *delivery, language use,* and *topic development.* All three are important to your score. Even if you speak perfect English, if you don't answer the question correctly, your score will suffer.

o **Don't try to be perfect.** You don't need to speak English as if you were a native speaker. The graders are concerned only with how easy it is to understand what you say. It's acceptable to have errors in your speech.

o **Speak smoothly and confidently**, even if you make mistakes.

o **Connect your ideas** with transitions.

o **Use the templates.** It is very easy to lose track of what you are saying, and 60 seconds is not much time, so it's hard to recover if you get sidetracked. Practice the templates so you know exactly how your responses will be structured.

Let's go over the templates again:
- **Personal preference:** State your preference and list three reasons with details.
- **Choose an option:** Choose whichever option you have more to say about, state it, and present your reasons and details.
- **Summarize an opinion:** Repeat the speaker's opinions and reasons but restate them in your own words.

- **Summarize/contrast:** Compare the points in the reading and the lecture and say why they are similar or different.
- **Summarize/preference:** State the problem and the possible solutions, say which you prefer, and then give reasons and details why you think that one is better.
- **Summarize a passage or lecture:** Listen carefully and state the main idea of the lecture. Restate the points of the lecture in your own words and explain the reasons and details given in the lecture.

o **Practice, practice, practice.** There is no substitute for practice. Keep working on your speaking ability. Have an English-speaking friend listen to you as you speak, if possible.

Practice your speaking skills with the drills in the next chapter, and then we'll tackle cracking the Writing section. Almost done!

Chapter 14
Speaking Practice
Drills

Now you're ready to practice the Speaking section. If possible, record or ask a friend to record your responses so you can review them later. Remember to use the templates we covered in the previous chapter. Then compare your responses with those in the next chapter.

Throughout the Speaking section on the actual test, you will be instructed to listen carefully with a screen that looks like the one below.

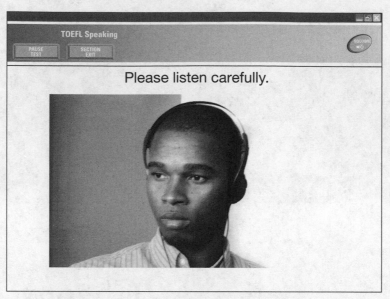

Questions will be introduced by a screen that looks like the one shown here.

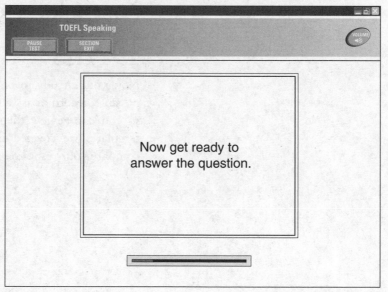

You will also see photographs of relevant scenes with each question. Some examples are included here with the question templates.

Choose an Option Question (Template #1)

Listen to Track 15 in your Student Tools. Here's the question.

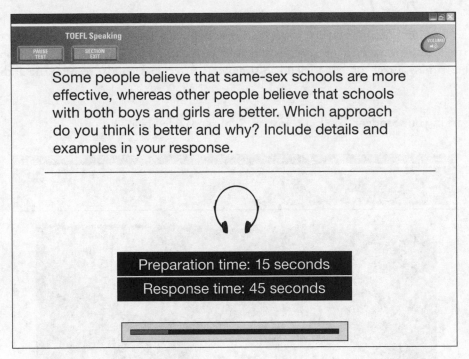

TOEFL Speaking

PAUSE TEST   SECTION EXIT

VOLUME

Some people believe that same-sex schools are more effective, whereas other people believe that schools with both boys and girls are better. Which approach do you think is better and why? Include details and examples in your response.

Preparation time: 15 seconds

Response time: 45 seconds

Summarize An Opinion Question (Template #2)

For the summarize an opinion questions on the actual test, you will see a series of screens similar to the ones that follow and hear a prompt to read a passage in 45 seconds. For our purposes here, you will need to stop the audio to read the passage and either time yourself or ask a friend to time you. After 45 seconds, resume the audio and listen to the conversation.

Now listen to Track 16 in your Student Tools (a transcript is also provided below).

Narrator: The University of Hartsdale has responded to budget constraints by eliminating some academic departments from its College of Liberal Arts. The campus newspaper printed the following report about the announcement of the department cuts. You have 45 seconds to read the report. Begin reading now.

[Pause the audio for 45 seconds.]

> The university has announced that, effective at the beginning of the fall semester, three departments will be eliminated from the College of Liberal Arts: Ecology, Folklore Studies, and Textile Sciences. Arrangements have been made to ensure that currently enrolled majors will receive their degrees as planned, but no new major applications have been approved for the affected departments during this past academic year. A statement by the dean of the College of Liberal Arts expressed confidence that the money thus saved would be put to good use elsewhere in the university.

[Restart the audio.]

Narrator: Now listen to two students as they discuss the announcement.

Woman: Did you see about those three departments being cut next year? It's a shame.

Man: Maybe. But you know, there were only two or three professors in each of those programs, and none of them are being let go. They're just being moved to bigger departments—you know, like, the folklore professors are going to be in anthropology. They'll still do the same research and teach the same classes.

W: They haven't let any professors go? I thought this was supposed to save money.

M: Well, it will. Each department has to have an administrative office, with a secretary and a budget manager. Those things add up. Moving the professors to bigger departments means a big savings on operations.

W: But it still means students have fewer options for majors.

M: You could say that, I guess. On the other hand, each of those departments only had, like, one major per year to begin with. They just weren't very popular. I really don't think we're going to be losing any important scholarship just because those things aren't full departments anymore.

Narrator: The man explains his opinion of the announcement made by the College of Liberal Arts. State his opinion, and explain the reasons he gives for holding that opinion.

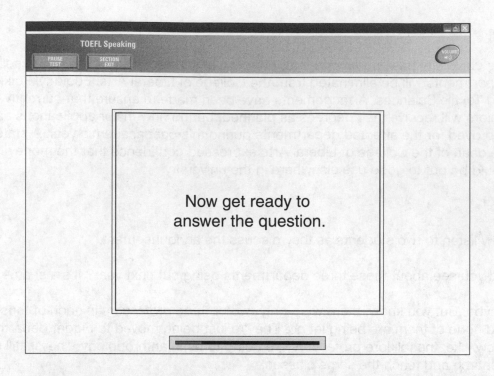

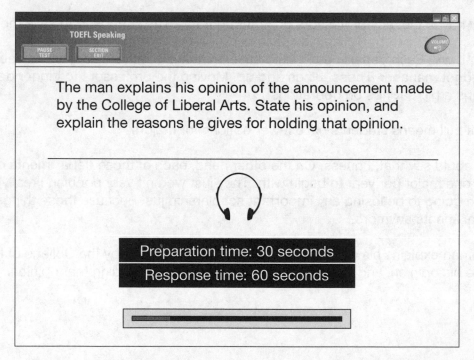

Summarize/Contrast Question (Template #3)

Now, let's look at a contrast question. On the actual test, you will see a series of screens similar to the ones that follow and hear a prompt that will ask you to read a passage in 45 seconds. For our purposes here, you will need to stop the audio to read the passage and either time yourself or ask a friend to time you. After 45 seconds, resume the audio for the listening passage. After the narrator reads the question, the track is finished.

Listen to Track 17 in your Student Tools (a transcript is also provided on the next page).

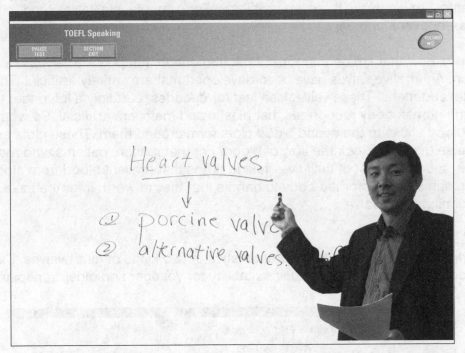

Narrator: Now read the passage about surgery to replace heart valves. You have 45 seconds to read the passage. Begin reading now.

[Stop the audio for 45 seconds.]

Heart Valve Replacement

Valves in the heart regulate the flow of blood, like gates or the locks of a canal. When a valve malfunctions and needs to be replaced, several factors need to be considered. The biggest is the age of the patient. Younger patients require valves that will last for many years; they also tend to be healthy enough to withstand courses of supplementary treatment that are hard on the body. Older patients, on the other hand, are often too weak for such supplementary treatments and can make do with replacement valves that are less durable.

[Restart the audio.]

Narrator: Now listen to part of a lecture on this topic given in a biology class.

Professor: People with defective heart valves need them replaced, and what's often used is the heart valve from a pig. It's called a "porcine valve" because of that. A pig's valve is very similar to a person's, and because pig valves are natural and tend to be accepted by the body, patients who receive them require little treatment after surgery...relatively, for transplant patients, I mean. Now, there *are* problems. For example, pig valves tend to last around ten years—not very long.

Actually, now that I'm on that topic, I might mention that porcine valves are not the only option. Alternative valves have been developed that are entirely artificial. They're made of plastic and metal. These valves can last for decades, certainly a lot longer than pig valves. But the human body recognizes that plastic and metal are artificial. So what happens is that blood sticks to them, and blood clots form around them. These clots are dangerous because they can block the flow of blood. For that reason, patients who receive artificial valves spend the rest of their lives taking drugs that prevent blood from clotting. The drugs can be tough for the body to handle, but they're worth it for the sake of having a functioning heart valve.

Narrator: The professor discussed the characteristics of two kinds of heart valves. Explain how their characteristics are related to their suitability for younger and older transplant patients.

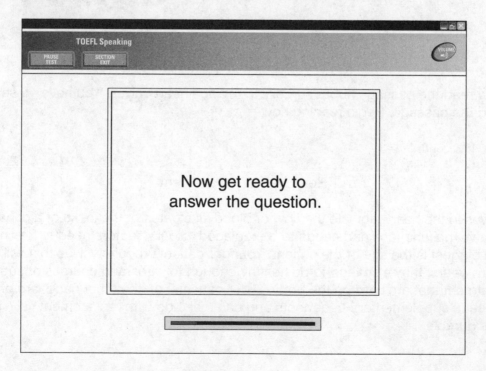

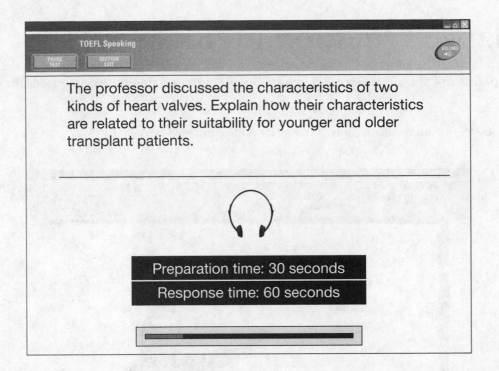

The professor discussed the characteristics of two kinds of heart valves. Explain how their characteristics are related to their suitability for younger and older transplant patients.

Preparation time: 30 seconds

Response time: 60 seconds

Summarize Question (Template #4)

Now let's look at a summarize question. On the actual test, you will see a series of screens similar to the ones that follow and hear a prompt that will ask you to listen to a lecture. For our purposes, after the narrator reads the question, the track is finished.

Now listen to Track 18 in your Student Tools (a transcript is also provided below).

Narrator: Now listen to part of a talk in an archaeology class.

Professor: Most gems weren't formed by life processes, so they're very durable. If you're one of the lucky few archaeologists who discovers an ancient crown inlaid with, say, rubies, you'll probably have to worry more about damage to the metal than to the stones themselves. But, some gemstones *are* organic. They're more fragile and can present special problems if you've dug them up and need to preserve them.

One example is amber, which formed millions of years ago from tree sap. The tree sap breaks down on exposure to air, but if the tree died and was buried in an airtight space before decaying, the sap could harden into amber. That's where amber gets its liquid clarity and smoothness. Uh, now, once it's hardened, you don't need to worry about oxygen breaking it down. What you do need to worry about is...well, think of it as being like hardened wax. If it comes too near to heat, it might melt or deform. Also, contact with oils or strong acids can injure the surface and make it cloudy. The basic thing to remember is, avoid sudden temperature changes and any contact with cleaning solutions and other such chemicals.

Another organic gem is coral. Coral is sort of the skeleton of creatures from the ocean floor, made of calcium carbonate, often with carotene mixed in. That's what makes it pinkish and orangish. You don't have to worry about melting coral, but you do have to worry about scratching it. Calcium carbonate is naturally rather powdery, so it chips easily. Also, it's very porous, so it absorbs liquids quickly. You need to make sure that you never soak coral in water or pour chemicals over it.

Narrator: Using points and examples from the talk, explain how archaeologists must take the origins of amber and coral into consideration when caring for them.

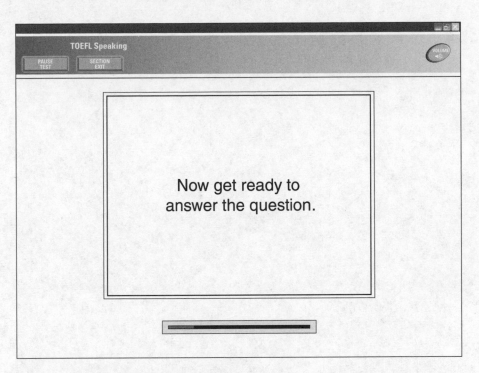

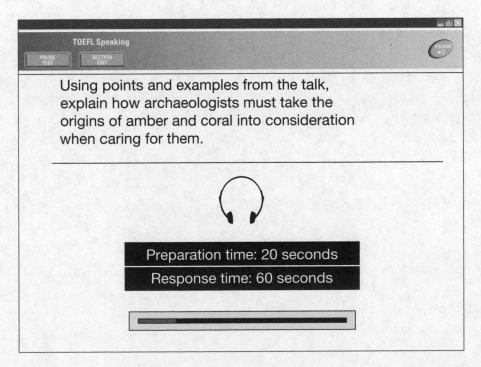

Chapter 15
Speaking Practice
Answers and
Explanations

In this chapter, you'll find transcripts of the questions in the previous chapter and sample responses. Use these to help you pinpoint areas for improvement in your speaking. Your answers will vary from the samples, but make sure you stick to the templates and fulfill the tasks.

CHOOSE AN OPTION QUESTION (TEMPLATE #1)

Narrator: Some people believe that same-sex schools are more effective, whereas other people believe that schools with both boys and girls are better. Which approach do you think is better and why? Include details and examples in your response.

Preparation time: 15 seconds

Response time: 45 seconds

Sample Response

State option	I **believe that** schools should have both male and female students in order to be effective.
Reason #1	**The first reason** I believe this is that a mixed school is a better example of the real world.
Specific detail for reason #1	Most jobs that a student gets will involve both men and women, so a mixed school will prepare the student for that.
Reason #2	**Secondly,** going to a same-sex school may cause some difficulties for students.
Specific detail for reason #2	**For example,** students at a same-sex school may not know how to get along well with the opposite sex.
Reason #3	**Finally,** I think that being exposed to a variety of opinions is important to education.
Specific detail for reason #3	A mixed school exposes students to more opinions, which is very important.

SUMMARIZE AN OPINION QUESTION (TEMPLATE #2)

Narrator: The University of Hartsdale has responded to budget constraints by eliminating some academic departments from its College of Liberal Arts. The campus newspaper printed the following report about the announcement of the department cuts. You have 45 seconds to read the report. Begin reading now.

The university has announced that, effective at the beginning of the fall semester, three departments will be eliminated from the College of Liberal Arts: Ecology, Folklore Studies, and Textile Sciences. Arrangements have been made to ensure that currently enrolled majors will receive their degrees as planned, but no new major applications have been approved for the affected departments during this past academic year. A statement by the dean of the College of Liberal Arts expressed confidence that the money thus saved would be put to good use elsewhere in the university.

Narrator: Now listen to two students as they discuss the announcement.

Woman: Did you see about those three departments being cut next year? It's a shame.

Man: Maybe. But you know, there were only two or three professors in each of those programs, and none of them is being let go. They're just being moved to bigger departments—you know, like, the folklore professors are going to be in anthropology. They'll still do the same research and teach the same classes.

W: They haven't let any professors go? I thought this was supposed to save money.

M: Well, it will. Each department has to have an administrative office, with a secretary and a budget manager. Those things add up. Moving the professors to bigger departments means a big savings on operations.

W: But it still means students have fewer options for majors.

M: You could say that, I guess. On the other hand, each of those departments only had, like, one major per year to begin with. They just weren't very popular. I really don't think we're going to be losing any important scholarship just because those things aren't full departments anymore.

Narrator: The man explains his opinion of the announcement made by the College of Liberal Arts. State his opinion, and explain the reasons he gives for holding that opinion.

Preparation time: 30 seconds

Response time: 60 seconds

Sample Response

State opinion	The man **believes that** the decision to cut the departments is a good one.
Reason #1	The man **contends that** no professors will lose their jobs when the departments are eliminated.
Details for reason #1	**According to** the student, the professors will simply join other departments.
Reason #2	**Furthermore,** the student states that there were not many majors in those departments.
Detail for reason #2	There was only one major per year in the eliminated departments.

SUMMARIZE/CONTRAST QUESTION (TEMPLATE #3)

Narrator: Now read the passage about surgery to replace heart valves. You have 45 seconds to read the passage. Begin reading now.

Heart Valve Replacement

Valves in the heart regulate the flow of blood, like gates or the locks of a canal. When a valve malfunctions and needs to be replaced, several factors need to be considered. The biggest is the age of the patient. Younger patients require valves that will last for many years; they also tend to be healthy enough to withstand courses of supplementary treatment that are hard on the body. Older patients, on the other hand, are often too weak for such supplementary treatments and can make do with replacement valves that are less durable.

Narrator: Now listen to part of a lecture on this topic given in a biology class.

Professor: People with defective heart valves need them replaced, and what's often used is the heart valve from a pig. It's called a "porcine valve" because of that. A pig's valve is very similar to a person's, and because pig valves are natural and tend to be accepted by the body, patients who receive them require little treatment after surgery...relatively, for transplant patients, I mean. Now, there *are* problems. For example, pig valves tend to last around ten years—not very long.

Actually, now that I'm on that topic, I might mention that porcine valves are not the only option. Alternative valves have been developed that are entirely artificial. They're made of plastic and metal. These valves can last for decades—certainly a lot longer than pig valves. But the human body recognizes that plastic and metal are artificial. So what happens is that blood sticks to them, and blood clots form around them. These clots are dangerous because they can block the flow of blood. For that reason, patients who receive artificial valves spend the rest of their lives taking drugs that prevent blood from clotting. The drugs can be tough for the body to handle, but they're worth it for the sake of having a functioning heart valve.

Narrator: The professor discussed the characteristics of two kinds of heart valves. Explain how their characteristics are related to their suitability for younger and older transplant patients.

Preparation time: 30 seconds

Response time: 60 seconds

Sample Response

Main response	The professor **discussed** two types of valves. One is from a pig; the other is made of plastic and metal.
Characteristic #1 from reading	**One aspect** of heart valves that is very important is how long they last.
Detail #1 from lecture	Pig valves can be used, **but** they last for only ten years. This makes them unsuitable for younger patients.
Characteristic #2 from reading	**Another characteristic** that is important is the need for additional treatments.
Detail #2 from lecture	Plastic and metal valves require special drugs that stop the blood from clotting.
Characteristic #3 from reading	**According to** the reading, old patients and young patients have different needs. Old patients should avoid extra treatments, **whereas** young patients need a valve that lasts for a long time.
Detail #3 from lecture	**Thus**, pig valves may be suited to older patients, **and** plastic or metal valves for younger patients.

SUMMARIZE QUESTION (TEMPLATE #4)

Narrator: Now listen to part of a talk in an archaeology class.

Professor: Most gems weren't formed by life processes, so they're very durable. If you're one of the lucky few archaeologists who discovers an ancient crown inlaid with, say, rubies, you'll probably have to worry more about damage to the metal than to the stones themselves. But, some gemstones *are* organic. They're more fragile and can present special problems if you've dug them up and need to preserve them.

One example is amber, which formed millions of years ago from tree sap. The tree sap breaks down on exposure to air, but if the tree died and was buried in an airtight space before decaying, the sap could harden into amber. That's where amber gets its liquid clarity and smoothness. Now, once it's hardened, you don't need to worry about oxygen breaking it down. What you do need to worry about is... well, think of it as being like hardened wax. If it comes too near to heat, it might melt or deform. Also, contact with oils or strong acids can injure the surface and make it cloudy. The basic thing to remember is, avoid sudden temperature changes and any contact with cleaning solutions and other such chemicals.

Another organic gem is coral. Coral is sort of the skeleton of creatures from the ocean floor, made of calcium carbonate, often with carotene mixed in—that's what makes it pinkish and orangish. You don't have to worry about melting coral, but you do have to worry about scratching it. Calcium carbonate is naturally rather powdery, so it chips easily. Also, it's very porous, so it absorbs liquids quickly. You need to make sure that you never soak coral in water or pour chemicals over it.

Narrator: Using points and examples from the talk, explain how archaeologists must take the origins of amber and coral into consideration when caring for them.

Preparation time: 20 seconds

Response time: 60 seconds

Sample Response

State main idea	**According to** the professor, both amber and coral can be harmed by certain processes.
Reason #1	Amber is made from hardened tree sap.
Detail for reason #1	**Because of** this fact, amber can be damaged by heat, oils, and acids.
Link between reason #1 and main idea	**Thus,** archaeologists have to be careful not to expose amber to high temperatures, which can affect the shape of the amber. **Also,** some liquids will make the amber cloudy.
Reason #2	Coral is made up of the skeletons of ocean creatures.
Detail for reason #2	**Because** it is brittle, it can be scratched or chipped. **Additionally,** it can absorb liquid.
Link between reason #2 and main idea	Archaeologists **therefore** must be careful not to soak coral or handle it roughly.

Chapter 16
Cracking the
Writing Section

This section of the TOEFL measures your ability to communicate in an academic environment. This is supposed to check to see whether you can write a college-level paper in English. There are only two writing tasks, and they require many of the same skills you need in order to ace the Reading, Listening, and Speaking sections. On the Writing section, you'll be asked to do the following:

Task 1: Integrated Writing—Read, Listen, Write
- **Read** a passage on an academic subject, **listen** to a lecture on the same topic, and **write** an essay that discusses the relationship between the two. You'll have three minutes to read and 20 minutes to respond.

Task 2: Independent Task
- **Write** an essay that states, explains, and supports your position on an issue. You'll have 30 minutes to write this essay.

You will have 50 minutes to complete both tasks.

Each of the two Writing responses you'll have to provide will be graded on a scale from 0 to 30. As we mentioned in the early part of this book, the Writing scores are subdivided into five sections:

Advanced (24–30). An "Advanced" score indicates that you can write clearly on a wide range of topics using an appropriate variety of vocabulary and grammar.

High-Intermediate (17–23). A "High-Intermediate" score indicates that you can organize your thoughts well and present them cogently in written form. Any difficulties that exist may be in the form of occasional incorrect grammar or phrases that are unidiomatic.

Low-Intermediate (13–16). A "Low-Intermediate" score indicates that you were able to respond to the tasks appropriately, but may have been unclear in some of the points you tried to make. Additional grammatical errors may contribute to the perception that your essays aren't as strong as they could be.

Basic (7–12). A "Basic" score indicates that you were able to answer the question, but provided little detail to support your ideas. Grammatical errors and incorrect vocabulary may make it difficult for a reader to understand these essays.

Below Basic (0–6). A score in the "Below Basic" range indicates that either you didn't understand the prompt or other source, and have significant areas of improvement in vocabulary and grammar.

WRITING SECTION DIRECTIONS

It is important to know that your first writing task will require both a reading and listening part, so you'll need to leave your headset on. Your essays must be typed, so you should have some familiarity with the keyboard before you take the TOEFL. The word processor used for the TOEFL is very simple: it has only *cut*, *copy*, and *paste* functions.

Task 1: Integrated Task—Read, Listen, Write

The first task begins with 3 minutes to read a 230- to 300-word passage about an academic topic. After the 3 minutes expire, the passage disappears from the screen and a 2-minute lecture on the same topic begins automatically. When the lecture is finished, the reading passage will reappear and you'll have 20 minutes to write an essay on the relationship between the reading and the lecture. Your response must not include personal opinions.

Task 2: Independent Task

The second task is much simpler. You will have 30 minutes to write a response to a prompt. There is no reading or lecture, and you are asked to provide your personal views on a subject.

HOW THE WRITING SECTION IS SCORED

Your TOEFL essays are graded on a 0–5 scale by 2–4 different graders. The average score on both essays is converted to the 0–30 scale. A top-scoring essay on the TOEFL accomplishes the following:

- addresses the topic and the task
- is well organized and uses appropriate examples
- displays unity, progress, and coherence
- demonstrates consistent facility in the use of language

It is worth noting that only one of the four criteria focuses on your use of language. The rest are concerned with how well you complete the task and how organized your writing is. So keep in mind that overall structure and content are more important than perfect grammar.

Your goal in the Writing section is to make the grader's job as easy as possible by writing a focused, organized essay. If you present your thoughts in a clear, focused way, you'll make it easy for the grader to give you a score of 4 or 5.

CRACKING THE WRITING SECTION: BASIC PRINCIPLES

There are a few things to keep in mind when writing your essays for the TOEFL. As with the Speaking section, the graders are not expecting perfection. They realize that you are essentially writing the first draft of an essay. Given the limited amount of time provided, they expect you to make a few grammatical mistakes and misspell a few words. Furthermore, in many ways the graders are looking more at *how* you write, not *what* you write. The structure and organization of your essay is just as important as the content of your essay.

When writing your essay, be aware of the following important points:

1. Make sure you answer the question appropriately.
2. Make sure your essay is long enough.
3. Make sure your essay is clearly organized.

Paying attention to these three basic points will put you on the right track. Let's explore them in further detail.

Basic Principle #1: Make Sure You Answer the Question Appropriately

One of the first things the graders will evaluate is whether you answered the question in the prompt. Well-written essays that don't address the task will lose points. Therefore, it is important that you know about the two different tasks you will be asked to do.

Task 1: Integrated Task—Read, Listen, Write

The first task asks you to **summarize** and **relate** the points presented in a lecture to those given in a reading. Therefore, your essay should contain *only* facts from the material. All you need to do is report the main points mentioned and show how they relate to each other. You should *not* give your opinion on any of the topics. The first task should be written entirely in the third person—that is, using words such as *he, she, the professor, the student,* and so on. You should never use *I* or *me* in the first essay.

Task 2: Independent Task

The second task requires you to state your **opinion**. This task requires you to argue what option or choice you believe to be better. Therefore, the essay should be written in the first person—it's acceptable to use *I* and *me* for the second essay.

Basic Principle #2: Make Sure Your Essay Is Long Enough

On the TOEFL, quantity makes a difference. To a grader, a longer essay is a better essay. Why? Because a longer essay shows the grader that you are comfortable writing and are able to produce a sustained, focused piece. When writing, you must make sure your essay falls within the TOEFL's suggested guidelines for length.

Task 1: Integrated Task—Read, Listen, Write

- For the first task, the TOEFL states that an "effective" response is between 150 and 225 words.

Task 2: Independent Task

- A minimum of 300 words is required for the second task.

For more reading and writing practice, check out *TOEFL Reading & Writing Workout.*

Although these word counts may seem intimidating, they're not as bad as you may think. For example, the section that you are now reading is more than 100 words. In fact, a 200-word essay basically consists of an introduction, one or two body paragraphs, and a conclusion—about the same length as half of this page. That's it.

A 300-word essay is approximately two-thirds of this page. You'll find that when you use the essay templates in this chapter, you shouldn't have any problem writing 300 words. Nonetheless, count the words of your practice essays to make sure they are long enough.

Basic Principle #3: Make Sure Your Essay Is Clearly Organized

Organized essays are easy to read. Essays that are easy to read are easy to understand. TOEFL graders like both of those qualities. Your written responses on the TOEFL should contain the following:

- **An introduction,** containing your thesis statement
- **Body paragraphs,** containing examples and details that support your thesis
- **A conclusion,** containing a final restatement of your thesis
- **Appropriate transitions,** linking your paragraphs and ideas together

Now would be a good time to return to Core Concept: Writing (Chapter 5), especially if you haven't read through it yet. That chapter provides all the necessary information on how to organize your essay and use transitions.

CRACKING THE WRITING SECTION: BASIC APPROACH

You will achieve a good score on the TOEFL Writing section if you do the following:

Essay Tip: There are only a few commonly used essay questions on the first TOEFL Writing section. By studying the templates on the following pages, you can walk into the test totally prepared.

1. **Know what you're going to write *before* you write.** Master the writing templates in this chapter so you are confident on test day.
2. **Organize your essay first.** Don't just start writing; spend a few minutes outlining your essay. It will make writing it much easier.
3. **Consider your audience.** TOEFL graders are trained to look for certain things in an essay. Make sure your essay contains these key elements. (These elements are explained later in this chapter.)
4. **Use your time wisely.** You have only 20 or 30 minutes to write. Make efficient use of your time.

Let's look at each of these steps.

Step 1: Know What You're Going to Write

The biggest danger in trying to write under timed conditions is writer's block—that is, you have absolutely no idea what to write. While you struggle with how to put your thoughts on paper, valuable time slips away. Fortunately, there is an easy solution to this problem: know exactly what you need to write *before* you sit down at the testing center.

We're going to look at templates for each of the writing tasks. Use these templates and familiarize yourself with their basic structures. That way, all you'll do is adjust the template to the specific topic.

Task 1: Integrated Task—Read, Listen, Write

Template #1: Casting Doubt on a Lecture

For the first essay, you will usually be asked to perform the following task:

Summarize the points made in the lecture, explaining how they cast doubt on the reading.

The template for this task is as follows:

Paragraph #1: Introduction	
Topic Sentence	**In the lecture, the** (professor/teacher/instructor) **made several points about** (topic).
State main idea of lecture	**The** (professor/teacher/instructor) **argues that** (main idea of lecture).
Transition/main idea of reading	**However, the author of the passage contends that** (main idea of reading).
Thesis statement	**The professor's lecture casts doubt on the reading by using a number of points that are contrary to** (main idea of reading).
Paragraph #2: Body Paragraph	
Transition/point #1 from lecture	**The first point that the** (professor/teacher/instructor) **uses to cast doubt on the reading is** (point #1 from lecture).
Detail for point #1 from lecture	**According to the** (professor/teacher/instructor), (detail for point #1 from lecture).
Opposing point from reading	**(Point #1) differs from the reading in that the reading states** (point #1 of the reading).
Explanation of relationship between reading and lecture	**The point made by the** (professor/teacher/instructor) **casts doubt on the reading because** (how lecture is different from reading).
Paragraph #3: Body Paragraph	
Transition/point #2 from lecture	**Another point that the** (professor/teacher/instructor) **uses to cast doubt on the reading is** (point #2 from lecture).
Detail for point #2 from lecture	**The** (professor/teacher/instructor) **claims that** (detail for point #2 from lecture).
Opposing point from reading	**However, the reading states** (point #2 from reading).
Explanation of relationship between reading and lecture	**This point is contradicted by** (point #2 from lecture).
Paragraph #4: Conclusion	
Topic Sentence	**In conclusion, the points made in the lecture contrast with the reading.**
Summary	(Points #1 and #2 from the lecture) **demonstrate that** (main idea of the reading) **is in doubt.**

The words in bold are suggestions; you don't have to use them exactly. You may also find that you have time to write a third body paragraph. If so, repeat the formula from the first two body paragraphs. However, your writing should still follow the general pattern established in the outline. In the next chapter, you'll have the opportunity to see the template in action on a sample question.

Template #2: Showing Support for a Reading Passage

While it's more likely that you'll see the previous prompt in the Integrated Writing assessment, you may see a different question:

> Summarize the points made in the lecture, explaining how they support the reading.

This task is simply the opposite of the first: instead of attacking it, we need to support it. Thus the template is fairly similar.

Paragraph #1: Introduction	
Topic Sentence	**In the lecture, the** (professor/teacher/instructor) **made several points about** (topic).
State main idea of lecture	**The** (professor/teacher/instructor) **argues that** (main idea of lecture).
Transition/main idea of reading	**The points made by the** (professor/teacher/instructor) **support** (main idea of reading passage).
Thesis statement	**In fact, the examples used by the** (professor/teacher/instructor) **support** (main idea of reading)
Paragraph #2: Body Paragraph	
Transition/point #1 from lecture	**The first point that the** (professor/teacher/instructor) **uses to support the reading is** (point #1 from lecture).
Detail for point #1 from lecture	**According to the** (professor/teacher/instructor), (detail for point #1 from lecture).
Supporting point from reading	**(Point #1) supports the reading, which holds that** (point #1 of the reading).
Explanation of relationship between reading and lecture	**The point made by the** (professor/teacher/instructor) **supports the reading because** (why lecture agrees with the reading).
Paragraph #3: Body Paragraph	
Transition/point #2 from lecture	**Furthermore, the** (professor/teacher/instructor) **bolsters the reading by stating that** (point #2 from lecture).
Detail for point #2 from lecture	**The** (point #2 from lecture) **claims that** (detail for point #2 from lecture).
Supporting point from reading	**This point agrees with the reading, which contends that** (point #2 from reading).
Explanation of relationship between reading and lecture	**The** (point #2 from lecture) **shows the truth of the reading because** (how point #2 agrees with the reading).
Paragraph #4: Conclusion	
Topic Sentence	**In conclusion, the points made in the lecture support the reading.**
Summary	(Points #1 and #2 from the lecture) **demonstrate that** (main idea of the reading) **is valid.**

Task 2: Independent Task

Template #3: Using Specific Details and Examples to Support Your Opinion

The second task on the TOEFL simply asks for your opinion on a matter. The prompt will look something like the example shown below.

> Do you agree or disagree with the following statement?
>
> *(statement)*
>
> Use specific details and examples to support your answer.

For the second task, use the following template:

Paragraph 1: Introduction	
Topic Sentence/Paraphrase Prompt	**The issue at hand is** (choice offered by the prompt).
Interpret the prompt	**This issue is** (important/difficult/troubling) **because** (what is important/difficult/troubling about the prompt).
Tie reason #1 back to thesis	**I believe** (state your choice) **is the better option because…** (reasons you believe your option is preferable).
Paragraph 2: Body Paragraph	
Transition/first reason	(Your choice of options) **is preferable because…** (reason #1).
Detail for reason #1	(details about reason #1)
Tie reason #1 back to thesis	**I believe** (state your choice) **is the better option because…** (reasons you believe your option is preferable).
Paragraph 3: Body Paragraph	
Transition/second reason	**Additionally,** (your choice of options) **is better because…** (reason #2).
Detail for reason #2	(details about reason #2)
Tie reason #2 back to thesis	**I believe** (state your choice) **is the better option because…** (reasons you believe your option is preferable).
Paragraph 4: Body Paragraph	
Transition/third reason	**Also,** (state your choice) **is the right choice because…** (reason #3).
Detail for reason #3	(details about reason #3)
Tie reason #3 back to thesis	**Finally, I think** (state your choice) **is the right choice because…** (reasons you believe your option is preferable).
Paragraph 5: Conclusion	
Transition/restate thesis	**Ultimately, I feel that** (your choice) **is the correct one**.
Final Statement	**I believe this because…** (why you believe your choice is best).

In summary, familiarize yourself with these templates. If you know exactly what your essay is supposed to look like, you'll have a much easier time writing.

Step 2: Organize Your Essay

In the first step, we looked at how your essay should be *structured*. Now we need to talk about what your essay will *contain*. Before you start writing, spend about five minutes brainstorming examples and points for your essay. Failing to do so may lead you to write an essay that lacks focus and coherence.

Task 1: Integrated Task—Read, Listen, Write

For the first task, you'll be presented with a short reading passage. While reading, take notes on the main idea and some of the major facts presented. Your notes do not have to be very detailed—you'll be able to refer back to the passage while you are writing. However, it is important to know the general idea of the reading so that you can relate it back to the lecture.

During the lecture, try to note the major points presented by the professor. There will usually be three to five points, but you won't need all of them: two or three points will be sufficient for the task. You will not be able to hear the lecture again, so it is important to remember some of the points.

Try to organize your notes in the following way:

> **Reading:**
> **Main idea:** _____
> **Example/reason:** _____
> **Example/reason:** _____
> **Example/reason:** _____

Remember, if it's too difficult to read and take notes, then do not attempt to do so. The reading passage will be available for reference while you write. For the lecture, the main idea is generally opposite that of the reading, so don't worry about noting that. The examples offered in the lecture are the parts you have to concentrate on. During the lecture, try to organize your notes as follows.

> **Lecture:**
> **Point #1:** _____
> **Detail #1:** _____
> **Point #2:** _____
> **Detail #2:** _____
> **Point #3:** _____
> **Detail #3:** _____

Even if you are unable to write down the details for the example, you'll need to try to remember them so you can refer to them in your essay. If you don't mention specific points from the lecture, you will receive a lower score.

For the second task, it is very important that you come up with good reasons for your viewpoint. You need to tell the reader why you believe your opinion is better. Here's a good way to organize your thoughts.

Issue:

Your opinion: _____

Why? _____

Reason #1: _____

Detail #1: _____

Reason #2: _____

Detail #2: _____

Reason #3: _____

Detail #3: _____

A Sample Response: A Well-Organized Essay

Let's look at a sample response for the second writing task. Here's the prompt.

Do you agree or disagree with the following statement?

The purpose of education should be to teach skills, not values.

Support your position with details and examples.

Before you start writing, take time to organize. First, write down the issue.

Issue: Should schools teach only skills and not values?

Putting the statement into your own words or rephrasing it as a question is a helpful way to approach the prompt. Now, figure out which side of the issue you agree with.

Your opinion: Disagree—I believe schools should teach values as well as skills.

After figuring out your opinion, ask yourself why you have that opinion. This information will be useful for your introduction.

Why? Because students need to know how to act in the world.

Once you ask yourself why you have your opinion, you then need to list some specific examples.

Reason #1: Students may not get educated about values at home.

Detail #1: Some parents don't teach values to their children. Thus, schools should teach them.

Reason #2: Education is more than just skills.

Detail #2: Students are going to use their education in the outside world. They need to know what's right and wrong.

Reason #3: <u>It is easier to teach values when students are younger.</u>

Detail #3: <u>Education plays an important role in a young person's life, so schools are a good place to teach values.</u>

Your Turn: Practice Writing a Well-Organized Essay

Now it's your turn to organize your thoughts on the prompt that follows.

Do you agree or disagree with the following statement?

Students should be required to take regular standardized tests to prove that they are learning.

Support your position with details and examples.

Issue: _____

    Your opinion: _____

          Why? _____

    Reason #1: _____

    Detail #1: _____

    Reason #2: _____

    Detail #2: _____

    Reason #3: _____

    Detail #3: _____

Now try it again, and time yourself. See if you can brainstorm some examples within five or six minutes.

Do you agree or disagree with the following statement?

The best way to teach is by example.

Support your position with details and examples.

Issue: _____

    Your opinion: _____

          Why? _____

    Reason #1: _____

    Detail #1: _____

    Reason #2: _____

    Detail #2: _____

    Reason #3: _____

    Detail #3: _____

Step 3: Consider Your Audience

TOEFL graders are trained to look for certain features in your writing. By ensuring that your essay contains these features, you'll improve your score. Make sure your essay contains the following:

1. **An introduction, body paragraphs, and a conclusion.** More details on these can be found in Core Concept: Writing (Chapter 5).
2. **Specific examples.** Your essay must use specific examples. The more detail you use, the better your essay will be.
3. **Transitions.** One of the things TOEFL graders look for in an essay is "unity and coherence." That means that all the ideas must flow easily. They should be linked together with appropriate transitions.

Similarly, there are some elements to avoid in your writing. Make sure you avoid the following:

1. **Repeating phrases from the reading or prompt word for word.** Always put the examples and reasons into your own words. Although repeating a word or two is acceptable, you should *never* copy long phrases directly from the text on screen. TOEFL graders will penalize you for this.
2. **Writing your essay as one long paragraph.** Make sure you divide your essay into separate paragraphs. *Do not* just write a single block of text.
3. **Including material not relevant to the task.** Your essay must remain on topic. *Do not* include any reasons or examples that do not connect or relate to the task.

By keeping these points in mind, you'll ensure that your essay is well received by the TOEFL graders.

Step 4: Use Your Time Wisely

If you had unlimited time, you would surely be able to achieve a top score on the Writing section. Unfortunately, your time on the TOEFL is extremely limited. Thus, you must make sure to use your time wisely. The following tables provide a good guide for how to spend your time.

Task #1: 20 minutes

Time	Task
5 minutes	Organize your essay.
2 minutes	Write your introduction.
10 minutes	Write your body paragraphs.
2 minutes	Write your conclusion.
1 minute	Proofread your essay to correct any mistakes.

Task #2: 30 minutes

Time	Task
7 minutes	Organize your essay.
2 minutes	Write your introduction.
16 minutes	Write your body paragraphs.
2 minutes	Write your conclusion.
3 minutes	Proofread your essay to correct any mistakes.

To stick to these guidelines, you'll have to know exactly what your essay is going to look like. Use the templates from Step 1 to focus as you read.

Now you're ready to try some practice writing drills.

Writing Summary

Congratulations! You now know how to crack all parts of the TOEFL. But before you move on, keep the following points in mind for cracking the Writing section:

o **Answer the question!** Even if you write well, you won't receive a top score unless you address the task. Make sure you know what each task requires.

o **Focus on form.** The structure and organization of your essay is crucial. Make sure you know how to put your essay together.

o **Make the graders' jobs easy.** You know what the TOEFL graders are looking for, so make them happy by giving them a structured essay that uses detailed examples and good transitions.

Let's practice some writing with the drills in the next chapter. Then, if you feel ready, go on to Part IV and take the full-length practice TOEFL exam. If not, review the lessons in the previous chapters until you are confident you know how to crack the test.

Chapter 17
Writing Practice Drills

You're now ready to crack the Writing section. Try the following practice prompts. After you've finished, read through the sample essays in the next chapter to get an idea of what TOEFL graders are looking for in the essay responses.

Writing Practice Drill #1

The first type of writing question will provide you with the following directions:

> You will have 3 minutes to read the following passage. You may take notes during your reading. After the 3 minutes are up, you will hear a lecture on the topic. You may take notes during the lecture as well.
>
> After the lecture ends, you will have 20 minutes to write your response. An effective response is generally 150–225 words long. You may use your notes to help you answer, and you may refer to the reading passage. Your essay will be graded on the quality of your writing and on the completeness of the content.

Now let's look at a writing question. On the actual test, you will hear a prompt that will ask you to read a passage in 3 minutes. For our purposes here, you will need to stop the audio to read the passage and either time yourself or ask a friend to time you. After 3 minutes, resume the audio for the listening passage.

Begin playing Track 19 in your Student Tools.

Narrator: Now read the passage about the first grain-based food. You have 3 minutes to read the passage. Begin reading now.

[Stop the audio for 3 minutes while you read the passage on the next page.]

Scant physical evidence remains of the first human domestication of grain. Still, there is enough to conclude that ancient peoples, motivated by the nutritional value of bread or cakes made of wild wheat, looked for controlled ways to grow it to provide a consistent food supply. Three related discoveries are likely to have led to the introduction of bread as the first grain-based food.

The first discovery was that wheat could be prepared for use by grinding. People probably began consuming wheat by chewing it raw. Because wheat is very hard, they gradually discovered that it was less trouble to eat if crushed to paste between two stones. The result would have been the ancestor of the drier, more powdery wheat flour we use today.

From there, it was a short step to the next breakthrough—baking the simplest bread, which requires no technology but fire. Loaves of wheat paste, when baked into bread, could be stored for long periods, certainly longer than raw seeds. This kept the food value of wheat available for an extended period after it had been harvested.

Finally, ancient peoples found that if the paste was allowed to sit in the open, yeast spores from the air settled on it and began fermenting the wheat. This natural process of fermentation caused bubbles to form in the wheat paste, suggesting that it would be lighter in texture and even easier to eat when baked.

Resume playing Track 19.

N: Now listen to part of a lecture on the topic you just read about.

N: Summarize the points made in the lecture you just heard, explaining how they cast doubt on the contents of the reading. You may refer to the passage as you write.

For the Writing Drills, make sure you have a word processing document open on your computer and practice typing your response, as you will on test day.

TOEFL Writing

PAUSE
TEST

SECTION
EXIT

VOLUME

HELP
?

NEXT
→

HIDE TIME   00:29:57

Directions: You have 20 minutes to plan and write your response. Your response will be graded on the quality of your writing and on how well your response presents the points in the lecture and their relationship to the reading passage. Typically, an effective response will be 150–225 words.

Question: Summarize the points made in the lecture you just heard, explaining how they cast doubt on the contents of the reading. You may refer to the passage as you write.

Word Count: 0

Copy   Cut   Paste

Scant physical evidence remains of the first human domestication of grain. Still, there is enough to conclude that ancient peoples, motivated by the nutritional value of bread or cakes made of wild wheat, looked for controlled ways to grow it to provide a consistent food supply. Three related discoveries are likely to have led to the introduction of bread as the first grain-based food.

The first discovery was that wheat could be prepared for use by grinding. People probably began consuming wheat by chewing it raw. Because wheat is very hard, they gradually discovered that it was less trouble to eat if crushed to paste between two stones—the result would have been the ancestor of the drier, more powdery wheat flour we use today.

From there, it was a short step to the next breakthrough: baking the simplest bread, which requires no technology but fire. Loaves of wheat paste, when baked into bread, could be stored for long periods, certainly longer than raw seeds. This kept the food value of wheat available for an extended period after it had been harvested.

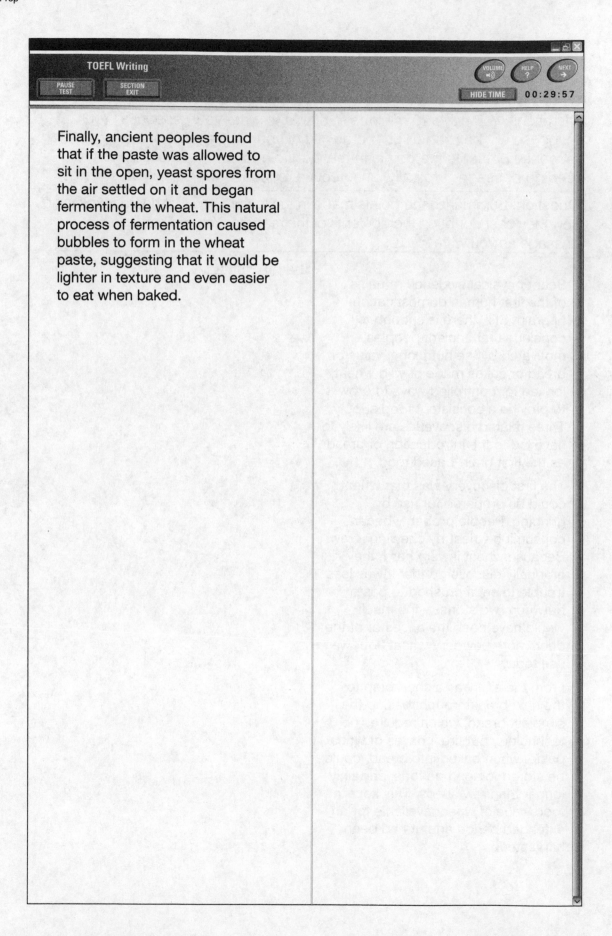

Finally, ancient peoples found that if the paste was allowed to sit in the open, yeast spores from the air settled on it and began fermenting the wheat. This natural process of fermentation caused bubbles to form in the wheat paste, suggesting that it would be lighter in texture and even easier to eat when baked.

Writing Practice Drill #2

The second type of writing question asks you to write a response to a question in 30 minutes. It will look something like the following:

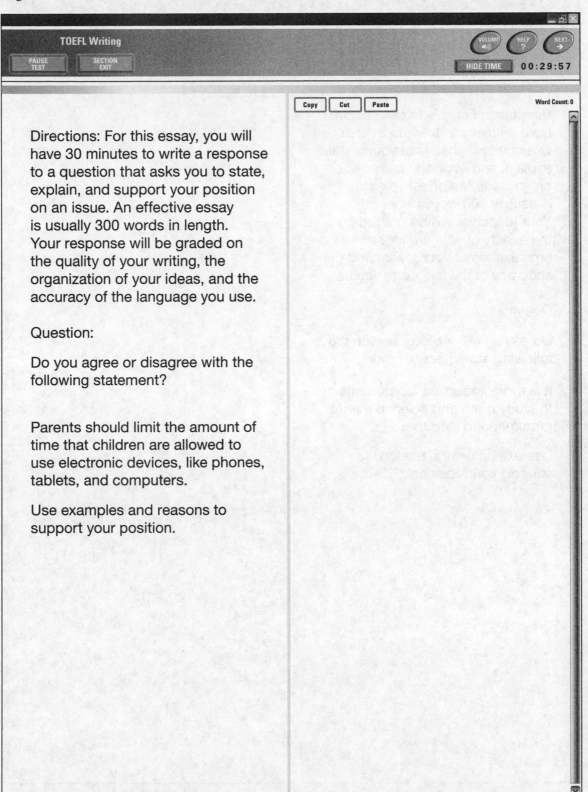

Writing Practice Drill #3

This drill again asks you to write a response to a question in 30 minutes.

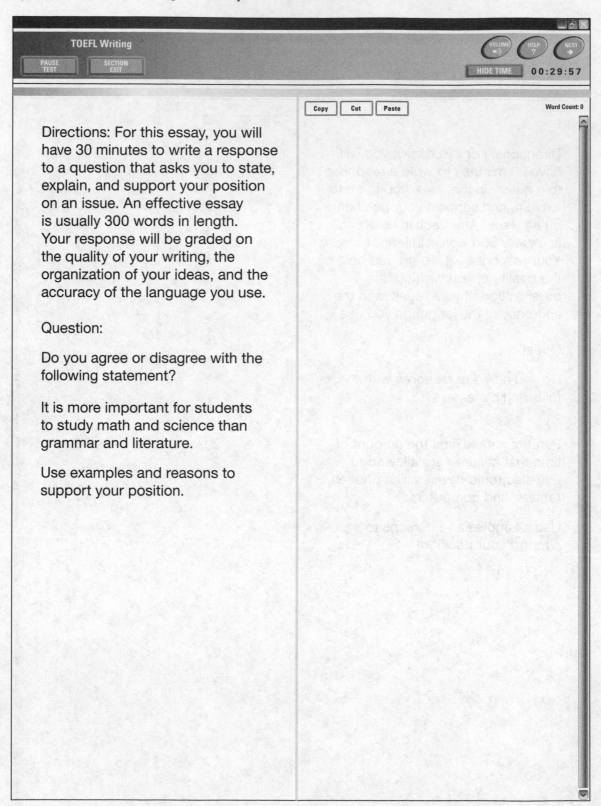

TOEFL Writing

PAUSE TEST | SECTION EXIT

VOLUME | HELP ? | NEXT →

HIDE TIME | 00:29:57

Copy | Cut | Paste

Word Count: 0

Directions: For this essay, you will have 30 minutes to write a response to a question that asks you to state, explain, and support your position on an issue. An effective essay is usually 300 words in length. Your response will be graded on the quality of your writing, the organization of your ideas, and the accuracy of the language you use.

Question:

Do you agree or disagree with the following statement?

It is more important for students to study math and science than grammar and literature.

Use examples and reasons to support your position.

Writing Practice Drill #4

This is another opportunity for you to write a response to a question in 30 minutes.

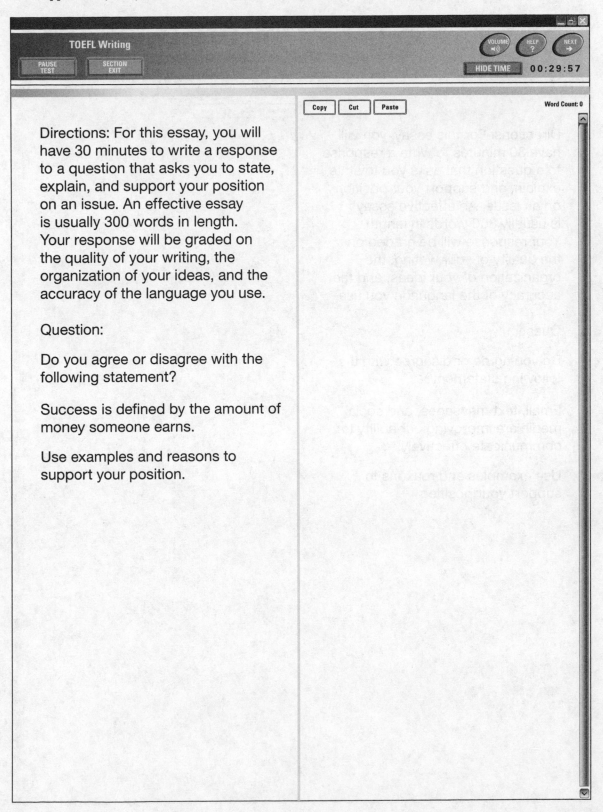

TOEFL Writing

PAUSE TEST · SECTION EXIT

VOLUME · HELP ? · NEXT →

HIDE TIME · 00:29:57

Copy · Cut · Paste · Word Count: 0

Directions: For this essay, you will have 30 minutes to write a response to a question that asks you to state, explain, and support your position on an issue. An effective essay is usually 300 words in length. Your response will be graded on the quality of your writing, the organization of your ideas, and the accuracy of the language you use.

Question:

Do you agree or disagree with the following statement?

Success is defined by the amount of money someone earns.

Use examples and reasons to support your position.

Writing Practice Drill #5

Here's another chance to write a response to a question in 30 minutes.

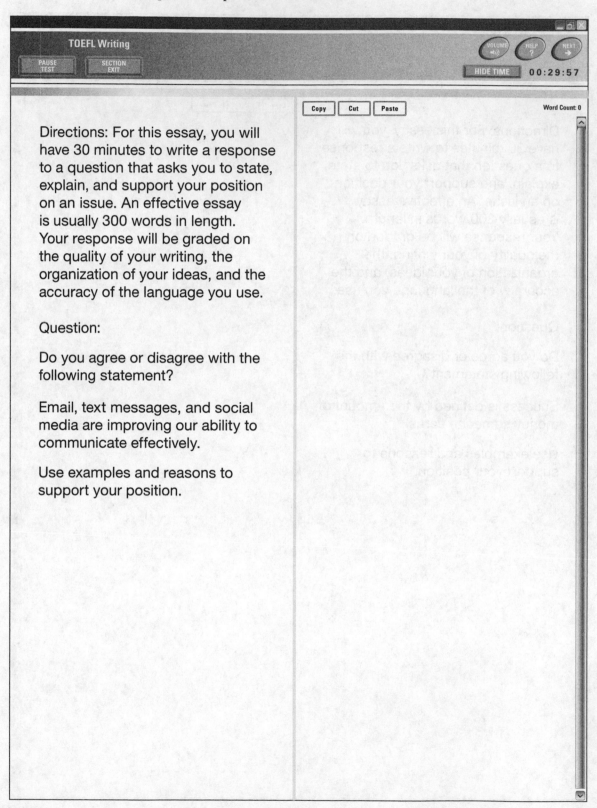

TOEFL Writing

PAUSE TEST   SECTION EXIT

VOLUME   HELP ?   NEXT →

HIDE TIME   00:29:57

Copy   Cut   Paste   Word Count: 0

Directions: For this essay, you will have 30 minutes to write a response to a question that asks you to state, explain, and support your position on an issue. An effective essay is usually 300 words in length. Your response will be graded on the quality of your writing, the organization of your ideas, and the accuracy of the language you use.

Question:

Do you agree or disagree with the following statement?

Email, text messages, and social media are improving our ability to communicate effectively.

Use examples and reasons to support your position.

Chapter 18
Writing Practice
Answers and
Explanations

Read through the following sample responses to the drills you completed in the previous chapter and compare your essays with them. If possible, have a friend who is a native speaker or highly proficient in English look over your essays.

As always, your writing does not have to match ours exactly. Just check to see if your essay accomplishes the important points highlighted in the high-scoring essays.

WRITING PRACTICE DRILL #1
Take a look at the first task.

> *Narrator:* Now read the passage about the first grain-based food. You have 3 minutes to read the passage. Begin reading now.

Scant physical evidence remains of the first human domestication of grain. Still, there is enough to conclude that ancient peoples, motivated by the nutritional value of bread or cakes made of wild wheat, looked for controlled ways to grow it to provide a consistent food supply. Three related discoveries are likely to have led to the introduction of bread as the first grain-based food.

The first discovery was that wheat could be prepared for use by grinding. People probably began consuming wheat by chewing it raw. Because wheat is very hard, they gradually discovered that it was less trouble to eat if crushed to paste between two stones—the result would have been the ancestor of the drier, more powdery wheat flour we use today.

From there, it was a short step to the next breakthrough: baking the simplest bread, which requires no technology but fire. Loaves of wheat paste, when baked into bread, could be stored for long periods, certainly longer than raw seeds. This kept the food value of wheat available for an extended period after it had been harvested.

Finally, ancient peoples found that if the paste was allowed to sit in the open, yeast spores from the air settled on it and began fermenting the wheat. This natural process of fermentation caused bubbles to form in the wheat paste that suggested it would be lighter in texture and even easier to eat when baked.

> *Narrator:* Now listen to part of a lecture on the topic you just read about.

> *Professor:* Conventional wisdom says that a very primitive kind of bread was the first grain food that human societies ate. But, you know, for the last few decades, there's been an alternative hypothesis that quite a few anthropologists are starting to give a closer look. That hypothesis says that it was, in fact, beer—not bread—that was the first grain food. Sound strange? Consider a couple of things.
>
> For one thing, you don't have to grind wheat to make it easier to eat. If you keep it in a moist environment, it naturally starts sprouting, with a new baby plant splitting the hard seed case in half. Sprouted wheat is sweeter, softer, and actually more nutritious than whole wheat seeds—and it would have developed without human

effort. In order to discover the usefulness of ground wheat, someone had to get the bright idea of crushing it. To discover the usefulness of sprouted wheat, people just had to do nothing and let it sit. Which do you think happened first?

Another thing: What turns grain into beer is fermentation, and wheat begins to ferment almost as soon as it's stored—from water and yeasts in the air. After the wheat sprouted, it would have started to ferment. The process would have been obvious because of the bubbles and foam that formed. People could have experimented by tasting it and discovering the first beer.

And even if you assume that people were already grinding wheat to paste, think about it. The paste ferments and bubbles. Is it likely that early peoples would have thought to fire it before eating? We're used to cooking our food, but in prehistoric times, the idea that you would take fire to food to improve it for eating was not obvious.

N: Summarize the points made in the lecture you just heard, explaining how they cast doubt on the contents of the reading. You may refer to the passage as you write.

Let's look at some notes you may have jotted down.

Reading:
    Main Idea: <u>Bread was the first grain-based food.</u>
    Example/reason: <u>Wheat is hard to eat, and people probably ground it into a paste.</u>
    Example/reason: <u>The wheat paste could be baked with fire.</u>
    Example/reason: <u>Wheat ferments naturally, which makes it easier to eat when baked.</u>

Lecture:
    Point #1: <u>Wheat doesn't need to be ground.</u>
    Detail #1: <u>Sprouted wheat is easy to eat and tastes better than normal wheat.</u>
    Point #2: <u>Fermenting happens very quickly.</u>
    Detail #2: <u>People tasting the foam from fermenting may have created the first beer.</u>
    Point #3: <u>It's unlikely that people would think to bake wheat.</u>
    Detail #3: <u>Early people did not cook things.</u>

With that information, let's construct our essay. The following sections offer a variety of responses, scored from high to low. All spelling and grammatical errors are intentional—to demonstrate the factors behind an assigned score. As you read the response, think of what numerical value the grader might have assigned, and check to see how your assessment matches up to the actual score. As you know, the scale is from 0–5.

A Higher-Scoring Response

The following is an example of a higher-scoring response:

In the lecture, the profesor makes several points about the first wheat product. The profesor argues that beer was the first wheat product. This is different from the reading, which states that bread came first. However, the teacher cast doubt on the reading with several points.

First of all, the teacher says that wheat doesn't have to be ground. It is easy for people to eat wheat when it sprouts. This is not what the reading states, it says that early people ground wheat into a paste because it is hard to eat. The lecture casts doubt on this by showing another way to eat wheat.

Also, the talk says that fermenting happens very fast. This fermenting leads to a foam, which people probably tasted as the first beer. In the reading, it is argued that fermenting made people think to bake the bread. The professor doubts this point by stating it is unlikely.

Finally, the profesor argues that people would not think to bake the wheat. The point is made that early people do not cook things. These points made by the teacher cast doubt on the reading. It seems like beer not bread was the first wheat food.

Score and Analysis of This Response

Score: 5 This essay received the highest possible score of 5 because it does many things well.

- First, it is extremely well organized. It has a clear introduction, body paragraphs, and a conclusion. It is also easy to follow because the essay uses appropriate transitions to link ideas.
- Also, the essay has a good length: 199 words.
- More important, the author mentions several specific examples from the talk and shows how they are different from the points in the reading. That level of detail is necessary for a top score on the TOEFL.

This essay is by no means perfect. The writer misspelled "professor" throughout the essay and makes a number of errors with subject-verb agreement (for example, "the teacher cast doubt" instead of "casts doubt"). The important thing is that those errors do not detract from the overall message of the essay.

A Lower-Scoring Response

Following is an example of a lower-scoring response to the first practice drill.

In early cultures there were different ways of using wheat. Some cultures use wheat for making bread and some ohers used it to make beer. It is said by the instructor though that it is the beer that was made first.

Another thing is that fermenting of the wheat created beer, not bread. The professor said that the people would not bake the foam but instead they would drink it like beer.

The lecture shows that early peoples rarely used fire to make things. They didn't think to make the bread form the wheat that they had ground. That is to say that it seems like beer was more likely to be make by people than was bread.

Score and Analysis of This Response

Score: 2   This weaker response scored much lower because the essay has numerous problems.

- The first problem is that the ideas in the essay are not clearly expressed. The writing style makes it difficult to understand exactly what the author is trying to demonstrate.
- Also, the ideas are not linked together, making the essay difficult to follow.
- The first two sentences indicate that the writer did not grasp the main point of the reading and the lecture. Plus, the first sentence of the third paragraph is not mentioned in either the reading or the lecture.
- The response is also rather short, only 118 words long.

On the positive side, the response does include some points from the lecture, even if they are slightly unclear.

WRITING PRACTICE DRILL #2

Now let's look at the second task from the previous chapter.

Question:

Do you agree or disagree with the following statement?

Parents should limit the amount of time that children are allowed to use electronic devices, like phones, tablets, and computers.

Use examples and reasons to support your position.

Here are some sample notes for this topic.

Issue: *Should parents limit the amount of time their children use electronic devices?*

Your opinion:	Agree—parents should limit children's screen time.
Why?	Because devices aren't safe and they prevent children from learning how to communicate.
Reason #1:	Studies show a lot of electronics are harmful.
Detail #1:	Children ignore things around them when they focus on the device.
Reason #2:	Children don't learn how to interact.
Detail #2:	If children always play on an iPad, they don't learn to interact with people around them.
Reason #3:	Devices can cause health problems.
Detail #3:	Some people believe that WiFi and cellular signals can increase the chance of cancer.

Now let's put it together in our essay.

A Higher-Scoring Response

The following is a higher-scoring essay.

The question being asked is if parents should limit the amount of time their children spend using devices. This is a very important question because it has to do with children's health and futures. In my opinion, I believe that parents should limit the time their children spend on devices because there are health risks and it is possible for the children not to be able to communicate well. The first reason I believe that parents should limit their children's use of electronic devices is because studies have shown that using devices a lot can be not healthy. For example, when children get focused on looking at the screen, they don't pay attention to the scene around them. They don't see other people walking nearby or they don't see cars coming. There are stories in the news every day about children who are in accidents because they pay attention to the phone instead.

Moreover, it can be that children do not learn to interact with each other when they spend so much time looking at electronic devices. If they spend all their time looking at devices, they don't have opportunity to talk to other children or other adults. So they don't learn to be polite or to say pleasantries. Yesterday when I was walking into a store a girl was on her device the whole time and almost walked in to me. She did not see how close she came to me, and therefore she also did not apologize for almost walking in to me.

Lastly, I believe that the signal from wireless devices like WiFi and cellular signals can help cause cancer. Some studies show that there is relationship, and if I was a parent I wouldn't want to take any chances.

In conclusion, I believe parents should limit the amount of time their children spend looking at electronic devices. There are too many bad possibilities from using them too much.

Score and Analysis of This Response

Score: 5   This response received the highest possible score for the following reasons:

- The writer keeps the essay focused on the topic. Everything relates to the thesis.
- The essay is just the right length.
- There are clear transitions, and the essay is easy to follow.
- The writer does a nice job of tying the conclusion back to the introduction by repeating the line about limiting children's use of devices.

Again, the essay is not perfect. There are several grammatical and other errors, but nothing big enough to detract from the overall meaning. It's good enough to get a top score on the TOEFL.

A Lower-Scoring Response

Now take a look at a lower-scoring response.

Some people say is better to limit childrens' use of devices. I don't really know. I think sometimes is good, sometimes is bad. I do think sometimes devices is bad, but sometimes is necesary. For example, when parents is at dinner and childrens are noisy, giving them device to use can keep quiet, and so then parents can enjoy diner and not be rude to people around. But sometimes parents use device too much and can be bad for childrens.

For example, when childrens use device all time when not in school, childrens don't learn to talk to other childrens and they don't pay atention to area around. They can get in accidents by walking into people because they can't see them when they are looking at devices, and they don't learn to say nice things to other children because they do not interact with each others.

So its hard to say if parents should limit. Sometimes is good, sometimes is bad. Each parents has to decide what is write for her childrens.

Score and Analysis of This Response

Score: 2   This essay received a much lower score than the previous response for the following reasons:

- One of the most glaring problems with this essay is that it does not satisfy the task. The assignment asks you to state whether you agree or disagree, so make sure you pick a side. Don't try to defend both sides of the issue.
- Furthermore, this essay is not very well planned out. It is clear that the author didn't think before writing.
- There are not enough examples.
- The author tries to write a conclusion, but still does not address the essay task.
- There are too many grammatical errors.

Although this is not the worst possible essay, it is not going to receive a good score.

WRITING PRACTICE DRILL #3

Here are sample responses to Drill #3 from the previous chapter.

> Question:
>
> Do you agree or disagree with the following statement?
>
> It is more important for students to study math and science than grammar and literature.
>
> Use examples and reasons to support your position.

Here are some sample notes for the topic.

Issue: *Should students focus more on math and science than on grammar and literature?*

Your opinion:	Disagree—students need to study both.
Why?	Because you need a basic understanding of both to be successful.
Reason #1:	If you don't understand basics of science and math, you can't understand the world around you.
Detail #1:	If you can't count money, people can steal from you easier.
Reason #2:	If you don't understand how to conduct an experiment, you won't know if people are lying to you.
Detail #2:	Scientific method is the basis of any experiment. If someone claims something is caused by something else, if you don't know about scientific method you won't know if they're lying.
Reason #3:	If you can't spell or write well, you won't succeed in business.
Detail #3:	You need communication skills to get a job.

Let's see how we can put this information into an essay.

A Higher-Scoring Response

Here's an example of a higher-scoring response.

I believe it is just as important to study grammar and literature as it is to study maths and science. This is because you need to understand basics of all areas in order succeed in life.

First, math is basis of our economy. If you don't understand basics of maths people can steal from you easier. For example, if you can't count change, you won't know if a cashier gave you right amount when you buy a soda at a gas station. Also, you need to understand math to know if you were charged the right amount at restaurant or store.

Second, science gives the basics of understanding any study. Scientific method says you can only change one thing at time when you conduct a study. So, if someone says that something caused an effect, you can ask if something else might have caused it. If two things changed, maybe something else caused the effect, instead. If you don't know that only one thing can change, you won't know to ask.

Third, bosses wants to hire people who can write correctly. To do this, must know grammar and how to spell. If your resume has lots of wrong words and grammar mistakes, you will not even get an interview.

In conclusion, it is important to study grammar and literature, not just maths and science.

Score and Analysis of This Response

Score: 4 This response scored a solid grade of 4. There are several good things in this essay.

- The essay stays on topic.
- The essay is well-organized, with a clear introduction, body paragraphs, and conclusion. The writer uses obvious transitions.
- There are three good examples provided for the topic and the writer gives some details for each of them.

However, there are a few issues that prevented the writer from achieving the top score.

- The essay is too short, using only 218 words.
- The conclusion is very simple.
- There are too many grammatical errors (typos, misspellings, incidents where the verb doesn't agree with the subject).

Overall, however, this is a good response for the TOEFL. It is a good example to show that you don't need to write like a native English speaker or have perfect spelling or grammar in order to get a strong score.

A Lower-Scoring Response

Now look at a lower-scoring essay. What are some of its problems?

Must learn gramer and literature, not just math and science. Very important becuase need basics of all to understand world. Without math, you can not count money so people can lie. Plus need understand sientifi method to understand experiments. People can say smething caused something else, but can be lying. If you do not under stand sientific method you will not know to question. Also, need to write good to get a job. Boss only wants to hire people who can write. Therefore, must stury all area in school.

Score and Analysis of This Response

Score: 1 This essay received only a 1, the lowest score possible for an essay that is written in English. Here are some reasons why.

- Although the essay does address the task, there is no organization. The essay contains only one paragraph.
- The examples are not explained in sufficient detail.
- The essay is too short.

The writer needs to better organize this essay and develop the examples more to gain a higher score.

WRITING PRACTICE DRILL #4

The following are sample responses to Drill #4 from the previous chapter.

> Question:
>
> Do you agree or disagree with the following statement?
>
> Success is defined by the amount of money someone earns.
>
> Use examples and reasons to support your position.

Here are some sample notes for the topic.

Issue: Does money define success?

Your opinion:	Disagree. Money is not the only way to define success.
Why?	Other ways to be successful
Reason #1:	Other ways to be successful: help other people
Detail #1:	Malala Yousafzai
Reason #2:	Other ways to be successful: change your community
Detail #2:	My friend's father volunteered a lot and did many things to support veterans.
Reason #3:	Other ways to be successful: earn a degree
Detail #3:	First-generation college graduate.

Let's see how we can put this information into an essay.

A Higher-Scoring Response

Here's an example of a higher-scoring response.

Unfortunately, in todays society, many people believe that how much you earn tells how successful you are. How do people tell? They look at the clothes you wear, the cars you drive, and more. But I believe money is only one way of being successful. There are many other ways to achieve success.

One way you can be success is by helping other people. Like Malala Yousafzai. As a younger girl in Pakistan, she was shot in the face for defying authority and going to school. After her recovery, she went on to fight for the rights of other girls to go to school and became a humanitarian. I think she is very successful.

Another way you can be successful is by changing your community. My friend's father is a veteran and so wanted to help other veterans. He was very active in his community and did a lot of things to help make life better for other veterans. By his actions he encouraged other people to also help veterans, and people began to care more about taking care of veterans as a result.

A third way to be successful without money is to earn university degree. For example, I was first person in my family to earn a degree in the United States. My parents moved here when I was very small hoping to offer me and my brother a better life. They sacrificed much things in order to give us opportunity. I really appreciate all the things they did to make it possible for us to go to university.

As you can see, earning a lot of money is not the only way to earn success.

Score and Analysis of This Response

Score: 4   This is a higher-scoring essay. Here's why.

- The essay is focused and clearly addresses the question task, right from the first paragraph.
- The essay is well organized, with a straightforward introduction, body paragraphs with clear transitions, and a distinct conclusion.
- Each example is supported by relevant examples, but more details could have been included.
- The essay has 283 words, which is an appropriate length for a response earning a 4.

A Lower-Scoring Response

Here is a lower-scoring essay. As you read it, think about how the essay could be improved.

Success is defined by the amount of money someone earns. This is not true idea. Money is root of evil.

Money make peoples steal so can have nice thing. Money make peoples lie so they get benefit. Money make peoples do bad, like sell drugs.

Success not defined by amount of money someone earn.

Score and Analysis of This Response

Score: 2   Although this essay is organized into paragraphs and manages to address the topic, it has several significant problems.

- The essay is too short; it barely has 50 words!
- The response does not have enough content to show true organization. The writer should include more examples and details to lengthen the essay.

Despite these problems, the graders will give credit for the attempt at organization of the essay and the fact that it does answer the question in the prompt.

WRITING PRACTICE DRILL #5

The following are sample responses to Drill #5 from the previous chapter.

Question:

Do you agree or disagree with the following statement?

Email, text messages, and social media are improving our ability to communicate effectively.

Use examples and reasons to support your position.

Here are some sample notes for the topic.

Issue: *Are email, text messages, and social media improving our ability to communicate effectively?*

Your opinion: Yes. These are making it easier to communicate.

Why? Faster, shorter, more friendly

Reason #1: Text is fast, efficient, doesn't interrupt the other person like a phone call.

Detail #1: I text with my husband regularly instead of calling - it doesn't take as long to call, wait for him to answer, and wait for him to respond. I just wait for his response.

Reason #2: Text is easy to send information that does not need a response.

Detail #2: Massage appointment

Reason #3: Easy to stay in touch with friends

Detail #3: Facebook makes it easy to share pictures of friends and family.

Let's see how we can put this information into an essay.

A Higher-Scoring Response

Here's an example of a higher-scoring response.

Some people say technologies like social media, texting, and email make people communicate worse. Because communicating in person is better. I see what they say, but I think these technologies like these help people communicate better. There is definitely benefits to communicating in person, especially with important topics, but in person not always necessary.

For example, texting makes many communications very easy. My husband and I use text or use Facebook messenger all the time. We send short notes just to say hello or to share a little bit of news. Not all news requires a phone call, and I do not always have the flexibility to make a phone call. But I can send a quick text very easily without anyone around me knowing.

Text or instant messenger is also very convenient for when a message does not need an immediate response. Something like a reminder for a doctor appointment is perfect to send by text, just to make sure client does not forget. The client does not need to respond to the text, but is a good reminder for the client. It is a good customer service.

Also, social media like Facebook is really nice to keep in touch with friends or family who live far away. Sometimes it is hard to plan to call or Skype with my family because they are twelev hours different from where we are. Most times they are sleeping when we are awake. So being able to look at pictures on Facebook or send short messages makes it easier to communicate with them.

In conclusion, while I agree that in person communication is sometimes better, it does not mean that technologies make us communicate worse. Sometimes, technologies make us communicate better.

Score and Analysis of This Response

Score: 5   This is a top-scoring essay. Here's why.

- The essay stays on topic; everything in it is relevant to the topic and the thesis.
- The essay's organization is very good. Each body paragraph flows well by introducing a reason, providing details, and providing a summary.
- The essay is detailed and of a good length.
- There are very few grammatical and spelling mistakes.

This qualifies as a great essay on the TOEFL.

A Lower-Scoring Response

Here is a lower-scoring essay. As you read it, think about how the essay could be improved.

Technology is improving many aspects of our world, from cars to communication.

Today's cars are almost able to drive themselves because of the technology they have. Rear view cameras help you make sure not to back into anything. Bluetooth allows you to make calls from the steering wheel without even looking at the phone. It also lets you play music from your phone through the car's stereo system. We've come a long way since the early cars were made.

Technology also helps around the house. People now have Roomba vacuums that vacumm the house on their own. A new technology today is Alexa, which can let you play music or order things online just by talking to the device and saying, "Alexa, do something." We also have Bluetooth headphones that let you watch TV without distrubing the people around you.

Technology also helps you keep in contact with family better. You can text them or use Skype or Facetime to talk to them and see them at the same time.

Overall, technology has improved our world a lot.

Score and Analysis of This Response

Score: 1   This essay is very weak and has two main problems:

- The essay does not respond to the prompt.
- The essay is too short.

This essay demonstrates that it doesn't matter how strong your command of the English language is—if you do not respond to the prompt, you will not get a strong score. For example, this essay talks about advancements in technology, but not the way that technology affects communication, which is what the prompt asked for. It is much more important to answer the question, even if your writing is not as strong.

Part IV:
Taking a
Practice Test

Now that you've completed your TOEFL preparation, it's time to try a full-length TOEFL practice exam. Use the test in the next chapter to practice the techniques and approaches you've worked on throughout the book and to familiarize yourself with the types of questions you'll see on test day. Make sure to time yourself as accurately as possible while taking the test.

EVALUATING YOUR PERFORMANCE

Because of the nature of the TOEFL iBT, it is difficult to obtain a scaled score that precisely matches the one you'll receive after taking your actual exam. However, it is still possible to evaluate your performance and get an idea of how you'll do on the real thing.

Also, remember that on the actual test, you'll be doing the whole thing on the computer. Try to practice doing as much of the test as possible on the computer, even if you just type up your essays on the writing portion.

Reading and Listening Sections

For these two sections, go through each question and analyze your performance. Keep track of questions that you answered correctly and see if you can categorize them as follows (jot down the abbreviations in parentheses next to the question numbers).

- **Correct (C):** These are questions that you fully understood. You had no problem answering them and spent very little time on them.
- **Correct, guessed (CG):** These are questions you answered correctly, but you guessed the correct answer. For these questions, make sure you try to figure out *why* the answer is correct. Also, look at the other choices. What made you eliminate them?
- **Incorrect, mistake (I):** This abbreviation means that you answered the question incorrectly, but you see your mistake. This type of situation is very common. Often, it results from not using the techniques described in this book or from going too quickly on the test and not reading carefully enough. Minimize the number of questions that fall into this category, and you'll do well on the TOEFL.
- **Incorrect, don't understand (I?):** This abbreviation is for the questions that you answered incorrectly and you're not sure why. It could be a comprehension problem. Or maybe you misunderstood what the question was asking. For these questions, look back at the choices. Were there any obviously wrong answers? Did you fall for a *trap* answer? What could you have done differently?

Speaking and Writing Sections

If at all possible, try to record your spoken responses. Listen to them, and see how closely they match the templates we've provided. If possible, play the responses for an English speaker and ask that person to evaluate your response.

Do the same for your written responses. Compare what you've written with the samples provided in this book. Do you have a clear introduction? Does your response include transition words? Do you use examples appropriately?

WHAT NOW?

After you've finished our practice test and your self-evaluation, you should take the full-length practice test available from ETS (www.ets.org). This will give you an opportunity to receive a scored result.

Don't forget to refer back to the section on "The Week Before the Test" on pages 24 and 25 of the Introduction of this book for more tips on your final preparation.

Chapter 19
TOEFL iBT
Practice Test

THE READING SECTION

For this section, you will read three passages and answer questions about their content. You will have 54 minutes to answer all the questions. You may begin.

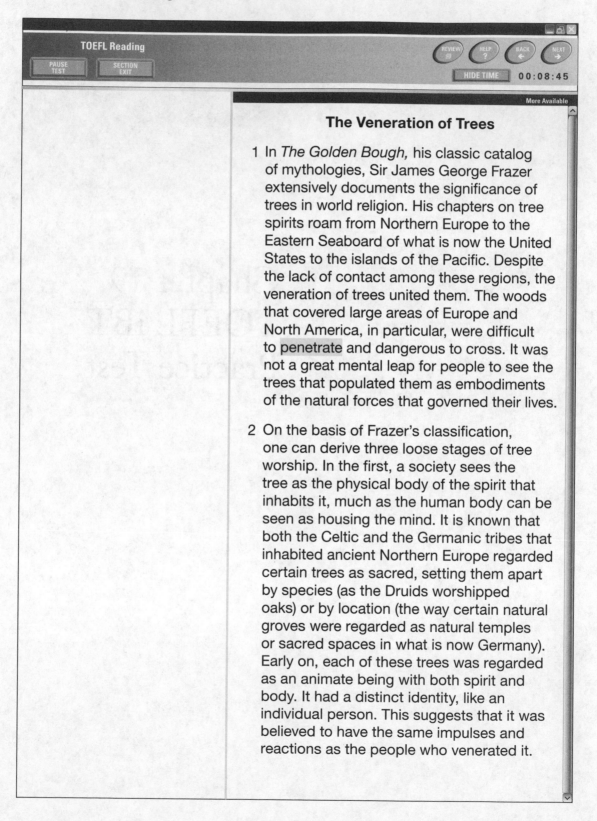

PAUSE TEST   SECTION EXIT

REVIEW   HELP ?   BACK ←   NEXT →

HIDE TIME   00:08:45

More Available

The Veneration of Trees

1 In *The Golden Bough,* his classic catalog of mythologies, Sir James George Frazer extensively documents the significance of trees in world religion. His chapters on tree spirits roam from Northern Europe to the Eastern Seaboard of what is now the United States to the islands of the Pacific. Despite the lack of contact among these regions, the veneration of trees united them. The woods that covered large areas of Europe and North America, in particular, were difficult to penetrate and dangerous to cross. It was not a great mental leap for people to see the trees that populated them as embodiments of the natural forces that governed their lives.

2 On the basis of Frazer's classification, one can derive three loose stages of tree worship. In the first, a society sees the tree as the physical body of the spirit that inhabits it, much as the human body can be seen as housing the mind. It is known that both the Celtic and the Germanic tribes that inhabited ancient Northern Europe regarded certain trees as sacred, setting them apart by species (as the Druids worshipped oaks) or by location (the way certain natural groves were regarded as natural temples or sacred spaces in what is now Germany). Early on, each of these trees was regarded as an animate being with both spirit and body. It had a distinct identity, like an individual person. This suggests that it was believed to have the same impulses and reactions as the people who venerated it.

3 Accordingly, ancient peoples had elaborate taboos designed to avoid causing offense to trees. These taboos were taken very seriously. In some places, one could be punished severely for injuring the bark of a tree or stealing its fruit. Before a tree was felled for human use, woodcutters in many world cultures would offer it both apologies and thanks for the resources it was about to provide them. This was necessary to avoid insulting the tree and inviting bad fortune. It was also the case, however, that injuries were said to cause suffering to trees as they did to people. In some societies, it was claimed that trees cry out in pain when struck or cut into. A tree's spirit and body are considered inseparable in this first stage.

4 A society makes a leap in sophistication and reaches Frazer's second stage when it begins to regard them as separate. That is, the spirit exists independently of the physical tree, even if it chooses to dwell there most of the time. The same spirit may thus take up residence in any tree of a forest; it is not killed when an individual tree is cut down. It is not bound to a single tree but rather stands for a group. The distinction may seem small, but it is a significant first step toward symbolic thinking. A forest, after all, is more than the sum of its parts. It encompasses not only its trees but also the animals and brush that flourish among them. The dangers of the forest are hidden; a traveler may or may not encounter them on a given journey. To think about a tree spirit identified with the forest as a whole, therefore, people had to think about phenomena that were removed from them in time and space—ideas rather than things. Such a tree spirit represented the potential and abstract rather than the concrete and immediate.

5 That transition is completed in the third stage. Liberated from each other, trees and their spirits can begin to be seen as symbols and embodiments of other natural processes of significance to primitive life: the power of weather and seasons to produce good or bad harvests, the mysteries of childbirth and disease. At that point, the veneration of trees reaches its stage of greatest complexity. Societies in both Eastern Europe and the South Pacific brought ceremonial offerings to trees in the hopes that they would furnish rain and sunshine. Women who hoped to bear children might be instructed to embrace special trees thought to give fertility. The appearance of these beliefs, in which the fruitfulness of trees suggests the fruitfulness of harvests and family-building, indicates that a society has made its first steps toward symbolic and abstract thinking.

TOEFL Reading

1 of 30

PAUSE TEST

SECTION EXIT

REVIEW | HELP | BACK | NEXT

HIDE TIME 00:08:45

More Available

1. It can be inferred from paragraph 1 of the passage that the peoples of Europe and North America associated trees with:

   a. travel to distant places
   b. the religions of older tribes
   c. dangerous forces of nature
   d. the common culture of humanity

Paragraph 1 is marked with an arrow [➜]

The Veneration of Trees

1 ➜ In *The Golden Bough,* his classic catalog of mythologies, Sir James George Frazer extensively documents the significance of trees in world religion. His chapters on tree spirits roam from Northern Europe to the Eastern Seaboard of what is now the United States to the islands of the Pacific. Despite the lack of contact among these regions, the veneration of trees united them. The woods that covered large areas of Europe and North America, in particular, were difficult to penetrate and dangerous to cross. It was not a great mental leap for people to see the trees that populated them as embodiments of the natural forces that governed their lives.

2 On the basis of Frazer's classification, one can derive three loose stages of tree worship. In the first, a society sees the tree as the physical body of the spirit that inhabits it, much as the human body can be seen as housing the mind. It is known that both the Celtic and the Germanic tribes that inhabited ancient Northern Europe regarded certain trees as sacred, setting them apart by species (as the Druids worshipped oaks) or by location (the way certain natural groves were regarded as natural temples or sacred spaces in what is now Germany). Early on, each of these trees was regarded as an animate being with both spirit and body. It had a distinct identity, like an individual person. This suggests that it was believed to have the same impulses and reactions as the people who venerated it.

3 Accordingly, ancient peoples had elaborate taboos designed to avoid causing offense to trees. These taboos were taken very seriously. In some places, one could be punished severely for injuring the bark of a tree or stealing its fruit. Before a tree was felled for human use, woodcutters in many world cultures would offer it both apologies and thanks for the resources it was about to provide them. This was necessary to avoid insulting the tree and inviting bad fortune. It was also the case, however, that injuries were said to cause suffering to trees as they did to people. In some societies, it was claimed that trees cry out in pain when struck or cut into. A tree's spirit and body are considered inseparable in this first stage.

4 A society makes a leap in sophistication and reaches Frazer's second stage when it begins to regard them as separate. That is, the spirit exists independently of the physical tree, even if it chooses to dwell there most of the time. The same spirit may thus take up residence in any tree of a forest; it is not killed when an individual tree is cut down. It is not bound to a single tree but rather stands for a group. The distinction may seem small, but it is a significant first step toward symbolic thinking. A forest, after all, is more than the sum of its parts. It encompasses not only its trees but also the animals and brush that flourish among them. The dangers of the forest are hidden; a traveler may or may not encounter them on a given journey. To think about a tree spirit identified with the forest as a whole, therefore, people had to think about phenomena that were removed from them in time and space—ideas rather than things. Such a tree spirit represented the potential and abstract rather than the concrete and immediate.

5 That transition is completed in the third stage. Liberated from each other, trees and their spirits can begin to be seen as symbols and embodiments of other natural processes of significance to primitive life: the power of weather and seasons to produce good or bad harvests, the mysteries of childbirth and disease. At that point, the veneration of trees reaches its stage of greatest complexity. Societies in both Eastern Europe and the South Pacific brought ceremonial offerings to trees in the hopes that they would furnish rain and sunshine. Women who hoped to bear children might be instructed to embrace special trees thought to give fertility. The appearance of these beliefs, in which the fruitfulness of trees suggests the fruitfulness of harvests and family-building, indicates that a society has made its first steps toward symbolic and abstract thinking.

More Available

2. The word penetrate in the passage is closest in meaning to:

a.   enter
b.   locate
c.   survive
d.   consider

The Veneration of Trees

1   In *The Golden Bough,* his classic catalog of mythologies, Sir James George Frazer extensively documents the significance of trees in world religion. His chapters on tree spirits roam from Northern Europe to the Eastern Seaboard of what is now the United States to the islands of the Pacific. Despite the lack of contact among these regions, the veneration of trees united them. The woods that covered large areas of Europe and North America, in particular, were difficult to penetrate and dangerous to cross. It was not a great mental leap for people to see the trees that populated them as embodiments of the natural forces that governed their lives.

2   On the basis of Frazer's classification, one can derive three loose stages of tree worship. In the first, a society sees the tree as the physical body of the spirit that inhabits it, much as the human body can be seen as housing the mind. It is known that both the Celtic and the Germanic tribes that inhabited ancient Northern Europe regarded certain trees as sacred, setting them apart by species (as the Druids worshipped oaks) or by location (the way certain natural groves were regarded as natural temples or sacred spaces in what is now Germany). Early on, each of these trees was regarded as an animate being with both spirit and body. It had a distinct identity, like an individual person. This suggests that it was believed to have the same impulses and reactions as the people who venerated it.

3   Accordingly, ancient peoples had elaborate taboos designed to avoid causing offense to trees. These taboos were taken very seriously. In some places, one could be punished severely for injuring the bark of a tree or stealing its fruit. Before a tree was felled for human use, woodcutters in many world cultures would offer it both apologies and thanks for the resources it was about to provide them. This was necessary to avoid insulting the tree and inviting bad fortune. It was also the case, however, that injuries were said to cause suffering to trees as they did to people. In some societies, it was claimed that trees cry out in pain when struck or cut into. A tree's spirit and body are considered inseparable in this first stage.

4   A society makes a leap in sophistication and reaches Frazer's second stage when it begins to regard them as separate. That is, the spirit exists independently of the physical tree, even if it chooses to dwell there most of the time. The same spirit may thus take up residence in any tree of a forest; it is not killed when an individual tree is cut down. It is not bound to a single tree but rather stands for a group. The distinction may seem small, but it is a significant first step toward symbolic thinking. A forest, after all, is more than the sum of its parts. It encompasses not only its trees but also the animals and brush that flourish among them. The dangers of the forest are hidden; a traveler may or may not encounter them on a given journey. To think about a tree spirit identified with the forest as a whole, therefore, people had to think about phenomena that were removed from them in time and space—ideas rather than things. Such a tree spirit represented the potential and abstract rather than the concrete and immediate.

5   That transition is completed in the third stage. Liberated from each other, trees and their spirits can begin to be seen as symbols and embodiments of other natural processes of significance to primitive life: the power of weather and seasons to produce good or bad harvests, the mysteries of childbirth and disease. At that point, the veneration of trees reaches its stage of greatest complexity. Societies in both Eastern Europe and the South Pacific brought ceremonial offerings to trees in the hopes that they would furnish rain and sunshine. Women who hoped to bear children might be instructed to embrace special trees thought to give fertility. The appearance of these beliefs, in which the fruitfulness of trees suggests the fruitfulness of harvests and family-building, indicates that a society has made its first steps toward symbolic and abstract thinking.

3. The author mentions the Druids in paragraph 2 as an example of a people that:

a.   exhibited all three stages of tree worship

b.   punished people for stealing fruit

c.   worshipped a particular species of tree

d.   cut down many trees as its civilization expanded

Paragraph 2 is marked with an arrow [➔]

The Veneration of Trees

1   In *The Golden Bough,* his classic catalog of mythologies, Sir James George Frazer extensively documents the significance of trees in world religion. His chapters on tree spirits roam from Northern Europe to the Eastern Seaboard of what is now the United States to the islands of the Pacific. Despite the lack of contact among these regions, the veneration of trees united them. The woods that covered large areas of Europe and North America, in particular, were difficult to penetrate and dangerous to cross. It was not a great mental leap for people to see the trees that populated them as embodiments of the natural forces that governed their lives.

2   ➔ On the basis of Frazer's classification, one can derive three loose stages of tree worship. In the first, a society sees the tree as the physical body of the spirit that inhabits it, much as the human body can be seen as housing the mind. It is known that both the Celtic and the Germanic tribes that inhabited ancient Northern Europe regarded certain trees as sacred, setting them apart by species (as the Druids worshipped oaks) or by location (the way certain natural groves were regarded as natural temples or sacred spaces in what is now Germany). Early on, each of these trees was regarded as an animate being with both spirit and body. It had a distinct identity, like an individual person. This suggests that it was believed to have the same impulses and reactions as the people who venerated it.

3   Accordingly, ancient peoples had elaborate taboos designed to avoid causing offense to trees. These taboos were taken very seriously. In some places, one could be punished severely for injuring the bark of a tree or stealing its fruit. Before a tree was felled for human use, woodcutters in many world cultures would offer it both apologies and thanks for the resources it was about to provide them. This was necessary to avoid insulting the tree and inviting bad fortune. It was also the case, however, that injuries were said to cause suffering to trees as they did to people. In some societies, it was claimed that trees cry out in pain when struck or cut into. A tree's spirit and body are considered inseparable in this first stage.

4   A society makes a leap in sophistication and reaches Frazer's second stage when it begins to regard them as separate. That is, the spirit exists independently of the physical tree, even if it chooses to dwell there most of the time. The same spirit may thus take up residence in any tree of a forest; it is not killed when an individual tree is cut down. It is not bound to a single tree but rather stands for a group. The distinction may seem small, but it is a significant first step toward symbolic thinking. A forest, after all, is more than the sum of its parts. It encompasses not only its trees but also the animals and brush that flourish among them. The dangers of the forest are hidden; a traveler may or may not encounter them on a given journey. To think about a tree spirit identified with the forest as a whole, therefore, people had to think about phenomena that were removed from them in time and space—ideas rather than things. Such a tree spirit represented the potential and abstract rather than the concrete and immediate.

5   That transition is completed in the third stage. Liberated from each other, trees and their spirits can begin to be seen as symbols and embodiments of other natural processes of significance to primitive life: the power of weather and seasons to produce good or bad harvests, the mysteries of childbirth and disease. At that point, the veneration of trees reaches its stage of greatest complexity. Societies in both Eastern Europe and the South Pacific brought ceremonial offerings to trees in the hopes that they would furnish rain and sunshine. Women who hoped to bear children might be instructed to embrace special trees thought to give fertility. The appearance of these beliefs, in which the fruitfulness of trees suggests the fruitfulness of harvests and family-building, indicates that a society has made its first steps toward symbolic and abstract thinking.

More Available

4. Which of the following is NOT mentioned as evidence that ancient peoples believed trees had individual spirits?

a. They apologized to a tree before cutting it down.
b. They had rules against injuring tree bark.
c. They thought trees could express pain.
d. They gave each tree a personal name.

The Veneration of Trees

1 In *The Golden Bough,* his classic catalog of mythologies, Sir James George Frazer extensively documents the significance of trees in world religion. His chapters on tree spirits roam from Northern Europe to the Eastern Seaboard of what is now the United States to the islands of the Pacific. Despite the lack of contact among these regions, the veneration of trees united them. The woods that covered large areas of Europe and North America, in particular, were difficult to penetrate and dangerous to cross. It was not a great mental leap for people to see the trees that populated them as embodiments of the natural forces that governed their lives.

2 On the basis of Frazer's classification, one can derive three loose stages of tree worship. In the first, a society sees the tree as the physical body of the spirit that inhabits it, much as the human body can be seen as housing the mind. It is known that both the Celtic and the Germanic tribes that inhabited ancient Northern Europe regarded certain trees as sacred, setting them apart by species (as the Druids worshipped oaks) or by location (the way certain natural groves were regarded as natural temples or sacred spaces in what is now Germany). Early on, each of these trees was regarded as an animate being with both spirit and body. It had a distinct identity, like an individual person. This suggests that it was believed to have the same impulses and reactions as the people who venerated it.

3 Accordingly, ancient peoples had elaborate taboos designed to avoid causing offense to trees. These taboos were taken very seriously. In some places, one could be punished severely for injuring the bark of a tree or stealing its fruit. Before a tree was felled for human use, woodcutters in many world cultures would offer it both apologies and thanks for the resources it was about to provide them. This was necessary to avoid insulting the tree and inviting bad fortune. It was also the case, however, that injuries were said to cause suffering to trees as they did to people. In some societies, it was claimed that trees cry out in pain when struck or cut into. A tree's spirit and body are considered inseparable in this first stage.

4 A society makes a leap in sophistication and reaches Frazer's second stage when it begins to regard them as separate. That is, the spirit exists independently of the physical tree, even if it chooses to dwell there most of the time. The same spirit may thus take up residence in any tree of a forest; it is not killed when an individual tree is cut down. It is not bound to a single tree but rather stands for a group. The distinction may seem small, but it is a significant first step toward symbolic thinking. A forest, after all, is more than the sum of its parts. It encompasses not only its trees but also the animals and brush that flourish among them. The dangers of the forest are hidden; a traveler may or may not encounter them on a given journey. To think about a tree spirit identified with the forest as a whole, therefore, people had to think about phenomena that were removed from them in time and space—ideas rather than things. Such a tree spirit represented the potential and abstract rather than the concrete and immediate.

5 That transition is completed in the third stage. Liberated from each other, trees and their spirits can begin to be seen as symbols and embodiments of other natural processes of significance to primitive life: the power of weather and seasons to produce good or bad harvests, the mysteries of childbirth and disease. At that point, the veneration of trees reaches its stage of greatest complexity. Societies in both Eastern Europe and the South Pacific brought ceremonial offerings to trees in the hopes that they would furnish rain and sunshine. Women who hoped to bear children might be instructed to embrace special trees thought to give fertility. The appearance of these beliefs, in which the fruitfulness of trees suggests the fruitfulness of harvests and family-building, indicates that a society has made its first steps toward symbolic and abstract thinking.

More Available

5. The second stage of tree worship discussed in the passage involves a distinction between:

a.   sacred trees and ordinary trees

b.   the spirit and the body of a tree

c.   trees with and without spirits

d.   single trees and trees in forests

The Veneration of Trees

1   In *The Golden Bough,* his classic catalog of mythologies, Sir James George Frazer extensively documents the significance of trees in world religion. His chapters on tree spirits roam from Northern Europe to the Eastern Seaboard of what is now the United States to the islands of the Pacific. Despite the lack of contact among these regions, the veneration of trees united them. The woods that covered large areas of Europe and North America, in particular, were difficult to penetrate and dangerous to cross. It was not a great mental leap for people to see the trees that populated them as embodiments of the natural forces that governed their lives.

2   On the basis of Frazer's classification, one can derive three loose stages of tree worship. In the first, a society sees the tree as the physical body of the spirit that inhabits it, much as the human body can be seen as housing the mind. It is known that both the Celtic and the Germanic tribes that inhabited ancient Northern Europe regarded certain trees as sacred, setting them apart by species (as the Druids worshipped oaks) or by location (the way certain natural groves were regarded as natural temples or sacred spaces in what is now Germany). Early on, each of these trees was regarded as an animate being with both spirit and body. It had a distinct identity, like an individual person. This suggests that it was believed to have the same impulses and reactions as the people who venerated it.

3   Accordingly, ancient peoples had elaborate taboos designed to avoid causing offense to trees. These taboos were taken very seriously. In some places, one could be punished severely for injuring the bark of a tree or stealing its fruit. Before a tree was felled for human use, woodcutters in many world cultures would offer it both apologies and thanks for the resources it was about to provide them. This was necessary to avoid insulting the tree and inviting bad fortune. It was also the case, however, that injuries were said to cause suffering to trees as they did to people. In some societies, it was claimed that trees cry out in pain when struck or cut into. A tree's spirit and body are considered inseparable in this first stage.

4   A society makes a leap in sophistication and reaches Frazer's second stage when it begins to regard them as separate. That is, the spirit exists independently of the physical tree, even if it chooses to dwell there most of the time. The same spirit may thus take up residence in any tree of a forest; it is not killed when an individual tree is cut down. It is not bound to a single tree but rather stands for a group. The distinction may seem small, but it is a significant first step toward symbolic thinking. A forest, after all, is more than the sum of its parts. It encompasses not only its trees but also the animals and brush that flourish among them. The dangers of the forest are hidden; a traveler may or may not encounter them on a given journey. To think about a tree spirit identified with the forest as a whole, therefore, people had to think about phenomena that were removed from them in time and space—ideas rather than things. Such a tree spirit represented the potential and abstract rather than the concrete and immediate.

5   That transition is completed in the third stage. Liberated from each other, trees and their spirits can begin to be seen as symbols and embodiments of other natural processes of significance to primitive life: the power of weather and seasons to produce good or bad harvests, the mysteries of childbirth and disease. At that point, the veneration of trees reaches its stage of greatest complexity. Societies in both Eastern Europe and the South Pacific brought ceremonial offerings to trees in the hopes that they would furnish rain and sunshine. Women who hoped to bear children might be instructed to embrace special trees thought to give fertility. The appearance of these beliefs, in which the fruitfulness of trees suggests the fruitfulness of harvests and family-building, indicates that a society has made its first steps toward symbolic and abstract thinking.

More Available

6. The author of the passage uses the phrase ideas rather than things to indicate that:

a. the forest was actually much less dangerous than people thought it to be

b. people stopped fearing the forest at the second stage of tree worship

c. some aspects of the forest can be imagined but not seen

d. many travelers were seriously hurt in the forest

The Veneration of Trees

1 In *The Golden Bough*, his classic catalog of mythologies, Sir James George Frazer extensively documents the significance of trees in world religion. His chapters on tree spirits roam from Northern Europe to the Eastern Seaboard of what is now the United States to the islands of the Pacific. Despite the lack of contact among these regions, the veneration of trees united them. The woods that covered large areas of Europe and North America, in particular, were difficult to penetrate and dangerous to cross. It was not a great mental leap for people to see the trees that populated them as embodiments of the natural forces that governed their lives.

2 On the basis of Frazer's classification, one can derive three loose stages of tree worship. In the first, a society sees the tree as the physical body of the spirit that inhabits it, much as the human body can be seen as housing the mind. It is known that both the Celtic and the Germanic tribes that inhabited ancient Northern Europe regarded certain trees as sacred, setting them apart by species (as the Druids worshipped oaks) or by location (the way certain natural groves were regarded as natural temples or sacred spaces in what is now Germany). Early on, each of these trees was regarded as an animate being with both spirit and body. It had a distinct identity, like an individual person. This suggests that it was believed to have the same impulses and reactions as the people who venerated it.

3 Accordingly, ancient peoples had elaborate taboos designed to avoid causing offense to trees. These taboos were taken very seriously. In some places, one could be punished severely for injuring the bark of a tree or stealing its fruit. Before a tree was felled for human use, woodcutters in many world cultures would offer it both apologies and thanks for the resources it was about to provide them. This was necessary to avoid insulting the tree and inviting bad fortune. It was also the case, however, that injuries were said to cause suffering to trees as they did to people. In some societies, it was claimed that trees cry out in pain when struck or cut into. A tree's spirit and body are considered inseparable in this first stage.

4 A society makes a leap in sophistication and reaches Frazer's second stage when it begins to regard them as separate. That is, the spirit exists independently of the physical tree, even if it chooses to dwell there most of the time. The same spirit may thus take up residence in any tree of a forest; it is not killed when an individual tree is cut down. It is not bound to a single tree but rather stands for a group. The distinction may seem small, but it is a significant first step toward symbolic thinking. A forest, after all, is more than the sum of its parts. It encompasses not only its trees but also the animals and brush that flourish among them. The dangers of the forest are hidden; a traveler may or may not encounter them on a given journey. To think about a tree spirit identified with the forest as a whole, therefore, people had to think about phenomena that were removed from them in time and space—ideas rather than things. Such a tree spirit represented the potential and abstract rather than the concrete and immediate.

5 That transition is completed in the third stage. Liberated from each other, trees and their spirits can begin to be seen as symbols and embodiments of other natural processes of significance to primitive life: the power of weather and seasons to produce good or bad harvests, the mysteries of childbirth and disease. At that point, the veneration of trees reaches its stage of greatest complexity. Societies in both Eastern Europe and the South Pacific brought ceremonial offerings to trees in the hopes that they would furnish rain and sunshine. Women who hoped to bear children might be instructed to embrace special trees thought to give fertility. The appearance of these beliefs, in which the fruitfulness of trees suggests the fruitfulness of harvests and family-building, indicates that a society has made its first steps toward symbolic and abstract thinking.

TOEFL Reading

PAUSE
TEST

SECTION
EXIT

REVIEW

HELP
?

BACK
←

NEXT
→

7 of 30

HIDE TIME   00:08:45

More Available

7. The author implies that the most complex phase of tree worship involves:

a.   the belief that all trees are sacred

b.   distinguishing between male and female tree spirits

c.   different ceremonies for different seasons

d.   the use of trees as symbols

The Veneration of Trees

1   In *The Golden Bough,* his classic catalog of mythologies, Sir James George Frazer extensively documents the significance of trees in world religion. His chapters on tree spirits roam from Northern Europe to the Eastern Seaboard of what is now the United States to the islands of the Pacific. Despite the lack of contact among these regions, the veneration of trees united them. The woods that covered large areas of Europe and North America, in particular, were difficult to penetrate and dangerous to cross. It was not a great mental leap for people to see the trees that populated them as embodiments of the natural forces that governed their lives.

2   On the basis of Frazer's classification, one can derive three loose stages of tree worship. In the first, a society sees the tree as the physical body of the spirit that inhabits it, much as the human body can be seen as housing the mind. It is known that both the Celtic and the Germanic tribes that inhabited ancient Northern Europe regarded certain trees as sacred, setting them apart by species (as the Druids worshipped oaks) or by location (the way certain natural groves were regarded as natural temples or sacred spaces in what is now Germany). Early on, each of these trees was regarded as an animate being with both spirit and body. It had a distinct identity, like an individual person. This suggests that it was believed to have the same impulses and reactions as the people who venerated it.

3   Accordingly, ancient peoples had elaborate taboos designed to avoid causing offense to trees. These taboos were taken very seriously. In some places, one could be punished severely for injuring the bark of a tree or stealing its fruit. Before a tree was felled for human use, woodcutters in many world cultures would offer it both apologies and thanks for the resources it was about to provide them. This was necessary to avoid insulting the tree and inviting bad fortune. It was also the case, however, that injuries were said to cause suffering to trees as they did to people. In some societies, it was claimed that trees cry out in pain when struck or cut into. A tree's spirit and body are considered inseparable in this first stage.

4   A society makes a leap in sophistication and reaches Frazer's second stage when it begins to regard them as separate. That is, the spirit exists independently of the physical tree, even if it chooses to dwell there most of the time. The same spirit may thus take up residence in any tree of a forest; it is not killed when an individual tree is cut down. It is not bound to a single tree but rather stands for a group. The distinction may seem small, but it is a significant first step toward symbolic thinking. A forest, after all, is more than the sum of its parts. It encompasses not only its trees but also the animals and brush that flourish among them. The dangers of the forest are hidden; a traveler may or may not encounter them on a given journey. To think about a tree spirit identified with the forest as a whole, therefore, people had to think about phenomena that were removed from them in time and space—ideas rather than things. Such a tree spirit represented the potential and abstract rather than the concrete and immediate.

5   That transition is completed in the third stage. Liberated from each other, trees and their spirits can begin to be seen as symbols and embodiments of other natural processes of significance to primitive life: the power of weather and seasons to produce good or bad harvests, the mysteries of childbirth and disease. At that point, the veneration of trees reaches its stage of greatest complexity. Societies in both Eastern Europe and the South Pacific brought ceremonial offerings to trees in the hopes that they would furnish rain and sunshine. Women who hoped to bear children might be instructed to embrace special trees thought to give fertility. The appearance of these beliefs, in which the fruitfulness of trees suggests the fruitfulness of harvests and family-building, indicates that a society has made its first steps toward symbolic and abstract thinking.

TOEFL Reading

PAUSE TEST   SECTION EXIT

8 of 30

REVIEW   HELP   BACK   NEXT

HIDE TIME   00:08:45

More Available

8. The word furnish in the passage is closest in meaning to:

a. explain
b. provide
c. avoid
d. refuse

The Veneration of Trees

1 In *The Golden Bough,* his classic catalog of mythologies, Sir James George Frazer extensively documents the significance of trees in world religion. His chapters on tree spirits roam from Northern Europe to the Eastern Seaboard of what is now the United States to the islands of the Pacific. Despite the lack of contact among these regions, the veneration of trees united them. The woods that covered large areas of Europe and North America, in particular, were difficult to penetrate and dangerous to cross. It was not a great mental leap for people to see the trees that populated them as embodiments of the natural forces that governed their lives.

2 On the basis of Frazer's classification, one can derive three loose stages of tree worship. In the first, a society sees the tree as the physical body of the spirit that inhabits it, much as the human body can be seen as housing the mind. It is known that both the Celtic and the Germanic tribes that inhabited ancient Northern Europe regarded certain trees as sacred, setting them apart by species (as the Druids worshipped oaks) or by location (the way certain natural groves were regarded as natural temples or sacred spaces in what is now Germany). Early on, each of these trees was regarded as an animate being with both spirit and body. It had a distinct identity, like an individual person. This suggests that it was believed to have the same impulses and reactions as the people who venerated it.

3 Accordingly, ancient peoples had elaborate taboos designed to avoid causing offense to trees. These taboos were taken very seriously. In some places, one could be punished severely for injuring the bark of a tree or stealing its fruit. Before a tree was felled for human use, woodcutters in many world cultures would offer it both apologies and thanks for the resources it was about to provide them. This was necessary to avoid insulting the tree and inviting bad fortune. It was also the case, however, that injuries were said to cause suffering to trees as they did to people. In some societies, it was claimed that trees cry out in pain when struck or cut into. A tree's spirit and body are considered inseparable in this first stage.

4 A society makes a leap in sophistication and reaches Frazer's second stage when it begins to regard them as separate. That is, the spirit exists independently of the physical tree, even if it chooses to dwell there most of the time. The same spirit may thus take up residence in any tree of a forest; it is not killed when an individual tree is cut down. It is not bound to a single tree but rather stands for a group. The distinction may seem small, but it is a significant first step toward symbolic thinking. A forest, after all, is more than the sum of its parts. It encompasses not only its trees but also the animals and brush that flourish among them. The dangers of the forest are hidden; a traveler may or may not encounter them on a given journey. To think about a tree spirit identified with the forest as a whole, therefore, people had to think about phenomena that were removed from them in time and space—ideas rather than things. Such a tree spirit represented the potential and abstract rather than the concrete and immediate.

5 That transition is completed in the third stage. Liberated from each other, trees and their spirits can begin to be seen as symbols and embodiments of other natural processes of significance to primitive life: the power of weather and seasons to produce good or bad harvests, the mysteries of childbirth and disease. At that point, the veneration of trees reaches its stage of greatest complexity. Societies in both Eastern Europe and the South Pacific brought ceremonial offerings to trees in the hopes that they would furnish rain and sunshine. Women who hoped to bear children might be instructed to embrace special trees thought to give fertility. The appearance of these beliefs, in which the fruitfulness of trees suggests the fruitfulness of harvests and family-building, indicates that a society has made its first steps toward symbolic and abstract thinking.

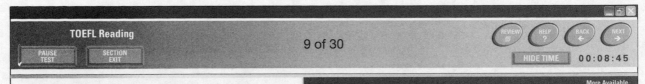

More Available

9. According to paragraph 5 of the passage, ancient peoples saw special meaning in:

a.   the ability of trees to bear fruit

b.   the three stages in the life cycle of a tree

c.   trees that required little rain and sun

d.   the raising of trees by women

Paragraph 5 is marked with an arrow [➜]

The Veneration of Trees

1   In *The Golden Bough,* his classic catalog of mythologies, Sir James George Frazer extensively documents the significance of trees in world religion. His chapters on tree spirits roam from Northern Europe to the Eastern Seaboard of what is now the United States to the islands of the Pacific. Despite the lack of contact among these regions, the veneration of trees united them. The woods that covered large areas of Europe and North America, in particular, were difficult to penetrate and dangerous to cross. It was not a great mental leap for people to see the trees that populated them as embodiments of the natural forces that governed their lives.

2   On the basis of Frazer's classification, one can derive three loose stages of tree worship. In the first, a society sees the tree as the physical body of the spirit that inhabits it, much as the human body can be seen as housing the mind. It is known that both the Celtic and the Germanic tribes that inhabited ancient Northern Europe regarded certain trees as sacred, setting them apart by species (as the Druids worshipped oaks) or by location (the way certain natural groves were regarded as natural temples or sacred spaces in what is now Germany). Early on, each of these trees was regarded as an animate being with both spirit and body. It had a distinct identity, like an individual person. This suggests that it was believed to have the same impulses and reactions as the people who venerated it.

3   Accordingly, ancient peoples had elaborate taboos designed to avoid causing offense to trees. These taboos were taken very seriously. In some places, one could be punished severely for injuring the bark of a tree or stealing its fruit. Before a tree was felled for human use, woodcutters in many world cultures would offer it both apologies and thanks for the resources it was about to provide them. This was necessary to avoid insulting the tree and inviting bad fortune. It was also the case, however, that injuries were said to cause suffering to trees as they did to people. In some societies, it was claimed that trees cry out in pain when struck or cut into. A tree's spirit and body are considered inseparable in this first stage.

4   A society makes a leap in sophistication and reaches Frazer's second stage when it begins to regard them as separate. That is, the spirit exists independently of the physical tree, even if it chooses to dwell there most of the time. The same spirit may thus take up residence in any tree of a forest; it is not killed when an individual tree is cut down. It is not bound to a single tree but rather stands for a group. The distinction may seem small, but it is a significant first step toward symbolic thinking. A forest, after all, is more than the sum of its parts. It encompasses not only its trees but also the animals and brush that flourish among them. The dangers of the forest are hidden; a traveler may or may not encounter them on a given journey. To think about a tree spirit identified with the forest as a whole, therefore, people had to think about phenomena that were removed from them in time and space—ideas rather than things. Such a tree spirit represented the potential and abstract rather than the concrete and immediate.

5   ➜ That transition is completed in the third stage. Liberated from each other, trees and their spirits can begin to be seen as symbols and embodiments of other natural processes of significance to primitive life: the power of weather and seasons to produce good or bad harvests, the mysteries of childbirth and disease. At that point, the veneration of trees reaches its stage of greatest complexity. Societies in both Eastern Europe and the South Pacific brought ceremonial offerings to trees in the hopes that they would furnish rain and sunshine. Women who hoped to bear children might be instructed to embrace special trees thought to give fertility. The appearance of these beliefs, in which the fruitfulness of trees suggests the fruitfulness of harvests and family-building, indicates that a society has made its first steps toward symbolic and abstract thinking.

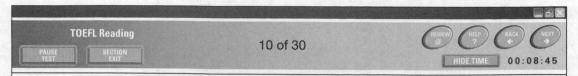
10. Directions: An introductory sentence for a brief summary of the passage is provided below. Complete the summary by selecting the THREE answer choices that express the most important ideas in the passage. Some sentences do not belong in the summary because they express ideas that are not presented in the passage or are minor ideas in the passage. *This question is worth 2 points.*

Three basic levels of tree worship can be observed in *The Golden Bough*.

-
-
-

Answer Choices	
It was forbidden to cut down certain trees because they would be seriously offended by an injury.	Ancient Germans believed certain groves were sacred and used them as temples, but Druids venerated the oak tree in particular.
Certain peoples came to believe that tree spirits were independent of individual trees and, instead, resided in the whole forest.	Some societies believed each tree was the body for an individual spirit, the way the human body houses an individual's mind.
More is known about the ceremonies of Europe than about the ceremonies of North America and the South Pacific.	Society progressed toward more symbolic and abstract thinking when tree spirits were believed to control natural forces such as crops and human fertility.

Mercury Pollution

1 When most people think or talk about dangers to our environment, they focus on general terms like "pollution," "smog," and "acid rain." Also, they often focus on the impact of supposedly man-made chemicals and compounds. But to truly understand the risks to our environment, it's helpful to focus on the danger of specific chemicals, which are often otherwise naturally-occurring elements that have been spread harmfully by man. One of the largest threats to our environment is mercury: Hg on the periodic table of elements.

2 At room temperature, mercury, a metal, exists as a silvery-white liquid. However, it vaporizes readily when heat is applied, and it can stay suspended in the air for more than a year. The largest sources of mercury pollution in the United States are coal-fired power plants. Emissions from these plants account for 70 percent of the mercury that enters our oceans, lakes, and streams. Air currents carry these particles far from the source and are capable of polluting bodies of water thousands of miles away.

3 Mercury particles released into the air fall into these waterways and quickly enter aquatic food chains. First, mercury attaches to sediments (fragments of organic and inorganic material that settle to the bottom of the body of water). Second, bacteria change the mercury into methyl mercury, a highly toxic substance. Third, phytoplankton feed on the organic matter in sediments and absorb the methyl mercury. Fourth, fish then eat the mercury-contaminated phytoplankton; the larger the fish and the longer it lives, the more concentrated the methyl mercury in its system becomes.

TOEFL Reading

PAUSE TEST

SECTION EXIT

REVIEW

HELP ?

BACK

NEXT

HIDE TIME   00:08:45

More Available

The mercury can then move higher up the food chain when humans eat fish that have absorbed high amounts of mercury.

4 Studies indicate that mercury levels in U.S. waterways have increased anywhere from 100 to 400 percent over the course of the last century, and no river, lake, or ocean seems immune. It is important to note that, thanks to the U.S. Clean Air Act and efforts by industry to curb unnecessary discharges as well as better sewage treatment methods, the levels have been in slow decline since the 1970s. However, this minor decline is relatively miniscule in comparison to the major increase in the years prior.

5 If you've ever experienced that "rotten egg" smell during low tide at a coastal area, you've seen (or smelled) methylation in action. Methylation is the conversion of mercury in sediments to methyl mercury by sulfate-reducing bacteria. While this methylation is a natural process, the industrial discharge of mercury has greatly accelerated the process beyond what the ecosystem is able to absorb safely. This methylation not only impacts aquatic species, but also harms humans and other land-based wildlife.

6 Most of the fish and shellfish that humans eat live solely in coastal areas or frequent coastal areas and feed on the fish that live there. At the same time, most methylation takes place in coastal areas. Therefore, methyl mercury moves up the food chain from plankton to lobster, bluefish, winter flounder, tuna, and many other species eaten extensively by man. The methyl mercury binds to the protein in fish, residing in the muscle of the fish. This muscle is exactly what we eat: the fillet.

7 The short-term impact of digestion of toxic methyl mercury is obviously a concern. ■ More troubling, however, is its long-term impact on species up and down the food chain. ■ In Wisconsin, scientists have studied the decline of chick production in loons (aquatic birds). ■ They have made a positive link to mercury concentration in eggs which exceeds the concentration found to be toxic in laboratory studies. ■ Through that example, the lasting impact of methyl mercury far from the source of the pollution can be seen.

8 One of the great wonders of the Earth is the interconnectivity of all the world's ecosystems. This interconnectivity gives us the range and diversity of wildlife that we all enjoy and it also allowed life on the planet to endure through cataclysmic events, such as asteroid impacts and the ice ages. However, it is this very interconnectivity that makes our ecosystems so vulnerable. Mercury pollution is unfortunately one of many examples of an environmental impact far removed from the source of the pollution; understanding the process by which the pollution spreads up the food chain is one of many steps to ameliorate the impact of such pollution.

More Available

11. According to paragraph 2, what accounts for 70% of toxic mercury pollution?

a.   Air currents
b.   Vaporization
c.   Coal-fired power plants
d.   A silvery-white liquid

Paragraph 2 is marked with an arrow [→]

Mercury Pollution

1   When most people think or talk about dangers to our environment, they focus on general terms like "pollution," "smog," and "acid-rain." Also, they often focus on the impact of supposedly man-made chemicals and compounds. But to truly understand the risks to our environment, it's helpful to focus on the danger of specific chemicals, which are often otherwise naturally-occurring elements that have been spread harmfully by man. One of the largest threats to our environment is mercury: Hg on the periodic table of elements.

2   → At room temperature, mercury, a metal, exists as a silvery-white liquid. However, it vaporizes readily when heat is applied, and can stay suspended in the air for more than a year. The largest sources of mercury pollution in the United States are coal-fired power plants. Emissions from these plants account for 70 percent of the mercury that enters our oceans, lakes, and streams. Air currents carry these particles far from the source and are capable of polluting bodies of water thousands of miles away.

3   Mercury particles released into the air fall into these waterways and quickly enter aquatic food chains. First, mercury attaches to sediments (fragments of organic and inorganic material that settle to the bottom of the body of water). Second, bacteria change the mercury into methyl mercury, a highly toxic substance. Third, phytoplankton feed on the organic matter in sediments and absorb the methyl mercury. Fourth, fish then eat the mercury-contaminated phytoplankton; the larger the fish and the longer it lives, the more concentrated the methyl mercury in its system becomes. The mercury can then move higher up the food chain when humans eat fish that have absorbed high amounts of mercury.

4   Studies indicate that mercury levels in U.S. waterways have increased anywhere from 100 to 400 percent over the course of the last century, and no river, lake, or ocean seems immune. It is important to note that, thanks to the U.S. Clean Air Act and efforts by industry to curb unnecessary discharges as well as better sewage treatment methods, the levels have been in slow decline since the 1970s. However, this minor decline is relatively miniscule in comparison to the major increase in the years prior.

5   If you've ever experienced that "rotten egg" smell during low tide at a coastal area, you've seen (or smelled) methylation in action. Methylation is the conversion of mercury in sediments to methyl mercury by sulfate-reducing bacteria. While this methylation is a natural process, the industrial discharge of mercury has greatly accelerated the process beyond what the ecosystem is able to absorb safely. This methylation not only impacts aquatic species, but also harms humans and other land-based wildlife.

6   Most of the fish and shellfish that humans eat live solely in coastal areas or frequent coastal areas and feed on the fish that live there. At the same time, most methylation takes place in coastal areas. Therefore, methyl mercury moves up the food chain from plankton to lobster, bluefish, winter flounder, tuna, and many other species eaten extensively by man. The methyl mercury binds to the protein in fish, residing in the muscle of the fish. This muscle is exactly what we eat: the fillet.

7   The short-term impact of digestion of toxic methyl mercury is obviously a concern. ■ More troubling, however, is its long-term impact on species up and down the food chain. ■ In Wisconsin, scientists have studied the decline of chick production in loons (aquatic birds). ■ They have made a positive link to mercury concentration in eggs which exceeds the concentration found to be toxic in laboratory studies. ■ Through that example, the lasting impact of methyl mercury far from the source of the pollution can be seen.

8   One of the great wonders of the Earth is the interconnectivity of all the world's ecosystems. This interconnectivity gives us the range and diversity of wildlife that we all enjoy and it also allowed life on the planet to endure through cataclysmic events, such as asteroid impacts and the ice ages. However, it is this very interconnectivity that makes our ecosystems so vulnerable. Mercury pollution is unfortunately one of many examples of an environmental impact far removed from the source of the pollution; understanding the process by which the pollution spreads up the food chain is one of many steps to ameliorate the impact of such pollution.

More Available

12. The word concentrated in the passage is closest in meaning to:

a. clustered
b. thought
c. separated
d. reduced

Mercury Pollution

1 When most people think or talk about dangers to our environment, they focus on general terms like "pollution," "smog," and "acid-rain." Also, they often focus on the impact of supposedly man-made chemicals and compounds. But to truly understand the risks to our environment, it's helpful to focus on the danger of specific chemicals, which are often otherwise naturally-occurring elements that have been spread harmfully by man. One of the largest threats to our environment is mercury: Hg on the periodic table of elements.

2 At room temperature, mercury, a metal, exists as a silvery-white liquid. However, it vaporizes readily when heat is applied, and can stay suspended in the air for more than a year. The largest sources of mercury pollution in the United States are coal-fired power plants. Emissions from these plants account for 70 percent of the mercury that enters our oceans, lakes, and streams. Air currents carry these particles far from the source and are capable of polluting bodies of water thousands of miles away.

3 Mercury particles released into the air fall into these waterways and quickly enter aquatic food chains. First, mercury attaches to sediments (fragments of organic and inorganic material that settle to the bottom of the body of water). Second, bacteria change the mercury into methyl mercury, a highly toxic substance. Third, phytoplankton feed on the organic matter in sediments and absorb the methyl mercury. Fourth, fish then eat the mercury-contaminated phytoplankton; the larger the fish and the longer it lives, the more concentrated the methyl mercury in its system becomes. The mercury can then move higher up the food chain when humans eat fish that have absorbed high amounts of mercury.

4 Studies indicate that mercury levels in U.S. waterways have increased anywhere from 100 to 400 percent over the course of the last century, and no river, lake, or ocean seems immune. It is important to note that, thanks to the U.S. Clean Air Act and efforts by industry to curb unnecessary discharges as well as better sewage treatment methods, the levels have been in slow decline since the 1970s. However, this minor decline is relatively miniscule in comparison to the major increase in the years prior.

5 If you've ever experienced that "rotten egg" smell during low tide at a coastal area, you've seen (or smelled) methylation in action. Methylation is the conversion of mercury in sediments to methyl mercury by sulfate-reducing bacteria. While this methylation is a natural process, the industrial discharge of mercury has greatly accelerated the process beyond what the ecosystem is able to absorb safely. This methylation not only impacts aquatic species, but also harms humans and other land-based wildlife.

6 Most of the fish and shellfish that humans eat live solely in coastal areas or frequent coastal areas and feed on the fish that live there. At the same time, most methylation takes place in coastal areas. Therefore, methyl mercury moves up the food chain from plankton to lobster, bluefish, winter flounder, tuna, and many other species eaten extensively by man. The methyl mercury binds to the protein in fish, residing in the muscle of the fish. This muscle is exactly what we eat: the fillet.

7 The short-term impact of digestion of toxic methyl mercury is obviously a concern. ■ More troubling, however, is its long-term impact on species up and down the food chain. ■ In Wisconsin, scientists have studied the decline of chick production in loons (aquatic birds). ■ They have made a positive link to mercury concentration in eggs which exceeds the concentration found to be toxic in laboratory studies. ■ Through that example, the lasting impact of methyl mercury far from the source of the pollution can be seen.

8 One of the great wonders of the Earth is the interconnectivity of all the world's ecosystems. This interconnectivity gives us the range and diversity of wildlife that we all enjoy and it also allowed life on the planet to endure through cataclysmic events, such as asteroid impacts and the ice ages. However, it is this very interconnectivity that makes our ecosystems so vulnerable. Mercury pollution is unfortunately one of many examples of an environmental impact far removed from the source of the pollution; understanding the process by which the pollution spreads up the food chain is one of many steps to ameliorate the impact of such pollution.

More Available

13. All of the following are mentioned in the passage as reasons why mercury levels in the environment have been in slow decline since the 1970s EXCEPT:

a. the Clean Air Act
b. reduction in sulfate-producing bacteria
c. better sewage treatment
d. changes in industrial practice

Mercury Pollution

1 When most people think or talk about dangers to our environment, they focus on general terms like "pollution," "smog," and "acid-rain." Also, they often focus on the impact of supposedly man-made chemicals and compounds. But to truly understand the risks to our environment, it's helpful to focus on the danger of specific chemicals, which are often otherwise naturally-occurring elements that have been spread harmfully by man. One of the largest threats to our environment is mercury: Hg on the periodic table of elements.

2 At room temperature, mercury, a metal, exists as a silvery-white liquid. However, it vaporizes readily when heat is applied, and can stay suspended in the air for more than a year. The largest sources of mercury pollution in the United States are coal-fired power plants. Emissions from these plants account for 70 percent of the mercury that enters our oceans, lakes, and streams. Air currents carry these particles far from the source and are capable of polluting bodies of water thousands of miles away.

3 Mercury particles released into the air fall into these waterways and quickly enter aquatic food chains. First, mercury attaches to sediments (fragments of organic and inorganic material that settle to the bottom of the body of water). Second, bacteria change the mercury into methyl mercury, a highly toxic substance. Third, phytoplankton feed on the organic matter in sediments and absorb the methyl mercury. Fourth, fish then eat the mercury-contaminated phytoplankton; the larger the fish and the longer it lives, the more concentrated the methyl mercury in its system becomes. The mercury can then move higher up the food chain when humans eat fish that have absorbed high amounts of mercury.

4 Studies indicate that mercury levels in U.S. waterways have increased anywhere from 100 to 400 percent over the course of the last century, and no river, lake, or ocean seems immune. It is important to note that, thanks to the U.S. Clean Air Act and efforts by industry to curb unnecessary discharges as well as better sewage treatment methods, the levels have been in slow decline since the 1970s. However, this minor decline is relatively miniscule in comparison to the major increase in the years prior.

5 If you've ever experienced that "rotten egg" smell during low tide at a coastal area, you've seen (or smelled) methylation in action. Methylation is the conversion of mercury in sediments to methyl mercury by sulfate-reducing bacteria. While this methylation is a natural process, the industrial discharge of mercury has greatly accelerated the process beyond what the ecosystem is able to absorb safely. This methylation not only impacts aquatic species, but also harms humans and other land-based wildlife.

6 Most of the fish and shellfish that humans eat live solely in coastal areas or frequent coastal areas and feed on the fish that live there. At the same time, most methylation takes place in coastal areas. Therefore, methyl mercury moves up the food chain from plankton to lobster, bluefish, winter flounder, tuna, and many other species eaten extensively by man. The methyl mercury binds to the protein in fish, residing in the muscle of the fish. This muscle is exactly what we eat: the fillet.

7 The short-term impact of digestion of toxic methyl mercury is obviously a concern. ■ More troubling, however, is its long-term impact on species up and down the food chain. ■ In Wisconsin, scientists have studied the decline of chick production in loons (aquatic birds). ■ They have made a positive link to mercury concentration in eggs which exceeds the concentration found to be toxic in laboratory studies. ■ Through that example, the lasting impact of methyl mercury far from the source of the pollution can be seen.

8 One of the great wonders of the Earth is the interconnectivity of all the world's ecosystems. This interconnectivity gives us the range and diversity of wildlife that we all enjoy and it also allowed life on the planet to endure through cataclysmic events, such as asteroid impacts and the ice ages. However, it is this very interconnectivity that makes our ecosystems so vulnerable. Mercury pollution is unfortunately one of many examples of an environmental impact far removed from the source of the pollution; understanding the process by which the pollution spreads up the food chain is one of many steps to ameliorate the impact of such pollution.

More Available

14. According to paragraph 6, coastal areas are the locations for most:

a. tuna
b. methylation
c. mercury pollution sources
d. ecosystems

Paragraph 6 is marked with an arrow [→]

Mercury Pollution

1 When most people think or talk about dangers to our environment, they focus on general terms like "pollution," "smog," and "acid-rain." Also, they often focus on the impact of supposedly man-made chemicals and compounds. But to truly understand the risks to our environment, it's helpful to focus on the danger of specific chemicals, which are often otherwise naturally-occurring elements that have been spread harmfully by man. One of the largest threats to our environment is mercury: Hg on the periodic table of elements.

2 At room temperature, mercury, a metal, exists as a silvery-white liquid. However, it vaporizes readily when heat is applied, and can stay suspended in the air for more than a year. The largest sources of mercury pollution in the United States are coal-fired power plants. Emissions from these plants account for 70 percent of the mercury that enters our oceans, lakes, and streams. Air currents carry these particles far from the source and are capable of polluting bodies of water thousands of miles away.

3 Mercury particles released into the air fall into these waterways and quickly enter aquatic food chains. First, mercury attaches to sediments (fragments of organic and inorganic material that settle to the bottom of the body of water). Second, bacteria change the mercury into methyl mercury, a highly toxic substance. Third, phytoplankton feed on the organic matter in sediments and absorb the methyl mercury. Fourth, fish then eat the mercury-contaminated phytoplankton; the larger the fish and the longer it lives, the more concentrated the methyl mercury in its system becomes. The mercury can then move higher up the food chain when humans eat fish that have absorbed high amounts of mercury.

4 Studies indicate that mercury levels in U.S. waterways have increased anywhere from 100 to 400 percent over the course of the last century, and no river, lake, or ocean seems immune. It is important to note that, thanks to the U.S. Clean Air Act and efforts by industry to curb unnecessary discharges as well as better sewage treatment methods, the levels have been in slow decline since the 1970s. However, this minor decline is relatively miniscule in comparison to the major increase in the years prior.

5 If you've ever experienced that "rotten egg" smell during low tide at a coastal area, you've seen (or smelled) methylation in action. Methylation is the conversion of mercury in sediments to methyl mercury by sulfate-reducing bacteria. While this methylation is a natural process, the industrial discharge of mercury has greatly accelerated the process beyond what the ecosystem is able to absorb safely. This methylation not only impacts aquatic species, but also harms humans and other land-based wildlife.

6 → Most of the fish and shellfish that humans eat live solely in coastal areas or frequent coastal areas and feed on the fish that live there. At the same time, most methylation takes place in coastal areas. Therefore, methyl mercury moves up the food chain from plankton to lobster, bluefish, winter flounder, tuna, and many other species eaten extensively by man. The methyl mercury binds to the protein in fish, residing in the muscle of the fish. This muscle is exactly what we eat: the fillet.

7 The short-term impact of digestion of toxic methyl mercury is obviously a concern. ■ More troubling, however, is its long-term impact on species up and down the food chain. ■ In Wisconsin, scientists have studied the decline of chick production in loons (aquatic birds). ■ They have made a positive link to mercury concentration in eggs which exceeds the concentration found to be toxic in laboratory studies. ■ Through that example, the lasting impact of methyl mercury far from the source of the pollution can be seen.

8 One of the great wonders of the Earth is the interconnectivity of all the world's ecosystems. This interconnectivity gives us the range and diversity of wildlife that we all enjoy and it also allowed life on the planet to endure through cataclysmic events, such as asteroid impacts and the ice ages. However, it is this very interconnectivity that makes our ecosystems so vulnerable. Mercury pollution is unfortunately one of many examples of an environmental impact far removed from the source of the pollution; understanding the process by which the pollution spreads up the food chain is one of many steps to ameliorate the impact of such pollution.

More Available

15. The word its in the passage refers to:

a. long-term impact
b. methyl mercury
c. food chain
d. coal

Mercury Pollution

1 When most people think or talk about dangers to our environment, they focus on general terms like "pollution," "smog," and "acid-rain." Also, they often focus on the impact of supposedly man-made chemicals and compounds. But to truly understand the risks to our environment, it's helpful to focus on the danger of specific chemicals, which are often otherwise naturally-occurring elements that have been spread harmfully by man. One of the largest threats to our environment is mercury: Hg on the periodic table of elements.

2 At room temperature, mercury, a metal, exists as a silvery-white liquid. However, it vaporizes readily when heat is applied, and can stay suspended in the air for more than a year. The largest sources of mercury pollution in the United States are coal-fired power plants. Emissions from these plants account for 70 percent of the mercury that enters our oceans, lakes, and streams. Air currents carry these particles far from the source and are capable of polluting bodies of water thousands of miles away.

3 Mercury particles released into the air fall into these waterways and quickly enter aquatic food chains. First, mercury attaches to sediments (fragments of organic and inorganic material that settle to the bottom of the body of water). Second, bacteria change the mercury into methyl mercury, a highly toxic substance. Third, phytoplankton feed on the organic matter in sediments and absorb the methyl mercury. Fourth, fish then eat the mercury-contaminated phytoplankton; the larger the fish and the longer it lives, the more concentrated the methyl mercury in its system becomes. The mercury can then move higher up the food chain when humans eat fish that have absorbed high amounts of mercury.

4 Studies indicate that mercury levels in U.S. waterways have increased anywhere from 100 to 400 percent over the course of the last century, and no river, lake, or ocean seems immune. It is important to note that, thanks to the U.S. Clean Air Act and efforts by industry to curb unnecessary discharges as well as better sewage treatment methods, the levels have been in slow decline since the 1970s. However, this minor decline is relatively miniscule in comparison to the major increase in the years prior.

5 If you've ever experienced that "rotten egg" smell during low tide at a coastal area, you've seen (or smelled) methylation in action. Methylation is the conversion of mercury in sediments to methyl mercury by sulfate-reducing bacteria. While this methylation is a natural process, the industrial discharge of mercury has greatly accelerated the process beyond what the ecosystem is able to absorb safely. This methylation not only impacts aquatic species, but also harms humans and other land-based wildlife.

6 Most of the fish and shellfish that humans eat live solely in coastal areas or frequent coastal areas and feed on the fish that live there. At the same time, most methylation takes place in coastal areas. Therefore, methyl mercury moves up the food chain from plankton to lobster, bluefish, winter flounder, tuna, and many other species eaten extensively by man. The methyl mercury binds to the protein in fish, residing in the muscle of the fish. This muscle is exactly what we eat: the fillet.

7 The short-term impact of digestion of toxic methyl mercury is obviously a concern. ■ More troubling, however, is its long-term impact on species up and down the food chain. ■ In Wisconsin, scientists have studied the decline of chick production in loons (aquatic birds). ■ They have made a positive link to mercury concentration in eggs which exceeds the concentration found to be toxic in laboratory studies. ■ Through that example, the lasting impact of methyl mercury far from the source of the pollution can be seen.

8 One of the great wonders of the Earth is the interconnectivity of all the world's ecosystems. This interconnectivity gives us the range and diversity of wildlife that we all enjoy and it also allowed life on the planet to endure through cataclysmic events, such as asteroid impacts and the ice ages. However, it is this very interconnectivity that makes our ecosystems so vulnerable. Mercury pollution is unfortunately one of many examples of an environmental impact far removed from the source of the pollution; understanding the process by which the pollution spreads up the food chain is one of many steps to ameliorate the impact of such pollution.

More Available

16. Which of the following is mentioned in paragraph 7 as one of the long-term impacts of methyl mercury pollution?

a. Increase in sulfate-reducing bacteria in sediment

b. Reduction in the number of fish in coastal areas

c. Danger to the reproductive cycle of birds

d. Concentrated mercury in lobsters

Paragraph 7 is marked with an arrow [➔]

Mercury Pollution

1   When most people think or talk about dangers to our environment, they focus on general terms like "pollution," "smog," and "acid-rain." Also, they often focus on the impact of supposedly man-made chemicals and compounds. But to truly understand the risks to our environment, it's helpful to focus on the danger of specific chemicals, which are often otherwise naturally-occurring elements that have been spread harmfully by man. One of the largest threats to our environment is mercury: Hg on the periodic table of elements.

2   At room temperature, mercury, a metal, exists as a silvery-white liquid. However, it vaporizes readily when heat is applied, and can stay suspended in the air for more than a year. The largest sources of mercury pollution in the United States are coal-fired power plants. Emissions from these plants account for 70 percent of the mercury that enters our oceans, lakes, and streams. Air currents carry these particles far from the source and are capable of polluting bodies of water thousands of miles away.

3   Mercury particles released into the air fall into these waterways and quickly enter aquatic food chains. First, mercury attaches to sediments (fragments of organic and inorganic material that settle to the bottom of the body of water). Second, bacteria change the mercury into methyl mercury, a highly toxic substance. Third, phytoplankton feed on the organic matter in sediments and absorb the methyl mercury. Fourth, fish then eat the mercury-contaminated phytoplankton; the larger the fish and the longer it lives, the more concentrated the methyl mercury in its system becomes. The mercury can then move higher up the food chain when humans eat fish that have absorbed high amounts of mercury.

4   Studies indicate that mercury levels in U.S. waterways have increased anywhere from 100 to 400 percent over the course of the last century, and no river, lake, or ocean seems immune. It is important to note that, thanks to the U.S. Clean Air Act and efforts by industry to curb unnecessary discharges as well as better sewage treatment methods, the levels have been in slow decline since the 1970s. However, this minor decline is relatively miniscule in comparison to the major increase in the years prior.

5   If you've ever experienced that "rotten egg" smell during low tide at a coastal area, you've seen (or smelled) methylation in action. Methylation is the conversion of mercury in sediments to methyl mercury by sulfate-reducing bacteria. While this methylation is a natural process, the industrial discharge of mercury has greatly accelerated the process beyond what the ecosystem is able to absorb safely. This methylation not only impacts aquatic species, but also harms humans and other land-based wildlife.

6   Most of the fish and shellfish that humans eat live solely in coastal areas or frequent coastal areas and feed on the fish that live there. At the same time, most methylation takes place in coastal areas. Therefore, methyl mercury moves up the food chain from plankton to lobster, bluefish, winter flounder, tuna, and many other species eaten extensively by man. The methyl mercury binds to the protein in fish, residing in the muscle of the fish. This muscle is exactly what we eat: the fillet.

7   ➔ The short-term impact of digestion of toxic methyl mercury is obviously a concern. ■ More troubling, however, is its long-term impact on species up and down the food chain. ■ In Wisconsin, scientists have studied the decline of chick production in loons (aquatic birds). ■ They have made a positive link to mercury concentration in eggs which exceeds the concentration found to be toxic in laboratory studies. ■ Through that example, the lasting impact of methyl mercury far from the source of the pollution can be seen.

8   One of the great wonders of the Earth is the interconnectivity of all the world's ecosystems. This interconnectivity gives us the range and diversity of wildlife that we all enjoy and it also allowed life on the planet to endure through cataclysmic events, such as asteroid impacts and the ice ages. However, it is this very interconnectivity that makes our ecosystems so vulnerable. Mercury pollution is unfortunately one of many examples of an environmental impact far removed from the source of the pollution; understanding the process by which the pollution spreads up the food chain is one of many steps to ameliorate the impact of such pollution.

More Available

17. According to paragraph 8, the interconnectivity of the Earth's ecosystems is also:

a. the reason the ecosystems are so susceptible to pollution

b. the cause of mercury pollution

c. the reason methyl mercury is such a harmful substance

d. the cure for pollution from coal-fired power plants

Paragraph 8 is marked with an arrow [➔]

Mercury Pollution

1   When most people think or talk about dangers to our environment, they focus on general terms like "pollution," "smog," and "acid-rain." Also, they often focus on the impact of supposedly man-made chemicals and compounds. But to truly understand the risks to our environment, it's helpful to focus on the danger of specific chemicals, which are often otherwise naturally-occurring elements that have been spread harmfully by man. One of the largest threats to our environment is mercury: Hg on the periodic table of elements.

2   At room temperature, mercury, a metal, exists as a silvery-white liquid. However, it vaporizes readily when heat is applied, and can stay suspended in the air for more than a year. The largest sources of mercury pollution in the United States are coal-fired power plants. Emissions from these plants account for 70 percent of the mercury that enters our oceans, lakes, and streams. Air currents carry these particles far from the source and are capable of polluting bodies of water thousands of miles away.

3   Mercury particles released into the air fall into these waterways and quickly enter aquatic food chains. First, mercury attaches to sediments (fragments of organic and inorganic material that settle to the bottom of the body of water). Second, bacteria change the mercury into methyl mercury, a highly toxic substance. Third, phytoplankton feed on the organic matter in sediments and absorb the methyl mercury. Fourth, fish then eat the mercury-contaminated phytoplankton; the larger the fish and the longer it lives, the more concentrated the methyl mercury in its system becomes. The mercury can then move higher up the food chain when humans eat fish that have absorbed high amounts of mercury.

4   Studies indicate that mercury levels in U.S. waterways have increased anywhere from 100 to 400 percent over the course of the last century, and no river, lake, or ocean seems immune. It is important to note that, thanks to the U.S. Clean Air Act and efforts by industry to curb unnecessary discharges as well as better sewage treatment methods, the levels have been in slow decline since the 1970s. However, this minor decline is relatively miniscule in comparison to the major increase in the years prior.

5   If you've ever experienced that "rotten egg" smell during low tide at a coastal area, you've seen (or smelled) methylation in action. Methylation is the conversion of mercury in sediments to methyl mercury by sulfate-reducing bacteria. While this methylation is a natural process, the industrial discharge of mercury has greatly accelerated the process beyond what the ecosystem is able to absorb safely. This methylation not only impacts aquatic species, but also harms humans and other land-based wildlife.

6   Most of the fish and shellfish that humans eat live solely in coastal areas or frequent coastal areas and feed on the fish that live there. At the same time, most methylation takes place in coastal areas. Therefore, methyl mercury moves up the food chain from plankton to lobster, bluefish, winter flounder, tuna, and many other species eaten extensively by man. The methyl mercury binds to the protein in fish, residing in the muscle of the fish. This muscle is exactly what we eat: the fillet.

7   The short-term impact of digestion of toxic methyl mercury is obviously a concern. ■ More troubling, however, is its long-term impact on species up and down the food chain. ■ In Wisconsin, scientists have studied the decline of chick production in loons (aquatic birds). ■ They have made a positive link to mercury concentration in eggs which exceeds the concentration found to be toxic in laboratory studies. ■ Through that example, the lasting impact of methyl mercury far from the source of the pollution can be seen.

8   ➔ One of the great wonders of the Earth is the interconnectivity of all the world's ecosystems. This interconnectivity gives us the range and diversity of wildlife that we all enjoy and it also allowed life on the planet to endure through cataclysmic events, such as asteroid impacts and the ice ages. However, it is this very interconnectivity that makes our ecosystems so vulnerable. Mercury pollution is unfortunately one of many examples of an environmental impact far removed from the source of the pollution; understanding the process by which the pollution spreads up the food chain is one of many steps to ameliorate the impact of such pollution.

More Available

18. The word ameliorate in the passage is closest in meaning to:

a. enlarge
b. impact
c. summarize
d. lessen

Mercury Pollution

1   When most people think or talk about dangers to our environment, they focus on general terms like "pollution," "smog," and "acid-rain." Also, they often focus on the impact of supposedly man-made chemicals and compounds. But to truly understand the risks to our environment, it's helpful to focus on the danger of specific chemicals, which are often otherwise naturally-occurring elements that have been spread harmfully by man. One of the largest threats to our environment is mercury: Hg on the periodic table of elements.

2   At room temperature, mercury, a metal, exists as a silvery-white liquid. However, it vaporizes readily when heat is applied, and can stay suspended in the air for more than a year. The largest sources of mercury pollution in the United States are coal-fired power plants. Emissions from these plants account for 70 percent of the mercury that enters our oceans, lakes, and streams. Air currents carry these particles far from the source and are capable of polluting bodies of water thousands of miles away.

3   Mercury particles released into the air fall into these waterways and quickly enter aquatic food chains. First, mercury attaches to sediments (fragments of organic and inorganic material that settle to the bottom of the body of water). Second, bacteria change the mercury into methyl mercury, a highly toxic substance. Third, phytoplankton feed on the organic matter in sediments and absorb the methyl mercury. Fourth, fish then eat the mercury-contaminated phytoplankton; the larger the fish and the longer it lives, the more concentrated the methyl mercury in its system becomes. The mercury can then move higher up the food chain when humans eat fish that have absorbed high amounts of mercury.

4   Studies indicate that mercury levels in U.S. waterways have increased anywhere from 100 to 400 percent over the course of the last century, and no river, lake, or ocean seems immune. It is important to note that, thanks to the U.S. Clean Air Act and efforts by industry to curb unnecessary discharges as well as better sewage treatment methods, the levels have been in slow decline since the 1970s. However, this minor decline is relatively miniscule in comparison to the major increase in the years prior.

5   If you've ever experienced that "rotten egg" smell during low tide at a coastal area, you've seen (or smelled) methylation in action. Methylation is the conversion of mercury in sediments to methyl mercury by sulfate-reducing bacteria. While this methylation is a natural process, the industrial discharge of mercury has greatly accelerated the process beyond what the ecosystem is able to absorb safely. This methylation not only impacts aquatic species, but also harms humans and other land-based wildlife.

6   Most of the fish and shellfish that humans eat live solely in coastal areas or frequent coastal areas and feed on the fish that live there. At the same time, most methylation takes place in coastal areas. Therefore, methyl mercury moves up the food chain from plankton to lobster, bluefish, winter flounder, tuna, and many other species eaten extensively by man. The methyl mercury binds to the protein in fish, residing in the muscle of the fish. This muscle is exactly what we eat: the fillet.

7   The short-term impact of digestion of toxic methyl mercury is obviously a concern. ■ More troubling, however, is its long-term impact on species up and down the food chain. ■ In Wisconsin, scientists have studied the decline of chick production in loons (aquatic birds). ■ They have made a positive link to mercury concentration in eggs which exceeds the concentration found to be toxic in laboratory studies. ■ Through that example, the lasting impact of methyl mercury far from the source of the pollution can be seen.

8   One of the great wonders of the Earth is the interconnectivity of all the world's ecosystems. This interconnectivity gives us the range and diversity of wildlife that we all enjoy and it also allowed life on the planet to endure through cataclysmic events, such as asteroid impacts and the ice ages. However, it is this very interconnectivity that makes our ecosystems so vulnerable. Mercury pollution is unfortunately one of many examples of an environmental impact far removed from the source of the pollution; understanding the process by which the pollution spreads up the food chain is one of many steps to ameliorate the impact of such pollution.

More Available

19. Look at the four squares ■ that indicate where the following sentence can be added to the passage.

Thus, the harmful effects of methyl mercury are passed from adult to young and will impact the health of the species for years to come.

Where would the sentence best fit?

Click on a square ■ to add the sentence to the passage.

[Here, on this practice test, circle your answer below.]

a.   Square 1
b.   Square 2
c.   Square 3
d.   Square 4

Mercury Pollution

1   When most people think or talk about dangers to our environment, they focus on general terms like "pollution," "smog," and "acid-rain." Also, they often focus on the impact of supposedly man-made chemicals and compounds. But to truly understand the risks to our environment, it's helpful to focus on the danger of specific chemicals, which are often otherwise naturally-occurring elements that have been spread harmfully by man. One of the largest threats to our environment is mercury: Hg on the periodic table of elements.

2   At room temperature, mercury, a metal, exists as a silvery-white liquid. However, it vaporizes readily when heat is applied, and can stay suspended in the air for more than a year. The largest sources of mercury pollution in the United States are coal-fired power plants. Emissions from these plants account for 70 percent of the mercury that enters our oceans, lakes, and streams. Air currents carry these particles far from the source and are capable of polluting bodies of water thousands of miles away.

3   Mercury particles released into the air fall into these waterways and quickly enter aquatic food chains. First, mercury attaches to sediments (fragments of organic and inorganic material that settle to the bottom of the body of water). Second, bacteria change the mercury into methyl mercury, a highly toxic substance. Third, phytoplankton feed on the organic matter in sediments and absorb the methyl mercury. Fourth, fish then eat the mercury-contaminated phytoplankton; the larger the fish and the longer it lives, the more concentrated the methyl mercury in its system becomes. The mercury can then move higher up the food chain when humans eat fish that have absorbed high amounts of mercury.

4   Studies indicate that mercury levels in U.S. waterways have increased anywhere from 100 to 400 percent over the course of the last century, and no river, lake, or ocean seems immune. It is important to note that, thanks to the U.S. Clean Air Act and efforts by industry to curb unnecessary discharges as well as better sewage treatment methods, the levels have been in slow decline since the 1970s. However, this minor decline is relatively miniscule in comparison to the major increase in the years prior.

5   If you've ever experienced that "rotten egg" smell during low tide at a coastal area, you've seen (or smelled) methylation in action. Methylation is the conversion of mercury in sediments to methyl mercury by sulfate-reducing bacteria. While this methylation is a natural process, the industrial discharge of mercury has greatly accelerated the process beyond what the ecosystem is able to absorb safely. This methylation not only impacts aquatic species, but also harms humans and other land-based wildlife.

6   Most of the fish and shellfish that humans eat live solely in coastal areas or frequent coastal areas and feed on the fish that live there. At the same time, most methylation takes place in coastal areas. Therefore, methyl mercury moves up the food chain from plankton to lobster, bluefish, winter flounder, tuna, and many other species eaten extensively by man. The methyl mercury binds to the protein in fish, residing in the muscle of the fish. This muscle is exactly what we eat: the fillet.

7   The short-term impact of digestion of toxic methyl mercury is obviously a concern. ■ More troubling, however, is its long-term impact on species up and down the food chain. ■ In Wisconsin, scientists have studied the decline of chick production in loons (aquatic birds). ■ They have made a positive link to mercury concentration in eggs which exceeds the concentration found to be toxic in laboratory studies. ■ Through that example, the lasting impact of methyl mercury far from the source of the pollution can be seen.

8   One of the great wonders of the Earth is the interconnectivity of all the world's ecosystems. This interconnectivity gives us the range and diversity of wildlife that we all enjoy and it also allowed life on the planet to endure through cataclysmic events, such as asteroid impacts and the ice ages. However, it is this very interconnectivity that makes our ecosystems so vulnerable. Mercury pollution is unfortunately one of many examples of an environmental impact far removed from the source of the pollution; understanding the process by which the pollution spreads up the food chain is one of many steps to ameliorate the impact of such pollution.

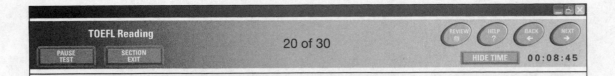

20. **Directions:** An introductory sentence for a brief summary of the passage is provided below. Complete the summary by selecting the THREE answer choices that express the most important ideas in the passage. Some sentences do not belong in the summary because they express ideas that are not presented in the passage or are minor ideas in the passage. *This question is worth 2 points.*

> Mercury pollution is one example of a type of pollution that has short-term and long-term effects far from the source of the pollution.

-
-
-

Answer Choices	
Air currents carry Mercury particles far from the source and are capable of polluting bodies of water thousands of miles away.	Mercury pollution is increasing in the United States despite the U.S. Clean Air Act and efforts of industry.
Mercury is transformed into the toxic methyl mercury and moves up the food chain to cause harm for organisms at every level all the way up to humans.	The methyl mercury binds to the protein in fish, residing in the muscle.
Sulfate-reducing bacteria cause the "rotten egg" smell that exists at coastal areas during low tide.	The harmful effects of methyl mercury are passed from adult to young and will impact the health of many species for years to come.

Hormones in the Body

1 Until the beginning of the twentieth century, the nervous system was thought to control all communication within the body and the resulting integration of behavior. Scientists had determined that nerves ran, essentially, on electrical impulses. These impulses were thought to be the engine for thought, emotion, movement, and internal processes such as digestion. However, experiments by William Bayliss and Ernest Starling on the chemical secretin, which is produced in the small intestine when food enters the stomach, eventually challenged that view. From the small intestine, secretin travels through the bloodstream to the pancreas. There, it stimulates the release of digestive chemicals. In this fashion, the intestinal cells that produce secretin ultimately regulate the production of different chemicals in a different organ, the pancreas.

2 Such a coordination of processes had been thought to require control by the nervous system; Bayliss and Starling showed that it could occur through chemicals alone. This discovery spurred Starling to coin the term *hormone* to refer to secretin, taking it from the Greek word *hormon,* meaning "to excite" or "to set in motion." A hormone is a chemical produced by one tissue to make things happen elsewhere.

3 As more hormones were discovered, they were categorized, primarily according to the process by which they operated on the body. Some glands which make up the endocrine system—such as the thyroid and pituitary glands—secrete hormones directly into the bloodstream. The exocrine system consists of organs and glands that

produce substances that are used outside the bloodstream, primarily for digestion. The pancreas is one such organ, although it secretes some chemicals into the blood and thus is also part of the endocrine system.

4 Much has been learned about hormones since their discovery. Some play such key roles in regulating bodily processes or behavior that their absence would cause immediate death. The most abundant hormones have effects that are less obviously urgent but can be more far-reaching and difficult to track: They modify moods and affect human behavior, even some behavior we normally think of as voluntary. Hormonal systems are very intricate. Even minute amounts of the right chemicals can suppress appetite, calm aggression, and change the attitude of a parent toward a child. Certain hormones accelerate the development of the body, regulating growth and form; others may even define an individual's personality characteristics. The quantities and proportions of hormones produced change with age, so scientists have given a great deal of study to shifts in the endocrine system over time in the hopes of alleviating ailments associated with aging.

5 In fact, some hormone therapies are already very common. ■ A combination of estrogen and progesterone has been prescribed for decades to women who want to reduce mood swings, sudden changes in body temperature, and other discomforts caused by lower natural levels of those hormones as they enter middle age. ■ Known as hormone replacement therapy (HRT), the treatment was also believed to prevent weakening of the bones. ■ At least one study has linked HRT with a heightened risk of heart disease and certain types of cancer.

TOEFL Reading

PAUSE TEST

SECTION EXIT

REVIEW

HELP ?

BACK ←

NEXT →

HIDE TIME 00:08:45

More Available

HRT may also increase the likelihood that blood clots—dangerous because they could travel through the bloodstream and block major blood vessels—will form. Some proponents of HRT have tempered their enthusiasm in the face of this new evidence, recommending it only to patients whose symptoms interfere with their abilities to live normal lives. ■

6　Human growth hormone may also be given to patients who are secreting abnormally low amounts on their own. Because of the complicated effects the growth hormone has on the body, such treatments are generally restricted to children who would be pathologically small in stature without it. Growth hormone affects not just physical size but also the digestion of food and the aging process. Researchers and family physicians tend to agree that it is foolhardy to dispense it in cases in which the risks are not clearly outweighed by the benefits.

More Available

21. The word engine in the passage is closest in meaning to:

a. desire
b. origin
c. science
d. chemical

Hormones in the Body

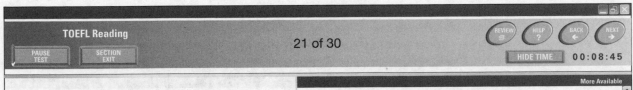

1 Until the beginning of the twentieth century, the nervous system was thought to control all communication within the body and the resulting integration of behavior. Scientists had determined that nerves ran, essentially, on electrical impulses. These impulses were thought to be the engine for thought, emotion, movement, and internal processes such as digestion. However, experiments by William Bayliss and Ernest Starling on the chemical secretin, which is produced in the small intestine when food enters the stomach, eventually challenged that view. From the small intestine, secretin travels through the bloodstream to the pancreas. There, it stimulates the release of digestive chemicals. In this fashion, the intestinal cells that produce secretin ultimately regulate the production of different chemicals in a different organ, the pancreas.

2 Such a coordination of processes had been thought to require control by the nervous system; Bayliss and Starling showed that it could occur through chemicals alone. This discovery spurred Starling to coin the term *hormone* to refer to secretin, taking it from the Greek word *hormon,* meaning "to excite" or "to set in motion." A hormone is a chemical produced by one tissue to make things happen elsewhere.

3 As more hormones were discovered, they were categorized, primarily according to the process by which they operated on the body. Some glands which make up the endocrine system—such as the thyroid and pituitary glands—secrete hormones directly into the bloodstream. The exocrine system consists of organs and glands that produce substances that are used outside the bloodstream, primarily for digestion. The pancreas is one such organ, although it secretes some chemicals into the blood and thus is also part of the endocrine system.

4 Much has been learned about hormones since their discovery. Some play such key roles in regulating bodily processes or behavior that their absence would cause immediate death. The most abundant hormones have effects that are less obviously urgent but can be more far-reaching and difficult to track: They modify moods and affect human behavior, even some behavior we normally think of as voluntary. Hormonal systems are very intricate. Even minute amounts of the right chemicals can suppress appetite, calm aggression, and change the attitude of a parent toward a child. Certain hormones accelerate the development of the body, regulating growth and form; others may even define an individual's personality characteristics. **The quantities and proportions of hormones produced change with age, so scientists have given a great deal of study to shifts in the endocrine system over time in the hopes of alleviating ailments associated with aging.**

5 In fact, some hormone therapies are already very common. ■ **A combination of estrogen and progesterone has been prescribed for decades to women who want to reduce mood swings, sudden changes in body temperature, and other discomforts caused by lower natural levels of those hormones as they enter middle age.** ■ Known as hormone replacement therapy (HRT), the treatment was also believed to prevent weakening of the bones. ■ At least one study has linked HRT with a heightened risk of heart disease and certain types of cancer. **HRT may also increase the likelihood that blood clots—dangerous because they could travel through the bloodstream and block major blood vessels—will form.** Some proponents of HRT have tempered their enthusiasm in the face of this new evidence, recommending it only to patients whose symptoms interfere with their abilities to live normal lives. ■

6 Human growth hormone may also be given to patients who are secreting abnormally low amounts on their own. **Because of the complicated effects the growth hormone has on the body, such treatments are generally restricted to children who would be pathologically small in stature without it.** Growth hormone affects not just physical size but also the digestion of food and the aging process. Researchers and family physicians tend to agree that it is foolhardy to dispense it in cases in which the risks are not clearly outweighed by the benefits.

More Available

22. The word it in the passage refers to:

a. secretin
b. small intestine
c. bloodstream
d. pancreas

Hormones in the Body

1 Until the beginning of the twentieth century, the nervous system was thought to control all communication within the body and the resulting integration of behavior. Scientists had determined that nerves ran, essentially, on electrical impulses. These impulses were thought to be the engine for thought, emotion, movement, and internal processes such as digestion. However, experiments by William Bayliss and Ernest Starling on the chemical secretin, which is produced in the small intestine when food enters the stomach, eventually challenged that view. From the small intestine, secretin travels through the bloodstream to the pancreas. There, it stimulates the release of digestive chemicals. In this fashion, the intestinal cells that produce secretin ultimately regulate the production of different chemicals in a different organ, the pancreas.

2 Such a coordination of processes had been thought to require control by the nervous system; Bayliss and Starling showed that it could occur through chemicals alone. This discovery spurred Starling to coin the term *hormone* to refer to secretin, taking it from the Greek word *hormon,* meaning "to excite" or "to set in motion." A hormone is a chemical produced by one tissue to make things happen elsewhere.

3 As more hormones were discovered, they were categorized, primarily according to the process by which they operated on the body. Some glands which make up the endocrine system—such as the thyroid and pituitary glands—secrete hormones directly into the bloodstream. The exocrine system consists of organs and glands that produce substances that are used outside the bloodstream, primarily for digestion. The pancreas is one such organ, although it secretes some chemicals into the blood and thus is also part of the endocrine system.

4 Much has been learned about hormones since their discovery. Some play such key roles in regulating bodily processes or behavior that their absence would cause immediate death. The most abundant hormones have effects that are less obviously urgent but can be more far-reaching and difficult to track: They modify moods and affect human behavior, even some behavior we normally think of as voluntary. Hormonal systems are very intricate. Even minute amounts of the right chemicals can suppress appetite, calm aggression, and change the attitude of a parent toward a child. Certain hormones accelerate the development of the body, regulating growth and form; others may even define an individual's personality characteristics. **The quantities and proportions of hormones produced change with age, so scientists have given a great deal of study to shifts in the endocrine system over time in the hopes of alleviating ailments associated with aging.**

5 In fact, some hormone therapies are already very common. ■ **A combination of estrogen and progesterone has been prescribed for decades to women who want to reduce mood swings, sudden changes in body temperature, and other discomforts caused by lower natural levels of those hormones as they enter middle age.** ■ Known as hormone replacement therapy (HRT), the treatment was also believed to prevent weakening of the bones. ■ At least one study has linked HRT with a heightened risk of heart disease and certain types of cancer. **HRT may also increase the likelihood that blood clots—dangerous because they could travel through the bloodstream and block major blood vessels—will form.** Some proponents of HRT have tempered their enthusiasm in the face of this new evidence, recommending it only to patients whose symptoms interfere with their abilities to live normal lives. ■

6 Human growth hormone may also be given to patients who are secreting abnormally low amounts on their own. **Because of the complicated effects the growth hormone has on the body, such treatments are generally restricted to children who would be pathologically small in stature without it.** Growth hormone affects not just physical size but also the digestion of food and the aging process. Researchers and family physicians tend to agree that it is foolhardy to dispense it in cases in which the risks are not clearly outweighed by the benefits.

TOEFL Reading

23 of 30

PAUSE TEST   SECTION EXIT

REVIEW   HELP ?   BACK ←   NEXT →

HIDE TIME   00:08:45

More Available

23. To be considered a hormone, a chemical produced in the body must:

a. be part of the digestive process

b. influence the operations of the nervous system

c. affect processes in a different part of the body

d. regulate attitudes and behavior

Hormones in the Body

1 Until the beginning of the twentieth century, the nervous system was thought to control all communication within the body and the resulting integration of behavior. Scientists had determined that nerves ran, essentially, on electrical impulses. These impulses were thought to be the engine for thought, emotion, movement, and internal processes such as digestion. However, experiments by William Bayliss and Ernest Starling on the chemical secretin, which is produced in the small intestine when food enters the stomach, eventually challenged that view. From the small intestine, secretin travels through the bloodstream to the pancreas. There, it stimulates the release of digestive chemicals. In this fashion, the intestinal cells that produce secretin ultimately regulate the production of different chemicals in a different organ, the pancreas.

2 Such a coordination of processes had been thought to require control by the nervous system; Bayliss and Starling showed that it could occur through chemicals alone. This discovery spurred Starling to coin the term *hormone* to refer to secretin, taking it from the Greek word *hormon,* meaning "to excite" or "to set in motion." A hormone is a chemical produced by one tissue to make things happen elsewhere.

3 As more hormones were discovered, they were categorized, primarily according to the process by which they operated on the body. Some glands which make up the endocrine system—such as the thyroid and pituitary glands—secrete hormones directly into the bloodstream. The exocrine system consists of organs and glands that produce substances that are used outside the bloodstream, primarily for digestion. The pancreas is one such organ, although it secretes some chemicals into the blood and thus is also part of the endocrine system.

4 Much has been learned about hormones since their discovery. Some play such key roles in regulating bodily processes or behavior that their absence would cause immediate death. The most abundant hormones have effects that are less obviously urgent but can be more far-reaching and difficult to track: They modify moods and affect human behavior, even some behavior we normally think of as voluntary. Hormonal systems are very intricate. Even minute amounts of the right chemicals can suppress appetite, calm aggression, and change the attitude of a parent toward a child. Certain hormones accelerate the development of the body, regulating growth and form; others may even define an individual's personality characteristics. **The quantities and proportions of hormones produced change with age, so scientists have given a great deal of study to shifts in the endocrine system over time in the hopes of alleviating ailments associated with aging.**

5 In fact, some hormone therapies are already very common. ■ **A combination of estrogen and progesterone has been prescribed for decades to women who want to reduce mood swings, sudden changes in body temperature, and other discomforts caused by lower natural levels of those hormones as they enter middle age.** ■ Known as hormone replacement therapy (HRT), the treatment was also believed to prevent weakening of the bones. ■ At least one study has linked HRT with a heightened risk of heart disease and certain types of cancer. **HRT may also increase the likelihood that blood clots—dangerous because they could travel through the bloodstream and block major blood vessels— will form.** Some proponents of HRT have tempered their enthusiasm in the face of this new evidence, recommending it only to patients whose symptoms interfere with their abilities to live normal lives. ■

6 Human growth hormone may also be given to patients who are secreting abnormally low amounts on their own. **Because of the complicated effects the growth hormone has on the body, such treatments are generally restricted to children who would be pathologically small in stature without it.** Growth hormone affects not just physical size but also the digestion of food and the aging process. Researchers and family physicians tend to agree that it is foolhardy to dispense it in cases in which the risks are not clearly outweighed by the benefits.

More Available

24. The hormones mentioned in paragraph 3 are categorized according to:

a.   whether scientists understand their function

b.   how frequently they release hormones into the body

c.   whether the hormones they secrete influence the aging process

d.   whether they secrete chemicals into the blood

Paragraph 3 is marked with an arrow [➔]

Hormones in the Body

1   Until the beginning of the twentieth century, the nervous system was thought to control all communication within the body and the resulting integration of behavior. Scientists had determined that nerves ran, essentially, on electrical impulses. These impulses were thought to be the engine for thought, emotion, movement, and internal processes such as digestion. However, experiments by William Bayliss and Ernest Starling on the chemical secretin, which is produced in the small intestine when food enters the stomach, eventually challenged that view. From the small intestine, secretin travels through the bloodstream to the pancreas. There, it stimulates the release of digestive chemicals. In this fashion, the intestinal cells that produce secretin ultimately regulate the production of different chemicals in a different organ, the pancreas.

2   Such a coordination of processes had been thought to require control by the nervous system; Bayliss and Starling showed that it could occur through chemicals alone. This discovery spurred Starling to coin the term *hormone* to refer to secretin, taking it from the Greek word *hormon,* meaning "to excite" or "to set in motion." A hormone is a chemical produced by one tissue to make things happen elsewhere.

3   ➔ As more hormones were discovered, they were categorized, primarily according to the process by which they operated on the body. Some glands which make up the endocrine system—such as the thyroid and pituitary glands—secrete hormones directly into the bloodstream. The exocrine system consists of organs and glands that produce substances that are used outside the bloodstream, primarily for digestion. The pancreas is one such organ, although it secretes some chemicals into the blood and thus is also part of the endocrine system.

4   Much has been learned about hormones since their discovery. Some play such key roles in regulating bodily processes or behavior that their absence would cause immediate death. The most abundant hormones have effects that are less obviously urgent but can be more far-reaching and difficult to track: They modify moods and affect human behavior, even some behavior we normally think of as voluntary. Hormonal systems are very intricate. Even minute amounts of the right chemicals can suppress appetite, calm aggression, and change the attitude of a parent toward a child. Certain hormones accelerate the development of the body, regulating growth and form; others may even define an individual's personality characteristics. **The quantities and proportions of hormones produced change with age, so scientists have given a great deal of study to shifts in the endocrine system over time in the hopes of alleviating ailments associated with aging.**

5   In fact, some hormone therapies are already very common. ■ **A combination of estrogen and progesterone has been prescribed for decades to women who want to reduce mood swings, sudden changes in body temperature, and other discomforts caused by lower natural levels of those hormones as they enter middle age.** ■ Known as hormone replacement therapy (HRT), the treatment was also believed to prevent weakening of the bones. ■ At least one study has linked HRT with a heightened risk of heart disease and certain types of cancer. **HRT may also increase the likelihood that blood clots—dangerous because they could travel through the bloodstream and block major blood vessels— will form.** Some proponents of HRT have tempered their enthusiasm in the face of this new evidence, recommending it only to patients whose symptoms interfere with their abilities to live normal lives. ■

6   Human growth hormone may also be given to patients who are secreting abnormally low amounts on their own. **Because of the complicated effects the growth hormone has on the body, such treatments are generally restricted to children who would be pathologically small in stature without it.** Growth hormone affects not just physical size but also the digestion of food and the aging process. Researchers and family physicians tend to agree that it is foolhardy to dispense it in cases in which the risks are not clearly outweighed by the benefits.

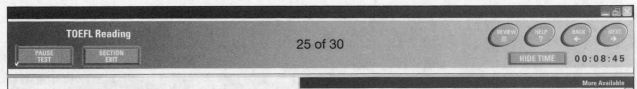

More Available

25. The word minute in the passage is closest in meaning to:

a. sudden
b. small
c. seconds
d. noticeable

Hormones in the Body

1   Until the beginning of the twentieth century, the nervous system was thought to control all communication within the body and the resulting integration of behavior. Scientists had determined that nerves ran, essentially, on electrical impulses. These impulses were thought to be the engine for thought, emotion, movement, and internal processes such as digestion. However, experiments by William Bayliss and Ernest Starling on the chemical secretin, which is produced in the small intestine when food enters the stomach, eventually challenged that view. From the small intestine, secretin travels through the bloodstream to the pancreas. There, it stimulates the release of digestive chemicals. In this fashion, the intestinal cells that produce secretin ultimately regulate the production of different chemicals in a different organ, the pancreas.

2   Such a coordination of processes had been thought to require control by the nervous system; Bayliss and Starling showed that it could occur through chemicals alone. This discovery spurred Starling to coin the term *hormone* to refer to secretin, taking it from the Greek word *hormon,* meaning "to excite" or "to set in motion." A hormone is a chemical produced by one tissue to make things happen elsewhere.

3   As more hormones were discovered, they were categorized, primarily according to the process by which they operated on the body. Some glands which make up the endocrine system—such as the thyroid and pituitary glands—secrete hormones directly into the bloodstream. The exocrine system consists of organs and glands that produce substances that are used outside the bloodstream, primarily for digestion. The pancreas is one such organ, although it secretes some chemicals into the blood and thus is also part of the endocrine system.

4   Much has been learned about hormones since their discovery. Some play such key roles in regulating bodily processes or behavior that their absence would cause immediate death. The most abundant hormones have effects that are less obviously urgent but can be more far-reaching and difficult to track: They modify moods and affect human behavior, even some behavior we normally think of as voluntary. Hormonal systems are very intricate. Even minute amounts of the right chemicals can suppress appetite, calm aggression, and change the attitude of a parent toward a child. Certain hormones accelerate the development of the body, regulating growth and form; others may even define an individual's personality characteristics. **The quantities and proportions of hormones produced change with age, so scientists have given a great deal of study to shifts in the endocrine system over time in the hopes of alleviating ailments associated with aging.**

5   In fact, some hormone therapies are already very common. ■ **A combination of estrogen and progesterone has been prescribed for decades to women who want to reduce mood swings, sudden changes in body temperature, and other discomforts caused by lower natural levels of those hormones as they enter middle age.** ■ Known as hormone replacement therapy (HRT), the treatment was also believed to prevent weakening of the bones. ■ At least one study has linked HRT with a heightened risk of heart disease and certain types of cancer. **HRT may also increase the likelihood that blood clots—dangerous because they could travel through the bloodstream and block major blood vessels—will form.** Some proponents of HRT have tempered their enthusiasm in the face of this new evidence, recommending it only to patients whose symptoms interfere with their abilities to live normal lives. ■

6   Human growth hormone may also be given to patients who are secreting abnormally low amounts on their own. **Because of the complicated effects the growth hormone has on the body, such treatments are generally restricted to children who would be pathologically small in stature without it.** Growth hormone affects not just physical size but also the digestion of food and the aging process. Researchers and family physicians tend to agree that it is foolhardy to dispense it in cases in which the risks are not clearly outweighed by the benefits.

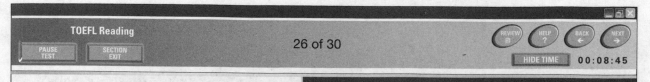

More Available

26. The word tempered in the passage is closest in meaning to:

a. decreased
b. advertised
c. prescribed
d. researched

Hormones in the Body

1 Until the beginning of the twentieth century, the nervous system was thought to control all communication within the body and the resulting integration of behavior. Scientists had determined that nerves ran, essentially, on electrical impulses. These impulses were thought to be the engine for thought, emotion, movement, and internal processes such as digestion. However, experiments by William Bayliss and Ernest Starling on the chemical secretin, which is produced in the small intestine when food enters the stomach, eventually challenged that view. From the small intestine, secretin travels through the bloodstream to the pancreas. There, it stimulates the release of digestive chemicals. In this fashion, the intestinal cells that produce secretin ultimately regulate the production of different chemicals in a different organ, the pancreas.

2 Such a coordination of processes had been thought to require control by the nervous system; Bayliss and Starling showed that it could occur through chemicals alone. This discovery spurred Starling to coin the term *hormone* to refer to secretin, taking it from the Greek word *hormon,* meaning "to excite" or "to set in motion." A hormone is a chemical produced by one tissue to make things happen elsewhere.

3 As more hormones were discovered, they were categorized, primarily according to the process by which they operated on the body. Some glands which make up the endocrine system—such as the thyroid and pituitary glands—secrete hormones directly into the bloodstream. The exocrine system consists of organs and glands that produce substances that are used outside the bloodstream, primarily for digestion. The pancreas is one such organ, although it secretes some chemicals into the blood and thus is also part of the endocrine system.

4 Much has been learned about hormones since their discovery. Some play such key roles in regulating bodily processes or behavior that their absence would cause immediate death. The most abundant hormones have effects that are less obviously urgent but can be more far-reaching and difficult to track: They modify moods and affect human behavior, even some behavior we normally think of as voluntary. Hormonal systems are very intricate. Even minute amounts of the right chemicals can suppress appetite, calm aggression, and change the attitude of a parent toward a child. Certain hormones accelerate the development of the body, regulating growth and form; others may even define an individual's personality characteristics. **The quantities and proportions of hormones produced change with age, so scientists have given a great deal of study to shifts in the endocrine system over time in the hopes of alleviating ailments associated with aging.**

5 In fact, some hormone therapies are already very common. ■ **A combination of estrogen and progesterone has been prescribed for decades to women who want to reduce mood swings, sudden changes in body temperature, and other discomforts caused by lower natural levels of those hormones as they enter middle age.** ■ Known as hormone replacement therapy (HRT), the treatment was also believed to prevent weakening of the bones. ■ At least one study has linked HRT with a heightened risk of heart disease and certain types of cancer. **HRT may also increase the likelihood that blood clots—dangerous because they could travel through the bloodstream and block major blood vessels—will form.** Some proponents of HRT have tempered their enthusiasm in the face of this new evidence, recommending it only to patients whose symptoms interfere with their abilities to live normal lives. ■

6 Human growth hormone may also be given to patients who are secreting abnormally low amounts on their own. **Because of the complicated effects the growth hormone has on the body, such treatments are generally restricted to children who would be pathologically small in stature without it.** Growth hormone affects not just physical size but also the digestion of food and the aging process. Researchers and family physicians tend to agree that it is foolhardy to dispense it in cases in which the risks are not clearly outweighed by the benefits.

More Available

27. Which patients are usually treated with growth hormone?

   a. Adults of smaller stature than normal
   b. Adults with strong digestive systems
   c. Children who are not at risk from the treatment
   d. Children who may remain abnormally small

Hormones in the Body

1 Until the beginning of the twentieth century, the nervous system was thought to control all communication within the body and the resulting integration of behavior. Scientists had determined that nerves ran, essentially, on electrical impulses. These impulses were thought to be the engine for thought, emotion, movement, and internal processes such as digestion. However, experiments by William Bayliss and Ernest Starling on the chemical secretin, which is produced in the small intestine when food enters the stomach, eventually challenged that view. From the small intestine, secretin travels through the bloodstream to the pancreas. There, it stimulates the release of digestive chemicals. In this fashion, the intestinal cells that produce secretin ultimately regulate the production of different chemicals in a different organ, the pancreas.

2 Such a coordination of processes had been thought to require control by the nervous system; Bayliss and Starling showed that it could occur through chemicals alone. This discovery spurred Starling to coin the term *hormone* to refer to secretin, taking it from the Greek word *hormon,* meaning "to excite" or "to set in motion." A hormone is a chemical produced by one tissue to make things happen elsewhere.

3 As more hormones were discovered, they were categorized, primarily according to the process by which they operated on the body. Some glands which make up the endocrine system—such as the thyroid and pituitary glands—secrete hormones directly into the bloodstream. The exocrine system consists of organs and glands that produce substances that are used outside the bloodstream, primarily for digestion. The pancreas is one such organ, although it secretes some chemicals into the blood and thus is also part of the endocrine system.

4 Much has been learned about hormones since their discovery. Some play such key roles in regulating bodily processes or behavior that their absence would cause immediate death. The most abundant hormones have effects that are less obviously urgent but can be more far-reaching and difficult to track: They modify moods and affect human behavior, even some behavior we normally think of as voluntary. Hormonal systems are very intricate. Even minute amounts of the right chemicals can suppress appetite, calm aggression, and change the attitude of a parent toward a child. Certain hormones accelerate the development of the body, regulating growth and form; others may even define an individual's personality characteristics. **The quantities and proportions of hormones produced change with age, so scientists have given a great deal of study to shifts in the endocrine system over time in the hopes of alleviating ailments associated with aging.**

5 In fact, some hormone therapies are already very common. ■ **A combination of estrogen and progesterone has been prescribed for decades to women who want to reduce mood swings, sudden changes in body temperature, and other discomforts caused by lower natural levels of those hormones as they enter middle age.** ■ Known as hormone replacement therapy (HRT), the treatment was also believed to prevent weakening of the bones. ■ At least one study has linked HRT with a heightened risk of heart disease and certain types of cancer. **HRT may also increase the likelihood that blood clots—dangerous because they could travel through the bloodstream and block major blood vessels—will form.** Some proponents of HRT have tempered their enthusiasm in the face of this new evidence, recommending it only to patients whose symptoms interfere with their abilities to live normal lives. ■

6 Human growth hormone may also be given to patients who are secreting abnormally low amounts on their own. **Because of the complicated effects the growth hormone has on the body, such treatments are generally restricted to children who would be pathologically small in stature without it.** Growth hormone affects not just physical size but also the digestion of food and the aging process. Researchers and family physicians tend to agree that it is foolhardy to dispense it in cases in which the risks are not clearly outweighed by the benefits.

More Available

28. Click on the sentence in bold text in the passage, that is repeated below, where the author explains the primary goal of hormone replacement therapy.

   a. The quantities and proportions of hormones produced change with age, so scientists have given a great deal of study to shifts in the endocrine system over time in the hopes of alleviating ailments associated with aging.

   b. A combination of estrogen and progesterone has been prescribed for decades to women who want to reduce mood swings, sudden changes in body temperature, and other discomforts caused by lower natural levels of those hormones as they enter middle age.

   c. HRT may also increase the likelihood that blood clots—dangerous because they could travel through the bloodstream and block major blood vessels—will form.

   d. Because of the complicated effects the growth hormone has on the body, such treatments are generally restricted to children who would be pathologically small in stature without it.

Hormones in the Body

1 Until the beginning of the twentieth century, the nervous system was thought to control all communication within the body and the resulting integration of behavior. Scientists had determined that nerves ran, essentially, on electrical impulses. These impulses were thought to be the engine for thought, emotion, movement, and internal processes such as digestion. However, experiments by William Bayliss and Ernest Starling on the chemical secretin, which is produced in the small intestine when food enters the stomach, eventually challenged that view. From the small intestine, secretin travels through the bloodstream to the pancreas. There, it stimulates the release of digestive chemicals. In this fashion, the intestinal cells that produce secretin ultimately regulate the production of different chemicals in a different organ, the pancreas.

2 Such a coordination of processes had been thought to require control by the nervous system; Bayliss and Starling showed that it could occur through chemicals alone. This discovery spurred Starling to coin the term *hormone* to refer to secretin, taking it from the Greek word *hormon,* meaning "to excite" or "to set in motion." A hormone is a chemical produced by one tissue to make things happen elsewhere.

3 As more hormones were discovered, they were categorized, primarily according to the process by which they operated on the body. Some glands which make up the endocrine system—such as the thyroid and pituitary glands—secrete hormones directly into the bloodstream. The exocrine system consists of organs and glands that produce substances that are used outside the bloodstream, primarily for digestion. The pancreas is one such organ, although it secretes some chemicals into the blood and thus is also part of the endocrine system.

4 Much has been learned about hormones since their discovery. Some play such key roles in regulating bodily processes or behavior that their absence would cause immediate death. The most abundant hormones have effects that are less obviously urgent but can be more far-reaching and difficult to track: They modify moods and affect human behavior, even some behavior we normally think of as voluntary. Hormonal systems are very intricate. Even minute amounts of the right chemicals can suppress appetite, calm aggression, and change the attitude of a parent toward a child. Certain hormones accelerate the development of the body, regulating growth and form; others may even define an individual's personality characteristics. **The quantities and proportions of hormones produced change with age, so scientists have given a great deal of study to shifts in the endocrine system over time in the hopes of alleviating ailments associated with aging.**

5 In fact, some hormone therapies are already very common. ■ **A combination of estrogen and progesterone has been prescribed for decades to women who want to reduce mood swings, sudden changes in body temperature, and other discomforts caused by lower natural levels of those hormones as they enter middle age.** ■ Known as hormone replacement therapy (HRT), the treatment was also believed to prevent weakening of the bones. ■ At least one study has linked HRT with a heightened risk of heart disease and certain types of cancer. **HRT may also increase the likelihood that blood clots—dangerous because they could travel through the bloodstream and block major blood vessels— will form.** Some proponents of HRT have tempered their enthusiasm in the face of this new evidence, recommending it only to patients whose symptoms interfere with their abilities to live normal lives. ■

6 Human growth hormone may also be given to patients who are secreting abnormally low amounts on their own. **Because of the complicated effects the growth hormone has on the body, such treatments are generally restricted to children who would be pathologically small in stature without it.** Growth hormone affects not just physical size but also the digestion of food and the aging process. Researchers and family physicians tend to agree that it is foolhardy to dispense it in cases in which the risks are not clearly outweighed by the benefits.

29. Look at the four squares [■] that indicate where the following sentence could be added to the passage.

The body is a complex machine, however, and recent studies have called into question the wisdom of essentially trying to fool its systems into believing they aren't aging.

Where would the sentence best fit?

Click on a square [■] to add the sentence to the passage.

[Here, on this practice test, circle your answer below.]

a. Square 1
b. Square 2
c. Square 3
d. Square 4

More Available

Hormones in the Body

1   Until the beginning of the twentieth century, the nervous system was thought to control all communication within the body and the resulting integration of behavior. Scientists had determined that nerves ran, essentially, on electrical impulses. These impulses were thought to be the engine for thought, emotion, movement, and internal processes such as digestion. However, experiments by William Bayliss and Ernest Starling on the chemical secretin, which is produced in the small intestine when food enters the stomach, eventually challenged that view. From the small intestine, secretin travels through the bloodstream to the pancreas. There, it stimulates the release of digestive chemicals. In this fashion, the intestinal cells that produce secretin ultimately regulate the production of different chemicals in a different organ, the pancreas.

2   Such a coordination of processes had been thought to require control by the nervous system; Bayliss and Starling showed that it could occur through chemicals alone. This discovery spurred Starling to coin the term *hormone* to refer to secretin, taking it from the Greek word *hormon,* meaning "to excite" or "to set in motion." A hormone is a chemical produced by one tissue to make things happen elsewhere.

3   As more hormones were discovered, they were categorized, primarily according to the process by which they operated on the body. Some glands which make up the endocrine system—such as the thyroid and pituitary glands—secrete hormones directly into the bloodstream. The exocrine system consists of organs and glands that produce substances that are used outside the bloodstream, primarily for digestion. The pancreas is one such organ, although it secretes some chemicals into the blood and thus is also part of the endocrine system.

4   Much has been learned about hormones since their discovery. Some play such key roles in regulating bodily processes or behavior that their absence would cause immediate death. The most abundant hormones have effects that are less obviously urgent but can be more far-reaching and difficult to track: They modify moods and affect human behavior, even some behavior we normally think of as voluntary. Hormonal systems are very intricate. Even minute amounts of the right chemicals can suppress appetite, calm aggression, and change the attitude of a parent toward a child. Certain hormones accelerate the development of the body, regulating growth and form; others may even define an individual's personality characteristics. **The quantities and proportions of hormones produced change with age, so scientists have given a great deal of study to shifts in the endocrine system over time in the hopes of alleviating ailments associated with aging.**

5   In fact, some hormone therapies are already very common. ■ **A combination of estrogen and progesterone has been prescribed for decades to women who want to reduce mood swings, sudden changes in body temperature, and other discomforts caused by lower natural levels of those hormones as they enter middle age.** ■ Known as hormone replacement therapy (HRT), the treatment was also believed to prevent weakening of the bones. ■ At least one study has linked HRT with a heightened risk of heart disease and certain types of cancer. **HRT may also increase the likelihood that blood clots—dangerous because they could travel through the bloodstream and block major blood vessels—will form.** Some proponents of HRT have tempered their enthusiasm in the face of this new evidence, recommending it only to patients whose symptoms interfere with their abilities to live normal lives. ■

6   Human growth hormone may also be given to patients who are secreting abnormally low amounts on their own. **Because of the complicated effects the growth hormone has on the body, such treatments are generally restricted to children who would be pathologically small in stature without it.** Growth hormone affects not just physical size but also the digestion of food and the aging process. Researchers and family physicians tend to agree that it is foolhardy to dispense it in cases in which the risks are not clearly outweighed by the benefits.

30. Directions: An introductory sentence for a brief summary of the passage is provided below. Complete the summary by selecting the THREE answer choices that express the most important ideas in the passage. Some sentences do not belong in the summary because they express ideas that are not presented in the passage or are minor ideas in the passage. *This question is worth 2 points.*

The class of chemicals called hormones was discovered by two researchers studying a substance produced in the small intestine.

-
-
-

Answer Choices	
The term *hormone* is based on a Greek word that means "to excite" or "to set in motion."	Researchers are looking for ways to decrease the dangers of treatments with growth hormone so that more patients can benefit from it.
Hormones can be given artificially, but such treatments have risks and must be used carefully.	Hormones can affect not only life processes such as growth but also behavior and emotion.
Scientists have discovered that not only the nervous system but also certain chemicals can affect bodily processes far from their points of origin.	Hormone replacement therapy (HRT) may increase the risk of blood clots and heart disease in middle-age women.

THE LISTENING SECTION

This section measures your ability to understand lectures and conversations in English. You will hear each selection only once. Each lecture or conversation will be followed by a series of questions, typically about the main idea and supporting details. Answer the questions in the order they appear. You may not skip a question and return to it. You may take notes while you listen and use your notes to help you answer the questions.

On the actual test, you will have 41–57 minutes to answer the questions. The time will not run down while you are listening to the test material. You will see screens similar to the ones shown below and in the next pages to introduce questions or provide instructions, such as "listen again to."

To most closely simulate the actual test conditions, listen to each track in your Student Tools, and then set a timer or ask a friend to time you for 41 minutes. Remember, give yourself only 41 minutes to finish the entire section. Begin now.

Listening 1
Please play Track 20 in your Student Tools.

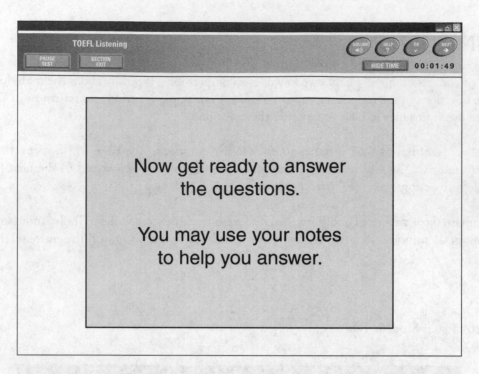

Now get ready to answer
the questions.

You may use your notes
to help you answer.

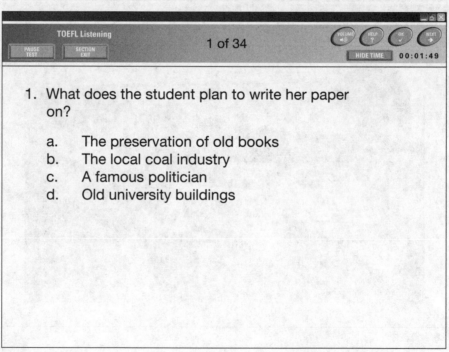

1. What does the student plan to write her paper on?

    a.   The preservation of old books
    b.   The local coal industry
    c.   A famous politician
    d.   Old university buildings

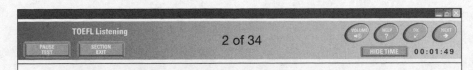

2. What security procedures does the librarian
   tell the student she must follow?

   Click on 2 answers.

   a.   Show her her note cards before leaving
   b.   Allow her ID card to be copied
   c.   Submit a deposit of five dollars
   d.   Sign in and out of the archives room

3. Why does the librarian say the archives need
   to be kept secure?

   a.   Students from other universities frequently
        use the collection.
   b.   Some items are worth a lot of money.
   c.   Many items cannot be replaced.
   d.   There have been several thefts recently.

4. Why did the librarian mention the age of the books?

    a.   They need to be handled with gloves.
    b.   The student can look only at photographs of them.
    c.   They were added to the collection recently.
    d.   They have increased in value.

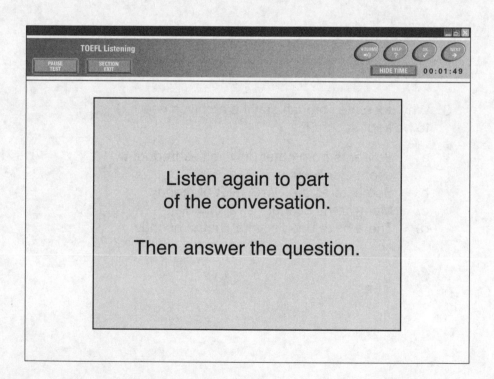

Listen again to part
of the conversation.

Then answer the question.

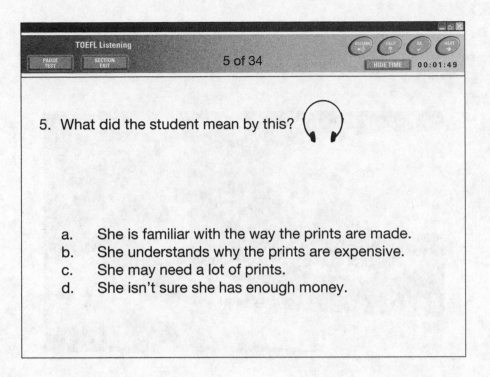

5. What did the student mean by this?

a. She is familiar with the way the prints are made.
b. She understands why the prints are expensive.
c. She may need a lot of prints.
d. She isn't sure she has enough money.

Listening 2

Please play Track 21 in your Student Tools.

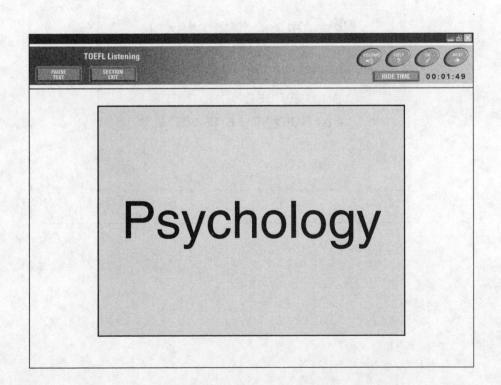

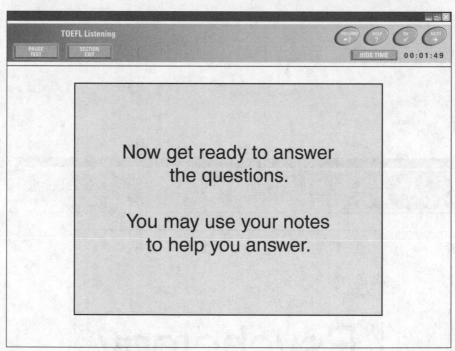

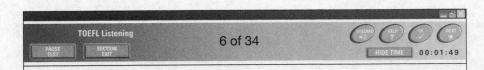

6. What is the lecture mainly about?

    a. Why some events are more memorable than others
    b. The process by which memories form in the brain
    c. Research on animals that may help explain human memory
    d. Ways students can strengthen their abilities to remember things

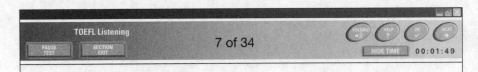

7. Why does the professor say Walter Freeman mentioned two types of crowds?

    a. People can be taught to recall information that has fallen into disuse.
    b. Scientists are studying why some people have a better sense of direction than others.
    c. Impulses in the brain may follow a pattern researchers don't yet understand.
    d. Each individual person has a unique way of remembering things.

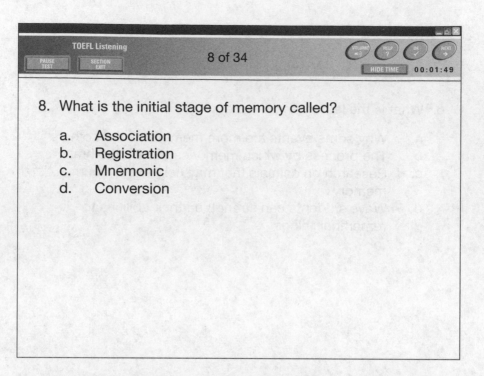

8. What is the initial stage of memory called?

   a. Association
   b. Registration
   c. Mnemonic
   d. Conversion

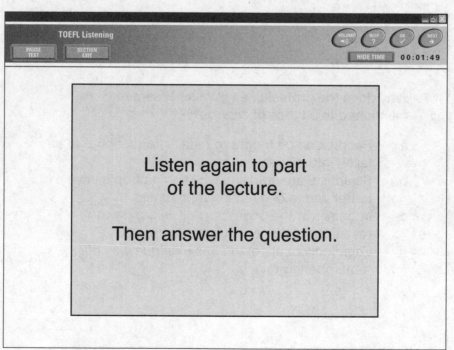

Listen again to part
of the lecture.

Then answer the question.

9. What is the professor trying to illustrate?

    a. People have an easier time remembering unusual images.
    b. The most memorable images come from nature.
    c. Some people have names with few easy associations.
    d. Large objects are easier to remember than small objects.

10. What does the professor imply about a memory that has passed through the long-term retention stage?

    a. It usually takes a long time to recall.
    b. It could still be lost if not used frequently.
    c. It can be recalled even if the brain is injured.
    d. It often comes back suddenly in old age.

11. What will the class do next?

    a.   Look at scans of the brain
    b.   Discuss what will be tested on the final
    c.   Practice inventing memorable visual images
    d.   Talk about methods for improving memory

Listening 3

Please play Track 22 in your Student Tools.

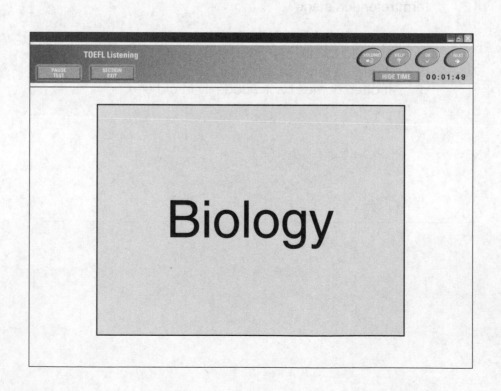

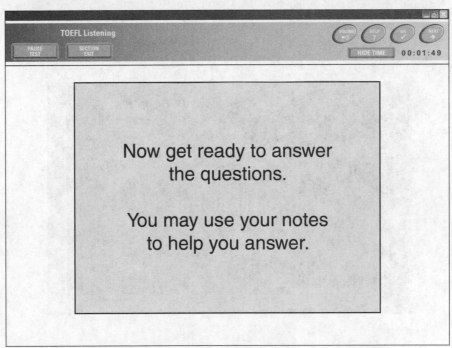

12. What is the discussion mainly about?

    a.   The symptoms of joint injury
    b.   Which joints are used in different sports
    c.   How to distinguish different types of joints
    d.   How people can improve the flexibility of their joints

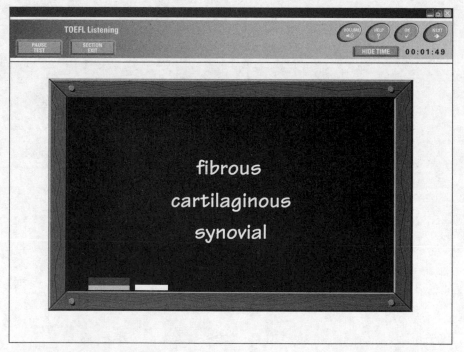

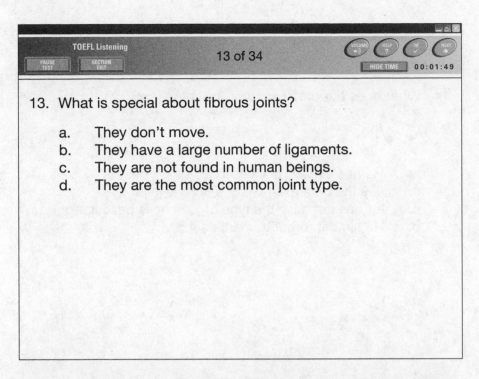

13. What is special about fibrous joints?

    a.   They don't move.
    b.   They have a large number of ligaments.
    c.   They are not found in human beings.
    d.   They are the most common joint type.

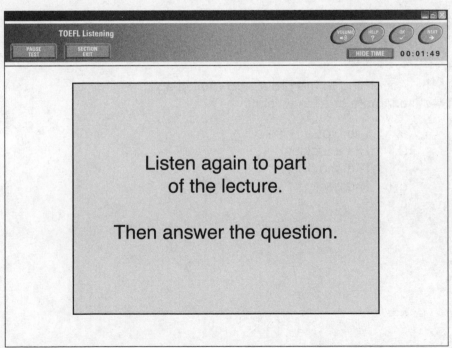

Listen again to part
of the lecture.

Then answer the question.

14. What does the professor say about the jaw?

    a.   He has already discussed its joint type.
    b.   It is the best example of a fibrous joint.
    c.   It does not have the type of joint he is describing.
    d.   He almost forgot to mention it.

15. According to the professor, what is an example of a hinge joint?

    a.   The hip
    b.   The knuckles
    c.   The shoulder
    d.   The neck

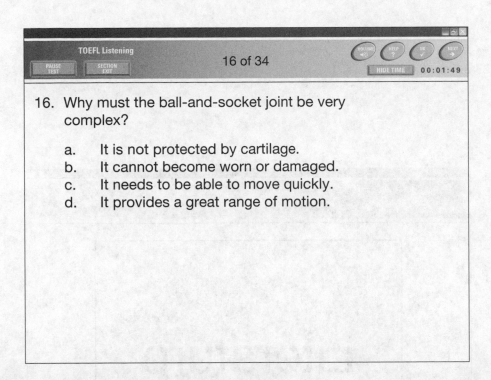

16. Why must the ball-and-socket joint be very complex?

    a.   It is not protected by cartilage.
    b.   It cannot become worn or damaged.
    c.   It needs to be able to move quickly.
    d.   It provides a great range of motion.

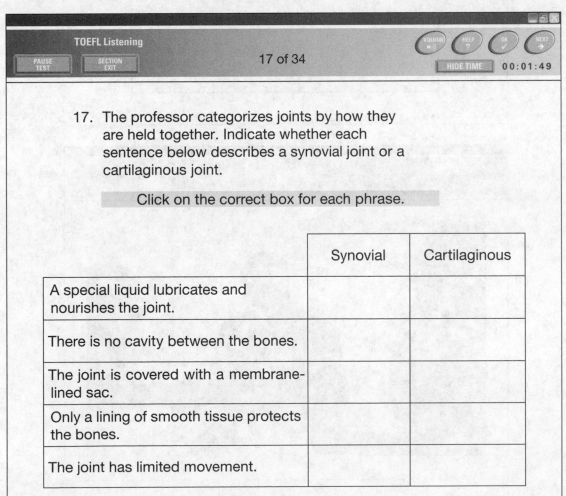

17. The professor categorizes joints by how they are held together. Indicate whether each sentence below describes a synovial joint or a cartilaginous joint.

        Click on the correct box for each phrase.

	Synovial	Cartilaginous
A special liquid lubricates and nourishes the joint.		
There is no cavity between the bones.		
The joint is covered with a membrane-lined sac.		
Only a lining of smooth tissue protects the bones.		
The joint has limited movement.		

Listening 4

Please play Track 23 in your Student Tools.

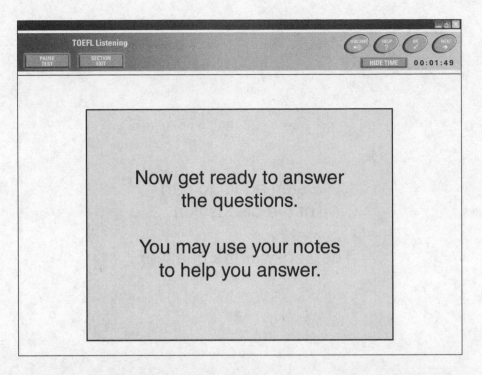

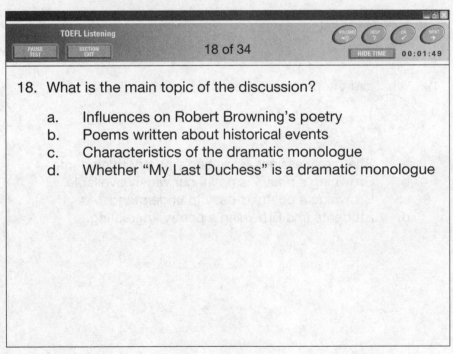

18. What is the main topic of the discussion?

    a.   Influences on Robert Browning's poetry

    b.   Poems written about historical events

    c.   Characteristics of the dramatic monologue

    d.   Whether "My Last Duchess" is a dramatic monologue

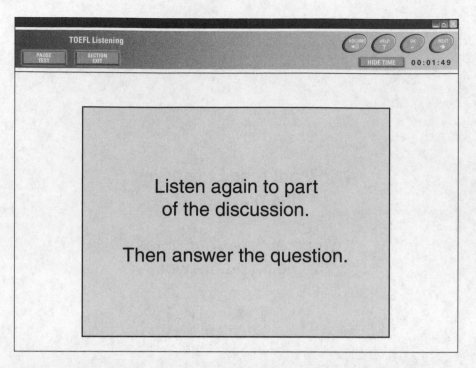

19. What did the professor mean by this?

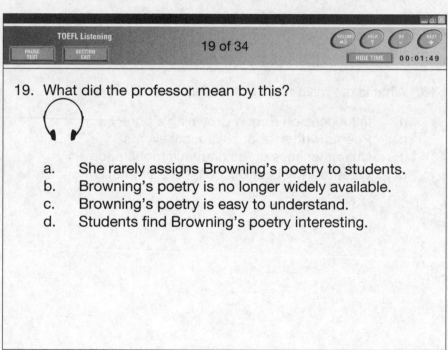

a.   She rarely assigns Browning's poetry to students.
b.   Browning's poetry is no longer widely available.
c.   Browning's poetry is easy to understand.
d.   Students find Browning's poetry interesting.

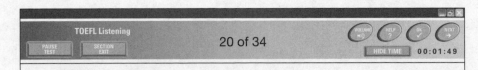

20. According to the professor, what is a monologue?

    a.   A speech given by a single person
    b.   A profile of one historical character
    c.   A description of a specific historical event
    d.   A poet who writes in the voice of a different person

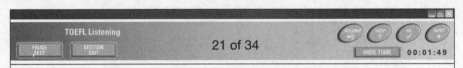

21. According to the professor, what are the primary characteristics of the poetic form called the dramatic monologue?

Click on 3 answers.

    a.   The speaker in the poem tries to justify his thinking.
    b.   The reader identifies with the listener addressed in the poem.
    c.   The speaker in the poem is a person of high status.
    d.   Readers must use their own inferences to complete the story.

22. What was the woman's reaction to the poem "My Last Duchess"?

    a.   She liked the character of the duke.
    b.   She found it disturbing.
    c.   She thought it unlike Browning's other poems.
    d.   She doubted its historical accuracy.

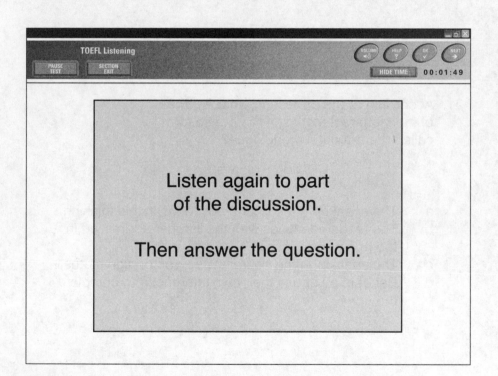

Listen again to part of the discussion.

Then answer the question.

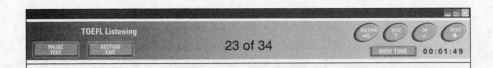

TOEFL Listening

23 of 34

VOLUME   HELP   OK   NEXT
?

PAUSE   SECTION
TEST   EXIT

HIDE TIME   00:01:49

23. What does the professor ask the woman to do?

a. Consider a different interpretation
b. Allow her classmates to give their opinions
c. Wait until later to analyze the specific meanings of
    the poem
d. Explain what she thought the poem was saying

Listening 5

Please play Track 24 in your Student Tools.

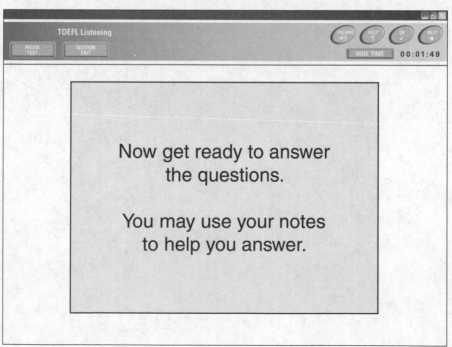

Now get ready to answer
the questions.

You may use your notes
to help you answer.

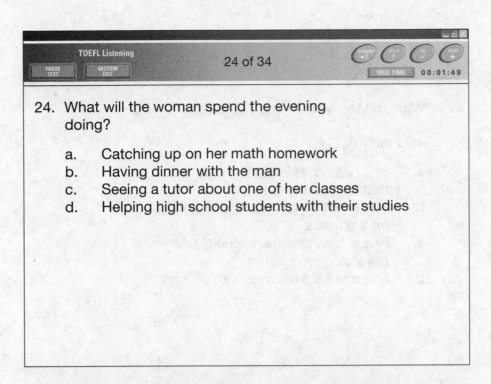

24. What will the woman spend the evening doing?

    a.   Catching up on her math homework
    b.   Having dinner with the man
    c.   Seeing a tutor about one of her classes
    d.   Helping high school students with their studies

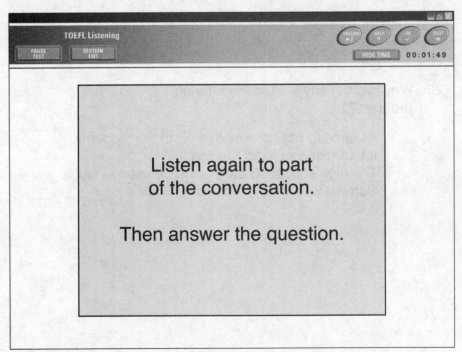

Listen again to part
of the conversation.

Then answer the question.

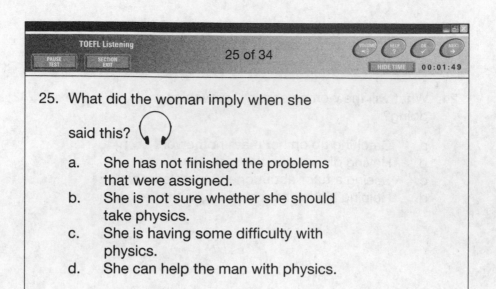

25. What did the woman imply when she said this?

a. She has not finished the problems that were assigned.
b. She is not sure whether she should take physics.
c. She is having some difficulty with physics.
d. She can help the man with physics.

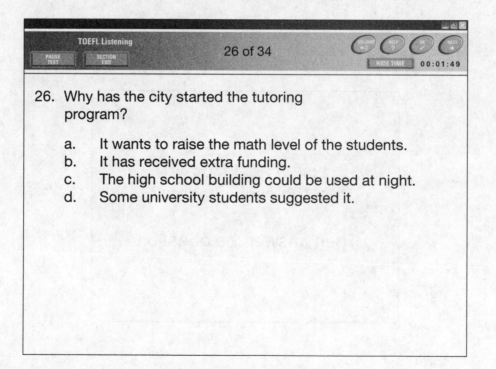

26. Why has the city started the tutoring program?

a. It wants to raise the math level of the students.
b. It has received extra funding.
c. The high school building could be used at night.
d. Some university students suggested it.

27. What does the education department like
about the tutors?

    a.   Most of them have taught students before.
    b.   The tutors are available in the afternoon.
    c.   Most of them went to the city high school.
    d.   The department doesn't have to pay them.

28. What does the woman think tutoring will
prepare her for?

    a.   Her upcoming math tests
    b.   Her duties as a graduate student
    c.   A job as a high school teacher
    d.   A job at the City Department of Education

Listening 6

Please play Track 25 in your Student Tools.

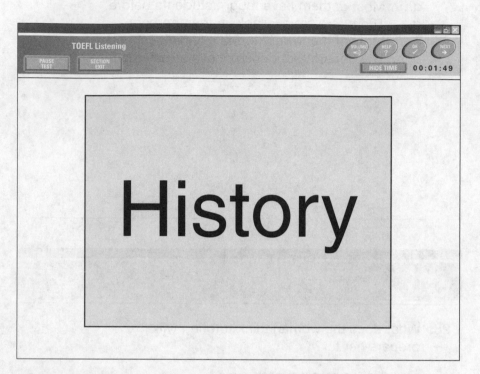

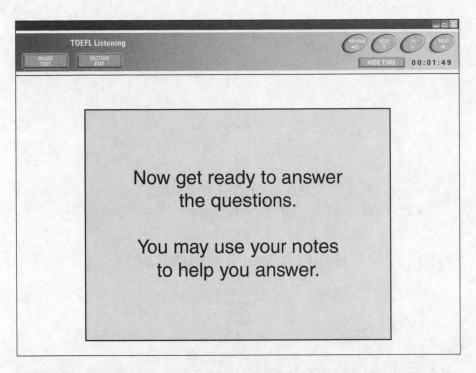

Now get ready to answer
the questions.

You may use your notes
to help you answer.

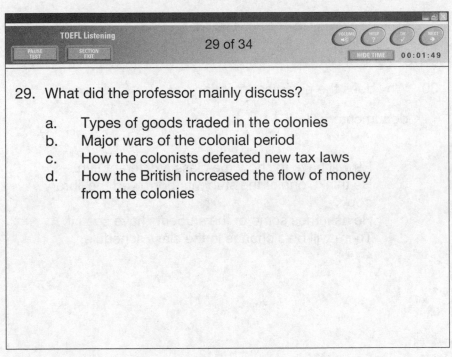

29. What did the professor mainly discuss?

    a.   Types of goods traded in the colonies
    b.   Major wars of the colonial period
    c.   How the colonists defeated new tax laws
    d.   How the British increased the flow of money
        from the colonies

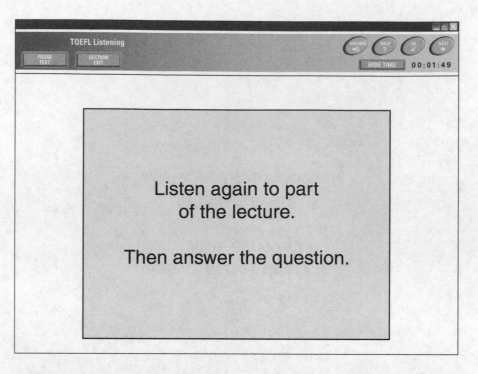

Listen again to part
of the lecture.

Then answer the question.

30. Why does the professor mention the documentary film?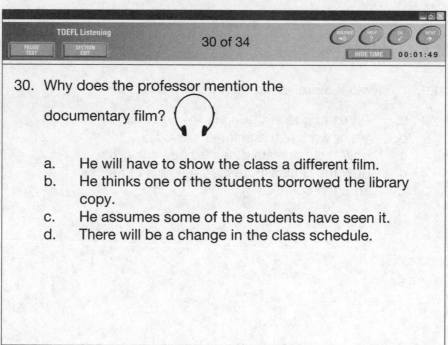

   a. He will have to show the class a different film.
   b. He thinks one of the students borrowed the library copy.
   c. He assumes some of the students have seen it.
   d. There will be a change in the class schedule.

31. Why did Britain want to receive more money
from the American colonies?

 a. It had just finished a costly war.
 b. Colonial paper currency had increased in value.
 c. The colonies were producing more sugar.
 d. Taxes in Britain had been lowered.

32. Which of the following did the professor
mention as changes that accompanied the
Sugar Act?

Click on 2 answers.

 a. A greater number of commodities were taxed.
 b. The taxes were collected more carefully.
 c. The tax on sugar replaced the tax on coffee and
   wines.
 d. The Stamp Act was no longer necessary.

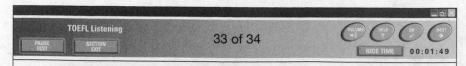

33. Why does the professor say the colonists developed their own paper currency?

   a.   They needed more money to pay the sugar tax.

   b.   Their British currency was used to pay for British goods.

   c.   Property could be bought only with paper currency.

   d.   Paper currency was easier for laborers to transport.

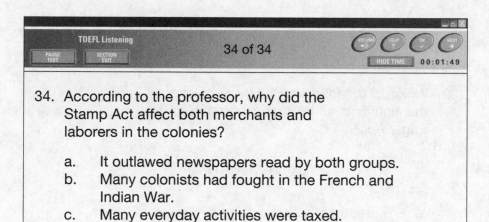

34. According to the professor, why did the Stamp Act affect both merchants and laborers in the colonies?

   a.   It outlawed newspapers read by both groups.

   b.   Many colonists had fought in the French and Indian War.

   c.   Many everyday activities were taxed.

   d.   Both groups consumed large amounts of sugar.

THE SPEAKING SECTION

In this section, you will demonstrate your ability to speak about various topics. You will answer four questions. Answer each question as completely as possible.

Question 1 will ask you about a familiar topic. For question 2, you will first read a short text and then answer a question about what you have read. For question 3, you will read a text and listen to a lecture on the same topic. You will then be asked a question about what you have read and heard. Question 4 requires you to listen to a lecture first. You will then be asked questions about what you just heard. You may take notes while you read and listen. You may use your notes to help you prepare.

For each task, you will be given a short period of time to prepare your response; to most closely simulate actual test conditions, you will need to pause and restart the audio as instructed in the following pages.

Note to students: If possible, record your responses or have someone proficient in English listen to your response. Compare your responses with the samples in Chapter 21.

Speaking 1

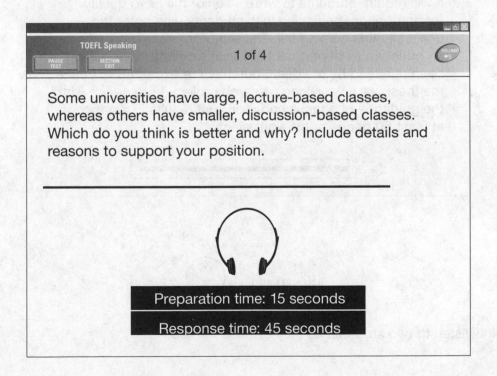

TOEFL Speaking   1 of 4

Some universities have large, lecture-based classes, whereas others have smaller, discussion-based classes. Which do you think is better and why? Include details and reasons to support your position.

Preparation time: 15 seconds
Response time: 45 seconds

Speaking 2

Please play Track 27 in your Student Tools.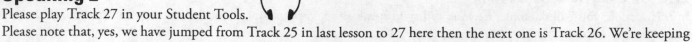
Please note that, yes, we have jumped from Track 25 in last lesson to 27 here then the next one is Track 26. We're keeping you on your toes!

Narrator: The College of Arts and Sciences at Eastern University has decided to add a senior project to its existing graduation requirements. The campus newspaper printed the following report about the announcement of the new requirement. You have 45 seconds to read the report. Begin reading now.

[Pause the audio for 45 seconds.]

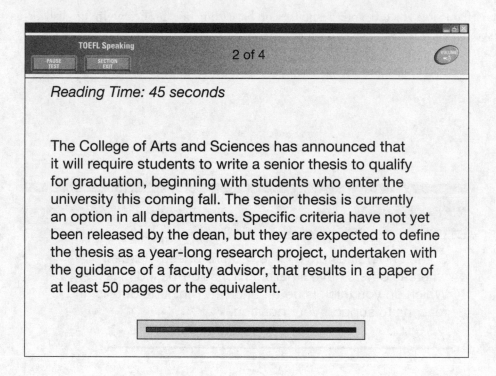

Reading Time: 45 seconds

The College of Arts and Sciences has announced that it will require students to write a senior thesis to qualify for graduation, beginning with students who enter the university this coming fall. The senior thesis is currently an option in all departments. Specific criteria have not yet been released by the dean, but they are expected to define the thesis as a year-long research project, undertaken with the guidance of a faculty advisor, that results in a paper of at least 50 pages or the equivalent.

[Restart audio.]

Narrator: Now listen to two students as they discuss the report.

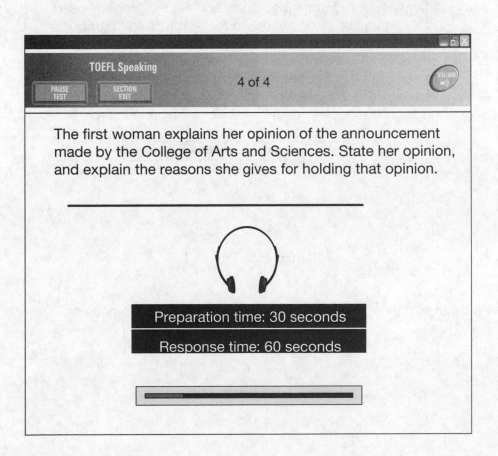

The first woman explains her opinion of the announcement made by the College of Arts and Sciences. State her opinion, and explain the reasons she gives for holding that opinion.

Preparation time: 30 seconds

Response time: 60 seconds

Speaking 3

Please play Track 26 in your Student Tools.
Please note that, yes, we have jumped from Track 27 in last lesson to 26 here. We're keeping you on your toes!

Narrator: Now read the passage about birds of prey. You have 45 seconds to read the passage. Begin reading now.

[Pause the audio for 45 seconds]

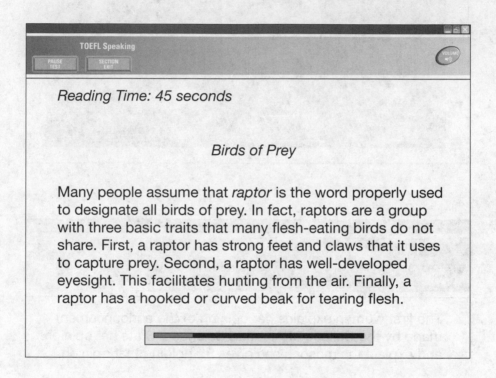

Reading Time: 45 seconds

Birds of Prey

Many people assume that *raptor* is the word properly used to designate all birds of prey. In fact, raptors are a group with three basic traits that many flesh-eating birds do not share. First, a raptor has strong feet and claws that it uses to capture prey. Second, a raptor has well-developed eyesight. This facilitates hunting from the air. Finally, a raptor has a hooked or curved beak for tearing flesh.

[Restart audio.]

Narrator: Now listen to part of a lecture on this topic given in a biology class.

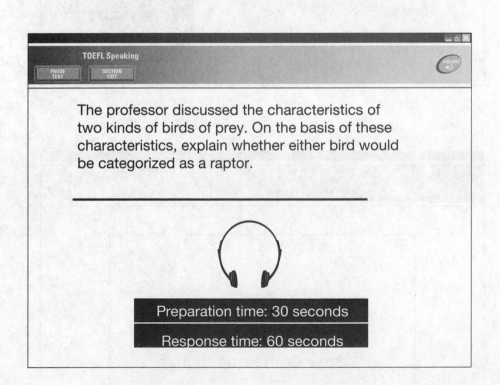

The professor discussed the characteristics of two kinds of birds of prey. On the basis of these characteristics, explain whether either bird would be categorized as a raptor.

Preparation time: 30 seconds

Response time: 60 seconds

Speaking 4

Please play Track 28 in your Student Tools.

Narrator: Now listen to part of a lecture in a history class.

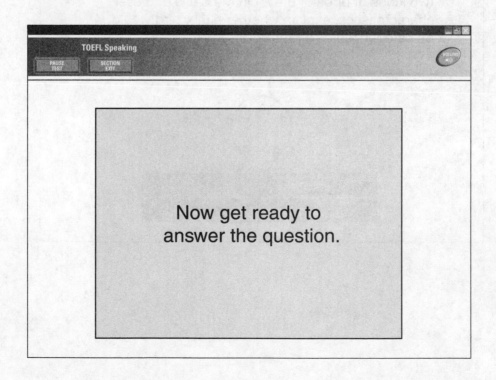

Now get ready to
answer the question.

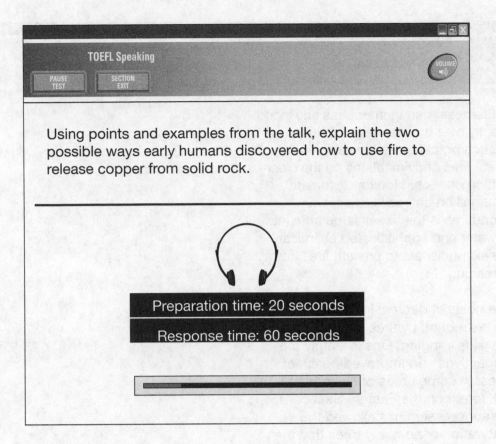

Using points and examples from the talk, explain the two possible ways early humans discovered how to use fire to release copper from solid rock.

_____

Preparation time: 20 seconds

Response time: 60 seconds

THE WRITING SECTION

This section measures your ability to communicate in an academic environment. There are two writing tasks. The first task asks you to read a passage, listen to a lecture, and respond. You will answer the second question based on your own knowledge and experience. To most closely simulate actual test conditions, you will need to pause and restart the audio as instructed throughout this section.

Writing 1

Directions: You will have 20 minutes to plan and write your response. The break between the reading and lecture is not timed in the online audio, because some students may need to practice untimed. Therefore, you will need to stop the audio for the duration of the break. You have three minutes to read the selection.

Please play Track 29 in your Student Tools.

Narrator: Now read the passage about the suppression of forest fires. You have three minutes to read the passage. Begin reading now.

[Stop audio for 3 minutes.]

TOEFL Writing

VOLUME   HELP   NEXT

PAUSE
TEST

SECTION
EXIT

HIDE TIME   00:29:57

Wilderness management has advanced greatly over the last century, due in part to such practices as the suppression of forest fires and limitations on the clear-cutting of trees. Monitoring forests for small brushfires is easier with aircraft, as is the use of large amounts of water and sophisticated chemical fire extinguishers to prevent fires from spreading.

The goals of decreasing the amount of destruction by fires and cutting are wide-ranging. One is simply the longer lives and improved health of trees. In some areas of hickory and oak forest on the Eastern Seaboard, fire suppression has allowed the maturation of so many trees that the treetops form a continuous canopy.

There is evidence of the healthful effects of fire suppression closer to the ground as well. Vines and low bushes that would be burned out in a forest fire can flourish when fires are suppressed, of course, but there is a more indirect way fires harm plant life. Chemical tests on areas that have recently experienced forest fires demonstrate that burning decreases the overall amount of nutrients in the soil. Suppressing fires prevents such a decrease. Ferns, wildflowers, and herbs grow without disturbance.

Finally, wildlife can benefit. In the eastern hickory and oak forests, the suppression of fires has meant that forest animals—ranging from small insects and birds to large deer and bears—are not burned to death. Deer populations, in particular, have increased notably.

[Restart audio.]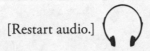

Narrator: Now listen to part of a lecture on the topic you just read about.

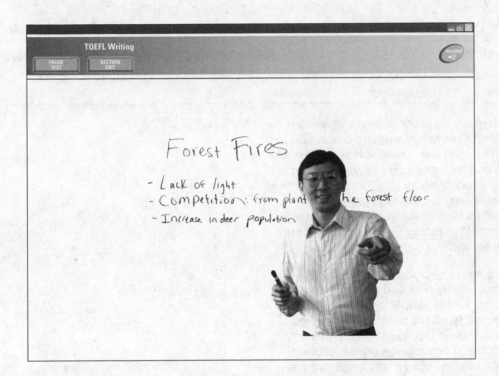

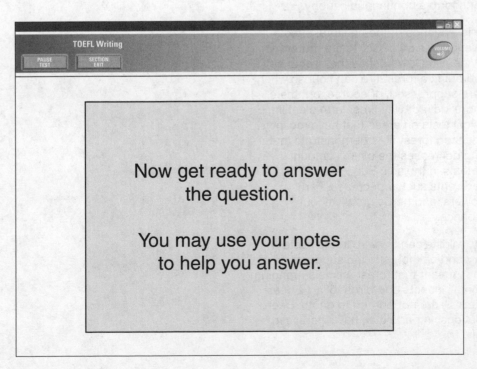

Directions: You have 20 minutes to plan and write your response. Your response will be graded on the quality of your writing and on how well your response presents the points in the lecture and their relationship to the reading passage. Typically, an effective response will be 150–225 words.

Question: Summarize the points made in the lecture you just heard, explaining how they cast doubt on the contents of the reading. You may refer to the passage as you write.

Copy   Cut   Paste   Word Count: 0

Wilderness management has advanced greatly over the last century, due in part to such practices as the suppression of forest fires and limitations on the clear-cutting of trees. Monitoring forests for small brushfires is easier with aircraft, as is the use of large amounts of water and sophisticated chemical fire extinguishers to prevent fires from spreading.

The goals of decreasing the amount of destruction by fires and cutting are wide-ranging. One is simply the longer lives and improved health of trees. In some areas of hickory and oak forest on the Eastern Seaboard, fire suppression has allowed the maturation of so many trees that the treetops form a continuous canopy.

There is evidence of the healthful effects of fire suppression closer to the ground as well. Vines and low bushes that would be burned out in a forest fire can flourish when fires are suppressed, of course, but there is a more indirect way fires harm plant life. Chemical tests on areas that have recently experienced forest fires demonstrate that burning decreases the overall amount of nutrients in the soil. Suppressing fires prevents such a decrease. Ferns, wildflowers, and herbs grow without disturbance.

Finally, wildlife can benefit. In the eastern hickory and oak forests, the suppression of fires has meant that forest animals—ranging from small insects and birds to large deer and bears—are not burned to death. Deer populations, in particular, have increased notably.

Writing 2

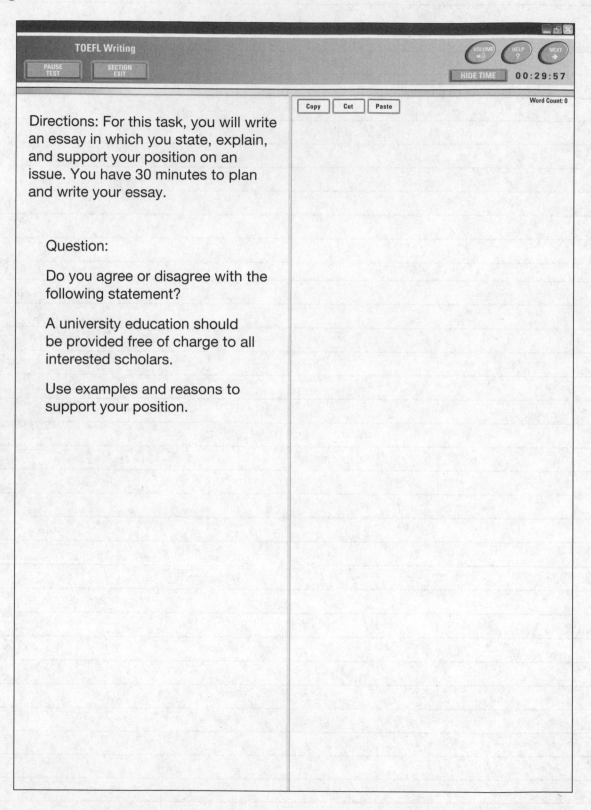

Directions: For this task, you will write an essay in which you state, explain, and support your position on an issue. You have 30 minutes to plan and write your essay.

Question:

Do you agree or disagree with the following statement?

A university education should be provided free of charge to all interested scholars.

Use examples and reasons to support your position.

TOEFL Writing

PAUSE TEST   SECTION EXIT

VOLUME   HELP ?   NEXT

HIDE TIME   00:29:57

Copy   Cut   Paste

Word Count: 0

Chapter 20
Practice Test
Answer Key

READING

1. C
2. A
3. C
4. D
5. D
6. C
7. D
8. B
9. A
10. See explanations
11. C
12. A
13. B
14. B
15. B
16. C
17. A
18. D
19. D
20. See explanations
21. B
22. A
23. C
24. D
25. B
26. A
27. D
28. A
29. C
30. See explanations

LISTENING

1. B
2. B, D
3. C
4. A
5. B
6. B
7. C
8. B
9. A
10. B
11. D
12. C
13. A
14. C
15. B
16. D
17. See explanations
18. C
19. D
20. A
21. A, B, D
22. B
23. C
24. D
25. C
26. A
27. D
28. B
29. D
30. D
31. A
32. A, B
33. B
34. C

SPEAKING AND WRITING

Because the Speaking and Writing section questions are not multiple choice, see the explanations in the next chapter for examples of how these questions may be answered.

Chapter 21
Practice Test
Answers and
Explanations

THE READING SECTION

The number one rule to remember in the Reading section is that if the information in the answer choice is NOT provided in the text, that answer choice is NOT correct. Please read the following explanations for more information.

Reading Passage #1: The Veneration of Trees

1.   **C**   Refer back to the first paragraph for the answer to this question. The text says

> It was not a great mental leap for people to see the trees that populated them
> as embodiments of the natural forces that governed their lives.

Choice (C) is the only choice close in meaning to these lines. Here's why the other choices are incorrect.

- Fortunately, neither (A) nor (B) is mentioned at all in this paragraph.
- Choice (D) is a trap. Although the paragraph does say that the veneration of trees united people, this is not how people viewed the trees.

2.   **A**   Here is the line in question:

> The woods that covered large areas of Europe and North America, in particular,
> were difficult to _____ and dangerous to cross.

Look for an answer that refers to woods that are "dangerous to cross." *Enter* is closest in meaning to "cross." The other answer choices are not close in meaning to the word *cross*.

3.   **C**   This question asks why the author mentions Druids? Go back to the second paragraph and read the lines about Druids.

> It is known that both the Celtic and the Germanic tribes that inhabited ancient
> Northern Europe regarded certain trees as sacred, setting them apart by
> species (as the Druids worshipped oaks)...

These lines tell you that the Druids "worshipped oaks," which is what (C) states. Here's why the other answer choices are incorrect.

- Eliminate (A) because the author has not introduced the other two stages yet.
- And (B) and (D) are not mentioned in relationship to Druids.

4. **D** For a NOT question, return to the passage and look for evidence for each answer. If you're having trouble figuring out where to look, remember that the questions appear roughly in the sequence of the passage. Here's each answer choice, with the corresponding lines of text that contradict each choice, thereby eliminating them.

(A) "Before a tree was felled for human use, woodcutters in many world cultures would offer it both apologies and thanks for the resources it was about to provide them."

(B) "In some places, one could be punished severely for injuring the bark of a tree or stealing its fruit."

(C) "In some societies, it was claimed that trees cry out in pain when struck or cut into."

(D) This information is not in the passage, so this is the correct answer.

5. **D** This question asks for the distinction mentioned in the second state of tree worship. That means the answer is where the passage discusses the "second stage of tree worship." The lines you need are in paragraph 4:

> It is not bound to a single tree but rather stands for a group. The distinction
> may seem small, but it is a significant first step toward symbolic thinking.

These lines say that the distinction is not a "single tree" but a "group," which is a paraphrase of (D). The other choices are not mentioned as a distinction in the paragraph.

6. **C** With questions that seem confusing, remember to break them down to the basics. The question asks why the author use this phrase. Return to the passage to see these lines.

> To think about a tree spirit identified with the forest as a whole, therefore,
> people had to think about phenomena that were removed from them in time
> and space—ideas rather than things. Such a tree spirit represented the
> potential and abstract rather than the concrete and immediate.

These lines tell you that people had to think of things that were "removed from them in time and space." The spirits also represent "the potential and abstract." Both these lines point to (C) as the answer. Here's why the other choices are incorrect.

- These lines do not mention danger, so eliminate (A).
- Similarly, these lines do not say the people stopped fearing the forest, so (B) is incorrect.
- Choice (D) is extreme and also not mentioned.

7. **D** This is an *inference* question, meaning that you have to figure out what the author is trying to say based on clues in the passage. Inference questions tend to be a bit more difficult than other types of questions, so if you're pressed for time, skip it and come back to it later. The question is asking about the "most complex" phase of tree worship. Look in the last paragraph, where the author talks about "complexity." Here are the appropriate lines.

Liberated from each other, trees and their spirits can begin to be seen as symbols and embodiments of other natural processes of significance to primitive life: the power of weather and seasons to produce good or bad harvests, the mysteries of childbirth and disease. At that point, the veneration of trees reaches its stage of greatest complexity.

Also, later in the paragraph, it states, "The appearance of these beliefs...indicates that a society has made its first steps toward symbolic and abstract thinking." Thus, (D), which talks of trees as "symbols" is best. Here's why the other choices are incorrect.

- Eliminate (A) because it is extreme—there is no information about "all" trees provided.
- Male and female tree spirits are not mentioned, so (B) must be wrong.
- And no evidence is offered about different "ceremonies" for different seasons, so eliminate (C).

8.   **B**   Read the following sentence for the clue to this question:

Societies in both Eastern Europe and the South Pacific brought ceremonial offerings to trees in the hopes that they would furnish rain and sunshine.

The passage states that the societies "brought offerings" to the trees so the trees would give them something in return (rain and sunshine). Thus, you should look for a word that has a meaning similar to *give*. The best match is (B). Here's why the other choices are incorrect.

- Choice (A) doesn't make sense in this sentence.
- Choices (C) and (D) are the opposite of what we need.

9.   **A**   Return to paragraph 5 for the answer to this question. It may be best to use POE on the answer choices.

- Choice (B) refers to the "three stages in the life" of a tree, but the paragraph discusses the third stage of the people's beliefs in trees, not *the life cycle of a tree*. So eliminate (B).
- Choice (C) talks about trees that required "little" rain or sun; however, the passage mentions that *people* asked trees to provide rain and sunshine. Therefore, (C) is wrong since the trees did need the rain and sunshine.
- Choice (D) mentions trees "raised by women." The paragraph says that women "embraced" trees, but it doesn't say they "raised" them.
- Thus, (A) is the correct choice, since paragraph 5 talks about the fruitfulness of trees.

10. From the previous question and any active reading you've done, you may have noted that the main idea of the passage is the three stages of tree veneration. Here are summaries of the main points.

Three basic levels of tree worship can be observed in *The Golden Bough*.

- Certain peoples came to believe that tree spirits were independent of individual trees and, instead, resided in the whole forest.

- Some societies believed each tree was the body for an individual spirit, the way the human body houses an individual's mind.

- Society progressed toward more symbolic and abstract thinking when tree spirits were believed to control natural forces such as crops and human fertility.

Here's why the other choices are incorrect.

- It was forbidden to cut down certain trees because they would be seriously offended by an injury

    This choice is wrong because it mentions only a detail about one of the stages.

- More is known about the ceremonies of Europe than about the ceremonies of North America and the South Pacific.

    This choice is wrong because it talks about ceremonies, not stages of beliefs.

- Ancient Germans believed certain groves were sacred and used them as temples, but Druids venerated the oak tree in particular.

    This choice is also a specific detail that is mentioned only once in the passage.

Reading Passage #2: Mercury Pollution

11. **C** This is a *lead word* question. The question asks you which choice accounts for 70 percent of the toxic mercury pollution. The passage states that "The largest sources of mercury pollution in the United States are coal-fired power plants. Emissions from these plants account for 70 percent of the mercury that enters our oceans, lakes, and streams." This matches (C).

12. **A** This is a *vocabulary in context* question. Read a few lines above and below the word in question. Try to predict your own word for the shaded word based on the clues in the sentence. Eliminate answer choices that either are not supported by the words or phrases in the passage or are dictionary definitions of the word but are incorrect in the context of the sentence. *Concentrated* means "made less dilute" (as in a solution or mixture) and is used in this context to describe how the mercury becomes more prevalent as it moves up the food chain. Therefore, "clustered" is the closest to the meaning of concentrated. Choice (A) is correct.

13. **B** This is an EXCEPT question. Rephrase the question, eliminating the EXCEPT, go back to the passage, and look for each answer choice, marking each choice as TRUE OR FALSE. Choose the answer that is different from the other three. The passage states, "It is important to note that, thanks to the U.S. Clean Air Act and efforts by industry to curb unnecessary discharges as well as better sewage treatment methods, the levels have been in slow decline since the 1970s." Choices (A), (C), and (D) are all mentioned in the passage so the correct answer is (B).

14. **B** This is a *lead word* question, so go back to the passage to find out what it says about coastal areas. The passage states "most methylation takes place in coastal areas." Choice (A), tuna, is a trap answer because it is mentioned in paragraph 6, but it does not say that most tuna live there. Choice (B) is the correct answer.

15. **B** This is a *reference* question. The question is asking what noun the pronoun *its* replaces. In context "its" refers to the digestion of toxic methyl mercury in the previous sentence. Therefore, Choice (B) is the correct answer.

16. **C** This is a *lead word* question. This question asks you to understand what the passage says about longterm effects of mercury pollution. The paragraph states, "[Scientists] have made a positive link to mercury concentration in eggs which exceeds the concentrations found to be toxic...." Therefore, (C) is correct.

17. **A** This is a *lead word* question. This question asks you to understand what the passage says about Earth's ecosystems. The paragraph states that "it is this very interconnectivity that makes our ecosystem so vulnerable." Thus, the interconnectivity is the reason why the ecosystems are susceptible to pollution as described in (A). Choices (B) and (D) are incorrect because the interconnectivity is not the cause of the mercury pollution nor is it the cure for the pollution. Cross out (C) because methyl mercury is harmful long before it comes in contact with an interconnected ecosystem.

18. **D** This is a *vocabulary in context* question. Read a few lines above and below the word in question. Try to predict your own word for the shaded word based on the clues in the sentence. Eliminate answer choices that either are not supported by the words or phrases in the passage or are dictionary definitions of the word but are incorrect in the context of the sentence. "Ameliorate" means to make or become better, more bearable, or more satisfactory and is used in this context to describe improving the environment by reducing the impact of mercury. Therefore, "lessen" is closest to the meaning of "ameliorate," and (D) is the correct answer.

19. **D** This is a *sentence insertion* question. Remember to make sure the ideas in the new sentence match up with the sentences before and after the black square. Eliminate answers that do not match or only half-match. The statement about the long-term impact of mercury pollution best fits after the findings have been thoroughly explained and before the paragraph is summarized. Therefore, (D) has the correct placement.

20.   This is a *summary* question. Remember to separate main ideas from details. Use your understanding of passage structure to help. Make sure to eliminate answers that are too specific or not mentioned. The question asks you to find three points that support the following idea:

Mercury pollution is one example of a type of pollution that has short-term and long-term effects far from the source of the pollution.

- Air currents carry Mercury particles far from the source and are capable of polluting bodies of water thousands of miles away.

- Mercury is transformed into the toxic methyl mercury and moves up the food chain to cause harm for organisms at every level all the way up to humans.

- The harmful effects of methyl mercury are passed from adult to young and will impact the health of many species for years to come.

Here's why the other choices are incorrect:
- Mercury pollution is increasing in the United States despite the U.S. Clean Air Act and efforts of industry.

  This choice is too detailed to be a main idea.

- The methyl mercury binds to the protein in fish, residing in the muscle.

  This choice is also wildly specific so it is not a good response to a main idea question.

- Sulfate-reducing bacteria cause the "rotten egg" smell that exists at coastal areas during low tide.

  This choice is also extremely specific and not a good summary response.

Reading Passage #3: Hormones in the Body

21. **B** This *vocabulary in context* question refers to the lines below.

> Until the beginning of the twentieth century, the nervous system was thought
> to control all communication within the body and the resulting integration of
> behavior....These impulses were thought to be the engine for thought, emotion,
> movement, and internal processes such as digestion.

These lines assert that the nervous system was believed to "control all communication." We need a word that shows that all things are *started* by the nervous system. Choice (B), which means "beginning," is the only match. Here's why the other choices are incorrect.

- Choices (A) and (C) don't make sense.
- Choice (D) is contradicted by the lines stating that the nervous system is *electrical,* not chemical.

22. **A** Look at the following lines:

> From the small intestine, secretin travels through the bloodstream to the
> pancreas. There, _____ stimulates the release of digestive chemicals.

The shaded word in paragraph 1 of the passage refers to the noun that "stimulates the release of... chemicals." That can only be secretin, (A). Here's why the other answer choices are incorrect.

- The small intestine, (B), doesn't "stimulate the release of...chemicals."
- Nor does the pancreas, (D).
- The secretin does travel through the bloodstream, (C), but the bloodstream doesn't release chemicals.

23. **C** Use the word "hormone" to lead you to the correct answer. The author states,

> This discovery spurred Starling to coin the term *hormone* to refer to secretin,
> taking it from the Greek word *hormon,* meaning "to excite" or "to set in motion."
> A hormone is a chemical produced by one tissue to make things happen
> elsewhere.

Thus, a hormone is something that "makes things happen elsewhere," which means the same thing as (C). Here's why the other choices are incorrect.

- Choice (A) is not part of the definition of a hormone.
- Choice (B) is partially correct, but the problem is that it refers only to the "nervous system."
- The definition of "hormone" in the passage does not mention attitudes and behavior, so (D) is wrong.

24. **D** This question asks how hormones are categorized. The answer is in the following lines:

> As more hormones were discovered, they were categorized, primarily according to the process by which they operated on the body. Some glands which make up the endocrine system—such as the thyroid and pituitary glands—secrete hormones directly into the bloodstream… The exocrine system consists of organs and glands that produce substances that are used outside the bloodstream, primarily for digestion.

From this excerpt, it appears that classification is based on whether the hormones are dispensed into the bloodstream or not, which is what (D) states. Here's why the other choices are incorrect.

- The issue is not whether scientists understand the function or not, as in (A).
- The passage doesn't talk about how frequently the hormones work, so (B) is wrong.
- The aging process, the subject of (C), is not mentioned at all in paragraph 3.

25. **B** This question is tougher because you have to pay attention to a key word, "minute." The passage states

> Even _____ amounts of the right chemicals can suppress appetite, calm aggression, and change the attitude of a parent toward a child.

The sentence describes some very powerful effects—calming aggression, changing attitudes—and the word *even* means that we need something opposite of these major changes; (B), *small,* comes closest to the opposite of *major.* Here's why the other choices are incorrect.

- Choice (A), *sudden,* is not the opposite of *major* or *powerful.*
- Nor is (C), *seconds.* This is a trap answer; if you didn't read the lines in the passage, you might think that *minute* was referring to a unit of time.
- Choice (D) is the opposite of what you're looking for because the word *noticeable* is akin to the word *major*; that is, when something *major* happens, it's *noticeable.*

26. **A** The answer to this question is in the following lines:

> Some proponents of HRT have _____ their enthusiasm in the face of this new evidence, recommending it only to patients whose symptoms interfere with their abilities to live normal lives.

If the proponents now recommend HRT "only" to a small group of patients, their enthusiasm for it must have decreased. This makes (A) the best choice. Here's why the other choices are incorrect.

- There is no mention of advertising, so (B) is wrong.
- The shaded word refers to the "enthusiasm" of the proponents, not to the prescribing or researching of hormones. Therefore, (C) and (D) are incorrect.

27. **D** To answer this question, you need to look at the final paragraph. It states,

> Because of the complicated effects the growth hormone has on the body, such treatments are generally restricted to children who would be pathologically small in stature without it.

Now use POE.
- Because the treatment is for children, eliminate (A) and (B), which pertain to adults only.
- Eliminate (C) because it contradicts the passage, which states that the treatment is risky no matter who the patient is.
- Thus, (D) is correct because the passage says they would be "small in stature without it."

28. **A** This question asks you to find the purpose of hormone therapy. The correct answer is Choice (A).

> (A) The quantities and proportions of hormones produced change with age, so scientists have given a great deal of study to shifts in the endocrine system over time in the hopes of alleviating ailments associated with aging.

This is the correct answer because the purpose is "alleviating ailments associated with aging." Here's why the other choices are incorrect.

> (B) A combination of estrogen and progesterone has been prescribed for decades to women who want to reduce mood swings, sudden changes in body temperature, and other discomforts caused by lower natural levels of those hormones as they enter middle age.

This answer is incorrect because it refers to a *specific type* of hormone treatment (estrogen and progesterone), not the overall *purpose* of the therapy.

> (C) HRT may also increase the likelihood that blood clots—dangerous because they could travel through the bloodstream and block major blood vessels—will form.

> (D) Because of the complicated effects the growth hormone has on the body, such treatments are generally restricted to children who would be pathologically small in stature without it.

Both of these answer choices are incorrect because they talk about *problems* with the therapy, rather than the purpose of hormone therapy.

29. **C** This sentence should be inserted here.

> Known as hormone replacement therapy (HRT), the treatment was also believed to prevent weakening of the bones. The body is a complex machine, however, and recent studies have called into question the wisdom of essentially trying to fool its systems into believing they aren't aging. At least one study has linked HRT with a heightened risk of heart disease and certain types of cancer.

This is the best place because the new sentence talks about "recent studies" that are mentioned in the next sentence. It also uses the word *however* to indicate a transition from the first sentence, which discusses a positive aspect of the treatment, to the other sentence, which mentions a negative aspect.

30. This passage focuses on the discovery of hormones, what they do, and what new medical techniques may result from them. This corresponds to the following correct answers:

> The class of chemicals called hormones was discovered by two researchers studying a substance produced in the small intestine.

- Scientists have discovered that not only the nervous system but also certain chemicals can affect bodily processes far from their points of origin.

- Hormones can affect not only life processes such as growth but also behavior and emotion.

- Researchers are looking for ways to decrease the dangers of treatments with growth hormone so that more patients can benefit from it.

Here's why the other choices are incorrect.
- The term *hormone* is based on a Greek word that means "to excite" or "to set in motion."

> This choice is wrong because it details only the origin of the word; it has nothing to do with hormones or how they work.

- Hormones can be given artificially, but such treatments have risks and must be used carefully.

> This choice is wrong because it is too specific. It mentions hormone treatment, but focuses on the risks.

- Hormone replacement therapy (HRT) may increase the risk of blood clots and heart disease in middle-age women.

> This choice is wrong because it mentions problems encountered by only a small group of people, a detail that doesn't belong in the main idea.

THE LISTENING SECTION

Listening 1

Here is a transcript of the conversation (Track 20 in your Student Tools). Pay attention to the structure and main idea/purpose.

N: Listen to part of a conversation at a university library.

S: Hi. May I speak to the...uh, the archives librarian?

L: I'm the archives librarian. What can I help you with?

S: Well, actually, I'm not a student here. I'm studying history at State U. across town, but there's a collection of—

L: Oh, wait. Are you the...sorry, I don't remember your name, but the librarian over there asked me about giving someone access to the Jacobson collection. Is that you?

S: Yes, that's right. See, my paper is on the development of the coal-mining industry here in the city, and the Jacobson collection has a lot of information about John Jacobson... like, when he founded the company and things, right?

L: Yes, it does. More than you'll be able to fit into a paper, I'd bet. Did your librarian explain what our system is here?

S: A little. She told me to make sure I brought my college ID so I could get in the door.

L: Yes, well, I'll need to take a copy of it too. Even our own students who look at items from our archive collections have to leave a copy of their ID with us. You'll also have to sign into the archives room whenever you enter and sign out whenever you leave. There's a desk. You know, for security.

S: Wow. So a lot of this stuff is valuable?

L: Hmm. Well, I don't know whether you'd get much money for it, but a lot of it is one-of-a-kind, so if it were taken...that's it. It'd be gone.

S: I'll be careful.

L: Thank you. The other thing is, the things in the Jacobson collection are more than 100 years old, so I'll have to ask you to wear special gloves while handling the books. Also, I'm afraid you won't be able to photocopy anything.

S: I figured that. I ought to…I mean, I can probably get everything I need on note cards, but suppose there's a page or two I really want a copy of? Can I…I don't know, take a picture, or something?

L: Well, I can't let you take a picture. But we have scans…images…of all the pages in the collection. You can buy a print of any page you want, but they're expensive—five dollars apiece. So be sure you know which pages you want before you ask for them.

S: Five dollars! Well, I guess given how rare these things are... Okay, so you want a copy of my ID, and then can you tell me how to get to the archives room so I can get started?

1. **B** The student states the topic of her paper in her third statement: "My paper is on the development of the coal-mining industry here in the city." Here's why the other choices are incorrect.

   - If you were unsure and had to guess, (A) would be a good choice to avoid because it is a trap—the student needs to *use* old books for her paper, but the paper isn't *about* old books.
   - Eliminate (C) and (D). These two subjects were not mentioned at all in the discussion.

2. **B, D**

   The librarian tells the student, "I'll need to take a copy of it" (it = her ID). At the end of the conversation, she tells the student that she'll have to sign in and out of the archives room. Here's why the other choices are incorrect.

   - Choice (A) is incorrect because the librarian never said that the student has to show her notes.
   - The five-dollar fee was for copying images, not entering the room, which is why (C) is incorrect.

3. **C** The librarian says, "a lot of it is one-of-a-kind, so if it were taken…that's it. It'd be gone" (it = archival material). Here's why the other choices are incorrect.

   - Choice (B) is the opposite of what the librarian said: "Well, I don't know if you'd get much money for it…"
   - Choices (A) and (D) were not mentioned in the conversation.

4.   **A**   The librarian mentions the age of the books to explain why the student needs to wear gloves to handle them. Specifically, the librarian says, "The things in the Jacobson collection are more than 100 years old, so I'll have to ask you to wear special gloves while handling the books." Here's why the other choices are incorrect.

- Eliminate (B) because it is extreme; it says that the student can "only" look at photographs, whereas she can actually buy a print of any page she wants.

- Choice (C) is incorrect because the passage does not mention when the books were added to the collection.

- Choice (D), again, is the opposite of what the librarian said about the value of the books (see the explanation for question 3).

5.   **B**   This question asks you to listen again to the following part of the conversation and to determine what the student meant in the part excerpted below:

L: Well, I can't let you take a picture. But we have scans…images…of all the pages in the collection. You can buy a print of any page you want, but they're expensive—five dollars apiece. So be sure you know which pages you want before you ask for them.

S: Five dollars! Well, I guess given how rare these things are…

Choice (B) is correct because the student admits "…given how rare these things are…." Here's why the other choices are incorrect.

- Eliminate (A) and (C) because they have nothing to do with money.
- Choice (D) is not mentioned by the student.

Listening 2

Here is a transcript of the lecture (Track 21 in your Student Tools).

N: Listen to a professor lecture on the process of memory.

P: A popular saying goes, "An elephant never forgets." But how about people? Have you ever forgotten the name of someone you just met at a party? Sure, we all have. This is because our memories are complex processes.

We're not going to be able to talk much about the physiology of memory here...both because, well, it's not our subject, and because there's a lot we still need to learn about how the brain stores things. One thing we do know is that the mechanism isn't simple. When researchers scan the brain as a memory is forming, parts seem to light up—by "light up" I mean, you know, become active—in random, scattered formations. But of course they can't be random because memory produces very orderly results.

One researcher...this is Walter Freeman of the University of California at Berkeley... compares it to two kinds of crowds. The impulses in the brain look completely random, like the movement of a mob of people who are frightened. You know, they just keep moving, and they're not really going anywhere, and there's no pattern to their movement. That's the way impulses in the brain look at first. But since memory does, in fact, work, the impulses must be moving more like people in a crowded train station. You know, if you've got people running in and out and from one train line to another, it seems like complete confusion. But really they all know where they're going. They're following a set of instructions—the timetable for the trains, the board that tells which track is for which train, all that stuff. So you have to look carefully to see that there's actually organization, a system, involved. That's how memory impulses must function. Freeman figures we just haven't figured out what the timetable and track numbers are!

So we'll leave the physiology there; we're going to talk about the psychology of memory...the actual process. Psychologists divide memory into three stages: registration, long-term retention, and recall.

In the initial stage, registration, information is perceived and understood, like when you first hear a name or address. This information is then retained in the short-term memory system. Unfortunately, the short-term memory is limited in the amount of material it can store at one time. And, unless refreshed by constant repetition, the new contents are lost within minutes when replaced by even newer information. To solve this dilemma, the information needs to be transformed into the second stage, long-term retention.

The conversion to the long-term retention stage is most easily accomplished using what the research team labeled association. Associating the new information with the visual imagery evoked by it gives the individual a sort of "memory" crutch to rely on. For example, let's say you're at a party, and you've just met a woman named Lily. To remember her name, visualize it in connection to the flower, the lily. Oh, and be sure to make it outlandish…kind of silly, even. Those images are most memorable. Picture her with a big basket of lilies, or wearing a hat with a lily on it, or even sitting inside a giant lily.

The third stage, recall, is when the information stored—stored through long-term retention—at an unconscious level is then deliberately brought into the conscious mind. However, this final stage primarily depends on how well the material was stored in stage two. Of course, there are disturbances that may affect the recall stage—age, for example. The older a person gets, the less new information he can recall. Disuse is another example. Here, forgetting occurs because stored information is not used and, therefore, is lost. Memory loss can also be physiological. If a person receives an injury to the head, he may experience what is known as amnesia, the failure to remember certain or even all events preceding the accident.

Of course, many self-help books on how to improve your memory have been published, and many other mnemonic methods have been tried and tested. Let's take a closer look at some of the more widely accepted approaches to memory enhancement. Perhaps you may even incorporate some of them into your study habits as you prepare for the upcoming finals.

6. **B** Here's why the other choices are incorrect.
    - Choice (A) wrongly focuses on "events" instead of memory.
    - Choice (C) is also a good candidate for POE because animals are not the main focus.
    - Eliminate (D) because the professor doesn't mention this topic (of how to strengthen memory) until the very end of the lecture.

7. **C** Here's why the other choices are incorrect.
    - You may have recalled that the information in (A) doesn't appear until later in the lecture.
    - For this question, (B) is not related to the main idea, so eliminate it—this idea of "direction" was used only in the crowded train station analogy.
    - Choice (D) is extreme; it says that each person has a "unique" way of remembering things.

8. **B** This is a question in which there isn't much you can do if you missed the part of the lecture that gives the definition. (The three stages, "registration, long-term retention, and recall," were first introduced; then each stage was discussed in detail.) If you did miss this, just guess and move on.

9. **A** This question asks you to listen again to the following part of the lecture, which directly states the answer (that outlandish images are most memorable):

> For example, let's say...you've just met a woman named Lily. To remember her name, visualize it in connection to the flower, the lily. Oh, and be sure to make it outlandish…kind of silly, even. Those images are most memorable. Picture her with a big basket of lilies, or wearing a hat with a lily on it, or even sitting inside a giant lily.

Here's why the other choices are incorrect.
- Choice (B) is extreme, eliminate it. The "lily" example was exactly that—an example, not a recommendation of how to help one's memory by thinking of something from nature.
- Choice (C) wrongly focuses on the specifies of the example rather than the point of the professor's illustration.
- Choice (D), which refers to the size of objects, has nothing to do with remembering a person's name.

10. **B** Toward the end of the lecture, the professor talks about the "disturbances" that may affect the recall of stored memories. He says, "Disuse… Here, forgetting occurs because stored information is not used and, therefore, is lost," which supports (B). Here's why the other choices are incorrect.
- Choices (A) and (C) are not mentioned by the professor (note that brain injury, the topic of (C) *is* mentioned but only in the context of amnesia).
- Choice (D) is the opposite of what is stated in the lecture. ("The older a person gets, the less new information he can recall.")

11. **D** The professor ends the lecture with these words: "Let's take a closer look at some of the more widely accepted approaches to memory enhancement. Perhaps you may even incorporate some of them into your study habits as you prepare for the upcoming finals."
Here's why the other choices are incorrect.
- Choices (A) and (C) are not mentioned.
- Eliminate (B) because it has nothing to do with the main idea.

Listening 3

Here is a transcript of the class discussion (Track 22 in your Student Tools).

N: Listen to part of a class discussion on the different types of joints.

P: Now, I know that most of you are healthy individuals who participate in some sort of physical activity pretty regularly. Some of you jog, others bicycle, you might throw around the Frisbee with your friends, or Rollerblade. Our movements are so easy and fluid that you may not have stopped to think that the system of joints that makes them possible is highly complex. A joint is the place where two or more bones connect, and because that's the technical definition, it actually includes some places that don't move. Since it's movement that we're interested in, I won't spend much time on the immovable joints. They're called fibrous joints. The reason is that...uh, well, they're joined together by bone fibers. It's kind of like welding or soldering two pieces of metal together. There are fibrous joints, for example, between the different bones that make up the top part of your skull. The bones don't move, right? I'm talking about the top of your head—forget your jaw for a second. If your jaw had a fibrous joint, you couldn't talk! The round dome of the skull is made of several bone plates with fibers holding them together.

Okay, so those are the fibrous joints. The other joints, the ones we're interested in, are movable. In a movable joint, the bones aren't fused to each other. They're held together with ligaments. Ligaments are long and flexible; they're kind of like ropes or cables. But because the bones have to slide or rub over each other when the joint moves, it also needs to be cushioned against abrasion. These joints are categorized by the types of tissues used to keep them working smoothly.

Cartilaginous joints have a tough, smooth lining over the parts of the bone. It's like a pad or cushion; it protects the bone from friction that could wear it down or cause it to splinter. And, in fact, if this cartilage—the protective tissue is called cartilage—if it becomes worn or damaged, joint movement may be painful or severely restricted because now you have bone hitting bone. That's because cartilaginous joints are tight; the bones fit very closely together—for example, the bones in your spine.

Some joints require more movement. They're called synovial joints. There has to be a space between the bones, a joint cavity. Those more mobile joints, in addition to being padded with cartilage, are lubricated with liquid that flows through the cavity. The knuckles of your fingers are examples of synovial joints. Of course, the fluid has to be held in place, otherwise it'll seep into the surrounding tissues and be absorbed back into the body, and what holds it in place is a little membrane-lined sac called a bursa. So the joint is encased in this membrane, and the membrane is a pocket for that lubricating fluid. By the way, the fluid also keeps the joint nourished—it doesn't have an independent blood supply in adults, so the fluid absorbs nutrients from the blood through the joint's outer membrane. That's a synovial joint.

Tony, do you have a question?

M: Yeah, I'm kind of confused. When we learned about the joints in high school, I don't remember talking about them this way. I thought we talked about them more like machines…uh, like, the directions in which they moved.

P: Uh-huh, we're getting to that. Okay, now that we have joints categorized by how their surfaces are put together—fibrous, synovial, and cartilaginous—we can talk about how the movable joints actually move. I mentioned your knuckles a few minutes ago, and they're good examples of hinge joints. They work kind of like the hinge on a door, so the joint can flex and extend in one direction only. But hinge joints aren't the only movable joints in the body. The hip, as well as the shoulder, is an example of the ball-and-socket joint. The ball-and-socket joint allows the greatest range of movement, and therefore, it has to be the most anatomically complex. In a ball-and-socket, one bone has a rounded knob at the end, and it fits snugly into the socket, a round cavity, of another bone. The ball-and-socket joint is a type characteristically found in more evolved creatures, such as apes and us humans. It allows you to move through 360 degrees of motion, the way you can wind your arm back before you throw a ball.

While we're at it, can anyone think of another type of joint?

W: Well, I know that when I rollerblade, I have to turn my head constantly to make sure I don't crash into anyone. But the neck doesn't seem to be an example of either a hinge joint or a ball-and-socket joint.

P: Good example, Louise. The neck is actually a type of pivot joint. Pivot joints permit rotation, the way you can twist your head around. Well, it doesn't go all the way around, but it moves around your neck. It pivots on an axis.

12. **C** Here's why the other choices are incorrect.
    - There is no mention of injuries, so (A) is wrong.
    - Eliminate (B) because sports are mentioned only at the very beginning of the lecture, as a way of introducing the main topic.
    - Flexibility, (D), is not mentioned either.

13. **A** Here's why the other choices are incorrect.
    - Choice (B), regarding ligaments, pertains to the *other* type of joint: movable joints, not fibrous joints.
    - Of the choices, (C) is the best candidate for POE. The entire lecture talked about humans, so it wouldn't make sense for (C) to be correct.
    - You can also eliminate (D) because of the word "most."

14. **C** This question asks you to listen again to the following part of the discussion, which directly states the answer:

    > There are fibrous joints, for example, between the different bones that make up the top part of your skull. The bones don't move, right? I'm talking about the top of your head—forget your jaw for a second. If your jaw had a fibrous joint, you couldn't talk!

    Here's why the other choices are incorrect.
    - Choice (A) is incorrect because the professor has not yet discussed the type of joint in the jaw.
    - Choice (B) is extreme; it uses the word *best*.
    - Choice (D) is a good trap because the instructor said "forget your jaw…." However, if you're unsure of the correct answer and one choice seems too easy, it's probably a trap.

15. **B** This is a question in which POE doesn't help much. If you didn't quite catch the part of the lecture, take your best guess and move on. If you remember that shoulders and hips are the same type of joint, you can eliminate both of them because you can choose only one answer.

16. **D** The professor stated this at the end of the lecture: "The ball-and-socket joint allows the greatest range of movement, and therefore, it has to be the most anatomically complex." Here's why the other choices are incorrect.
    - Cartilage was mentioned earlier in the talk, so eliminate (A).
    - Eliminate (B) because it is too strong—it is unlikely that the joint "cannot" be damaged at all.
    - Eliminate (C) because the professor never says that ball-and-socket joints need to move quickly. He says they allow for the "greatest range of movement."

17.   This one's tough. The completed chart is shown below.

	Synovial	Cartilaginous
A special liquid lubricates and nourishes the joint.	X	
There is no cavity between the bones.		X
The joint is covered with a membrane-lined sac.	X	
Only a lining of smooth tissue protects the bones.		X
The joint has limited movement.		X

Listening 4

Here is a transcript of the class discussion (Track 23 in your Student Tools).

N: Listen to part of a discussion in a class on English literature.

P: Everyone here? Okay, I hope that you all did the readings for this week. I know it's midterm time, and you're all busy, but Robert Browning is one of the most important poets in the history of English literature. He deserves all your attention. Actually, it's usually not hard to sell Browning on my students, I find—his poetry really draws people in. Uh, so, what did you all think?

W: Well, you're certainly right that it draws you in, but I have to say, it really confused me at first.

P: What was it that confused you?

W: Well, I mean, the poems we've read so far have been—it's like, the poet is just kind of writing the poem. The poems we read by this Browning guy...it took me a few minutes to realize that he was using the voice of some historical character. It was supposed to be someone else speaking.

P: Sure. The reason I assigned this particular set of poems by Browning was so you could see what his most famous style was. He perfected a style called the *dramatic monologue*. And its major features are what you saw in the readings. It's called dramatic because a poem of this type takes place at some sort of dramatic moment in the middle of a story. And a monologue is a long speech given by an individual, right? And so are these poems. You have Browning writing as if he were a different person, usually someone from history, speaking at length. And he talks about something that's happening to him when the poem takes place.

M: Professor, I kind of cheated and looked up information about Browning when I did the readings—I was like Karen; I was really confused at first. It seemed strange that this form of poetry, you know, the dramatic monologue, is so new. Browning only lived in the nineteenth century. Was he really the first person to develop a kind of poetry where he pretended to be someone from history giving a speech? It surprised me to read that.

P: Well, you see, the dramatic monologue is actually a more complex style of poetry than it might seem to be at first. For one thing, a lot of poems are addressed to the world in general, sort of, but a dramatic monologue isn't. The speaker in a dramatic monologue is addressing a particular person involved in the story. So for example in the poem "My Last Duchess," the duke is doing the speaking...and he's specifically speaking to a servant of his future father-in-law. That's important. A lot of the poem doesn't make sense unless you bear in mind that he's trying to give a message to the father of his new wife.

W: It took me a while to figure that out. And then, when I realized what was going on, it really creeped me out. I mean, did I read it right? He seemed to be admitting—

P: Karen, why don't we hold off on analyzing the poem too much for right now. I don't want to shut you down, but I do want to stick to the general structure of the poems for a bit.

I will say that when Karen talks about finding the poem a little spooky, part of that probably comes from the fact that...well, you figure, within the poem, the speaker is talking to someone in particular. So when you read the poem, you kind of take that person's role—the role of the person being addressed. That's one chief characteristic of the dramatic monologue.

Now, obviously, the other thing Karen was probably unsettled by, in the case of "My Last Duchess," is that the duke doesn't sound like a very nice character! We know that because of another key element of the dramatic monologue. What the speaker says is designed to make an argument—he's trying to persuade the listener...and you the reader by extension...that what he did was right, or that his viewpoint is correct, or whatever. He makes a case, kind of like a lawyer with a judge or jury, and in the process he reveals his way of thinking, something of his psychology. And you have to decide whether you believe him.

M: It's kind of hard because—I felt like a lot of the story was missing. The speaker in the poem only told his side of things, and you got the feeling that there had to be more going on, but it was all just guesswork.

P: Now you see why I said the form was complex, huh? Sure. You have to fill in the back story yourself. And that's the third big characteristic of a dramatic monologue. Now, with those things in mind, let's look at the actual poems you read for this week.

18. **C** Dramatic monologue was emphasized by the professor early in the lecture. Here's why the other choices are incorrect.

- Choice (A) is wrong because the discussion is about Browning, not what influenced him.
- Choice (B) is too broad. Make sure your choice reflects the topic of the discussion.
- Eliminate (D) because the professor doesn't mention "My Last Duchess" until halfway through the lecture.

19. **D** This question asks you to listen again to the following part of the discussion and to determine what the professor meant in part of it:

> Okay, I hope that you all did the readings for this week. I know it's midterm time, and you're all busy, but Robert Browning is one of the most important poets in the history of English literature. He deserves all your attention. Actually, it's usually not hard to sell Browning on my students, I find—his poetry really draws people in.

Here's why the other choices are incorrect.

- Choices (A) and (B) don't make sense; the professor stated that Browning is very popular.
- Choice (C) is pretty much contradicted by the fact that both students say they were "confused" and the professor says "the dramatic monologue is actually a *more complex* [emphasis added] style of poetry" and thus, not "easy to understand."

20. **A** The professor says, "a monologue is a long speech given by an individual, right?" Here's why the other choices are incorrect.

- The discussion is all about poems and people, not historical characters, (B), or events, (C).
- For this question, (D) is obviously out because a monologue is not a person.

21. **A, B, D**

Choice (C) is not mentioned. Although "My Last Duchess" may be about a duke, it doesn't mean that all poems of this sort are about people of high status.

22. **B** The student says, "...when I realized what was going on, it really creeped me out." Here's why the other choices are incorrect.

- Choice (A) is the opposite of what the woman felt.
- Choice (C) should be eliminated because no other poems are mentioned.
- The woman says she had trouble realizing that Browning was "using the voice of some historical character." She never questions the historical accuracy of the poem. Eliminate (D).

23. **C** This question asks you to listen again to the following part of the discussion:

> *W:* It took me a while to figure that out. And then, when I realized what was going on, it really creeped me out. I mean, did I read it right? He seemed to be admitting—
>
> *P:* Karen, why don't we hold off on analyzing the poem too much for right now. I don't want to shut you down, but I do want to stick to the general structure of the poems for a bit.

The professor said, "why don't we hold off on analyzing the poem too much for right now," meaning that he didn't want to talk about the specifics. Here's why the other choices are incorrect.

- Choice (D) is the opposite meaning of the sentence above.
- Choices (A) and (B) also invite further discussion, which is not what the professor is doing at this point.

Listening 5

Here is a transcript of the conversation (Track 24 in your Student Tools).

N: Listen to a conversation on a college campus.

M: Amy, a bunch of us are probably going to ditch the dining hall and go for pizza tonight. If you're free, you can meet us at the east gate at seven.

W: You know, I'd love to, but I have tutoring tonight.

M: Tutoring? I can't imagine you needing help with a class.

W: The tutoring I'm talking about is tutoring I'm doing for someone else—though, now that you mention it, physics has been giving me more problems than usual this semester.

M: I find that hard to believe. Uh, so are you tutoring one of the lower-classmen, or something?

W: Actually, no, I go downtown to tutor a few students at the high school.

M: High school kids? Wow. In math or something?

W: Right. You've probably read about this in the paper, but the city's trying to raise the standards for its math classes. The problem is, a lot of the kids are behind when they get to junior high school.

M: So you help them get caught up?

W: Basically. I have three students for forty-five minutes each on Wednesday night. So I'm there from 6:00 to 8:30 or so.

M: Isn't that late for kids to be still at school?

W: Well, they'd be doing homework at that hour if they were home, anyway. The thing is, most of the tutors are students here at the university, so our classes aren't over until late afternoon. And the city education department likes us. We're good at what we do, but we volunteer, so the program doesn't cost a lot beyond, you know, the heat and electricity to keep the high school open at night.

M: Can you afford to take that much time away from your own studying?

W: Some weeks it's kind of hard, but, I mean, when I go to grad school, I'm going to have to start teaching physics to students as a professor's assistant, anyway. I may as well get used to teaching with easier material and just one student at a time.

M: And it must be nice to help people.

W: Definitely. That goes without saying. Forty-five minutes a week isn't much time, but all three of my students have improved in the months we've worked together. It's really inspiring.

M: Cool.

W: So, anyway, sorry about dinner. It sounds like fun, and if it were any other night—

M: Hey, I understand. Have fun, and I guess I'll see you in class tomorrow morning.

24. **D** This is the main idea of the conversation: helping high school students with their studies. The other choices are not part of the conversation.

25. **C** This question asks you to listen again to the following part of the conversation and to determine what the woman meant in part of it:

M: Tutoring? I can't imagine you needing help with a class.

W: The tutoring I'm talking about is tutoring I'm doing for someone else—though, now that you mention it, physics has been giving me more problems than usual this semester.

The woman says "physics has been giving me more problems than usual this semester." Therefore, the correct answer is (C). Here's why the other choices are incorrect.

- Choice (A) isn't correct because the only mention of physics is the general comment that the class is giving her problems; there's no specific mention about any particular assignment.
- Choice (B) doesn't make sense because she wouldn't have problems with physics if she weren't taking it.
- She is not referring to the man, so eliminate (D).

26. **A** Here's the statement from the conversation that answers the question: "…the city's trying to raise the standards for its math classes." Here's why the other choices are incorrect.

   - Choice (B) is the opposite of what the woman states about the program; she says it doesn't have a lot of money.
   - Choice (C) doesn't answer the question of "why" the program was started.
   - Choice (D) doesn't work because there's no mention that the university students *initiated* or *suggested* the tutoring, just that they're doing it.

27. **D** Here's the statement from the conversation that answers the question: "…the city education department likes us. We're good at what we do, but we volunteer, so the program doesn't cost a lot…." Here's why the other choices are incorrect.

   - Eliminate (A) and (C) because the word *most* is an extreme word. Remember to avoid these.
   - Choice (B) is the opposite of what the woman says—she tutors at night.

28. **B** Here's the statement from the conversation that answers the question: "…when I go to grad school, I'm going to have to start teaching physics to students…anyway. I may as well get used to teaching…." Here's why the other choices are incorrect.

   - Choice (A) doesn't make sense: the woman is not being tutored; instead, she is tutoring other students.
   - The jobs mentioned in (C) and (D) are not mentioned by the woman. She mentions only her future teaching duties as a grad student.

Listening 6

Here is a transcript of the lecture (Track 25 in your Student Tools).

N: Listen to part of a lecture on events leading up to the American Revolution.

P: Okay, while I think of it, on Tuesday, I was originally going to show you a documentary film about a town in New England that was founded in the colonial period…uh, but it looks like we had a mix-up at the library, and they lent it out to someone, so I won't be able to show it until Thursday's class. So, instead of what I told you before, do the readings over the weekend and be prepared to discuss them on Tuesday. Hope that doesn't inconvenience you.

Okay, we're going to be talking about the American Revolution—what we often call the Revolutionary War—and we'll talk about two or three laws—the Sugar Act, the Currency Act, and the Stamp Act. They were all enacted soon after the French and Indian War ended in 1763. The British had won the war and, as a consequence, gained a lot of territory. But there was a downside to their victory: The war had cost a lot of money. So, British Parliament looked for ways to make sure that trade money from the American colonies came back to Britain. The increased money would help pay for the war. The way the British decided to get that money was to put taxes on certain purchases and to put limits on what kinds of goods the colonists could buy and sell, and that's where the trouble started.

The Sugar Act was passed in 1764. It was actually a revised version of an old tax on sugar by-products like molasses, and it had two big effects. One, Parliament lowered the tax on molasses but increased the tax on sugar and certain kinds of cloth, coffee, some wines, and fruits from the tropics. Second, it made sure the taxes were collected—the old tax on molasses hadn't been enforced very well. Now, what this did was, mostly, it made it more difficult for rich people—they were the ones buying the wines and tropical fruits and refined sugar, as you might imagine—to get things they wanted.

Now, that same year, Parliament passed the Currency Act. The colonists had to buy most of their goods from home, from England; that took up most of their British currency. So, what happened, of course, was that when they wanted to trade with each other within the colonies, they didn't have any money left over to use. That gave them an incentive to come up with their own paper currency. Some was backed by— meaning, its value was based on—people's property. It was useless for buying things from England, but it was very useful for workers with a little farmland who wanted to pay off their debts quickly. They could use the paper notes and then try to earn back the real value in produce from their farms. What did the Currency Act do? It invalidated all these colonial forms of paper currency. The colonists were told they couldn't use them anymore. So now you have the rich merchants, the traders, angered by the Sugar Act, and you have the laborers in debt who need to rely on paper money, and they're angered by the Currency Act.

Okay, so now the third law: the Stamp Act. The Sugar Act put a tax on sugar, so you might think the Stamp Act put a tax on stamps, but that wasn't the idea. The idea was that there would now be a tax on all sorts of official documents the colonists used to get for free: marriage licenses, newspapers, even playing cards. Well, these were the kinds of things people needed for everyday life, so everyone—merchants and laborers alike—was outraged.

Now, I'm leaving out some things in the sequence of events—such as that the British government adjusted some of the provisions of these laws when the colonists complained. But the main point I'm trying to make is, these laws were meant to get more money, more revenue, for the British government to pay for the French and Indian War, but the effect they had on the colonists was to make them feel as if they were being pushed around by a bunch of people in Parliament on the other side of the ocean. Up until this point, the taxes in the colonies had been administered by local governments in the colonies themselves. For the first time, Britain not only imposed taxes on the colonists but showed that it would use force to collect them. And this was the origin of the famous slogan "Taxation Without Representation," and it stoked the movement among the colonists to be free of British rule.

29. **D** Here's why the other choices are incorrect.
    - Choice (A) is not related to the main idea.
    - Choice (B) is far too broad.
    - No mention is made of (C).

30. **D** This question asks you to listen again to the following part of the lecture, which directly states the answer:

    P: Okay, while I think of it, on Tuesday, I was originally going to show you a documentary film about a town in New England that was founded in the colonial period…uh, but it looks like we had a mix-up at the library, and they lent it out to someone, so I won't be able to show it until Thursday's class. So instead of what I told you before, do the readings over the weekend and be prepared to discuss them on Tuesday. Hope that doesn't inconvenience you.

    Choice (D) is the answer. The other choices are not correct because they are not mentioned at all.

31. **A** This information is given in the professor's introduction: "They [the tax acts described in the rest of the lecture] were all enacted soon after the French and Indian War ended in 1763…the war had cost a lot of money." Here's why the other choices are incorrect.

- Choices (B) and (C) are related to the actual taxes, but they do not answer the question of "why" the British needed money.

- Choice (D) is incorrect because there's no mention of taxes in Britain, only in the American colonies.

32. **A, B**

Here's why the other choices are incorrect.

- Choice (C) is a little tricky because the lecture does say that the Sugar Act was "a *revised* version of an old tax on sugar by-products," [emphasis added] and it *does* mention taxes on coffee and wines, but not that they were *replaced;* instead, it says the Sugar Act "*increased* the tax on sugar and…coffee, some wines…." [again, emphasis added.]

- Of the choices, (D) is the best candidate for POE because it contradicts the main idea of the lecture, which is that there were too many taxes on the colonists.

33. **B** Here's the statement in the lecture: "The colonists had to buy most of their goods from home, from England; that took up most of their British currency." Therefore, (B) is the correct answer. Here's why the other choices are incorrect.

- Eliminate (A) because although the colonists *did* need more money to pay the higher Sugar Tax, this is not the reason they developed their own paper currency; instead, the reason is that "they wanted to trade with each other within the colonies, [and] they didn't have any money [i.e., British currency] left over to use. That gave them an incentive to come up with their own paper currency."

- Eliminate (C) because it is extreme.

- There is no mention of (D) in the lecture.

34. **C** Choice (C) is correct because the professor specifically states the following about the Stamp Act: "Well, these were the kinds of things people needed for everyday life, so everyone—merchants and laborers alike—was outraged."

- Choice (A) is wrong because newspapers are mentioned but only because the Stamp Act taxed them and other "official documents"; outlawing them isn't mentioned at all.

- Also, eliminate (B) because the war was mentioned in a different part of the lecture, and the professor never mentions that the colonists had fought in the war.

- Choice (D) refers to the wrong act (The Sugar Act), so eliminate it.

THE SPEAKING SECTION: SAMPLE RESPONSES

Compare your responses with the samples below. All the samples are of high-scoring responses. Try to copy the style and structure of the sample responses. Even if you feel you have a strong answer, practice saying our sample answers out loud to give yourself ideas of different ways of answering the same question.

Speaking 1

Narrator: Some universities have large, lecture-based classes, while others have smaller, discussion-based classes. Which do think is better and why? Include details and reasons to support your position.

Here's one way you could have answered this question.

State opinion	I believe that small classes are better than larger ones.
Reason #1	I think it is important for students to be able to talk about ideas.
Specific detail for reason #1	If you are in a large class, you will not be heard and will not be able to interact with the teacher.
Reason #2	Also, a small class is better because the student will get to know the professor.
Specific detail for reason #2	The student will have a better experience if he or she knows the professor well. The student will get more out of the class.
Reason #3	Finally, I prefer small classes because they are more interesting.
Specific detail for reason #3	It is easy to become distracted or lost during a lecture. But during a talk, you are more involved.

Speaking 2

Here is a transcript of the discussion (Track 27 in your Student Tools).

N: The College of Arts and Sciences at Eastern University has decided to add a senior project to its existing graduation requirements. The campus newspaper printed the following report about the announcement of the new requirement. You have 45 seconds to read the report. Begin reading now.

The College of Arts and Sciences has announced that it will require students to write a senior thesis to qualify for graduation, beginning with students who enter the university this coming fall. The senior thesis is currently an option in all departments. Specific criteria have not yet been released by the dean, but they are expected to define the thesis as a year-long research project, undertaken with the guidance of a faculty advisor, that results in a paper of at least 50 pages or the equivalent.

N: Now listen to two students as they discuss the report.

W1: Wow, look at this. The dean seems to be serious about tightening graduation requirements—they'll be forcing students to write a senior thesis in order to graduate.

W2: Yeah, you know, I read that at breakfast. It seems a little weird.

W1: Weird? Haven't you seen all those reports about how graduates with poor writing skills are having trouble finding jobs? Companies don't want to hire them.

W2: Uh-huh.

W1: And the ones that want to apply to graduate school—if they can't write, they can't present their research ideas effectively in their essays.

W2: I guess I'm more thinking about the science people—biology, physics. I mean, it seems strange to give them this big paper to do.

W1: Maybe. On the other hand, the paper—see here?—it says you have to write a paper "or equivalent." So presumably, you can do a project that ends up as a lot of data and stuff...maybe make it a presentation instead of a paper. But even so, I mean, don't biologists have to learn how to write up their research in order to get it published? It seems to me that having a writing requirement is long overdue.

N: The First woman explains her opinion of the announcement made by the College of Arts and Sciences. State her opinion, and explain the reasons she gives for holding that opinion.

Here's how you could have answered this question.

State opinion	The first woman states that the senior thesis is a good idea.
Reason #1	She thinks this is a good idea because students should know how to write.
Detail for reason #1	The first woman says that companies don't want to hire people who are bad writers.
Reason #2	The first woman also agrees with the idea because of graduate school.
Detail for reason #2	According to the first woman, students need to write well in order to succeed in graduate school.

Speaking 3

Here is a transcript of the passage (Track 26 in your Student Tools).

Narrator: Now read the passage about birds of prey. You have 45 seconds to read the passage. Begin reading now.

Birds of Prey

Many people assume that *raptor* is the word properly used to designate all birds of prey. In fact, raptors are a group with three basic traits that many flesh-eating birds do not share. First, a raptor has strong feet and claws that it uses to capture prey. Second, a raptor has well-developed eyesight. This facilitates hunting from the air. Finally, a raptor has a hooked or curved beak for tearing flesh.

N: Now listen to part of a lecture on this topic given in a biology class.

P: There are two bird species found in our local area that I think do a good job of exemplifying the range of ways birds of prey can adapt. One is the bald eagle, and the other is the great blue heron. They both feed largely on fish, and they're both large. But the more closely you observe them, the more the differences show.

The bald eagle is always on the lookout for dead fish at the side of a river or lake or for fish that it can grab from close to the surface of the water. That's because it has very sharp eyesight and strong talons. It can swoop down, grab a fish in its claws, and start eating it midair. Its beak curves; it has sort of a hook at the end so it can start pulling food into its mouth.

The great blue heron might eat those same fish, but it would have to go about it differently. The heron does have good eyesight—it'd be hard to see prey otherwise, right? But its claws aren't as strong as the eagle's, so it usually attacks by diving into the water headfirst. The heron has a long, straight beak that it can use either like a spear to impale a fish or like tongs to grab it.

N: The professor discussed the characteristics of two kinds of birds of prey. On the basis of these characteristics, explain whether either bird would be categorized as a raptor.

Here's one way you could have answered this question.

Main response	According to the reading, a raptor has several characteristics. The eagle is a raptor but the heron isn't.
Characteristic #1 from reading	First, a raptor has claws on its feet. It uses its claws to capture food.
Detail #1 from lecture	The eagle mentioned in the lecture has these types of claws. However, the heron uses its beak to capture food.
Characteristic #2 from reading	Another quality of the raptor is strong eyesight. Its eyesight helps the bird hunt.
Detail #2 from lecture	The professor said that the eagle has strong eyesight. The heron does as well.
Characteristic #3 from reading	The last thing about a raptor is a hooked beak.
Detail #3 from lecture	The eagle has this, but the heron doesn't.

Speaking 4

Here is the transcript of the lecture (Track 28 in your Student Tools).

N: Now listen to part of a lecture in a history class.

P: The discovery of copper was a great advance for civilization, but no one is quite sure how it happened. Of course, in nature, metal like copper is usually buried in rock. Early humans must have accidentally discovered that heating the rock melted the metal and released it. There are two interesting ways that might have happened.

One relates to the use of primitive campfires. Once humans figured out how to control fire for light and heat, they knew that they needed to keep their fires confined. One of the ways they did this was to take stones and cover the fire with them partially. That kept the fire enclosed, and it also made sure it didn't burn too fast and use up the fuel. Now, what do you think might have happened? Some of those stones contained copper, and before the fire died down, it was hot enough to melt the copper out of the stones. When people went back to the fire after it had burned out, they discovered small pieces of shiny metal that had melted out and cooled.

There's a second possibility that relates to pottery. Early humans discovered how to make pottery before they learned how to use copper. Of course, to make pottery, you have to bake it in an oven, right? Well, some societies got into the habit of decorating their containers with colored stones before baking them. One of those stones is a mineral called *malachite,* and malachite contains...that's right: copper. The hot temperature inside the oven released the copper metal from the other ingredients. When the people took their pottery out of the oven, they found pieces of copper at the bottom.

N: Using points and examples from the talk, explain the two possible ways early humans discovered how to use fire to release copper from solid rock.

Here's how you may have answered this question.

State main idea	The professor states that it was an accident that humans discovered copper.
Reason #1	Humans may have discovered copper by using campfires.
Detail for reason #1	Copper is stuck inside rocks, and people used rocks to contain their fires.
Link between reason #1 and main idea	If the fire was hot enough, the people would have noticed pieces of copper in their fires.
Reason #2	Another way people could have discovered copper was through pottery.
Detail for reason #2	Sometimes the people decorated their pottery with stones before they baked it in an oven.
Link between reason #2 and main idea	The heat in the oven caused the copper to melt and come out of the stones, and the people could have discovered it that way.

THE WRITING SECTION: SAMPLE RESPONSES

Look over your written responses. Make sure they answer the question effectively, are of the appropriate length, and are well organized. Use the following responses as guides.

Writing 1

Narrator: Now read the passage about the suppression of forest fires. You have three minutes to read the passage. Begin reading now.

Wilderness management has advanced greatly over the last century, due in part to such practices as the suppression of forest fires and limitations on the clear-cutting of trees. Monitoring forests for small brushfires is easier with aircraft, as is the use of large amounts of water and sophisticated chemical fire extinguishers to prevent fires from spreading.

The goals of decreasing the amount of destruction by fires and cutting are wide-ranging. One is simply the longer lives and improved health of trees. In some areas of hickory and oak forest on the Eastern Seaboard, fire suppression has allowed the maturation of so many trees that the treetops form a continuous canopy.

There is evidence of the healthful effects of fire suppression closer to the ground as well. Vines and low bushes that would be burned out in a forest fire can flourish when fires are suppressed, of course, but there is a more indirect way fires harm plant life. Chemical tests on areas that have recently experienced forest fires demonstrate that burning decreases the overall amount of nutrients in the soil. Suppressing fires prevents such a decrease. Ferns, wildflowers, and herbs grow without disturbance.

Finally, wildlife can benefit. In the eastern hickory and oak forests, the suppression of fires has meant that forest animals—ranging from small insects and birds to large deer and bears—are not burned to death. Deer populations, in particular, have increased notably.

Here is a transcript of the lecture (Track 29 in your Student Tools).

N: Now listen to part of a lecture on the topic you just read about.

P: For years, forest fires were regarded as uniformly destructive, and forest managers put a lot of effort into preventing them. But it turns out that fire suppression may have destructive long-term effects on the forests it's supposed to protect.

For instance, mature oaks have grown so thickly in some places that little light reaches the forest floor. But young oak trees need light in order to grow properly. The lack of light has meant that new oaks aren't maturing rapidly enough to replace the older oaks. It also means that other tree species that don't need so much light, such as maples, are invading oak and hickory forests and competing for resources.

There are competition problems at ground level too. What forest fires, both natural and artificial, used to do is burn off some of the plants on the forest floor before they could grow into huge thickets. Now they run wild over the ground—and again, that means it's hard for young trees and other native plants to grow.

Then there's the increase in the deer population—this partially results from the lack of forest fires and partially from limitations on hunting—but the thing is, deer like to eat the leaves off oak saplings. So if one of those oak seedlings somehow does manage to get a good start, despite the shade and all the other plants competing for nutrients, it's likely to be killed by having its leaves eaten.

Oh, and one other thing: scientists are now finding that forest fires release nutrients from the plants and animals that are burned. That means that, even though the total amount of nutrients is decreased, there can actually be more nutrients available on the soil surface for plants that are trying to grow back afterward.

N: Summarize the points made in the lecture you just heard, explaining how they "cast doubt on the contents of the reading." You may refer to the passage as you write.

Sample High-Scoring Response

In the lecture, the professor made several points about the effects of forest fires. The professor argues that forest fires can actually be good for the forests, not bad. The talk by the professor however, is different from the reading. According to the reading, forest fires are harmful to the land and should be stopped. But the professor casts doubt on that view with several points.

The first point the teacher makes is that if there are too many trees, it is hard for some trees to get light and nutrition. This means that the trees are not healthy. The professor's point is different from the reading. The reading states that it is good to have a lot of trees in the forest. But the lecture shows that too many trees is actually bad for the forest.

Another point made by the professor is that burning a forest actually puts more nutrients into the land. This is not what the reading says. The reading says that fires take nutrients out of the soil. However, the professor says there are more nutrients at the top for plants to use.

In conclusion, the professor challenges the claims made in the reading by showing that forest fires are sometimes needed for a healthy forest.

Writing 2

Directions: For this task, you will write an essay in which you state, explain, and support your position on an issue. You have 30 minutes to plan and write your essay.

Question:

Do you agree or disagree with the following statement?

A university education should be provided free of charge to all interested scholars.

Use examples and reasons to support your position.

Sample High-Scoring Response

The issue stated by the topic is whether or not a university education should be provided free to all that are interested. This is a very important issue because the cost of education is rising and because education is very important. However, I believe that universities should not give an education for free.

I do not think that university education should be free because who is going to pay for it if the students do not? If the government has to pay for it then that means taxes are raised. This is not fair to the people because if they have to pay higher taxes they might not want to go to the university. That means they are paying for something they won't even use, which is not fair.

Furthermore, I don't think university education should be free because universities that have more money can give better education. The only way for the universities to get more money is to charge the students. If the education is free, how will the universities get money to buy computers, books, and hire good professors to teach? For this reason, we should not have a free university.

Finally, I think the university should not be free because there are many schools available and they have different prices. Poor students can go to a school that doesn't cost as much and still learn a lot. Also, many universities give aid or scholarships so a student can attend even if they don't have money. So there is no need to make a university education free.

In conclusion, university education should not be made free. I believe this because the colleges need the money to make them better. If the universities are free, taxes will be raised and people will have to pay for things they might not use. Since there are many schools available with scholarships and aid, university should not be made free.

In Closing

Okay, got all that? It's a lot, but if you have made it all the way back here, then you have pushed through it and done some serious studying and preparation. Bravo! Walk into the TOEFL feeling confident and prepared because you are. Best of luck!

NOTES

NOTES